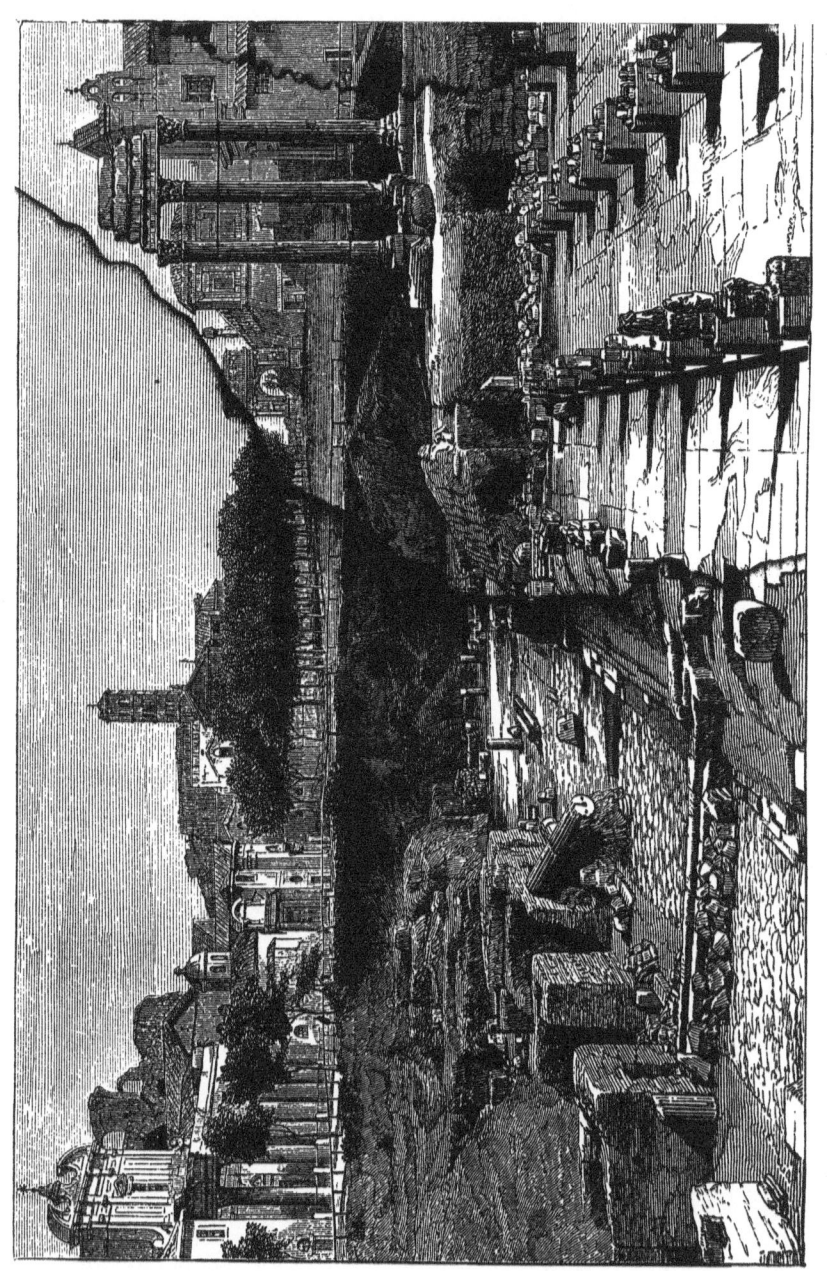

FORUM ROMANUM—VIEW IN BASILICA JULIA.

THE

HISTORY OF LAWYERS

ANCIENT AND MODERN

BY

WILLIAM FORSYTH

AUTHOR OF "HISTORY OF TRIAL BY JURY," "LIFE OF CICERO,"
ETC., ETC.

WITH ILLUSTRATIONS

THE LAWBOOK EXCHANGE, LTD.
Clark, New Jersey

ISBN-13: 9781886363144 (hardcover)
ISBN-13: 9781616190538 (paperback)

Lawbook Exchange edition 1996, 2010

The quality of this reprint is equivalent to the quality of the original work.

THE LAWBOOK EXCHANGE, LTD.
33 Terminal Avenue
Clark, New Jersey 07066-1321

*Please see our website for a selection of our other publications
and fine facsimile reprints of classic works of legal history:*
www.lawbookexchange.com

Library of Congress Cataloging-in-Publication Data

Forsyth, William, 1812-1899.
   The history of lawyers, ancient and modern / by William Forsyth.
     p.   cm.
   Originally published: Boston: Estes & Lauriat, 1875.
   ISBN 1-886363-14-5 (alk. paper)
   1. Lawyers—History. 2. Law-History. I. Title.
   K115.F668   1996
   340'.09-dc20   95-51103
                                                                     CIP

Printed in the United States of America on acid-free paper

THE

HISTORY OF LAWYERS

ANCIENT AND MODERN

BY

WILLIAM FORSYTH

AUTHOR OF "HISTORY OF TRIAL BY JURY," "LIFE OF CICERO,"
ETC., ETC

WITH ILLUSTRATIONS

NEW YORK
JAMES COCKCROFT & COMPANY
1875

PREFACE.

THE object of the following pages is to present in a popular form an historical sketch of the office and functions of an Advocate. It occurred to me that the subject afforded materials for work which would not be devoid of interest, and perhaps instruction, if, without going into minute and tedious detail, some of the more salient points were selected in the history of that profession. I therefore devoted the task to the unemployed hours of the legal vacation, confining my attention principally to the countries of Greece and Rome, France and England, where oratory, with which advocacy is so closely allied that in the Latin language they are almost synonymous terms, has been cultivated with the greatest reputation and success.

In the course of the work, translations, both in prose and verse, of passages from the classic authors frequently occur. These are in every case of my own, and the critical scholar may object that some of the terms have not been rendered with strict and technical accuracy. But this has been done advisedly. I have endeavored to express the meaning of the ancient writers, and to reflect the spirit rather than the mere letter of their works. In order to effect this, it is, I think, necessary to employ such terms as will, though not precisely equivalent, most readily convey the sense of the original. For instance, it would be easy to point out the difference between an Athenian and an English juryman; but in many respects their functions were analogous, and a modern reader will have a more lively idea of the scene presented in a Court of Justice at Athens, if we render ὠ ἄνδρες δικασταὶ, "Gentleman of the Jury!" than if, with pedantic propriety, we style them "O Dicasts!" We are too apt to cloth the ancients in buckram, and view them, as it were, through a magnifying glass, so that they loom before us in the dim distance in almost colossal proportions. But we forget that they were men very much like ourselves, and accustomed to talk and act like ordinary mortals. Pascal says, with as much truth as wit,—" On ne s'imagine d'ordinaire Platon et Aristote qu'avec de grandes robes, et comme des personnages toujours graves et sérieux. C'étaient d'honnêtes gens, qui riaient comme les autres avec leurs amis; et quand ils ont fait leurs lois et leurs traités de politique, c'a été en se jouant et pour se divertir." I know few things which serve more forcibly to link the past with the present, and prove the sameness of the great human family, than the sight of the dolls and toys in the British Museum which were the playthings of Egyptian children some three or four thousand years ago. Of course there are limits to the kind of license that may be used, and I fear we cannot applaud the taste of the Dutch commentator who always translated the word *consul* by "burgomaster." Sometimes, however, an opposite evil may arise, and false notions of institutions and manners may result, from too literal an adherence to the words of the original, where technical terms have been adopted into our language, but their meaning and force have been modified, or altogether changed to suit the exigencies of modern times. Bishop Thirlwall, in his "History of Greece," when speaking of the democratic form of government as treated of by Aristotle, says, "We shall not confine ourselves to the technical language of his system, but will endeavor to define the notion of democracy, as the word was commonly understood by the Greeks, so as to separate the essence of the theory from the various accidents which have sometimes been confounded with it by writers, who have treated Greek history as a vehicle for conveying their views on questions of modern politics, which never arose in the Greek republics."

In quoting Niebuhr's "History of Rome," which I do frequently, deeply impressed as I am with the conviction that he was the greatest genius that ever explored the dark recesses of antiquity and illumined the page of history, I have made use of the translation of his immortal work by Bishop Thirlwall and Archdeacon Hare. But the citations from his lectures are taken from the edition of Dr. Schmitz.

In conclusion I may observe that the chief difficulty with which I have had to contend has been that of compression—as the materials for a much longer treatise on the subject are abundant. But I was deterred by a fear lest, to use an expres- of King James, I should be thought especially in a first experiment, to "bestow my tediosity" upon the public. I believe the idea of such a work as the present is new; for although in France several essays, relative to the calling of advocates, have been written by Camus, Berryer, Dupin, and others, they are confined almost exclusively to the exercise of the profession in that country; and the works by Boucher d'Argis and Fournel are devoted to the French order of advocates. If the success of the present essay is at all commensurate with that of such publications in France, I shall be amply satisfied.

W F.

INNER TEMPLE.

LIST OF ILLUSTRATIONS

	PAGE
FORUM ROMANUM. VIEW IN THE BASILICA JULIA .	*Frontispiece*
FORUM. POMPEII	109
AN OLD ROMAN TOMB	127

CONTENTS.

CHAPTER I.

ADVOCACY IN THEORY.

PAGE.

Interest to the Subject.—Jealousy felt towards the Office.—Testimony borne by Antiquity.—Quotations from Cicero, Tacitus, Quintilian, and others.—Eulogy by Writers in France.—Terrasson.—Responsibility of the Office of an Advocate.—Lawyers of past times.—Early Struggles.—Arduous Requirements of the Law.—What is Advocacy?—Trial Scene from Homer's Description of the Shield of Achilles.—Account of the Legal Tribunals of Ancient Egypt.—More's Utopia.—Utility of the Office of an Advocate depends on the Character of Courts of Justice.—Influence of Democracy on Eloquence 1

CHAPTER II.

THE ATHENIAN COURTS.

Oratory in Greece confined to Athens.—Employment of Advocates there not usual.—Mock-trial in Lucian.—Speech-writers at Athens.—Instance of Barratry in an attempt to sink a Ship.—List of celebrated Orations never spoken.—Fondness of Athenians for Judicial Trials.—Aristophanes and the Comedy of the Wasps.—Plot of the play.—The Dicast's Merry Life.—Vicious Constitution of the Courts of Law.—Practice in Civil Actions.—Sentence upon Socrates.—Procedure in criminal Trials.—Rule as to hearsay Evidence.—Dying Declarations.—Use of Torture amongst the Ancients.—Case of Peacham in Reign of James I.—Cruel proceedings against Spreul in Scotland.—Clepsydras or Water Clocks.—Abusive Language in the Attic Orators.—Value of their Forensic Speeches.—Curious Case of *crim. con.* at Athens.— A Faithless Wife.—Specimen of a Will Cause.—Counsel acting for both Plaintiff and Defendant 20

CHAPTER III.

SKETCH OF THE ROMAN LAW AND THE ROMAN COURTS DURING THE REPUBLIC.

Account given by Pomponius in the digest.—The Lost Institutes of Gaius discovered by Niebuhr.—Mistakes of the Roman Jurists as to the early Constitution of Rome.—The Papirian Code, Twelve Tables, and Jus Flavianum.—Analogy to our own Law.—Distinction between *Populus* and *Plebs.*—Secession of the Plebs to the Sacred Hill. —The Jus Honorarium.—Province of Equity in this Country.— Explanation of the different kinds of Prætorian Edicts.—Constituent Elements of the Roman Law.—The Forum described.— Basilicæ or Halls.—A modern Trachallus.—Trials held in the open air.—State of the Forum when Cicero defended Milo.— Account of the death of Clodius.—Result of the Trial.—Vicissitudes of the Forum.—Jurisdiction of the Prætors.—The Emperor acting as a Judge at Chambers.—Court of the Centumviri.—Criminal Trials at Rome.—The Prætor sitting as President.—The Album Judicum 54

CHAPTER IV.

ADVOCACY IN ANCIENT ROME.

Meaning of term Orator.—Difference between Rome and England in this respect.—Relation of Patron and Client.—Meaning of *Advocatus.* —The Jurisconsults.—Calling to the Bar at Rome.—Roman Advocates ignorant of Law.—Distinction between questions of Law and Fact.—The Poetry of Action.—Brutus and Lucretia.—The old Soldier and his Creditor.—Virginius and his Daughter.—

CONTENTS.

Scene from Shakspeare.—Dramatic Scenes in Court.—Cicero defending Fonteius.—Unfortunate Attempts at Pathos.—Prerogative of Mercy in Roman Juries.—The accused on his trial clothed in sackcloth and ashes.—A Roman Advocate *cramming* for a case.—Ludicrous instances of legal Ignorance.—Some of the *Causes célèbres* at Rome.—The case of the Roman Soldier.—The case of Coponius *v.* Curius.—A will construed *cy pres* at Rome.—Caveat Emptor.—Question of Divorce.—Marius and the frail *Fanny*.—Instances of ambiguous Wills.—Case of Leon and *Pantaleon*.—Trials of Bassus and Priscus.—Defense by taking legal Objection, or on the Merits.—Cicero cross-examining.—The Advocate's Retinue at Rome.—Mistake of Erskine's patriotic Friends. . 83

CHAPTER V.

SOME ACCOUNT OF THE ADVOCATES OF ROME DURING THE REPUBLIC.

Early Orators of Rome.—The Forest Murders, and Sulpicius Galba.—Character of Caius Gracchus vindicated by Niebuhr.—Attack on Scaurus by Statius.—Rutilius Rufus, Caius Galba, and others.—Mark Antony the Orator.—Defense of Norbanus.—Prides himself on his ignorance of Law.—Lucius Licinius Crassus.—Comparison of his Death with that of Lord Chatham.—His Oratory compared with that of Canning.—His Defense of Lucinia, the frail Vestal.—Witty Argument of Crassus in the case of Coponius against Curius.—Cicero's Dialogue *de Oratore*.—Publius and Servius Sulpicius.—Celebrated Epistle of the latter to Cicero.—Beautiful Greek Epigram.—Sulpicius taunted by Mucius Scævola.—The Profession of a Soldier contrasted with that of a Lawyer by Cicero.—Noble Eulogium by Cicero upon Sulpicius.—Hortensius.—His prodigious Memory.—The Pains he took with his Dress and Personal Appearance.—His Retort upon Torquatus.—His care of his Fish-ponds.—Charge against him of Corruption.—His Defense of Verres.—Cicero's Jest at his expense.—Generous Tribute paid by Cicero to Hortensius.—Lady Advocates: Hortesia, Sentia, and Afrania.—Cicero as an Advocate.—His lofty

CONTENTS.

PAGE.

Idea of his Profession.—Narrative of his Studies and Practice.—His Theory of the perfect Orator.—Knowledge requisite for an Advocate.—Quotations from D'Aguesseau and Barrow.—Cicero more frequently for the Defense than the Prosecution.—Trial of Sextius Roscius on the Charge of Murder.—Facts of the Case, and Speech of Cicero.—Speech for Roscius the Actor.—Defense of Cluentius.—A Female Monster.—Cicero's Description of the Duties of a Juryman.—An accommodating Juror.—Speech on behalf of Licinius Murena.—State of Affairs at Rome.—Extracts from the Speech.—A Roman Consul charged by Cato with the Sin of *Dancing*.—A Consul should be an Orator.—Useful Hints for electioneering Tactics.—Ridicule of the Stoic Philosophy.—" Gentlemen of the Jury, you are none of you safe!"—Review of Cicero's Argument.—Speech for Ligarius.—St. Paul as an Orator.—Consummate Skill of Cicero.—Appeal to Tubero.—" Judge Festus Trembles."—Julius Cæsar an Advocate at the Roman Bar.—His Reputation as a Speaker.—Vicious State of Morals at Rome 113

CHAPTER VI.

THE BAR UNDER THE EMPIRE, AND IN THE MIDDLE AGES.

Forensic Oratory perished with the Republic.—Causes of this.—Tacitus on the Decline of Eloquence.—Complaints of Degeneracy made by Writers from earliest times.—Description by Juvenal of Condition of Advocates in his time.—Lord Ellenborough under drill.—*Claqueurs* introduced into Courts at Rome.—Curious Letter of Pliny recommending a Junior.—Names of famous Advocates in Imperial Rome.—Quintilian mourning for his Wife and Children.—Rights and Privileges of Advocates according to the Justinian Code.—Female Advocates prohibited.—Counsel assigned by Prætor.—Scurrility forbidden.—Ordinance of Charles VIII. of France on that Subject.—Advocates and Holy Orders.—Advocates in the Middle Ages.—La Haute Cour and La Cour des Bourgeois.—Letters du Sépulcre and Assises de Jerusalem.—A Coroner's Inquest in the eleventh century.—The true and constant Pleader.—Sage Advice given in the *Livre des Assises* to Advocates . 177

CHAPTER VII.

THE NOBLESSE DE LA ROBE.

PAGE

Proud Position of the Bar in France.—A French Advocate canonized. —Another becomes Pope.—Opposition by Advocates to the Pretensions of the Papal See—St. Louis appeals to the Lawyers.— Their bold and spirited Conduct.—Bull issued by Boniface VIII.— Parody by Pierre de Cugnières.—The "Bull" taken by the Horns. —Origin of the Parliament of Paris.—Cour Royale.—The Parliament becomes stationary.—Its Constitution.—Splendor of the Parliament in old times.—The Vavassour attending Pleadings.— Eulogy of the Parliament by Isabella, Queen of France.—Presence of the King.—Ancient Custom in England.—Punishment of corrupt Judges.—The Parliament strictly a Court of Justice.—Registration of Royal Edicts by the Parliament.—Refusal of Registration a proximate Cause of the first French Revolution.—Provincial Parliaments established.—The Parliaments swept away by the Revolution.—Sale of judicial Offices in France.—Evils of the System. —The Bar in France formed a lesser Order of Nobility.—Establishments of St. Louis.—The Advocate made a Chevalier.—His knightly Oath.—Institution of the ORDER OF ADVOCATES.— *Serment d'Advocacerie.*—Rules of the Order.—Judicial Combats in the Middle Ages.—Battle of the Liturgies.—Part played by Advocates in these Combats.—Rule *nisi* for a Duel.—Danger of Advocate identifying himself with his Client.—Philippe de Montespedon, and the Breach of Promise of Marriage.—A craven Lover.—Advocates *ecoutants, plaidants,* and *consultants.*—Citation of false Customs.—A Husband outwitted.—French Mode of "waging law."—Imaginary Trials, Bishop Sherlock's "Trial of the Witnesses."—A Bull and a Pig solemnly tried and hanged.— Curious Text-books.—Decrees of Love pronounced in the Court of Cupid.—The Stylus Parlamenti on the personal Appearance and Address of Advocates.—Loisel's *Dialogue des Avocats*—Inordinate Display of classical Learning in Speeches of Advocates of that Age.—Causes of this.—Racine's Comedy of *Les Plaideurs.*— Pedantic Speech of Anne Robert.—Helen Gillet the Infanticide.—

Dreadful Scene on the Scaffold.—Eloquent Speech of Févret.—
Julien Peleus and the Haunted House.—An English Case of
Nocturnal Dæmons.—Ingenious Argument of Peleus against
Ghosts.—New Trial granted to discuss Questions of Apparitions.
—Pasquier.—His famous Speech for the University of Paris
against the Jesuits.—Story of Pasquier's Flea.—*Contention mignarde* between him and Mlle. Catherine des Roches.—Epigrams
on the Subject.—Portrait of an Advocate of the olden Time.—
Age of Louis Quatorze a brilliant Period for the French Bar.—
Brinvilliers, the Great Poisoner.—Discovery of the Murders.—She
escapes from France, but is arrested at Liege.—Her Trial and Defense by Nivelle.—May the Secrets of the Confessional be divulged
in a Court of Law?—Masterly argument of Nivelle.—Conviction
of the Prisoner, and her Sentence.—D'Aguesseau.—Mysterious
case of De la Pivardière, in which he was engaged as counsel.—
The Dead alive again.—Disputed Question of Identity.—Abolition of the ORDER of Advocates at the Revolution.—The Revolutionary Tribunal.—Louis XVI. before the Convention.—Brave
conduct of Malesherbes.—His Epitaph.—The Girondists.—Eloquent Speech of Desèze.—Trial of Marie Antoinette.—Her Sublime Appeal to the Mothers of France.—Napoleon's dislike of the
Bar.—He decrees the Re-establishment of the Order of Advocates.
—Procedure in French Criminal Trials.—Story of Madame Lafarge.—The affair of the Diamonds.—She is tried for the Murder
of her Husband.—Cross-examination of Madame Lafarge by the
Attorney-General.—The Chemists report the Absence of Arsenic.
—The Corpse of Lafarge ordered to be exhumed.—Unfair Examination of the Prisoner.—MM. Orfila, Bussi, and Ollivier (d'Angers)
summoned from Paris.—The Diamonds again!—Conviction of the
Prisoner.—Guilty or not Guilty?—Comments on the Trial . . 200

CHAPTER VIII.

ADVOCACY IN ENGLAND.

Great State of the Sergeants in the olden Time.—Early Advocates of
England.—Wager of Battel in the Reign of Elizabeth.—Appeal
of Treason in the Court of Chivalry between Donald Lord Rea

CONTENTS.   xv

PAGE.

and David Ramsey.—Trial by Battel abolished.—Statute of Edward I. against Deceit on the part of Sergeants or Countors.—The *Mirroir des Justice*.—Rarity of forensic Eloquence in England.—Confession of Thomas Woodstock, Duke of Gloucester.—The piebald Language of the Law formerly.—Noble Address of Chief Justice Crewe.—Contrast of lay Speeches with Discourses of Divines.—Bishop Burnet and his Hour-glass.—Denial of Counsel to Prisoners on Questions of Fact in Cases of Treason or Felony. —Iniquity of this Rule illustrated in the Trials of the Duke of Norfolk, Colonel Lilburne, Sir Henry Vane, Algernon Sidney, and Colledge "the Prostestant Joiner."—Conduct of Jeffreys on the Trial of Mrs. Lisle.—Her affecting Speech on the Scaffold.—Hard Case of Rajah Nundocomar at Calcutta.—Cruelty of compelling a Prisoner to advocate his own Case.—Passing of Statute 7 Will. III. c. 3.—Presence of Mind shown by Lord Ashley at the time.—Rigorous Enforcement of the Law in the Case of Sir William Parkyn.—A cold Exordium by Sir Bartholomew Shower.—Prisoner's Counsel Act, 6 and 7 Will. IV. c. 114.—Criminal Trials formerly judicial Murders.—Arraignment of the Duke of Norfolk.—Trials in England for Witchcraft.—The Essex Witches.—Sir Matthew Hale declares his Belief in the Existence of Witches.—The "Wisdom of our Ancestors" not without Alloy.—Opposition made to Bill for abolishing Law Latin.—Retort on Lord Raymond, C. J., by the Duke of Argyle.—Trial of the Seven Bishops.—August Spectacle in Westminster Hall.—Speech of Somers.—Technicality of English Law one Cause of Absence of Eloquence. —Excessive Refinement of Special Pleading.—A "Negative Pregnant."—Necessity of a Knowledge of Pleading.—The immense Extent of the Law another Cause.—Fecundity of Reports.—The Neglect to cultivate Eloquence as an Art.—Different Theory and Practice of the Ancients.—D'Aguesseau on the Causes of the Decline of Eloquence.—Great Privilege of Speech accorded to Advocates.—Extent and Limits of their Privilege.—Curious Instance of professional immunity claimed by Cook the Regicide.—Distinction between the Office of Advocate and of Attorney.—Instances of legal Strategy at *Nisi Prius*.—Dexterity in Court only to be learnt by Practice.—Are our Rules of Evidence too strict?—Reason for keeping separate the Functions of Advocate and of Attorney   304

CHAPTER IX.

THE HONORARIUM.

PAGE.

Origin of the Theory of gratuitous Service by an Advocate.—The Cincian Law.—Reasons against a pecuniary Honorarium at Rome.—Payment of Members of the House of Commons in former Times.—Writ *de Expensis Burgensium levaudis.*—Change at the Downfall of the Roman Republic.—Suilius the informer.—Debate in the Roman Senate.—Decree of the Senate in the Reign of Nero. —Samius, betrayed by his Counsel, stabs himself.—Dishonorable conduct of Nominatus.—Law of Trajan on the Subject.—Edict of the Emperor Severus.—Argument of Quintilian.—The Case stated by Sir John Davys.—Rule at the English Bar.—African Barristers on Circuit.—Capitularies of Charlemagne.—Ordinance of Philip the Bold.—Witty Epigram by Pasquier.—Ordonnance de Blois. —*Emeute* of the Parisian Advocates 361

CHAPTER X.

FORENSIC CASUISTRY.

The Ethics of the Question stated.—Sarcasms of Writers.—Ben Jonson.—Bishop Hall.—Swift.— M. Cormenin or "Timon."—Mischievous Sophisms exposed.—An Advocate is not bound to undertake every Cause offered to him.—This proved by the authority of Cicero, Quintilian, and others.—Opinions of Sir Edward Coke, Sir John Davys, Cook, Sir Matthew Hale, and Lord Langdale.— Assize Sermon of Bishop Sanderson.—Contrary Theory maintained by Lord Erskine.—Gerald's Trial, and Henry Erskine.—Lord Brougham on the Duty of an Advocate.—His Theory considered. —Casuists perplexed by Question whether Falsehood is in all cases sinful.—Do Advocates violate a moral Duty by being ready to espouse either Side of a Question ?—The Peculiarity of their Position considered.—Fallacious Argument of Puffendorf.— Origin and Necessity of the Class of Lawyers.—Consequences of Counsel refusing to undertake a Cause.—The Duty of an Advocate in respect of fraudulent Claims.—Reasons why Advocates may in general act for either of two Parties in a Cause.—Distinction between his Duty and that of the Judge.—Objection, that of two Sides of an Argument, one only is right, considered.—Argument of Sir John Davys.—Sophistry of Paley.—Where Advocate knows his Client to be Guilty.—Mode of Defense in such Cases.—Necessity of Circumspection.—True Uses of Eloquence.—The Profession should be above Suspicion or Reproach.—Conclusion 377

CHAPTER I.

ADVOCACY IN THEORY.

U*N ordre aussi ancien que la magistrature, aussi noble que la vertu, aussi nécessaire que la justice.* Such is the glowing language in which D'Aguesseau, the great chancellor of France, speaks of the calling of advocates, of which it is the purpose in the following pages to give an historical sketch.

And I trust that I do not deceive myself by taking any exaggerated view of the importance of the subject, or of the degree of interest which it is likely to inspire. I have neither the wish nor the temptation unduly to "magnify mine office." But it is, perhaps, not unreasonable to suppose that the community may care to know something of the history and character of an order of men who have the varied and important duties to perform which devolve upon advocates; whose assistance may be required by the greatest as well as the meanest, individual in the most critical juncture of his life; who are the depositaries of the confidence, and the defenders of the lives and liberties, the reputation and fortunes, of their fellow citizens; and who form the links of a chain, extending from the highest pinnacle to which a subject can be raised, through the different gradations of the social scale, down to the humblest station. For the great feature of the profession is, that it is a republic open to all, where the promise of reward is held out without fear or favor to such as have industry and ability; and, as the prizes that await the successful are magnificent, no class or rank disdains to compete for them. Nor can it be unimportant to the state to inform itself what are the principles of a body of men, without whose aid the laws of their country can not be properly administered or enforced,—*nam et leges ipsæ nihil valent nisi actoris idoneâ voce munitæ* (*Quintil. Inst. Orat.* xii. 7.); and from amongst whom is taken every one of those magistrates of the commonwealth whose care should be, in the eloquent words of Bishop Horne, "when he goeth up to the judgment seat, to put on righteousness as a glorious and beautiful robe, and to render his tribunal a fit emblem of that eternal throne of which justice and judgment are the habitation."

In the admirable work of Meyer, in which he has investigated the origin and progress of judicial institutions in Europe, he strongly enforces this view of the relation subsisting between the advocate and the public. "He who has devoted himself to that profession which is as difficult as it is honorable; who receives in his chamber the most confidential communications; who directs by his counsel those who come to ask his advice and listen to him as though he were an oracle; who has the conduct of causes the most important; who constitutes himself the organ of those who claim the most sacred rights, or the defender of those who find themselves attacked in their persons, their honor, or their fortune; who brings forward and gives efficacy to their demand, or repels the charges brought against them; he, I say, who does all this, must necessarily require the support of the public. By his knowledge, his talents, his morality, he ought to endeavor to win the confidence and good will of his fellow citizens" (*Esprit, Origine*, vi. p. 540). And it may be not without advantage to consider what has been the position and what the estimation of the profession, in former ages and other countries, where it has been adorned by names that have survived the lapse of ages, and still live in the admiration of posterity.

It may, I think, be confidently affirmed, that the state has nowhere interfered so little with the conduct of advocates as in England. In a legislative sense it may be said to have almost ignored their existence. Very different was the case in imperial Rome; for the Code of Justinian bears ample testimony to the minute care with which their rights and privileges, and duties, were regulated by the emperors; and in the kingdoms of Europe, which were formed upon the ruins of the Roman empire, we find a long list of ordinances and edicts specially directed to the same subject. This was eminently the case in France, where the *noblesse de la robe* flourished with a splendor elsewhere unknown. But the inference that may be drawn from this is one not unfavorable to the advocates of England. *Obi plurimæ leges ibi pessima respublica* is, in one sense, a true maxim, and we may not unfairly presume, as indeed history warrants us in asserting, that many of the rules and prohibitions which have from time to time been required to check the malpractices of advocates in other countries, have been unnecessary here; and were it right or becoming to vindicate the claim of the bar of England, from the earliest times, to superior purity and a nicer sense of honor as contrasted with that of the rest of Europe, we might point to the significant fact that for centuries it has been subjected to no statutes, or rules, or discipline, other than those which it has framed for itself. It has adhered to its immemorial traditions, and they, when their spirit is rightly understood, ought to be, and have been, sufficient to preserve it as a body from all that is mean, base, and disreputable.

I say, "as a body," for it would be in the highest degree

visionary to expect that, amidst the numbers who crowd the ranks of the profession, no individuals should be found insensible to the dignity of their vocation, and unworthy of the society of honorable men. Such must always exist in every widely extended class; and even the sacred calling of the clergy does not prevent the intrusion into the priesthood of persons who bring disgrace upon the name. But most unfair would it be to judge of the character of either profession by such rare and melancholy exceptions; nor need we fear that the good sense and intelligence of the public will, in this matter, pronounce a partial and unjust verdict.

If, however, any one were to undertake a defense of the profession and professors of the law, there would be little cause for apprehension, lest, like the ancient sophist who proposed to write a panegyric upon Hercules, he should be met by the objection, *Quis vituperavit?* for it is impossible not to see that in some quarters an almost morbid jealousy is entertained of them. We need not stop to inquire into the causes of this feeling, which may, perhaps, admit of more than one explanation; the wiser course is to derive good out of the evil, and make use of such attacks as microscopes to detect whatever deformity is latent in the system. So far as they are directed against abuses which, though sanctioned by usage and by time, are indefensible, and bring to light defects which admit of an easy and immediate remedy at the hands of the profession itself—and who can deny that such abuses and defects do, to a certain extent, exist?—it ought to be thankful that its purity is carefully watched over by so vigilant a censorship, and diligently apply itself to correct the faults. But the taunts and carpings of malevolence it may safely disregard, in the confident assurance that if it does not deserve them they will fall like broken arrows to the ground, and that so long as it makes high and honorable principle the pole star of its conduct, public opinion will ratify and confirm the judgment which the voice of all ages has pronounced upon the value and necessity of the office of an advocate.

For were it necessary to vindicate that office it would be easy to cite the authority of great and venerable names. We might ask, with Cicero, " What is so kinglike, so generous, so munificent, as to bestow help on those who supplicate our aid? to raise the oppressed, and save our fellow citizens from peril, and preserve them to the state? What, on the other hand, is so necessary as to have always the command of weapons by which we may be protected from injury, or be enabled to attack the wicked or avenge ourselves if attacked by others?" (*De Orat.* i. 8.) Or with Tacitus, " For if all our thoughts and actions are to be directed with a view to expediency, what can be more safe than to practice that profession, whereby, being always armed, you will be able to afford protection to your friends, assistance to strangers, and safety to those who are in peril; and, on the other hand, spread terror and alarm among your enemies and the malevolent, while you yourself are meanwhile secure, and invested, as it were, with the panoply of power?" (*De Orat. Dialogus*, c. 5. *Lect. Hist. of Rome*, ii. 154.) We might also avail ourselves of that remarkable definition of an advocate which Cato gave,—*Vir bonus dicendi peritus*,—where we see the idea of moral worth inseparably connected with his character, and forming one of its constituent features, as though he were bound by the tenure of his office to eschew evil; and what Quintilian said of the power of forensic eloquence to gain the great prizes of ambition, and acquire for the speaker wealth and fame, has been confirmed by the experience of centuries which have rolled away since his voice was heard pleading in the courts at Rome: *Neque erat difficile vel veteribus vel novis exemplis palam facere, non aliunde majores honores, opes, amicitias, laudem præsentem, futuram, hominibus contigisse* (*Inst. Orat.* xii. 11).

We might appeal to the testimony borne by the constitutions of the Roman emperors, which declared that if advocates sustained their part in the state aright, they were no less the benefactors of mankind, than if they periled their lives in battle to save their country and families from ruin. For, as the Civil Law emphatically said, armed warriors, whose weapon was the sword, were not the only soldiers of the empire; advocates too, fought for imperial Rome, when they exerted the glorious gift of eloquence in defending the lives and fortunes of their fellow citizens, in upholding the cause of the poor and needy, and helping them to right who suffered wrong (*Cod. II.* vii. 14).

Not unworthy of being placed by the side of this passage is the quaint but eloquent testimony of Sir John Davys, who says: " Why may we not proceed further and affirm confidently, that the profession of the law is to be preferred before all other human professions and sciences, as being most noble for the matter and subject thereof, most necessary for the common and continued use thereof, and most meritorious for the good effects it doth produce in the commonwealth? For what is the matter and subject of our profession but justice, the lady and queen of all moral virtues? and what are our professors of the law but her counselors, her secretaries, her interpreters, her servants? Again, what is the king himself but the clear fountain of justice? and what are the professors of the law but conduit pipes deriving and conveying the streams of his justice unto all the subjects of his several kingdoms? So as if justice be rightly resembled to the sun in the firmament, in that she spreadeth her light and virtue unto all creatures, how can she but communicate part of her goodness and glory unto that science that is her handmaid, and waits upon her? And if kings be God's scholars (as Homer writeth), and that the rules of justice be their principal lesson, and if God do honor kings with his own name, *Dixi quod Dii estis* (as a more divine poet than Homer singeth), specially for that they sit upon God's own seat when they minister justice unto the people, do not kings again highly honor those persons, whose subordinate ministry and service they use in performing that principal part of their kingly office?

"Undoubtedly, touching the advancement of such persons, Solomon the king speaketh that they shall stand before kings; and God will set them, saith David, with princes, even with the princes of his people.

"Neither is the profession ennobled in regard of the dignity of her employment only, but she is to be honored so much the more for the necessity and continual use of her service in the common weal. For, if we must honor the physician, *propter necessitatem*, as the wise man prescribeth, much more must we honor for the same cause the professors and ministers of the law. For neither do all men at any time, nor any one man at all times, stand in need of the physician; for they that are in health (which are the greatest number of men) *non egent medico*, saith the great Physician of our souls, and our only Advocate which is in heaven. But all men, at all times and in all places, do stand in need of justice, and of law, which is the rule of justice, and of the interpreters and ministers of the law, which give life and motion unto justice."

But in no country has the office of an advocate been made the theme of eulogy so often as in France. Those who followed that profession there in former times seem to have been impressed with a deep conviction of the importance of its duties, and of the arduous nature of its manifold requirements. But they delighted to picture the ideal of the character which rose above the temptations that beset the path of the lawyer, and to dwell upon the bright reward, not merely of riches and honor, but of inward satisfaction, awaiting those who embarked in that career in a right spirit, and pursued it with success. Thus Terrasson, himself a distinguished lawyer, who flourished at the beginning of the last century, after speaking of the extent of the requirements which it is necessary for the advocate to possess (*Discours sur la Profession d'Avocat*), " that infinite variety of knowledge for which he has occasion; that immense number of volumes which he is obliged not only to read, but to meditate upon and fathom their depths; that multitude of laws which ought to be the object of his memory, and still more of his discernment and his reflections; that crowd of commentators whose scattered rays of interpretation he ought to collect,"—adds words of encouragement to the student, who might be terrified at the difficulties before him.—"At the sight of a labor so extensive the youthful orator, affrighted, is almost tempted to shrink back and retrace his steps; but let his courage withstand the first alarm. If he is astonished at the vastness of his duties, let him fix his attention upon the rewards which inseparably attend the fulfillment of them. The activity of continued occupation has for him the sweetness of repose, and in that profession every pain gives birth to a corresponding pleasure. The first recompense which he will reap consists in the daily augmentation of his treasures. With his memory enriched by facts, his imagination gratified by the view of different characters, his reason enlightened by the firm and unvarying principles of natural equity, which adapts itself to all the wants of mankind, as diversified in its means as it is uniform in its principles; the whole man, in short, within him wrought by study to the highest point of intellectual perfection,—he will feel the trouble less than he will enjoy the fruit of his labors; and as he advances step by step, and constantly acquires more facility in retaining, arranging, and comprehending the subject of his studies, he will at last derive enjoyment from that which at first occasioned him alarm."

And if we consider the momentous questions which are confided to his skill, involving all that is dear to man, and remember that when life or property is at stake, or the poisoned shaft of calumny is quivering in the heart, his office it is to stand forth and shield the person, or vindicate the character, of those who are assailed, and who fly to him for protection or redress, we shall be more disposed to acquiesce in the justice of such descriptions. And it is well to erect a lofty standard. There is little danger lest men should take an exaggerated view of the qualifications which are demanded by their profession. Vanity and self confidence are easily content with slight proficiency, and are unwilling to believe that they may not "rush in," however fearful genius may be "to tread." But without an adequate conception of the requirements of his office, it is utterly impossible that the advocate can perform the duties which, by its very tenure, he stands pledged to society to fulfill. How can he hope to thread the mazes of intricate argument, if his mind is not disciplined by the habit of accurate reasoning? or to advise safely in some perilous emergency, if he has not thoroughly digested and made himself master of legal principles ; or to plead successfully in behalf of the life or liberty of a fellow creature, if he has taken no pains to acquire grace or fluency as a speaker?

Great, indeed, is the responsibility which is incurred by him to whom are confided the weighty interests at stake in a court of justice. Who can set limits to their magnitude, or exaggerate the importance of his duties, who declares himself ready to undertake their defense? When a prisoner stands at the bar on trial for his life, and the moment has arrived when the advocate must rise, and, in the face of dark suspicions, and strong presumptions, and direct evidence of guilt, although in reality all these may be fallacious, persuade a jury of his countrymen, sworn solemnly to make a *true* deliverance, that the accused is innocent, or that, at all events, he can not safely be convicted;—amidst the breathless stillness of the audience, when every heart beats quickly, and *one* throbs with agonized and sickening fear, what mimic representation of passion on the stage, can equal that drama of reality?

It is no doubt difficult to sustain this feeling, and to regard the profession in the point of view presented by the writers who have been quoted. For it can not be denied that the cases in which an advocate is engaged in the ordinary exercise of his calling, are very frequently devoid of interest, and nothing seems better calculated to damp enthusiasm and deaden ambition, than the daily routine of practice in the courts. With a system so full of technicalities as the English law, where precedents govern with an iron sway, and the citation of them constitutes by far the greatest part of every legal argument; and in an age when, in order to avoid the reproach of being declamatory, we hardly venture to adorn our speeches with any of the flowers of rhetoric, much of the panegyric that has been lavished, by writers in former times, upon the eloquence of advocates and the dignity of their office, may appear unmeaning or extravagant. Perhaps, however, none are more conscious of the contrast between the ideal and the reality of that profession, than the majority of those who are its members. "Few men," says Gibbon, "without the spur of necessity, have resolution to force their way through the thorns and thickets of that gloomy labyrinth." He who does determine to succeed, has "the mettle of his pasture" tried in a manner and degree which they only who have descended into the arena, where the "garland is to be won, not without dust and heat," can understand and appreciate. The kind of struggle in which he has to engage is very different from what his imagination pictures to him beforehand. He enters upon his career, we will suppose, with a high and generous spirit, having girded up his loins to run the arduous race, and looking forward to the prizes of honor and distinction, which glitter in the distance, as the reward of his ambition. He thinks of the great names which shed an undying luster over the profession of the law. He remembers that of this profession was Bacon, the high priest of Nature, who "had taken all knowledge for his province;" and Clarendon, the wise and faithful servant of the Crown, doomed, like the great historian of Greece, to be the victim of ingratitude; and Hale, the depth of whose legal learning was only equaled by the fervor of his piety; and Somers, not more celebrated as a lawyer than a statesman, whose name is identified with that Revolution, to which we owe the safeguards of our liberties and rights; and Hardwicke, the oracle of equity; and Mansfield, whose eloquence and power of argument were such that before he adorned the bench, he alone was thought worthy to cope with Chatham in debate, and who, afterwards, as Chief Justice of England for thirty-two years, laid the deep and strong foundations of our commercial law; and Erskine, the orator of the forum, whose solitary statue in the hall where he sat for a brief period as Chancellor, attests the homage paid to his unrivaled power as an advocate; and Grant, the closest of reasoners, and most patient and excellent of judges; and Stowell, the profound jurist of modern times, whose judgments have commanded the admiration of the world, and whose comprehensive thoughts found utterance in language so fastidiously appropriate, that not a word can be altered without detriment to the sense.

But he soon finds how true, as applied to the profession in which he is engaged, are the words of the Preacher: "The race is not to the swift, nor the battle to the strong, neither yet bread to the wise, nor riches to men of understanding, nor yet favor to men of skill;

but time and chance happeneth to them all." Whereas formerly the chief concern of the student was to prepare himself for the demands which he fondly hoped would soon be made upon his intellect and skill, he now learns that the grand difficulty is not in undertaking causes, but in finding opportunity to do so. Months succeed months, and years are added to years, while he waits in vain for occupation. Unemployed and disheartened, he is obliged to sit in enforced idleness in the solitude of his chambers, or attend the courts of law in the character rather of a spectator than a counsel. For no case is intrusted to his care, and he begins at last to wonder that he ever cherished the thought of success in his profession. He gradually learns to contemplate failure as his appointed lot, and almost to acquiesce in the verdict which seems to be pronounced against his capacity for the bar.

He will not resort to unworthy means for his advancement, and he feels, therefore, that he is almost powerless to assist himself. He can not, like a tradesman, advertise his wares and solicit custom. He is like a vessel on the strand, which can not float until the tide flows and ripples round her. But the flowing of the tide must be caused by no underhand agency of his own, if he is careful to observe the honorable rule, and what ought to be the usage of his calling. All that he can do is to be ready for the summons whenever it may come, and prove his fitness whenever he is tried. But, in the meantime, how have the visions of his early youth melted into air? His heart is sick with hope deferred. He no longer fixes his eye upon the mountain tops, to which he once thought he was destined to climb. He feels, by sad experience, what a weary interval separates him from them, and is thankful if he can make any progress in the rough and barren ground over which he is obliged to toil. And even if he has a glimmering of success, nothing can be more likely to quench his ardor and extinguish his lofty aspirations, than the kind of cases which he will find committed to his care. Larcenies at sessions, pleadings at chambers, and undefended actions on bills of exchange in court, will most probably be all that he will be intrusted with for years.

There is need, therefore, of strong hope, and much patience, and steady perseverance in him who seeks to climb by the ladder of the law. But it is cheering to think how many travelers have passed on before him and attained success. They have had like difficulties and trials to overcome, and the remembrance of their triumphs inspires hope and sustains exertion. To the student, therefore, who is about to engage in the conflitc of the courts, it can not be uninteresting to know something of those who have preceded him in the race in other countries and in distant ages, nor unprofitable to learn in what discipline they were trained, and by what means so many of them gained an illustrious name. And the more we accustom ourselves to consider the calling of an advocate in the light and with the feelings with which antiquity regarded it, and the less we regard it as a profession followed merely for the sake of gain, and damaged, as no doubt it is in public estimation, by too much of careless indifference to the truth or justice of a cause undertaken for a fee, the more likely shall we be to satisfy its requirements, and render its exercise an ornament as well as a blessing to society.

D'Aguesseau has called the profession of an advocate "as ancient as the magistracy, and as necessary as justice;" and this is no mere figure of rhetoric or flight of fancy. It is the statement of a simple truth. From the period when men first adopted the forms of civil polity, the principle of advocacy must have existed, though the name may have been unknown. For what is it in theory, but the aid afforded by those whom God has gifted with the means and power, to such as are petitioners for right? Nay! what is the press itself but a mighty advocate at the bar of nations? And when did a time exist when there were not to be found the weak, the timid, and the oppressed, who either dared not, or could not, plead their own cause without assistance, at the footstool of justice? Even when the appeal was not to justice but to power, how often, in the infancy of the world, must the suppliant have needed the agency of a friend to stand between him and vengeance, and solicit mercy and pardon? That friend thereby became his advocate. All whom inability or diffidence prevented from speaking for themselves, because they were "not eloquent, being slow of speech, and of a slow tongue," must, like Moses, have required an Aaron to stand forward as the spokesman on their behalf. It was this feeling which wrung from Job, in the depth of his anguish, the bitter cry, "O that one might plead for a man with God, as a man pleadeth for his neighbor!"

We can not, however, expect to find, in the infancy of civilization, any formal recognition of the necessity of the office of an advocate as a distinct calling or profession. In those remote ages, when the transactions of life were of the simplest character, and education had not wrought such wondrous difference in the use of intellect as now exists between man and his fellow man, it might well be thought that the surest mode of eliciting the truth between contending parties was to bring the accuser and the accused face to face, and let each tell his own story, with such proofs as he could adduce, without allowing another to interfere. In that earliest account of a trial, where inquisition is made for blood, which Homer has given us in his description of the shield made by Hephæstus, at the request of Thetis, for Achilles, the parties are represented as pleading themselves before the judges, each his own advocate *Iliad*, xviii. 497–508).

> "The people thronged the forum, where arose
> The strife of tongues, and two contending stood;
> The one asserting he had paid the mulct,
> The price of blood, for having slain a man,
> The other claiming still the fine as due:
> Both eager to the judges made appeal.
> The crowd, by heralds scarce kept back, with shouts
> And cheers applauded loudly each in turn.
> On smooth and polished stones, a sacred ring,
> The elders sat, and in their hands their staves
> Of office held, to hear and judge the cause;
> While in the midst two golden talents lay,
> The prize of him who should most justly plead."

Diodorus Siculus tells us that the ancient Egyptians expressly forbade advocates to plead in their courts, on the ground that they darkened the administration of the laws. The account which this author gives of the legal tribunals in Egypt, in the olden time, is very interesting. From each of the cities, Heliopolis, Thebes, and Memphis, ten of the most eminent persons were selected to form the court; and when these thirty met, they chose one of their number, most competent for the office, to act as president ($\dot{\alpha}\rho\chi\iota\delta\iota\kappa\alpha\sigma\tau\acute{\eta}s$). In order to supply the vacancy thus occasioned among the *puisnes*, the city from which he had come then sent another in his place. The king provided all the judges with ample maintenance, but a much larger proportion fell to the share of the president, who wore, suspended round his neck by a gold chain (like that of the Lord Chief Justice or Chief Baron in England), a small image made of precious stones. The name of this image was Truth, and whenever the president put it on, it was the signal for the commencement of the trial. The whole of the laws of the realm were contained in eight books, which, for the convenience of reference, lay before the judges, and the proceedings were all conducted in writing.

The plaintiff first wrote down the nature of his cause of action, and the amount of damages which he claimed. The defendant then pleaded to the " declaration," either by denying the facts alleged, or confessing and avoiding them, or pleading in mitigation of damages. Upon this the plaintiff replied, and the defendant rejoined. This seems to have been the limit to the counter-allegations, and without straying into the regions of surrejoinder, rebutter, and surrebutter, the cause was now at issue, and the court having taken the "paper books," proceeded to consider the case. The mode in which judgment was delivered, was by the president placing his image of Truth upon the written pleadings of that party in whose favor the court had determined. Diodorus says that the Egyptians adopted this system from a conviction that it was most favorable to the administration of even-handed justice. Parties were thereby placed more upon a level, and the clever and tricky had no undue advantage over the simple and honest, as they could not avail themselves of rhetorical flourishes and appeals to the passions by set speeches. And he adds, that the law took care to allow sufficient time to each party to reply to the pleading of his adversary, and to the court to consider its judgment.

Sir Thomas More makes the absence of advocates one of the characteristic features of his Utopia. "They have no lawyers among them, for they consider them as a sort of people whose profession it is to disguise matters as well as to wrest laws; and therefore they think it is much better that every man should plead his own cause and trust it to the judge, as well as in other places the client does it to a counselor. By this means they both cut off many delays and find out truth more certainly. For after the parties have laid open the merits of their cause, without those artifices which lawyers are apt to suggest, the judge examines the whole matter, and supports the simplicity of such well-meaning persons whom otherwise crafty men would be sure to run down. And thus they avoid those evils which appear very remarkably among all those nations that labor under a vast load of laws." This is fiction; but Milton tells us the same of the hardly civilized Muscovites in his time. "They have no lawyers, but every man pleads his own cause, or else by bill or answer in writing delivers it with his own hand to the duke: yet justice by corruption of inferiors is much perverted. Where other proof is wanting they may try the matter by personal combat or by champion" (*Prose Works*, iv. 278).

It may seem to be almost a truism to assert that the profession of the advocate has flourished most amidst free institutions and under popular governments. For it is reasonable to suppose that the jealous tyranny of despotism would dread the searching investigation of facts and fearless comment upon them, which it is the duty of the orator of the courts to make. And yet history warrants us in asserting that, even where arbitrary power exists, his office may be held in the highest estimation. Nowhere do we find a more ample recognition of its use and importance than in the Code of Justinian, under a system where the will of the emperor was law, according to the famous maxim, *Quod principi placuit legis habet vigorem;* and in no country has it been more honored than in France under the old *régime*, when legislation was carried on by royal ordinances, and *l'Etat, c'est moi,* was the motto of her monarchs. A limit no doubt was drawn, both there and in imperial Rome, within which the advocate was obliged to confine himself: and he could not, with any safety to himself or advantage to his client, discuss matters of state policy, or reflect upon the acts of those in power. But in contests between parties for private rights, and in the defense of those who were charged with crimes against society as distinguished from the government, free scope was given to his exertions; and parties were enabled to pour their complaints into the ear of justice and make themselves heard, not by their own imperfect utterance, " with bated breath and whispering humbleness," but by means of the bold and fluent language of practiced speakers. And this is an advantage of no ordinary kind. It forms the best security for a pure administration of the laws, that no judicial verdict can be given without a full discussion of the merits of the case, and that the magistrate, before he decides against a party, is compelled to hear, in open court and in the face of the public, every argument which ingenuity and eloquence can urge in his behalf.

The utility of the office of an advocate depends much upon the character of the tribunals before which he has to plead. If they are notoriously corrupt, the consciousness of this fact paralyzes his efforts, and suitors dare not rely upon his assistance, but have recourse to bribery to secure a favorable hearing. And in the republics of Athens and Rome, the courts of justice were in a far worse condition in this respect than those which existed under the Roman empire and in France. According to Xenophon, the capricious fickleness of the Athenian courts was one of the reasons alleged by Socrates for refusing to make any preparation for his defense. He had seen them, he said, frequently condemning to death the innocent, and acquitting the guilty. It is sufficient here merely to notice the fact, as an opportunity will occur of considering it more fully hereafter.

In one point of view, indeed, popular institutions are essential to enable the advocate to achieve his highest triumphs. For it is obvious that the chief gift and attribute of his art is eloquence, and this must be trained and practiced in a very different school from that of despotism. Hobbes has defined democracy to be "a republic of orators, interrupted now and then by the monarchy of a single orator;" and, in the words of Giannone, "those who know how to speak well have a great advantage in assemblies of the people, which is willingly led by the ears (*il quale si mena volontieri per orecchie*); whence it happens that in a free state the advocates are generally those who have most power and authority." In order to learn what are the noblest efforts of which oratory is capable, we instinctively turn to Athens and Demosthenes, or to Rome and Cicero, and remember that both these great speakers gained their immortal fame under republican forms of government, and in the midst of popular tumults. France may seem to present an exception to this rule, for her advocates were distinguished for their eloquence at a time when the power of the crown was without check or control, and all the functions of government centered in the king and his ministers. But her parliaments were in reality a popular institution, which afforded scope and opportunity for the display of forensic oratory, such as has rarely been enjoyed in other countries. And it is a remarkable fact, that however arbitrary might be the conduct of the monarch in other respects, justice was generally administered in those courts with a firm and upright hand, and the crown seldom, if ever, attempted to interfere.

CHAPTER II.

THE ATHENIAN COURTS.

WHEN we speak of the eloquence of Greece, we mean that of Athens only, for no other city or state produced a single orator; and it is to her alone that we must look for anything relating to the profession of an advocate. But here we shall be somewhat disappointed. Among the Athenians there was no distinct class of men whose peculiar office it was to speak on behalf of parties in a court of justice. The practice was not uniform, but the rule, generally, seems to have been, that a speaker was not allowed to appear as an advocate, unless he had some interest in the cause himself. Thus, when Demosthenes defended Ctesiphon in the oration for the crown, it is obvious that he considered himself upon his trial; for the charge which Æschines had brought against Ctesiphon was, that he had illegally proposed that Demosthenes should be rewarded for his patriotic exertions by a golden crown; and the accusation was intended to give his great rival an opportunity of making an attack upon him. So, likewise, in the case where Demosthenes spoke on behalf of Phanus, he was interested in the result, for the action against the latter arose out of the proceedings which Demosthenes had been compelled to take against his guardians, to recover property which they had embezzled. But although originally parties were not allowed to avail themselves of the assistance of advocates to plead their causes for them. this rule was so far relaxed in after times, that a relative or friend was permitted to speak in their behalf, if they were prevented by illness or other inability from conducting their own case. It was upon this principle that, when Miltiades was impeached before the sovereign people, and, being incapacitated by disease from addressing the multitude, he appeared in the assembly borne upon a litter, his brother Tisagoras rose and spoke in his behalf; and, in the speech for the inheritance of Nicostratus, Isæus, who appeared for two of the claimants, commences by saying, "Gentlemen of the Jury, Agnon and Agnotheus, who are the plaintiffs in this suit, are friends and connections of mine; as their father was before them. It seems, therefore, to me to be reasonable that I should advocate their cause to the best of my ability." Sometimes several relatives were allowed to divide the task among them. Thus the party who opened the defense which Demosthenes wrote for Phormion, commences by saying, "You are well aware, Athenians, how incompetent Phormion is to make a speech, and it is necessary for us, who are his connections, to inform you of the facts which we know, having often heard them from his own lips."[1] Sometimes, however, we find a party to a suit lamenting his inefficiency as a

[1] In the mock trial that occurs in Lucian's *Bis Accusatus*, where Drunkenness brings an action against the Academy for enticing away and harboring one of her slaves, the plaintiff is allowed to be represented by counsel for a very sufficient reason:—

Justice (loquitur). "State your case, Madam Drunkenness. Why do you keep silence and nod your head in that way? Go, Mercury, and ascertain the reason."

Mercury. "She says that she can not speak, as she is tongue-tied from the effects of strong liquor, and is afraid of making herself ridiculous in court; and she says that she can scarce stand, as you perceive."

Justice. "Well, then, let her retain one of these clever fellows as her advocate; for there are many of them ready and willing to burst themselves for a fee—(ἐπὶ τριωβόλῳ διαρραγῆναι ἑτοιμοι.)"

speaker, which proves that it was by no means an universal rule to employ a friend as an advocate, even when there might be a valid plea for making use of his services. Thus, in the defense which Antiphon composed for Helus the Mitylenæan, who was prosecuted for the murder of Herodus in the course of a voyage, he makes him put forward his inexperience in legal proceedings, and his want of fluency, as reasons why the jury should be upon their guard, and pay strict attention to the evidence, and not suffer themselves to be led away by the eloquence of his accuser.

It is obvious that these are cases very different from the employment of counsel, who are strangers to the parties, and who have no personal interest in the issue of the trial. They were offices of friendship performed gratuitously, and can hardly be said to fall within the scope of the present work. The persons at Athens who corresponded most nearly to our idea of advocates, were not speakers in the courts, but those who composed speeches for clients (λογογράφοι,) to be delivered by the parties themselves in their own causes, as in the case in our own courts-martial. This was the ordinary occupation of a class of distinguished men at Athens, such as Antiphon, Lysias,[1] Isæus, Isocrates, Dinarchus, and Demades, who gained a livelihood by it, after Antiphon had first set the laudable example of receiving fees for his services, in thus providing litigént parties with the means of attack and defense in the courts of law. It was even thought by some of the ancients, that the spirited speeches in which Demosthenes attacked his fraudulent guardians when only nineteen years of age,

---

[1] Lysias did not speak in the courts of law himself, for in this sense we must understand what Cicero says of him *ipse quidem in causis forensibus non versatus,,* as he certainly composed forensic pleadings for others, of which we possess several specimens. The same remark applies to Isocrates, whom Cicero calls *magnus orator et perfectus magister, quanquam forensi luce caruit.* He gave lectures in rhetoric, and we are told that all Greece flocked to his house, as to a school of oratory.—*Cic. Brut. 8.*

were composed for him by Isæus. And he used to employ himself in the same vocation, until public affairs absorbed the whole of his attention. Thus many of the speeches which are found in the list of his extant orations were composed, but not delivered by him ; as, for instance, that against Androtion, which he wrote for Diodorus ; and that against Zenothemis for Demon, who was one of his relatives. In the latter case the plaintiff describes his application to Demosthenes to assist him. " I went to him and begged him to aid me and stand by me if he possibly could ; on which he said, ' Demon, I certainly will comply with your request ; for it would be a hard case if I did not. I must consider, however, my own interest as well as yours. It so happens that since I began to speak on political questions, I have never undertaken a single private cause." [1]

The occasion on which this rather reluctant consent was given by Demosthenes, was an action arising out of some curious circumstances, which may be shortly mentioned. Hegestratus was the master of an Athenian vessel on a voyage to Syracuse and back ; and Zenothemis, who seems to have been a sort of partner of his, was a passenger on board. While at Syracuse, these two worthies (if we are to believe the account as we find it in the speech written by Demosthenes) entered in a conspiracy to borrow money upon bottomry, that is, on the

[1] Quintilian says that there was a law at Athens which prohibited a person from pleading the cause of another in court: *Et tum maximè scribere litigatoribus, qvæ illi pro se ipsi dicerent, erat moris; atque ita* juri, quo non licebat pro altero agere, *fraus adhibebatur.*—Inst. Orat. ii. 15. In a learned note on this passage Spalding notices an exception to this law, namely, the case where a party had not the right of being heard himself in a court of justice, of which an instance occurs in the speech of Lysias on behalf of Callias, a *metic*, or alien *ami* resident in Athens. Other instances were speeches made for minors and females. But expressions are found in the ancient writers which seem to imply that no such law existed, and Spalding admits the difficulty of coming to an accurate conclusion on the point. He says, *Res ad liquidum deducta a VV. DD. non vid.tur.*

security of the vessel, and afterwards sink her, in order to avoid the necessity of payment. The ship was at the time loading a cargo of corn on account of Protus, an Athenian, who had purchased it with money which he had borrowed from Demon. Hegestratus and Zenothemis got the sum they wanted, by representing that the cargo belonged to them, and having put the money on board of another ship they sailed homewards. During the voyage the former proceeded to put their plan into execution, and one night he went down into the hold, and began to knock a hole in the bottom of the vessel, while Zenothemis, his accomplice, remained on deck with the passengers. The noise, however, attracted attention: the sailors hastened below, and Hegestratus was caught in the fact; but to escape seizure he threw himself over the side and was drowned. Zenothemis then tried to work upon the fears of the crew, and induce them to take to the boat and abandon the ship, as she was in a sinking state. The supercargo, however, of the corn was on board, and he offered large sums to the sailors if they would carry her into port. They accordingly exerted themselves to the utmost, and the leaky vessel reached a harbor in Cephallenia, "thanks," says the pious orator, "first to the good providence of the gods, and next to the skill and bravery of the crew." After being repaired, she proceeded to Athens; but on her safe arrival at the Piræus, Zenothemis claimed a lien upon the corn, alleging that it had been purchased by Hegestratus with money which he had lent to him. This gave rise to litigation, in the course of which the speech was delivered, from which the passage quoted above is taken.

It is a curious fact that some of the most celebrated orations of antiquity were never spoken. There is good reason to believe that Demosthenes never delivered his famous speech against Midias, and on this supposition it is amusing to read the self-complacent account he gives of the attempts which had been made to bribe him to suppress it, and his contemptuous rejection of the offer.

Of the fifteen speeches attributed to Antiphon, twelve were mere school exercises; and of Cicero's six orations against Verres only one was spoken, for Verres prudently withdrew into voluntary exile; and the second Philippic was never uttered in the senate, but after it was written, copies were sent to Brutus, Cassius, and others, and one of these, falling into the hands of Antony, filled him with the bitterest hatred against Cicero. Pericles is said to have been the first orator who prepared his speeches by writing them out beforehand, those who preceded him having spoken extempore. But if this be true, his example was soon universally followed, and Æschines tells us that when Demosthenes was at the court of Philip, and was delivering a set speech, he suddenly became confused and forgot what he had written, so that he was unable to go on, and made one or two ineffectual attempts to resume his argument.

The Athenians, a people versatile in character and gifted with extraordinary quickness of intellect, delighted in the excitement of forensic contests, but this was not the only attraction which rendered the office of a dicast or juror acceptable to them. Pericles introduced the custom of paying each of them for his attendance, and the demagogue Cleon, whose great object was to ingratiate himself with the populace, trebled the amount; so that the exercise of their judicial functions became, to a large number of the citizens, a means of livelihood as well as of amusement;[1] and they found

---

[1] The pay fixed by Pericles was an obolus a day. The value of this coin was a little more than three half-pence; and, therefore, when Cleon increased the amount, the Athenian juror had only five-pence for his attendance. Compared with this, the guinea which an English special juryman receives seems munificent; but money values are very deceptive, and prove nothing except when considered in relation to the prices of provisions and other commodities. At Athens the wages of the dicasts amounted to 150 talents yearly.

it more agreeable to meet their gossips on the bench, and listen to the speeches of the suitors or their friends, than devote themselves to the drudgery of their ordinary trades. Hence we find Isocrates complaining that the lower orders at Athens preferred to stay at home and sit as dicasts in the courts, rather than engage in the maritime service of the state. "The real power of the Athenian demus, as he himself well knew, lay in the courts of law. There was his throne, and there his scepter. There he found compliment, court, and adulations rained upon him so thick, that his imagination began at last to believe what his flatterers assured him, that he was a god, and not a man. And a god in some sense he was: for to no earthly tribunal lay there an appeal from him; his person was irresponsible, his decrees irreversible; and if ever there was a despotism complete in itself, 'pure, unsophisticated, dephlegmated, defæcated' despotism, it was that of an Athenian court of judicature."

This passionate fondness of the Athenians for the exercise of their judicial functions, which were such an agreeable source of income to the six thousand dicasts who sat as judges and jurymen in the courts, is satirized by Aristophanes in his comedy of the "Wasps," one of the most valuable, as well as amusing, pictures of the character and manners of that remarkable people, which time has spared us. We there see the vices of the system in full bloom, and one can not but admire the courage of the poet who ventured to bring the subject of "law reform" in such a shape before the sovereign people, and lash the abuses by which the temples of justice at Athens were profaned. He knew well the difficulty of the task he had undertaken, and says—

Χαλεπὸν μὲν καὶ δεινῆς γνώμης καὶ μείζονος ἢ 'πι τρυγῳδοῖς,
'Ιάσασθαι νόσον ἀρχαίαν ἐν τῇ πόλει ἐντετοκυῖαν.

> "'Tis more than comic art can do, however sharp and witty,
> To cure disease thus bred and born, the plague-spot of our city."

As the coffers of the state were replenished by the fines set upon those who were convicted, and a large portion of the money thus obtained was expended upon public shows and festivals, the temptation to give an unfavorable verdict was almost irresistible, and small was the chance of escape if the accused happened to be wealthy! Thus the chorus of dicast-wasps rejoices in the thought that they will soon have Laches before them in court, and—that the general is rich.

> Ἀλλ' ἐγκονῶμεν, ὦνδρες, ὡς ἔσται Λάχητι νυνί·
> Σίμβλον δέ φασι χρημάτων ἔχειν ἅπαντες αὐτόν.
>
> "But hasten, comrades, quickly on! for Laches stands for trial;
> And he has hived a store of wealth, of that there's no denial."

It will not be foreign to our subject to explain briefly the plot of this admirable comedy. Philocleon is an old gentleman who attends the court of Heliæa as one of the dicasts or jurymen, and his zeal in the discharge of his official duties amounts to a kind of insanity:

> Φιληλιαστής ἐστιν ὡς οὐδεὶς ἀνήρ.

He can not sleep for thinking of the bench, and prefers to his comfortable bed at home a shake-down at the door of the court, that he may secure a good seat in the front row when the business commences. There, with his staff in his hand, and his judicial cloak on his shoulders, his delight is to sit all day earning his three *oboli*, and having his ears tickled with the gross flattery by which litigant parties at Athens sought to conciliate the favor of the judges. His son Bdelycleon, who is much scandalized at his father's neglect of domestic affairs, determines to prevent him from getting out of the house; and the scene of the play represents the door of his mansion carefully guarded by two slaves, who have strict orders not to allow their master to go abroad. A net is stretched over the courtyard, and all avenues of escape seem to be closed. The cunning old dicast, however, whose legal experience has not been thrown away, makes many attempts, and his head is soon seen peering out of the chimney-pot. When he is dislodged from this, he tries in vain to burst open the door, against which the slaves place themselves. By and by he pretends that he wants to get out in order that he may sell an ass, but his son tells him that he will attend to that business, and brings out the animal for the purpose. Observing, however, that the poor beast can hardly walk, he stops to examine it, and discovers that Philocleon has strapped himself under its belly, and like another Ulysses, who played the same trick with one of Polyphemus's sheep, is making his escape. He is thrust back into the house, and afterwards is seen creeping along the tiles of the roof, but he is there *netted* like a bird, and fairly baffled. Now, however, up comes, buzzing and swarming, a chorus of fellow dicasts, dressed and painted to represent huge wasps, who, on their way to court, call upon their learned brother, and express their wonder at not finding him ready to accompany them. This gives rise to some amusing dialogue, in which Philocleon and his friends exhaust the vocabulary of abuse against his jailers; but at last Bdelycleon proposes an amicable parley, and undertakes to prove that his father has been grossly cozened and deceived, and that the life of a dicast is nothing better than miserable slavery. The old gentleman stoutly asserts that he reigns like a king, and the chorus is appointed umpire to decide which has the best of the argument. The contest then begins, and in the description which Philocleon gives of the sweets of judicial office, Aristophanes exposes its corruptions with unsparing severity. The following is a sample :—

"The dicast leads a jolly life, who happier is than he?
Though old in age he knows delight, and fares right daintily:

> When rising early in the morn to court he takes his way,
> The great and powerful at the door for him obsequious stay.
> Then some delinquent softly puts his oily palm in mine,
> And conscious of his frauds begins with doleful voice to whine—
> 'Have pity, if, when you yourself in office were, old fellow,
> Perchance you happened to commit some trifling peccadillo;'
> And yet he never would have known of my existence here,
> Had I not tried the rogue before, and—let him off, I fear.
> But when I take my seat in court, with coaxing flattery plied,
> Straightway the promises I break which I have made outside;
> And listen to the cries of those who loud for mercy pray,
> Each striving to avert our wrath in some peculiar way.
> Some plead their wretched poverty, and make a piteous case,
> (Almost as bad as my own plight in this accursed place);
> Some tell us tales of other times, and quote old Æsop's wit,
> And crack their jokes to make us smile, and say we will acquit;
> And if we will not yield, they take their children by the hand,
> And, bathed in tears, before the court the little suppliants stand—
> While tremblingly the father sues for grace and pardon then,
> As though I were a god to grant forgiveness unto men."

Bdelycleon, however, when his turn comes, shows that of the princely revenues of Athens the greater part is gorged by needy and noisy demagogues, while the dicast has to content himself with a wretched pittance of five pence a day, and that, in fact, his majesty is kept as poor as a rat by those who profess to be his devoted champions and warmest friends. A new light breaks in upon the chorus, and they supplicate Philocleon to yield to the entreaties of his son, who promises him all kinds of good things, if he will only "purge and live cleanly" for the future. But the ruling passion is still too strong, and since to him, as to Dandin in Racine's comedy of *Les Plaideurs*, "*Sans juger, la vie est un supplice*," Bdelycleon proposes that he shall preside over a domestic forum, and try causes at home. This jumps with the old man's humor, and he consents to the arrangement, but insists upon a trial taking place immediately. As luck will have it, the house-dog Labes (meaning Laches, has just run off with and devoured a Sicilian cheese, and the culprit is brought before Philocleon.[1] The prose-

---
[1] The scene refers to the expedition of the Athenians against Syracuse.

cutor is another dog (Cleon), and the indictment runs thus :—

> "The dog of Cydathenus doth present
> Dog Labes of Æxone, for that he
> Singly, alone, did swallow and devour
> One whole Sicilian cheese against the peace."

The trial commences: speeches are delivered for the prosecution and the defense, and the result is that the old dicast, for the first time in his life, drops into the box a verdict of acquittal. This completely staggers him, and he asks pardon of the gods for having been guilty of such an unheard-of act of mercy. His son, however, reassures him by telling him that he will take care of him; and so, after a serio-comic address by the chorus to the audience, the play ends. *Solvuntur risu tabulæ.*

The constitution of the courts of law at Athens was radically bad. Speaking of the legislative powers possessed by the select body drawn from the Heliæa, Bishop Thirlwall says: "But its beneficial effects were in a great measure counteracted by the vicious administration of the laws in the courts of justice, which introduced uncertainty and confusion into all the relations and transactions of private life, and contributed more than any other cause to the public disasters, while it corrupted the character of the people." One of the crying evils of the system was the number of dicasts who sat on every trial. The maxim of *Quicquid multis peccatur inultum* here powerfully applied. They were drawn out of a body of six thousand, who were chosen by lot for the service annually, and were taken indiscriminately from all classes, so that they included a large proportion of the lowest. They were divided into sections of five hundred each, which seems to have been the smallest number of which any tribunal consisted,

in which Laches was one of the generals. Hence the propriety of introducing the *Sicilian* cheese.

but frequently several of these sat together, according to the nature of the case to be tried. We may easily imagine the kind of scene that would take place when such a mob was called upon to decide important questions affecting the property and even lives of individuals. "Even in their best mood the Athenians came to the hearing of a cause with a disposition too like that with which they took their places at the theater, to compare the compositions of rival poets; and, in later times, at least, a skillful advocate seized every opportunity of interspersing his pleading with long poetical quotations." We have seen that Philocleon, in the "Wasps," relates that in this mode his ears were entertained while he sat as a juryman.

They were swayed by party feelings and private animosities; and suitors were not afraid to tell them that they dreaded lest the operation of unjust motives should influence their verdict. To our notions it seems that this line of remark must have been dangerous and almost suicidal, for an English jury would resent such an imputation upon their honesty as a grievous affront; and we know that the approved mode of address to them is the following: "I have the most unbounded confidence, gentlemen, in your integrity and intelligence; I know your reverence for your oaths, and I leave the case of my client in your hands without fear of the result, rejoicing in the thought that there exists for the protection of us all the palladium of a British jury." All must admit that the use of such compliments implies a better state of society, than reproachful advice to men to regard the interests of justice more than the gratification of their own private inclinations. If hypocrisy is the homage which vice pays to virtue, its very existence proves that virtue is acknowledged as the sovereign to whom allegiance is due. And this, in a national point of view, is a blessing of the first importance.

In criminal prosecutions the dicasts had, as has been

noticed, a direct interest in the conviction of the defendant, for by the confiscation of his property the state was enriched, and thus they themselves were benefited. The consequence was, that an odious class of men, the common imformers, *sycophants*, as they were called, were enabled to drive a gainful trade by extorting money from the fears of the wealthy, whom they threatened to denounce before the tribunals.

The number of these trials, and of lawsuits generally, was enormously increased at Athens during the period when she was acknowledged mistress of Greece, after the foolish conduct of Pausanias had alienated the other states from Sparta, and made them unwilling to submit to her supremacy. From the islands of the Ægæan and the shores of Asia Minor, as well as from the distant dependencies along the coast of Thrace, wealthy citizens were summoned before the Athenian tribunals, to answer charges of disaffection and sedition, the real object being to plunder them of their property under the mockery of legal forms. And, under various pretexts, a vast number of private causes, which ought to have been tried in the cities where the parties lived, found their way to Athens, and were decided there. In his Treatise on the Athenian Republic, Xenophon mentions several cogent reasons why the allies were compelled by the sovereign city to resort to her law courts for redress. First of all, he says, there were the court fees ($\pi\rho\upsilon\tau\alpha\nu\varepsilon\tilde{\iota}\alpha$); and, in the next place, the populace had, by this means, the power of obliging their friends, and ruining their enemies. Besides this, the customhouse at the Peiræus was benefited, and lodging-house keepers, and those who let out cattle and slaves for hire, were enabled to drive a thriving trade. But, beyond all these advantages, the people came in for a share of homage and flattery which they would not otherwise have enjoyed; "for, in the courts of justice, one is obliged to use entreaties, and, on entering in, to shake the dicasts by the hand." And this grasp of the hand implied more than mere friendship, for direct bribery was employed to obtain favorable verdicts, though here the number of the judges operated, in some degree, as a check. Xenophon says, " I must admit that many things are transacted at Athens by means of bribery, and that much more would be done, if more were ready to give bribes."

Let us now briefly notice some of the characteristic features of the modes of trial at Athens, avoiding, as much as possible, mere technical details. The process in a civil suit was shortly as follows. The plaintiff went before the magistrate who had jurisdiction in the subject-matter of the particular action, and obtained a summons for the appearance of the defendant before him. Between the summons and the appearance an interval of five days usually elapsed. Both parties afterwards attended, and a preliminary inquiry took place, when the magistrate had to determine whether or not the plaintiff had a *primâ facie* cause of action, and also whether there was any legal impediment to the further progress of the suit. If everything appeared to him to be regular, he appointed a day for another preliminary appearance, and a board or tablet was suspended outside his office to give notice to the public that such and such a cause was going on. When the appointed day arrived, the magistrate heard from each party a statement of his case, and the evidence of witnesses and other proofs were taken before him, not that he might decide judicially upon them, but that they might be carefully preserved by him, like depositions before a coroner or justice of the peace in England, and sealed up in a box (*echinus*) until the time came for laying the case before a jury. The use or object of this sort of interlocutory proceeding in a civil suit is not very obvious, but it may have been intended to give the parties an opportunity of effecting a compromise, or in order to inform the magistrate beforehand fully of the particulars of the cause, as it was his duty to preside at the jury-trial which afterwards took place; or, like the written pleadings in our own system, to facilitate the proceeding in court. No evidence was allowed to be given at the trial which had not been submitted to the magistrate at the preliminary investigation; and where a witness had been prevented from attending then, the party who wished to call him made a written statement of what he expected he would be able to prove, and this was deposited with the other documents in the cause in the magistrate's box, but at the trial the witness was obliged to appear, and by oath support or contradict the statement which had been prepared for him. And the other witnesses also were bound to be in attendance at the trial, not to state new matter, but to certify to the truth of the depositions they had already made, in order that the jury might have an opportunity of seeing them and observing their demeanor. The mode of giving a verdict was by putting into one of two urns, which stood ready for the purpose, a bean, or pebble, or mussel-shell, or brass ball, according to the nature of the trial.

The line between civil and criminal actions was not very accurately drawn, and we are sometimes at a loss to know whether we ought to designate the party, who set the law in motion, as plaintiff or prosecutor. For instance, in the speech of Demosthenes against Aphobus, his dishonest guardian, whose offense consisted in a breach of trust, he deals with it as a crime; and yet, if he succeeded at the trial, the only result would be that Aphobus must refund the money which he had wrongfully embezzled. And it was a peculiar feature in the trials at Athens, that they were divided into two classes, assessed ($\tau\iota\mu\eta\tau o\iota$) and non-assessed ($\dot{\alpha}\tau\iota\mu\eta\tau o\iota$). In the former, if the case was in the nature of a civil action, the plaintiff laid his damages at a certain amount; or, if it was a criminal case, the prosecutor named a certain penalty to be paid by the accused. The court then, after hearing the evidence, gave judgment first simply for or against the defendant, and if their verdict was unfavorable, provided it was not a capital case, he was allowed himself to name the punishment or penalty ($\mathring{\alpha}\nu\tau\iota\tau\acute{\iota}\mu\eta\mu\alpha$) which he thought ought to be inflicted upon him. Afterwards the dicasts voted a second time, and decided whether the original penalty or the one proposed by the defendant, or even, in some cases, one differing from both, should be finally adjudged. Those members of the court who were of opinion that the severer sentence should be pronounced, drew a long line ($\mu\alpha\varkappa\rho\grave{\alpha}\nu$) across the waxen tablet with which each of them was provided; those who took the more lenient view drew a short one. Hence we may understand the full force of the proud and lofty reply of Socrates, who, when he was asked by his judges after his conviction what sentence he deserved, said, "If I am to receive my deserts, I ought to have the highest honors paid to me, and be entertained at the public expense in the Prytaneum."[1] This answer, according to Cicero, so exasperated the court, that they immediately condemned him to death.

In the second class of actions the nature and amount of the penalty was determined by the law, and the judges, if they gave their verdict against a defendant, were obliged to award that punishment.

The mode of procedure in conducting State Trials at Athens is involved in more obscurity, owing to the scanty notices of them contained in the works which we possess

---

[1] *Plato, in Apolog. Soc.;* and *Cic. De Orat.* i. 54. From the narrative of Cicero it would seem that the sentence against Socrates was both iniquitous and illegal; for if the offense with which he was charged had been capital, there could not have been a *pœnæ æstimatio*. But perhaps the *fraus capitalis* may mean a crime for which the law fixed death as the penalty, leaving no discretion to the judges. In other cases they may have had power to award that punishment without being compelled to do so.

of the ancient writers. But the following is an outline of what took place. First of all, as a preliminary step, a motion was made in the popular assembly, or Ecclesia, by the prosecutor, that the accused should be put upon his trial, and this question was fully debated and put to the vote. We may call this the finding of the Grand Jury. If the people determined in favor of the motion, a day was fixed for the trial, and the party charged with the offense was, unless he gave sufficient bail, forthwith committed to prison. Shortly afterwards it was referred to an assembly of the people to decide upon the mode of trial, and the punishment that should be awarded, in case the party were found guilty. On the day of trial, if it took place before the people at large, the prosecutor rose, and formally stated the charge, supporting it with proofs, and he might be followed by any other speaker who wished to press the accusation. The prisoner then pleaded his own cause, and sometimes with fetters on his limbs, while officers stood on each side to prevent his escape. Two urns, or ballot-boxes, were placed for the use of each tribe, and into these the people cast the tablet of acquittal or condemnation, according as each wished to deliver his verdict. If found guilty, the prisoner underwent the punishment which had been previously appointed.

Sometimes, however, the people determined that they would not in a body try the accused, but ordered that he should be brought before the criminal judges, called Heliastæ; and it was the duty of certain public officers named Thesmothetæ, to undertake the management of the proceedings. In order that the interests of the State might be fully represented, it was customary to appoint, besides the prosecutor, who originally brought forward the impeachment, several public advocates, generally not less than ten, to assist him in enforcing the charge. These were called Synegori, and received each a drachm of the public money for their services;[1] but the office was not a permanent one, and they were selected as different occasions arose. Thus, when Cimon was accused of having corruptly, for a bribe, abandoned the invasion of Macedon, the conquest of which was supposed to be within his grasp, Pericles, a most formidable accuser, was appointed by the people to speak for the prosecution. But the party who brought forward the charge did so at his peril, for if he failed in obtaining the suffrages of a fifth part of the judges for a conviction, he was fined a thousand drachms, and in old times is said to have been punished still more severely.

A remarkable difference between the mode of conducting trials at Athens, and in England at the present day, consists in the degree of strictness required in supporting an accusation by proof. Among the Athenians we find the most lamentable deficiency in this first principle of justice. Common report was admitted as good evidence of guilt, and was held sufficient sometimes to warrant a conviction, though no specific proofs could be brought forward. Thus Æschines, in his speech against Timarchus, strongly insists upon the point that the prosecutor may proceed upon the notoriety of the facts charged against a party, and we find him constantly *presuming* the guilt of Timarchus, simply on the ground that everybody knew it, although he acknowledges his inability to bring direct evinence. Nay, he goes so far as to pronounce a panegyric upon the power of Rumor, to which, as a mighty goddess, he says the state formerly had erected an altar; and he

---

[1] Schol. ad Aristoph. Vesp. v. 689. The drachm was worth about tenpence of our money. "The wages of public advocates or orators ($\mu\iota\sigma\theta\grave{o}s$ $\sigma\upsilon\nu\eta\gamma o\rho\iota\varkappa\grave{o}s$) occasioned a small expense, which amounted every day, *i. e.* for the 300 days of business, to a drachm, and not for each speech, as the scholiast of Aristophanes erroneously asserts. As these advocates were ten in number, the whole expense amounted to half a talent a year."—*Bœckh*, i. 317.

quotes Homer, Hesiod, and Euripides, to prove the respect due to her influence. And this, too, in a criminal trial, where the character of the defendant was at stake, and the question was, whether he had been guilty of certain specific offenses of the most disgraceful nature. What more dangerous method for the destruction of the innocent can be imagined than this?

Although the rule in Athenian courts of justice, as in our own, was against the reception of hearsay evidence to prove particular facts, we find it was frequently violated in practice; and besides this, the speakers were in the habit of supporting their assertions, by appealing to the personal knowledge of the jurors themselves. We can well understand how, in a small community like that of Athens, where the jury on each trial bore no inconsiderable proportion to the whole number of citizens, many of those who sat as dicasts must have been cognizant beforehand of the facts of the case; and no doubt the verdict was often given, not upon the evidence adduced in court, but on the private information which they themselves possessed.[1] Indeed, Æschines tells us that it was the avowed system of the court of Areopagus (by far the most virtuous as well as most august tribunal at Athens), for the judges to give their votes, not merely according to the evidence and statements before them, but acting upon their own private information and inquiries.

The same effect seems to have been given to dying declarations, in cases of murder, by the Athenian as by the English law. An instance occurs in a speech composed by Antiphon for the prosecution of a wife, charged with having suborned a person to take off her husband

[1] It is hardly necessary to point out the resemblance, in this respect, between the Athenian dicasts and the English jury of ancient times. Among our ancestors, the jury originally were summoned rather as witnesses than triers. They came from the *vicinetum* or neighborhood (hence the word *venue*), and were such as had, or were supposed to have, personal knowledge of the fact in dispute.

by poison. He says, "You may be sure that those who design the death of their neighbors, do not plot and take their measures in the presence of witnesses, but do it as secretly as possible; and so that no one knows what they are about. And those whose lives are attempted, are in utter ignorance until they are attacked, and discover that destruction has overtaken them. Then, however, if they have sufficient time before they die, they summon their friends and relations, and take them to witness, and tell them who the persons are by whom they were murdered, and charge them to avenge their death, as my father charged me, when he lay dying in his miserable and mortal sickness. But if they can not get their friends around them, they write down the facts as they have occurred, and call upon their domestics to be witnesses, and make known to them the names of their assassins."

One of the most approved modes of obtaining evidence at Athens, and also at Rome, in civil as well as in criminal trials, was by the torture of slaves. We find the Grecian orators constantly appealing to this test, as the most infallible they can offer of the truth of their assertions. It seems to have been deliberately preferred to any other. In his speech against Onetor, Demosthenes makes the following astounding statement to an Athenian jury:—"You think with good reason, gentlemen, that both in public and private trials the application of torture is the most trustworthy of all modes of proof; and whenever slaves as well as freemen are offered as witnesses, and the question in dispute requires investigation, you prefer, not to avail yourselves of the depositions of freemen, but endeavor to ascertain the facts by putting slaves to the torture. For it has happened before now that the former, in the witness-box, have given false evidence, but it has never yet been proved, that what slaves have said under the influence of torture was untrue."

Now, dismissing for a moment all consideration of the monstrous cruelty involved in such a proposition, was there ever one more manifestly absurd? The use of torture in judicial inquiries, was the great practical fallacy of antiquity. It is inconceivable how men of sense could have lent themselves to the support of a system, as inimical to truth as perjury itself. For what had a slave to dread if he was convicted of a lie, but torture, and perhaps death? If, then, he had to endure the extremity of pain, unless he made a particular statement to suit the views of his tormentors, it is clear that, to avoid this, he would be irresistibly tempted to make the statement, though false, knowing that nothing worse could happen to him if his falsehood was discovered; and besides this, who could expect a poor illiterate creature to undergo with heroic firmness the worst agonies of human suffering, from which he might by a single word be immediately relieved, rather than speak that word because it was untrue?

The uselessness of the torture as a test of truth was, however, well known to the more intelligent among the Greeks, and this renders it the more surprising that it should have been continued in the courts of law. Antiphon thus speaks of it in a defense which he wrote for a party on his trial for murder, against whom some slaves had been examined under torture. "Just consider now the circumstances attending the use of the torture. My accusers promised freedom to the slave, and it was in their power to release him from suffering: so that, being under the influence of both these considerations, he bore false witness against me, hoping to gain his liberty, and wishing to be immediately released from torture. *For I fancy you all know perfectly well, that whoever have it in their power to inflict the greatest amount of pain, have at their command the testimony of those who will take care to say whatever is likely to gratify those who put them to the torture*" (*De Cæde Herod*).

The same idea is expressed in the following passage of Cicero, where he speaks of the examination by torture of some slaves:—"The effect of torture depends upon the pain, and in each case varies according to the nature of the mind as well as the body. It is under the control of the inquisitor, and is swayed by his caprice; hope and fear agitate the victim, so that in such a trying ordeal no room is left for truth" (*Pro Sulla*, 78).

It seems wonderful to us how Judges could bear to look upon the infliction of human suffering; but from habit they came no doubt to regard it with indifference, as in the following scene:—

"*Dandin.* N'avez vous jamais vu donner la question?
Isabelle. Non; et ne le verrai, que je crois, de ma vie.
Dandin. Venez, je vous en veux faire passer l'envie.
Isabelle. Hé, Monsieur! peut-on voir souffrir des malheureux?
Dandin. Bon! cela fait toujours passer une heure ou deux."
Les Plaideurs, act iii. sc. 4.

But the subject will not bear argument. The marvel is, that such a vile and iniquitous system should ever have suggested itself as a means for the discovery of truth. And we blush to think that it was practiced in Great Britain less than two centuries ago. There was, however, an important difference between ancient and modern times in this respect. For we do not find that it was at all usual in any country of modern Europe to torture *witnesses*, but only the party accused of a crime, in order to make him confess.

Although, to the honor of the English law, it was decided by all the judges in the case of Felton, who assassinated the Duke of Buckingham, that "he ought not by the law to be tortured by the rack, for no such punishment is known or allowed by our law," yet instances have undoubtedly occurred in our criminal annals, where the torture was applied. Thus, in the disgraceful proceedings against Peacham, in the reign of James I., who was indicted for high treason on account of some passages found in a manuscript sermon locked up in his desk, which he had never preached or in any way published, we find in a memorandum attached to some interrogatories upon which he was examined, the following statement: "Upon these interrogatories Peacham this day was examined, *before torture, in torture, between torture, and after torture;* notwithstanding, nothing could be drawn from him, he still persisting in his obstinate and insensible denials and former answers; and to this paper is set the name, among others, of Francis Bacon.[1]

In some trials the time during which a party might address the court was unlimited; but in others, it was regulated by a clepsydra, or water-clock. The former class of cases comprised actions brought by children against their parents for ill-treatment; by heiresses against their husbands; and wards against their guardians. In the latter, a certain quantity of water was measured out to each speaker, which ran something in the manner of sand in modern hour-glasses, and when it was exhausted he was obliged to stop. But while witnesses were under examination, or legal documents were read (which, by what seems to have been a most inconvenient practice, took place at different parts of the speaker's address, and interrupted its continuous thread), the water was stopped, and the time thus occupied was not taken into account. The pleader might, if he thought fit, give up a portion of his allotted water to another party interested in the cause, and thus enable him to speak at greater length. This water-system gave rise to a number of curious expressions which occur in the Attic orators, and it is necessary to be familiar with the usage, in order to understand them. It was a fre-

---

[1] *State Tr.* ii. 871. Some interesting particulars on this subject will be found in the *State Trials*, vols. ii. 774; x. 751, 753; xxx. 484, 541, 892. In Scotland the torture was in use until the union of the two kingdoms, and was only finally abolished by stat. 7 *Ann.* c. 21, § 5.

quent cause of complaint with them, that the time within which they were thus circumscribed, was not sufficient, and the greatest of them more than once laments that he is compelled to omit heavy charges against his opponents, because he is short of water. We might almost fancy he was speaking of a locomotive. Auger, the French translator of Demosthenes, seems to think that this circumstance may have given to the forensic speeches at Athens their terse and business-like character. The time, he says, was somewhat limited in private causes; the clepsydra, or water-clock, afforded but little, and the advocate had none to lose. It was therefore necessary for him not to extend too far his means of attack or defense, but confine them within certain limits: he was obliged to state his facts with brevity, and prove them by means of depositions and witnesses. But we must recollect that a similar custom prevailed at Rome, and the style of oratory there was the very opposite of the Athenian. The difference was chiefly caused by the genius of the two languages. The poverty of the Latin sought concealment in amplifications and the use of superlatives, of which the wondrous flexibility and force of the Greek disdained to avail itself.

In the speeches of the Attic orators, we can not help noticing the virulence of abuse in which they indulge against their opponents. Language is employed of the most insulting kind, and disgraceful epithets are scattered with a lavish hand. It seems to us at first sight unaccountable, that they should have ventured upon such personalities, and not have been deterred by a fear of unpleasant consequences to themselves. But we must bear in mind, that the ancients were far less sensitive in matters of this kind than ourselves. The point of honor was unknown to them, and they had no idea of that punctilio, which regulates the intercourse of educated men with each other in modern times. An

Athenian or Roman gentleman might apply, with impunity, terms to his adversary, which would not be tolerated among us. And moreover, that refinement of civilized society, whereby a man who has received an affront, fancies that he obtains satisfaction by exposing himself to the chance of being shot, does not seem to have ever occurred to the nations of antiquity.[1]

In making acquaintance with the remains of the ancient orators, we are too apt to confine our attention exclusively to a few great speeches, and fancy that a perusal of them is sufficient to give us a competent knowledge of this branch of classical learning. And, no doubt, if we wish merely to be able to appreciate the eloquence of antiquity, we can not do better than devote ourselves to the study of the Philippics, or the Crown oration, and the speeches of Cicero on behalf of Milo and against Antony; but we shall learn more of the private life, and customs and manners of the Athenian and Roman people, and become much more familiar with their laws and usages, if we read with attention what may be called their forensic speeches. Not many of these have been preserved; but such as are extant are most valuable and interesting, by bringing us into closer contact with the two most remarkable nations of antiquity. We see them, as it were, in undress before us. But, at the same time, these speeches reveal a state of society from which, in some points of view, the mind recoils with disgust, and we rise from the perusal of them with a deep conviction of the truth of the charges, which the great Apostle of the Gentiles brought against the heathen world, and see how it was that "God gave them up to uncleanness through the lusts of their own hearts."

The following graphic account of a case of *crim. con.* is

---

[1] By the Salic law, the price to be paid for blows was regulated by a graduated scale or tariff. So also among the Lombards. On the origin of dueling, see Montesquieu, *Esprit de Lois*, l. xxviii. c. 20.

contained in a speech composed by Lysias, on behalf of a client named Euphiletus, who having caught Eratosthenes, the paramour of his wife, in his house, and having clear proof of the adultery, had killed him on the spot, and was afterwards tried on the charge of murder. We must remember that this incident occurred upwards of two thousand years ago at Athens; and we shall see that the circumstances attending it are such as might have happened yesterday; and we might almost fancy that we were reading the report of a trial in one of our own courts in former days, and a statement by counsel of the facts, on which the injured husband founded a claim for heavy damages against the author of his dishonor.

"I will tell you, gentlemen, the whole circumstances from the beginning, omitting nothing, but speaking the truth; for I think that this is my only chance of safety, if I can succeed in making you understand everything that has happened. Well, then, gentlemen, when I determined to marry, and took a wife home with me, I at first observed a guarded line of conduct, and was neither harsh towards her, nor, on the other hand, allowed her to do just as she liked. But I kept my eye upon her as much as possible. However, after she had borne me a child, I at once placed confidence in her, and gave her the entire management of my household affairs, thinking that there was now the closest bond of union between us. And at first, gentlemen of the jury, her conduct was most excellent—for she was a clever and thrify housewife, and managed everything capitally. But afterwards my mother died, and this was the cause of all my misfortunes. For my wife followed her funeral, and being observed by this fellow, was at length seduced by him. By watching the maid-servant as she went to the market, and finding opportunities of conversing with her, he succeeded in effecting my wife's ruin. Now I must tell you that my house, which is a small one, consists of two stories, having rooms above and below exactly alike—the one set being the women's apartments, and the other the men's. And after the birth of our infant, its mother used to suckle it, and, in order that she might not, when she had occasion to wash herself, run any risk of falling, by having to go down stairs, I occupied a room above, and the females slept below. Accordingly, my wife used to leave me at night, and go down, as if for the purpose of sleeping with the child in order that she might give it the breast, and prevent it crying. This state of things continued for a long time, and I never suspected anything, but was foolish enough to think that my wife was one of the most chaste and modest women in the city. But by and by, gentlemen, I came home one day unexpectedly from the country, and after supper the child began to cry, and was very uneasy,—being teased on purpose by the nursery maid, in order that it might make a noise—for the fellow was in the house, as I was afterwards informed,—and I begged my wife to go and give the child the breast, that it might stop crying; but she at first pretended to be unwilling, as though she would rather stay with me after my long absence. I, however, became angry, and ordered her to go, on which she said, 'I suppose you want me to be away that you may flirt with the maid here;—I have not forgotten how, when you were tipsy, you pulled her about.' I laughed at this, and she rose, and as she went out of the room she shut to the door, and, pretending to carry on the joke, turned the key. I then fell asleep, being tired with my journey from the country, and utterly unsuspicious of what was going on. When it was daybreak, she came back and opened the door; and on my asking her why the doors made a noise during the night, said that the lamp that was kept burning beside the child went out, and she went and lighted it at the house of one of her neighbors. I said no more at the time, thinking that this was so. And yet I fancied, gentlemen, at the time that her face was rouged, though her brother had died not thirty days before:—however, I made no remark on this, but went out without saying anything. But some time afterwards, after I had long been ignorant of my own dishonor, there came to me an old woman, who, as I afterwards learnt, was privately sent by a lady with whom the deceased had an intrigue, and who being angry that he discontinued his visits, and thinking that she had a rival, kept a close watch, until she found out what was the cause of his absence. The old woman then, having waited for me near my house, said, 'Don't suppose, Euphiletus, that I have come to you from any desire for officious meddling, for the man who is dishonoring both you and your wife is an enemy of ours. If, however, you will lay hold of your servant girl who goes to market for you, and acts as your housekeeper, and put her to the torture, you will hear everything. And Eratosthenes from Œa is the man who has ruined not only your wife, but many other women.' After having told me this, gentlemen, she went away, and I was much disturbed, while everything rushed into my mind, and I became full of suspicion, when I recollected how I was, on the night that I have mentioned, locked in my chamber, and how one of the inner doors and the front door made a noise which never happened before, and that my wife seemed to have put rouge upon her cheeks. Upon this I went home, and desired the maid-servant to follow me to the market; and taking her to the house of one of my friends, I told her that I had heard what was going on at my house, and said that she might choose either to be whipped and put into the slave-prison for the rest of her life, or by telling the truth escape from this punishment, and be pardoned by me for her wicked conduct. 'But,' I added, 'tell me no lies, but the whole truth.' At first she denied everything, and told me to do what I pleased, for she said she knew nothing. But when I mentioned the name of Eratosthenes to her, and told her that he was the person who visited my wife, she was taken quite aback, and fancied that I knew accurately all that had happened. She thereupon fell on her knees, and having made me promise that I would do her no harm, she related to me in detail what had taken place. When she had finished her account, I charged her to let nobody know of this communication to me, and said, 'that if she did, I would not keep any of the promises I had made to her.' I then told her to give me ocular proof of the truth of her narrative, for I did not want words, but to have the fact demonstrated."

It is sufficient to add that Euphiletus was afterwards amply gratified in this respect; for one night his maid-servant awoke him, and told him that Eratosthenes was in the house; on which he slipped out and collected a posse of friends, with whom he returned home, and when they burst open the door of his wife's bed-chamber, they found Eratosthenes there. The injured husband immediately knocked him down, and afterwards tied his hands behind him, and killed him on the spot. This act he justified on his trial as sanctioned by the law.

As a specimen of the style of reasoning which it was hoped might be successful with an Athenian jury, we may take a few passages from a speech, prepared by Isœus for some clients in a will cause. The case was briefly this:—Cleonymus, having quarreled with his next of kin, made a will, whereby he left his property to the defendants, and deposited it in the archon's office; but the plaintiffs, who were his nearest relations, insisted that before his death he had become reconciled to them, and, intending to cancel his will, had sent a message to one of the archons, to come to his house and bring the will with him, in order that it might be legally revoked; but that the defendants had prevented him from entering the house, and Cleonymus died without having formally canceled the instrument. The defendants therefore relied upon the existing will; the plaintiffs upon the intended revocation. The question was reduced to a very simple issue of fact. Was there, on the part of the testator, an absolute intention to revoke, which had been improperly frustrated by the defendants? After calling several witnesses in their favor, the party who spoke on behalf of himself and his co-plaintiffs thus proceeded with his argument; " You ought, gentlemen, both on account of our near connection with the deceased, and the facts of this case, to give your verdict, as I am sure you will, for those who rely in this dispute upon their relationship to the testator, rather than for those who rely upon the will. For you are all aware of the fact of our being next of kin, and in this no falsehood can be played off upon you. But many have before now propounded false wills; sometimes such as were entire forgeries, and sometimes wills obtained by undue practices. And you all, as I have already said, know perfectly well our near relationship and terms of intimacy with the deceased, on which we found our claim; but none of you can be sure that the will, on which the defendants rely in their attempt to defraud us, was a valid instrument. In the next place, you will find that the fact of our relationship is admitted by our opponents, but the will is disputed by us. For they prevented him from canceling it, when he wished to do so. So that, gentlemen, it is much fairer that you should give your verdict in favor of a family connection which is allowed on both sides, than maintain a will which has been unjustly obtained. And, besides this, consider that Cleonymus wished to cancel it at a time when he was kindly disposed towards us; but he made it when he was angry and under the influence of bad advice; so that it will be the hardest of all possible things, if you give more effect to his fit of passion than his deliberate purpose and intention."

The above argument reduced to a logical form amounts to this: If the will is invalid, we are entitled as heirs at law; but you can not be certain of the validity of the will, for instances of forgery have before now occurred. You ought to prefer a certainty to an uncertainty, and support, therefore, the claims of the relationship which is admitted, rather than the will which is disputed. The fallacy of such reasoning is obvious. The issue in the cause was the fact of the revocation, and this could be in no way affected by the admission that the plaintiffs were the heirs of the deceased, but ought to be determined strictly by the evidence and probabilities of the case.

It is a common charge to bring against advocates at the present day, that they will indifferently espouse and argue upon either side of a question; but what shall we say of the speech-writers at Athens, who sometimes composed orations for both the contending parties in the same cause? It was once made a charge against Demosthenes that he showed a speech which he had prepared for his client to the opposite side. We possess three sets of tetralogies, or quartettes of speeches, which Antiphon wrote for the prosecution and defense in cases of trials for homicide; and an old scholiast mentions this approvingly, as a great feat of dexterity and skill. He says—"It is true that Antiphon always exhibits his native and peculiar power, but especially in those speeches, in which he counterpleads against himself. For having prepared two speeches on behalf of the accuser, he composed two for the accused also, and sustained his high reputation in both alike." One of these trials was of a curious nature. Two youths were practicing archery in a gymnasium, when one of them happened to run across the line of flight of an arrow shot by the other, and was killed. By the law of Athens a person who caused a death by what we call chance-medley, was liable to a prosecution, and the punishment awarded was exclusion from certain religious rites, under the notion that such an expiation was necessary to wipe off the pollution, which would otherwise rest upon the community. In this case the father of the young man who was slain was the accuser, and the defense set up was that, although it was perfectly just and proper that involuntary homicide should be punished, yet here the deceased could in no sense be said to have been killed by his companion, but was the author of his own misfortune; for if he had not gone himself in the direction of the arrow, he would not have been struck.[1] This seems obvious enough; but four speeches are devoted to the subject, and the arguments for and against each view of the case are not unamusing specimens of Athenian special pleading.

[1] This is something like a plea which we find in Bacon's Apophthegms. "A thief, being arraigned at the bar for stealing a mare, in his pleading urged many things in his own behalf; and at last, nothing availing, he told the bench the mare rather stole him than he stole the mare,—which, in brief, he thus related. That, passing over several grounds about his lawful occasions, he was pursued close by a fierce mastiff dog, and so was forced to save himself by leaping over a hedge, which, being of an agile body, he effected; and in leaping, a mare standing on the other side of the hedge, he leaped upon her back, who, running furiously away with him, he could not by any means stop her until he came to the next town, in which town the owner of the mare lived, and there was he taken and here arraigned." The reader will recollect the famous case of Bullum v. Boatum, where the question was, whether the bull went off with the boat, or the boat with the bull.

CHAPTER III.

SKETCH OF THE ROMAN LAW AND THE ROMAN COURTS DURING THE REPUBLIC.

BEFORE we proceed to give an account of the profession of an advocate in ancient Rome, it will be useful to inquire briefly, what was the nature of the Roman law with which he had to make himself acquainted, and what were the tribunals before which he had to plead. It will be sufficient for our present purpose to give merely a slight and imperfect sketch; for the difficult subject of the principles and rules of the early Roman law would require an elaborate treatise of itself, if it were discussed with the fullness which it admits of and deserves. Here, it is only necessary to trace the outlines of the different heads of law as administered at Rome, without staying to investigate the processes and forms peculiar to each separate jurisdiction, or discuss the rights of parties under them. We shall thus see what were the elements, of which the complex idea expressed by the term Roman law consisted, and what it would be understood to embrace in the days of Cicero; just as we might analyze the English law, by separating it into its different branches of common law, equity, statute law, and the civil and canon law administered in our ecclesiastical courts. For this purpose it will be convenient to follow the order of division, which we find in the Institutes and Digest of Justinian (*Inst.* I. tit. i., *Dig.* I.

ii. 2.); and I shall endeavor to render the subject more familiar to our ideas, by illustrations and analogies drawn from our own law.

The clear and interesting narrative given in the Digest is taken from a work which no longer exists, called the Enchiridion of Pomponius. But we can not, with implicit confidence, follow the Roman jurists as authorities on the subject of the early Roman law.[1] To understand this aright, a correct knowledge of the ancient constitution of Rome was necessary; and we know that in this respect they were singularly deficient. The writers in the later times of the republic had very inaccurate conceptions of the history of their country for the first few centuries; and Livy and Dionysius are constantly mistaken when they attempt to explain usages and institutions, of the origin of which no trustworthy record had been preserved. Popular traditions, however improbable as well as untrue, were accepted as a plausible account of bygone events, though often based upon no better foundation than that fertile source

---

[1] The only ancient work in which we have anything like a systematic account of the old Roman law, as it existed in the earlier times of the republic, is the Institutes of Gaius or Caius—for the name is spelt either way, according as the Greek or Latin orthography is preferred. Gaius lived in the reigns of Hadrian and Antoninus Pius, between 117 and 161 A. D.; but we know nothing of his history, except that he was a profound jurist and wrote a great work, called Institutiones, upon the ancient Roman law. Fragments of this were preserved by being incorporated into the Digest or Pandects of Justinian; but the work itself was supposed until recently to be wholly lost. Maffei had, indeed, at the beginning of the last century, discovered in the chapter library at Verona two pages of manuscript, containing a part of these Institutes; but it was not until 1816, that Niebuhr, during a two-days' residence at Verona, while on his way as Prussian ambassador to Rome, discovered nearly the whole work in a palimpsest, on which were written the letters of St. Jerome. Niebuhr was not at first aware of the value of the treasure he had found, not being able at the time to decipher more than satisfied him that it was the work of some old Roman jurist; but, on communicating with Savigny, the latter hazarded a conjecture that it was the lost Institutes of Gaius; and this happily proved to be correct.

of error, a false etymology. And the statements put forward by these historians were generally adopted, without any critical examination of their probability or truth. Indeed, historical criticism did not then exist. It was reserved for our own æra to discover the extent to which they were misled, and Niebuhr in his immortal history, first lifted the veil that shrouds in such deep obscurity the first ages of the republic, and, out of the minute and fragmentary materials which time has spared, shadowed forth the lineaments of truth.[1]

The earliest Roman laws of which any mention is made by Latin writers were those contained in the Papirian code. These were such as were from time to time enacted in the times of the kings, which Sextus Papirius collected in a volume, and they thence received their name. But of these little or nothing is now known. The next in order are those of the Twelve Tables. They were compiled by the Decemvirs at the beginning of the fourth century of Rome, and consisted of a revision of the then existing laws, and some new ones which, according to a very questionable tradition, had been imported from Greece by three Commissioners, who had been sent there for the purpose of collecting notices of such laws and customs as might be useful to the Romans. In the adaptation of these they are said to have been assisted by an Ionian Greek, named Hermodorus of Ephesus. The new code, when completed, was engraved on twelve

---

[1] Dion Cassius, who flourished at the end of the second and in the early part of the third century, had a far more accurate view of the early constitution of Rome than any of the Augustan writers. And yet he was not a Roman by birth, but a native of Nicæa in Bithynia. In speaking of Niebuhr as the author of the true theory of that constitution, it ought, in justice to the memory of Giambattista Vico, to be mentioned that he, in his Scienza di Nuovo, anticipated some of the discoveries of the German historian; especially the all-important difference between the *populus* and *plebs*. The same may be said of Perizonius, and, in a less degree, of Beaufort.

tablets of ivory or brass,[1] and set up publicly in front of the Rostra in the comitium, that the enactments might be seen and read by all the citizens. These were, in the strictest and most technical sense, *leges*, and may be considered as the early statute law of Rome. Cicero speaks of them in the most enthusiastic terms, and in the dialogue De Oratore makes Crassus, who there represents his own opinions, exclaim—"Let people clamor as they will, I shall say what I think. A single copy of the Twelve Tables seems to me to be more valuable and of more authority than the libraries of all the philosophers, for the purpose of investigating the sources and principles of law" (*De Orat.* 44).

At the same time certain forms of actions were framed, according to which legal rights and liabilities were to be determined, and these were called *legis actiones*. The knowledge of them, as well as the right of interpreting the Twelve Tables, was for nearly a century confined to the college of priests *(collegium pontificum)*, as a privilege or prerogative of their order; and it was deemed a kind of mystery or craft not to be communicated to the people. But, according to the tradition received at Rome, it happened that Appius Claudius composed, for the use of himself and his colleagues, a treatise upon these various forms of legal procedure; and his secretary Cnæus Flavius getting possession of the book, made it known to the public, so that thenceforth every man might make himself acquainted with the forms of action

---

[1] In the Digest we read, "quas in tabulas *eboreas* perscriptas pro rostris composuerunt;" but Dionysius, Hal. x. 57, says, στήλαις χαλκαῖς ἐγχαράξαντες αὐτούς. There may, however, be no real discrepancy between these statements; for probably the Digest refers only to the public exposition of the *ten* tablets which were hung up in the comitium to invite public criticism, the laws not being yet considered complete. Afterwards two more were added, and very possibly when the code was thus finally perfected, brazen tablets were used as being more durable. Livy, iii. 34, does not determine the question, as he simply uses the word *tabulæ.*

necessary to be observed in the courts of law. This act of his was so popular, that he was elected in consequence tribune of the commons, and afterwards Curule Ædile. The book which he had published, although he was not the author, was known by his name, and the *legis actiones* were thenceforth, by a kind of misnomer, called *jus civile Flavianum*. In process of time the want of additional forms of action was felt, and some new ones were in consequence framed by Sextus Ælius, who published them, and they thence derived the name of *jus Ælianum*.

These *legis actiones* remind us of our original writs at common law, which issued out of Chancery, as the Officina chartarum. It was a maxim of the English law, that *non potest quis sine brevi agere;* and formerly it was necessary to the due institution of all actions in the superior courts, that they should commence by original writ, which was a mandatory letter, issuing out of chancery, under the great seal, and in the king's name, directed to the sheriff of the county, and containing a short statement of the cause of action, and requiring him to summon the defendant to answer the claim. The most ancient writs provided for the most obvious kinds of wrong; but in the progress of society new cases arose, which were not embraced by any of the then known writs, and the clerks of chancery not having authority to devise new forms, the suitor was without remedy. It was therefore provided by the statute of Westminster II. (13 Edw. I. c. 24) that, "as often as it shall happen in the chancery that in one case a writ is found, and in a like case (*in consimili casu*) falling under the same right, and requiring like remedy, no writ is to be found, the clerks of the chancery shall agree in making a writ, or adjourn the complaint till the next parliament, and write the cases in which they can not agree, and refer them to the next parliament." This statute received a large interpretation; new writs were copiously produced, and actions "on the case," as they were called, added greatly to the stock of the ancient writs. If we wished to pursue a fanciful analogy, we might compare the books containing the *jus Flavianum* and *jus Ælianum* to our old *Registrum Brevium*, first published in the reign of Henry VIII.

Soon, however, as must always inevitably happen, disputes arose as to the meaning of different parts of these written laws, which, therefore, became the subject of discussion in the courts; and in order to understand their proper construction, the citizens resorted to certain learned members of the College of Priests, who alone were competent and authorized to interpret them. Afterwards this right of interpretation ceased to be an exclusive privilege, and was exercised by those who were competent, by education, to undertake the office. Their opinions or *Responsa Prudentum*, as they were called, formed a body of unwritten law, which was termed, in contradistinction to the written *leges*, Jus Civile, and may without much impropriety be considered as the common law of Rome. In its proper signification, it meant nothing more than the interpretations put by lawyers upon the written laws, when applied to the ever-varying cases that arise out of the multiplied transactions of human life. But it is often used in a wider sense, so as to embrace the whole of the municipal law of Rome, or that of any other state.

Besides the laws of the Twelve Tables, there were others, not mentioned by Pomponius, which were passed in the Comitia Centuriata or assemblies of the whole people, both *populus* and *plebs*, burghers and plebeians, held in the Campus Martius, under the auspices of the consuls, or, in their absence, the prætors. In these the chief magistrates, such as the consuls, prætors, and censors, were elected: — laws were passed affecting the Quirites, or whole body of citizens of Rome, and capital cases were determined when the offense was against the state.

This is not the place to attempt to give even the faintest outline of the constitution of Rome in the infancy of the republic; but no reader of Niebuhr requires to be reminded that the *populus* were the free burghers of the city, who claimed descent from its original founders, and as such were the patricians or old aristocracy of Rome, who alone had the right to assemble in the Comitia Curiata; while the *plebs* was an inferior population, personally free, but subject to many political disabilities, and made up of settlers from the neighborhood. Some of these were attracted to Rome by a natural desire to become members of so flourishing a community, and others, after their lands had been overrun and conquered by the Romans, migrated and amalgamated with their victors, though not on terms of political equality. We must not, however, imagine that the distinction between the patricians and plebeians was anything like that between the noblesse and the commonalty of modern times. There were many noble families belonging to the *plebs*. Perhaps the nearest analogy might be drawn from the case of a corporate town, where certain persons possess the privileges of freemen, and the rest of the inhabitants do not. A correct knowledge of the radical difference between the *populus* and the *plebs* is the master-key to the difficulties of the internal history of Rome. The Latin writers themselves did not understand the force of this distinction that prevailed in early times,—and were thereby led into the greatest mistakes. This partly arose from the fact, that the term *populus* came gradually to be applied to the whole of the community which composed the Roman state, including the *plebs*. Thus Gaius, when distinguishing the terms *lex* and *plebiscitum*, says,—*Plebs autem a populo eo distat, quod populi appellatione universi cives significantur, connumeratis etiam patriciis.* This, however, is an entirely erroneous definition, as applied to the *populus* of the early ages of the republic. To translate *plebs* by " plebeians," is very objectionable. It is not only inadequate, but suggests a fallacy; and yet we have no other more appropriate word.

Fifteen years after the expulsion of Tarquinius, the last of the kings, from Rome, the plebs, who had been cruelly oppressed by the patrician burghers, abandoned the city in a body and retired to the Sacred Hill. According to the account given by Pomponius in the Digest, they here passed laws or decrees by themselves, which were called Plebiscita; and when a reconciliation had been effected between them and the burghers, and they had returned to Rome, their right to make such laws was, after a short struggle, conceded; and the Plebiscita were, by the lex Hortensia, B.C. 286, recognized as part of the written Roman law, differing from the leges in the manner in which they were passed, but equally binding in their effect. But we can not accept this as an accurate statement of facts. Even Livy saw that the secession could not have lasted many days,— or the Volscians and Æquians, with whom the Romans were then at war, would have profited by the opportunity to attack the city; and we can hardly suppose that, in the brief and busy interval of negotiation and compromise between the two sections of the inhabitants of Rome, the plebs had time to establish for themselves a new species of legislation. It is very probable that, from the display of strength and serious determination which they then exhibited, and which secured for them the future inviolability of the persons of the tribunes, they were able afterwards to pass laws at their Comitia Tributa, by which they regulated their own affairs.

The Senate, according to Niebuhr, in its original form, directly represented the burghers or populus, and the three hundred members who composed it (which number remained unchanged for many centuries) corresponded to the same number of patrician houses. The decurion of each *gens* or clan was its representative in the Senate, and no plebeian is recorded to have sat there until the beginning of the fourth century after the foundation of the city, when we find Spurius Mælius mentioned as a senator. The extent of its legislative power and the force and meaning of the *senatus consulta* have been the subject of much controversy. But Cicero includes them as part of the jus civile, and Pomponius, after explaining how the Senate, as a smaller and more manageable body than the popular assemblies, took upon itself the administration of public affairs, says expressly that whatever it determined was observed, and this kind of law was called *senatus consultum.*

Besides these different sources of law there was another very important, though somewhat anomalous, branch called the Jus Honorarium. This consisted of the edicts which the prætors (originally two in number, *urbanus* and *peregrinus*) promulgated every year on their accession to office, and which were written on a white tablet and exposed to public view; wherein they announced the rules and principles, according to which they intended to administer the law during their year of office. And the prætors used, while the *legis actiones* were in force, to issue such new writs or forms of action as from time to time became necessary, in which respect there is a close analogy between their functions and those of the Court of Chancery in former times, as has been previously explained. The object of these edicts seems to have been to temper the strict rules of the common law, or *jus civile*, by the application of principles of natural equity, and to supply such deficiencies as experience discovered in the existing law. Hence the prætorian edict was defined to be *viva vox juris civilis*, and it was said to be promulgated "for the sake of assisting, or supplying, or correcting the law with the view of public benefit" (*Digest*, I. iii. 10). To this we have nothing in our law now strictly analogous. The common-law judges are only the interpreters and expounders of the law; they do not add to it or subtract from it, but simply administer it as they find it; and if any change is desired, resort must be had to the legislative power of Parliament and the Crown. Nor do courts of equity exercise any capricious jurisdiction. They are as much bound by precedent and authority as the courts of common law; and it is a mere vulgar error to suppose that the rules of equity fluctuate according to the exigencies of each particular case. Formerly, however, incorrect notions on this subject prevailed even among lawyers, as will be seen from the following passage taken from the writings of that eminent jurist, the late Mr. Justice Story (*Equity Jurisprudence*, Chap. I. § 19).

"If, indeed, a court of equity in England did possess the unbounded jurisdiction which has been thus generally ascribed to it, of correcting, controlling, moderating, and even superseding the law, and of enforcing all the rights, as well as the charities, arising from natural law and justice, and of forcing itself from all regard to former rules and precedents, it would be the most gigantic in its sway, and the most formidable instrument of arbitrary power, that could well be devised. It would literally place the whole rights and property of the community under the arbitrary will of the Judge, acting, if you please, *arbitrio boni judicis*, and, it may be, *ex æquo et bono*, according to his own notions and conscience; but still acting with a despotic and sovereign authority. A Court of Chancery might then well deserve the spirited rebuke of Selden: 'For law we have a measure, and know what to trust to. Equity is according to the conscience of him that is chancellor; and as that is larger or narrower, so is equity. 'Tis all one as if they should make the standard for the measure the chancellor's foot. What an uncertain measure would this be! One chancellor has a long foot; another a short foot; a third an indifferent foot. It is the same thing with the chancellor's conscience.' And notions of this sort were, in former ages, when the chancery jurisdiction was opposed with vehement disapprobation by common lawyers, very industriously propagated by the most learned of English antiquarians, such as Spelman, Coke, Lambard, and Selden. We might, indeed, under such circumstances, adopt the language of Mr. Justice Blackstone, and say: 'In short, if a court of equity in England did really act as many ingenious writers have supposed it (from theory) to do, it would rise above all law, either common or statute, and be a most arbitrary legislator in every particular case. So far, however, is this from being true, that one of the most common maxims, upon which a court of equity daily acts, is that equity follows the law, and seeks out and guides itself by the analogies of the law.'" And Mr. Justice Story afterwards quotes the words of Lord Redesdale, Lord Chancellor of Ireland, and one of our greatest equity judges: (1 *Shaw and Lefr.* 428) "There are certain principles on which courts of equity act, which are very well settled. The cases which occur are various; but they are decided on fixed principles. Courts of equity have in this respect no more discretionary power than courts of law. They decide new cases as they arise, by the principles on which former cases have been decided; and may thus illustrate or enlarge the operation of those principles. But those principles are as fixed and certain as the principles on which the courts of common law proceed."

Originally, the edicts of former prætors were not adopted by their successors, and their rules, or *ordines cancellarii*, if we may so designate them by an inadequate term, must have been greatly deficient in consistency and coherence. But gradually the inconvenience of this was felt to be so great, that it became a common practice for the prætors, on their accession to office, to incorporate the edicts of their predecessors, and make them part of the rules promulgated by themselves for the ensuing year. This was called the *edictum tralaticium;* and in course of time the collection of these constituted a separate and independent body of law; which was carefully studied by the Roman lawyers. The *perpetuum edictum* differed from the *repentinum* in this, that the former was the rule laid down to regulate the practice during the whole of the coming year; the latter was promulgated as any particular emergency arose. But the term " perpetuum edictum " came to be applied under the emperors, very generally, if not exclusively, to a treatise compiled by Salvius Julianus, who was prætor in the reign of Hadrian, in which he systematized the body of the prætorian edicts.

The *jus honorarium* was not confined exclusively to the prætorian edicts. Other magistrates, such as the tribunes, censors, curule ædiles, and pontiffs, had the power of publishing edicts within their peculiar jurisdictions, to which the same name was applied. But, in consequence of the more extensive jurisdiction of the prætors, their edictal authority was generally implied when this term was used.

In addition, however, to all these branches of law, we must mention the *consuetudines* or customs—that large body of unwritten law not to be found in statutes or edicts, but depending upon immemorial usage—to which the Romans, like ourselves, gave a binding and legal effect. Cicero says, *Consuetudinis autem jus esse putatur id, quod voluntate omnium, sine lege, vetustas comprobaverit.*

These, then, were the constituent elements of the Roman law, at the end of seven centuries from the foundation of the city: 1. The *leges* of the twelve Tables, and also those which were passed by the people, comprehending both populus and plebs, assembled in the Comitia centuriata. The Papirian code seems by that time to have become obsolete. 2. The *legis actiones*, or Flavian and Ælian collections of judicial forms and processes. 3. The *Responsa Prudentum*, or answers given by learned lawyers when consulted by clients on points of legal difficulty, whose opinions formed what was in strictness called *jus civile*, and corresponded in authority to the works of our ancient text writers, such as Glanville, Britton, Bracton, Fleta, Fitzherbert, and Coke. No treatise, however, embodying and systematizing these opinions, seems to have been compiled at Rome before Quintus Mucius Scævola undertook the task. 4 and 5. The *plebiscita* and *senatus consulta*, which, when all distinction between their binding effect was done away, still represented the original difference between the patrician burghers and unenfranchised plebs. 6. The *jus honorarium*, or prætorian equity, whereby a silent legislation was supplied, from year to year, according as transactions became more complicated and new exigencies arose; and lastly, 7. *Consuetudo*, or custom, the growth of centuries—a code framed by that omnipotent law-maker—Time.

We need not pursue the investigation beyond the downfall of the republic, nor examine the statement of the courtly jurists of imperial Rome, who pretended that, by a formal act (the lex regia), the people had stripped themselves of all their political rights, and committed to the sovereign the sole power of legislation. It is enough to know that the constitutions or edicts of the emperors had the force of law, and that, however they might veil their arbitrary proceedings under the ancient forms of the constitution, they were, in fact, absolute and irresponsible monarchs. It was but a mockery of departed freedom to invest themselves as they did with consular authority, and, when the trembling senate registered their edicts, to dignify them with the venerable name of Senatus consulta.

Having thus taken a rapid survey of the nature of the Roman law, let us add a few words on the subject of the legal tribunals or courts where that law was administered; and it will be necessary, in the first place, to gain a distinct notion of the Forum—the theater on which were displayed the greatest and most glorious triumphs of oratory. For this purpose we may avail ourselves of the account given of it by the late Dr. Arnold, as it existed in the fifth century of Rome.

"A spot so famous well deserves to be described, that we may conceive its principal features, and imagine to ourselves the scene as well as the actors in so many of the great events of the Roman History. From the foot of the Capitoline Hill to that of the Palatine, there ran an open space of unequal breadth, narrowing as it approached the Palatine, and inclosed on both sides between two branches of the Sacred Way. Its narrower end was occupied by the comitium, the place of meeting of the populus or great council of the burghers in the earliest times of the republic; while its wider extremity was the forum: in the stricter sense the market-place of the Romans, and therefore the natural place of meeting for the commons who formed the majority of the Roman nation. The comitium was raised a little above the level of the forum, like the dais or upper part of our old castle and college halls, and at its extremity nearest the forum stood the rostra, such as I have already described it; facing at this period toward the comitium, so that the speakers addressed, not indeed the patrician multitude as of old, but the senators, who had in a manner succeeded to their place, and who were accustomed to stand in this part of the assembly, immediately in front of the senate house, which looked out upon the comitium from the northern side of the Via Sacra. The magnificent basilicæ, which at a later period formed the two sides of the forum were not yet in existence, but in their place there were two rows of solid square pillars of peperino, forming a front to the shops of various kinds, which lay behind them. These shops were like so many cells, open to the street, and closed behind, and had no communication with the houses which were built over them. Those on the north side of the forum had been rebuilt or improved during the early part of the fifth century, and were called, in consequence, 'the new shops,' a name which as usual in such cases, they retained for centuries. On the south side, the line of shops was interrupted by the temple of Castor and Pollux, which had been built, according to the common tradition, by the dictator, A. Postumius, in gratitude for the aid afforded him by the twin heroes in the battle of the Lake Regillus. On the same side, also, but further to the eastward, and nearly opposite to the senate-house, was the temple of Vesta, and close to the temple was that ancient monument of the times of the kings, which went by the name of the court of Numa. In the open space of the forum might be seen an altar, which marked the spot once occupied by the Curtian pool, the subject of such various traditions. Hard by grew the three sacred trees of the oldest known civilization,—the fig, the vine, and the olive,—which were so carefully preserved or renewed, that they existed even in the time of the elder Pliny. Further towards the capitol, at the western extremity of the forum, were the equestrian statues of C. Mænius and L. Camillus, the conquerors of the Latins."

Such was the Roman forum in the middle of the fifth century from the foundation of the city, when she was just about to engage in the war with the Tarentines, and for the first time come into hostile collision with the Greeks under Pyrrhus, king of Epirus. In early times, the distinction between that part of the oblong space where the comitia curiata or assemblies of the patrician burghers were held, and what was properly the forum or market-place, was well known and recognized;

but afterwards the whole of the open ground embraced in the above description was called, generally, the forum, and chiefly used for proceedings of a judicial nature. Formerly the speakers, when they ascended the rostra, turned, as we have seen, towards the comitium (close to which stood the curia, or senate-house), in order to deliver their harangues; but Caius Licinius, as Cicero and Varro inform us, or Caius Gracchus, according to Plutarch, introduced the custom of facing the forum, and thereby doing homage to the power of the sovereign people.

But many other changes took place before the age of Cicero, both as to the physical aspect of the forum, and the uses that were made of it. Splendid basilicæ, or halls, which were used both as courts of law and marts of commerce, occupied the site of the old shops, and were distinguished by different names, such as Porcia, Fulvia, Opimia, and Julia. They were surrounded by colonnades, or porticoes, for the convenience of walking up and down, and of taking shelter when a shower of rain interrupted proceedings in the forum. At a still later period they became the models of, or were converted into, Christian churches. In these basilicæ were tried civil actions, such as came under the cognizance of the centumvirs; but public or state trials took place in the open air either in the comitium or the other part of the forum: in the former, if the matter was referred to the burghers at large as the judges; in the latter, if it was made the subject of an inquiry before the *judices decuriati*.[1]

[1] *Polleti Historia Fori Romani*; *Lugduni*, 1588. To this curious old work I am much indebted in this part of the subject. It contains many interesting particulars respecting the forms of legal procedure among the Romans, and is illustrated with a profusion of learning. In after times the number of forums was increased to five. The second was built by Julius Cæsar; a third by Augustus, which he appropriated exclusively to legal proceedings; a fourth by Nerva; a fifth, called forum Trajani or Ulpium, on a scale of great magnificence, by Trajan, where he erected his famous

In the basilica were four courts, called tribunalia, in which the different members of the centumviral body sat at the same time for the dispatch of business; as is the case in our own courts at Westminster and Lincoln's Inn; or, perhaps, still more like the Parliament House in Edinburgh; and Quintilian tells us of an advocate, named Trachallus, who had such a stentorian voice, that it overpowered every other sound, and was heard in all the courts at once, to the great annoyance of the other pleaders. A story is told of a barrister on the northern circuit, who had the lungs of Trachallus, and was addressing a jury in the civil court, while a criminal trial was proceeding in the crown court. His voice so overpowered that of the counsel in the latter, that the jury there fancied he was appealing to them, and found a verdict for *damages* against the *prisoner!* It seems, that on some occasions, all the judges of these four different courts sat together, in banc, for the purpose of hearing the same cause; a practice which we may compare to the sitting of the English judges in the Exchequer Chamber, when crown cases reserved were argued before them.

These tribunalia consisted of semicircular spaces, separated from the rest of the building, and appropriated to the business of the court, in order that the legal proceedings might not be interrupted by the crowd of persons who thronged the hall, to transact their mercantile and other affairs. The curule chair of the prætor, or other presiding magistrate, was in the center of a raised *dais* or tribune, on which sat the judges, and in front of this were the benches for the counsel and witnesses, and those whom business or curiosity attracted to the courts. The basilica had a kind of gallery

column. There were many other smaller forums at Rome used as markets, which were distinguished by the names of the things which were sold there—as boarium, olitorium, piscarium.—See Smith's *Dict. of Greek and Roman Antiq.*, Arts, Forum and Basilica.

running round it, with intervening pillars, where people of both sexes used to resort to hear interesting trials, just as in the Court of Queen's Bench, at present.

For the purpose of holding the public trials, a temporary stage seems to have been erected, consisting of *subsellia* or seats for the counsel and parties, and a tribunal or raised seat for the judges. At least we may, I think, infer this from a passage in Quintilian, who says that when a teacher of rhetoric, named Portius Latro, had to conduct a cause in the forum, he was so discomposed by having to plead in the open air, that he begged that the benches might be removed into one of the basilicæ, and that the court would adjourn there.[1] The accuser selected any part of the forum he pleased for holding the trial, and hence Cicero complained when he defended Flaccus, and Lælius, the prosecutor had chosen a spot near the Aurelian stairs, where a noisy and disorderly rabble could be collected, and clamor for a conviction.

That the public trials took place in the open air, is abundantly proved by many passages in the ancient authors; but it will be sufficient to mention an anecdote related by Valerius Maximus of Lucius Piso, during whose trial a sudden shower of rain came on, while the judges were deliberating upon their sentence. In order to move their compassion he threw himself upon the ground, and his face and clothes became all covered with mud. His miserable plight so affected the court, that they pronounced a verdict of acquittal.[2] At a later period Marcellus, the nephew of Augustus, furnished

---

[1] *Inst. Orat.* X. 5. The *Tribunal*, strictly speaking, was the seat of the presiding magistrate, who was quite distinct from the judices, whose duty it was to pronounce the verdict. The seats on which the latter sat, as well as those of the counsel, were called *subsellia*. See *Sueton. Nero*, c. 17; and *Heinece, Hist. Jur. Rom.* lib. i. c. 4, § 221.

[2] *Val. Max.* lib. viii. 6. The lucky accident of a shower of rain is said to have saved Appius Claudius also from a conviction.

part of the forum with an awning, for the express purpose of protecting the courts, which were held there, from the sun and rain. In like manner the judges at Athens, called Heilastæ, who had cognizance of murder and other capital crimes, sat in the open air; for which Antiphon, in one of his speeches, assigns as a reason the superstitious dread which the Greeks entertained, of being under the same roof with those whose hands were defiled with blood.

Let us now imagine to ourselves the Roman Forum surrounded by the temples of the gods; and thronged by an immense multitude, when Cicero rose to defend Milo against the charge of having murdered Clodius, one of the most profligate and abandoned citizens of Rome. He had made himself infamous by disgraceful acts of violence and riot, and intended to offer himself as a candidate for the office of prætor at the next election, when there was every probability that Titus Annius Milo, his personal enemy, would at the same time be chosen one of the consuls for the ensuing year. To prevent this, Clodius exerted all his influence, for he was conscious how much he would be " cabined, cribbed, confined," in his actions, under the consular authority of Milo. He is charged by Cicero with having deliberately determined to rid himself of this obstacle, by taking away the life of his opponent; and we may well believe that he would not have shrunk from perpetrating that crime. But we must of course receive with caution the statements made by Cicero against a man who was one of his bitterest enemies, and at a time when he was speaking with all the warmth and passion of an advocate.

Milo held an office at Lanuvium, a small town distant a few miles from Rome, which obliged him to be there on a particular occasion, and it so happened that Clodius left the city the preceding day with a band of retainers, and went to a villa which he possessed by the side of the Appian road. Next day, after the senate had risen, Milo quitted Rome, and proceeded in a carriage along the same road towards Lanuvium, accompanied by his wife and a numerous body of attendants. When he approached the villa of Clodius, the latter, whether accidentally or not is doubtful, met him, and an affray immediately took place between their adherents. Clodius was wounded, and fled for refuge to a wayside tavern, but Milo ordered his servants to attack the house, which they did, and having dragged Clodius out, they dispatched him on the spot. His body was left bleeding on the ground until it was taken up by a senator named S. Tedius, who happened to be passing in his chariot: he conveyed it to Rome, where it was exposed with all its gaping wounds to the view of the populace, and a dreadful uproar arose. The friends of Clodius demanded vengeance, and asserted that Milo was the first aggressor, accusing him of having gone along the Appian road for the purpose of attacking Clodius. The matter was brought before the senate, and there warmly debated, until at length, on the motion of Pompey, a special commission was appointed to try Milo on the charge of murder, and Cicero defended him. The rabble were furious at the death of their favorite leader, and were urged on by the Clodian family to acts of tumultuous violence; so that when the trial took place, in order to prevent bloodshed and preserve the peace of the city, Pompey stationed strong bodies of troops in the forum and the various avenues leading to it. It was a time of perilous excitement; all the shops were shut, and the whole city was in commotion;—and the boldest orator might have trembled when he saw on every side the glittering of arms, and heard the hoarse murmurs of the populace, who were only kept back by the spears of the soldiers from rushing upon the arena where he stood.

Strange, indeed, and unusual was the array which then

environed Cicero. His eye looked round in vain for the scene to which it had heretofore been accustomed at trials in the forum. Everything was changed. The ordinary crowd had been displaced by soldiers, and these, though intended as a guard against violence, could not but inspire alarm. The thought, however, that they had been stationed by the command of Pompey, reassured him, and he felt that he might banish fear, and rejoice that he was protected against the fury of the rabble. The rest of the vast multitude of citizens, who from windows and roofs and every eminence from which a glimpse of the forum could be caught, gazed down upon it with such thrilling interest, were, as he asserted, all on his side; for each knew that on the acquittal of Milo that day depended the safety of himself, his children, and his country.

The speech which has been handed down to us as that which Cicero delivered on this great occasion, is one of the most splendid of all his orations, and it seems impossible that it should not have been successful; but the truth is that we have it as it was composed, but not as it was spoken; for the orator lost his presence of mind when he rose to speak in defense of the accused, and, owing to the agitation under which he labored, he was unable to do justice to the cause of his client, who was convicted and sentenced to banishment. When in his exile from Rome he afterwards read the speech which we possess, and which his advocate had intended to deliver, he exclaimed, "If Cicero had spoken thus, I should not now have been eating figs at Marseilles."

In an eloquent passage of his description of Rome, Chevalier Bunsen expresses his regret that Niebuhr had not attempted to present to the mind's eye a picture of the mighty changes of which the eternal city has been the witness and the theater. And he asks, what would the great historian have told us of the Forum of the Roman people, if he had represented to us its countless vicissitudes from century to century, and called to new life its wasted ruins; he, who so often wandered in tears among them, uncertain whether he wept over the vanished virtue and heroic greatness of the Scipios and Catos, or rather over the imbecility and sloth of the men of the present day? There, he would have pointed out the place where so often and so long the destiny of Rome, Italy, the World, was debated and determined; where the manly eloquence of the senate strove with the fiery oratory of the Gracchi, and where Cicero, by the powers of his tongue, hurried along with him the entranced multitude, and vanquished the hostility of the patricians of Rome. Originally a sedgy marsh, it was drained by means of gigantic subterraneous works, and became the place of meeting for the curiæ and the senate; at first small, and adapted only for a priestly and royal conclave, but gradually embracing the assemblies of the two great divisions of the people. Afterwards, on the restoration of the city, it was adorned by Italian art with monuments and statues of heroes, until the splendor of marble halls and courts in the Grecian style overshadowed the simple majesty of old Rome. At last the embellishment of the spot was completed, just when, with its departed virtue, freedom fled from Rome, and all meaning and significance from the Forum. Images of the Cæsars succeeded, and these, too, crumbled into dust. For centuries the desolate scene of so many deeds, such high feelings, and such lofty destinies, was surrounded by the miserable hovels of the poor, and by churches, and convents, and gardens; but still preserved its identity, until the northern conqueror renewed the devastation wrought by the ancient Gauls, and compelled the neighboring population to leave their dwellings and take up their abode amidst the ruins of the buildings, in the plain below; so that gradually the whole of the hollow space was filled up, and even the steep side of the capitol made level with the adjoining ground by heaps of collected rubbish, through which, here and there, appeared some pillar or column struggling forth into day, like a sepulchral monument of the past.

Having thus briefly noticed the courts, let us consider who were the judges before whom the trials were held. The most general division of jurisprudence in every country must of course be into civil and criminal. In the former were embraced among the Romans all the judicia privata—in the latter the judicia publica. And first as to the former. In the earliest times of which we have any account, the kings of Rome themselves presided at the trials—just as was the case sometimes in France in the middle ages—for we are told that the good king St. Louis, in the thirteenth century, used, after hearing mass in the summer season, to lay himself at the foot of an oak in the wood of Vincennes, and make his courtiers sit round him; when all who wished were allowed to approach him, and he would ask aloud if there were any present who had suits. When the parties appeared, he used to bid two of his bailiffs determine their cause in his presence upon the spot.

But, after the expulsion of the kings, this jurisdiction was exercised by the consuls, and subsequently, and down to a very late period in Roman history, by the prætors. It is to the authority and forms of procedure under the latter, that we must chiefly pay attention. Their number was originally two—and they were called Prætor urbanus, and Prætor peregrinus—but afterwards they were increased, and the number varied at different periods. In the time of Cicero there appear to have been twelve.[1] They did not, however, personally attend the hearing of all causes, and give judgment themselves;

---

[1] *Polleti Hist. Fori Romani.* There has been much controversy as to the exact number of the prætors in the later ages of the republic. Some learned men maintain that, previous to the dictatorship of Julius Cæsar, there were only eight, others ten, others twelve.

but were empowered, and indeed, in many cases, obliged by law to appoint judges for the purpose. When the prætor tried causes he was said *cognoscere*,—either, *de tribunali*, or *de plano*. The former term was used when he sat upon a raised seat or tribunal, and heard the case formally argued before him : the latter when, as was frequently the case, he administered the law in a more familiar manner—conversing with the parties, and standing on the same level with themselves. Strange as this may appear, it was undoubtedly the custom at Rome. Suitors frequently addressed the prætor even in the street, or at his own house, for a redress of their grievances, and sometimes even in court he did not ascend the tribunal, but let the parties speak to him on the subject of their dispute, which he determined on the spot.[1] In all these cases he was said *cognoscere de plano*. The thing most analogous to this among ourselves is the practice before a judge at chambers, where a vast amount of most important business connected with litigation is transacted: but it is very certain that no such scene would be acted there, as we are told by Suetonius sometimes occurred, even when the imperial Cæsar himself disposed of causes in this manner. He says that the barristers ventured to presume so much upon the good-nature of Claudius, that when he descended from the tribunal they used to call out to him to stop, and pull him by his robe ; or even catch hold of his leg, and importune him to attend to the motions which they had to make.

When the prætor held his court *de tribunali*, he summoned to his aid a number of assessors, called judices, who sat on each side of him, a little behind his seat.

---

[1] *Heinecc. Syntag.* lib. iv. tit. 6. *Polleti Hist. Fori Rom.* lib. i. c. 5. Heineccius says that this mode of hearing causes must not be confounded with summary jurisdiction ; for many cases which were to be disposed of summarily, were obliged to be determined *de tribunali*. It is impossible, however, not to consider it as a very summary mode of settling disputes.

These were selected on ordinary occasions out of the centumviral body, who formed a kind of judicial college at Rome; but very little is known of their constitution or peculiar functions. According to Festus, three were chosen out of each tribe,—and as there were thirty-five tribes, these would amount to 105, which may have been the origin of their name, as being in round numbers a hundred men. We know that in the courts of the centumviri were tried causes involving the most dry and technical points of law. Questions were there discussed relating to adverse possession,[1] guardian and ward, pedigree, the law of debtor and creditor, party walls, ancient lights, easements, the validity of wills, and, in short, almost everything connected with the rights and liabilities of parties.

But let us now turn to the more important and interesting class of trials, those of a criminal nature. Although they are often confounded together, under the name of *judicia publica*, this term, in strictness, applied only to a particular division of them. They consisted, in fact, of four different kinds: 1. Actiones populares; 2. Actiones extraordinariæ; 3. Judicia publica; Judicia populi. The "actiones populares" were trials appointed at the instance of the prætor, for the punishment of a lesser kind of misdemeanors, and chiefly such as were offenses against municipal and sanitary regulations; as, for instance, sacrilegious disturbance of graves, impeding the streets or sewers, or doing anything whereby the public convenience was impaired. Any person might be the prosecutor in these cases, and the penalty of a fine

---

[1] *Usucapio.* This is sometimes incorrectly translated "prescription:" but there is no such thing as a right to the possession of real property by prescription known to the English law. *Usucapio* means the title to property, which is conferred by length of adverse possession. A man can not prescribe for an estate; but he may for an easement or *servitus, i. e.* a right to make use of the property of another in a particular manner, as, for instance, a right of way over his neighbor's field, or a right of common for his cattle.

was generally imposed. So far, we may compare them to *qui tam* actions among ourselves; but I am not aware that any portion of the fine went, in these actions at Rome, as in this country, to the informer.

There has been much controversy as to the exact difference between the "actiones extraordinariæ" (called sometimes "judicia extraordinaria"), and the "judicia publica;" but the better opinion seems to be, that the former embraced such crimes as were not specially provided against by any particular law, or to which no particular punishment was affixed, but it was left to the discretion of the tribunal. And the tribunal was of itself of a special nature, and appointed for the occasion, consisting sometimes of the whole senate, sometimes of the consuls, or other magistrates, as the case might be. For when crime occurred, the Romans dealt with it, if necessary, by an ex post facto law, and had no idea that a criminal should escape because there did not happen to be a law specifically applicable to his offense. The judicia publica, on the contrary, were trials for the violation of some established and particular law; as, for instance, the Julian, against treasons, the Cornelian, against stabbing and poisoning, the Pompeian, against parricide, and a variety of laws against bribery and corruption in canvassing for public offices. And the judicia populi of the earlier times, where the burghers at large tried and judged the accused, were, when these special laws were enacted, supplanted by the judicia publica; and, as we shall see, the number of judges was limited, and chosen out of a particular class.

But there was another mode of trying offenses anciently at Rome, by the appointment of commissioners called Quæsitores parricidii, or Quæsitores rerum capitalium. The tribunes of the commons used, in the first instance, to put the question to the people in one of the popular assemblies,—and ask them whether they willed and ordained that an inquiry should take place,—and that one of the prætors should refer it to the senate to determine who should conduct the trial. If the people voted for the accusation, the senate gave authority to some magistrate immediately to investigate the matter, and put the culprit upon his trial. But during the last century of the republic, this form was discontinued, and by various laws it became the province of the prætors to hold these trials themselves, without any special authority being delegated to them on each occasion. On entering their year of office it was determined by lot, what particular class of offenses each of them should take cognizance of during the ensuing twelve months. Thus Cicero assigns as one of the reasons why Sulpicius was beaten by Murena in the contest for the Consulship, that the former had as prætor obtained the unpopular office of *quæstor peculatus*, or "commissioner of embezzlement," which he calls "stern and odious; threatening, on the one hand, tears and misery, and on the other, trials and imprisonment."

But the prætor did not sit as a judge, in our sense of the word, at these trials. He acted as the president of the court, under whose auspices and authority the proceedings were conducted; but he seems to have had no voice in the sentence pronounced. He had the *imperium*, but not the *jurisdictio*. This belonged to the Judices, who were summoned by him to sit upon the trial, and of whom we find such constant mention made in the speeches and other writings of Cicero. It was their province to determine the question of guilt or innocence; and they were taken out of a particular class of citizens which varied at different times. The importance of the functions which they had to discharge made it a matter of vital interest that they should be men of pure and upright character; but nothing was more common at Rome, than to hear them charged with every kind of corruption and venality. Their names were inscribed on a list, or jury panel, *Album Judicum*, which is supposed to have been first brought into use by the Calpurnian law. There is much doubt as to their number, which, however, varied at different times. Some imagine that ten were originally chosen from each tribe, which would make them amount to about 300, and hence they explain the term, Decuria judicum. At first they seem to have been confined exclusively to the senatorian body; but by the Sempronian law, B.C. 123, of which Tiberius Gracchus was the author, this right or privilege was transferred from the senators to the equestrian order; and the latter enjoyed it for nearly fifty years, until Sylla, B.C. 80, deprived them of it, and restored it to the senators. By a later law, the Aurelia Lex, passed B.C. 70, it was enacted that the judices should be chosen from the senators, the knights, and the tribuni ærarii; the last of whom were taken from the body of the people. These formed the three decuriæ of judges, which existed until Julius Cæsar reduced them to two, by removing the decuriæ of the tribuni ærarii. The number that sat at a trial is uncertain; but it seems to have varied from fifty to seventy. After the reign of Augustus, the *album judicum* contained the names of all who were qualified to serve either on civil or criminal trials, and these amounted to not less than four thousand.

Such, then, was the nature of the Roman law, and such were the tribunals before which the advocate had to practice. The account has perhaps been tedious; but we shall find more to interest us, as we proceed to consider some of the peculiarities attending the exercise of his profession in the Eternal City.

CHAPTER IV.

ADVOCACY IN ANCIENT ROME.

THE word Orator in the Latin language had a more extensive application than with us. We generally confine it to those who pre-eminently excel in eloquence; whereas the Romans spoke of all as oratores, who accustomed themselves to public speaking, either in the popular assemblies or in the courts of law. Therefore, all advocates were orators in this sense, and Cicero constantly speaks of them as such. When he wishes to express a contemptuous opinion of a speaker, he calls him *mediocris*, or *sane tolerabilis*, or even *malus orator*. And the reason why he so seldom uses any other term than this, seems to be owing to one of the most remarkable points of difference between the profession of the bar in ancient and in modern times.

For we must not forget that at Rome there was no line of demarcation drawn between the advocate and the statesman. While appearing in the cause of his client, the eloquent speaker was, in fact, acquiring that popularity and influence which placed all public honors within his grasp. He was not, as with us, obliged to devote himself for years exclusively to legal studies, and endeavor to approve himself by success in his profession a sound and able lawyer, before he dared to enter upon public life. In England a man does not emerge from the courts until he is of mature age, and his habits of thought and powers of speaking have been exercised and molded there for so long a time, that he is almost unfit to contend in the new arena into which he is suddenly introduced. This is the chief reason why lawyers are so often said to fail in parliament, and why so few of them deserve the praise which Horace bestowed upon Asinius Pollio—

> " Insigne mœstis præsidium reis,
> Et consulenti, Pollio, curiæ." [1]

But the more technical name given to those who practiced in the courts at Rome was that of Patroni Causarum or simply Patroni, and the parties whom they there represented were called their Clientes. For the origin of these terms we must refer to one of the most peculiar of the political, or rather social, usages among the Roman people. This was the relation that subsisted between the patron and client, which may be traced back to the earliest times, and was founded upon a theory of reciprocal obligation and support.

"How the clientship arose," says Niebuhr, "admits as little of an historical exposition as the origin of Rome (*Hist. of Rome*, i. 277). Without, therefore, attempting to explain what this profound genius has declared to be hopelessly obscure, we may content ourselves with the following summary which he has given of the duties arising out of that relation. "But all, however different in rank and consequence, were entitled to paternal protection from the patron; he was bound to relieve their

---

[1] These lines are better than the couplet in which Pope complimented Murray, afterwards Lord Mansfield, when at the bar:

> " Grac'd as thou art with all the power of words,
> So known, so honor'd at the House of Lords."

The last line referred to a successful speech made by Murray at the bar of the House of Lords, after which he said that his income rose from nothing to three thousand a year.

The parody, by Colly Cibber, is well known :—

> " Persuasion tips his tongue whene'er he talks,
> And he has chambers in the King's Bench walks."

distress, *to appear for them in court, to expound the law to them, civil and pontifical.* On the other hand, the clients were obliged to be heartily dutiful and obedient to their patron, to promote his honor, to pay his mulcts and fines, to aid him, jointly with the members of his house, in bearing burdens for the commonwealth and defraying the charges of public offices, to contribute to the portioning of his daughters, and to ransom him or whoever of his family might fall into an enemy's hands." [1]

Among these duties of the patron not the least important was that of defending the rights of his client when attacked in a court of law, and throwing the shelter of his name and influence around his poorer dependent when his property or liberty was threatened. We may easily imagine how, in such cases, the client resorted to his patron for advice before it was necessary to claim his protection, and how, when he was interested in a question of construction of the Twelve Tables, or in the interpretation of some obscure prætorian edict, he referred the matter to the wealthy and educated patrician, and relied upon his opinion. In proportion as the state of society became less simple, and transactions more complicated, the necessity for these applications to the patron became more frequent, and it is not difficult to see how, in the case of a patron who had numerous clients, when a habit of answering legal questions arose, others who did not stand in that relation to him would seek to avail themselves of the benefit of his knowledge and experience. And thus, in the course of time, the delivery of legal opinions became the ordinary occupation and almost profession of some

---

[1] *Hist. of Rome*, i. 279. How strongly this description reminds us of the ancient feudal aids which were rendered by the vassal to his lord! These were principally three: 1. to ransom the lord's person if taken prisoner; 2. to make the lord's eldest son a knight; 3. to provide a portion for the lord's eldest daughter on her marriage. BLACKSTONE, in his *Commentaries*, ii. 63, 64, has pointed out the resemblance.

learned men at Rome. The name of Tiberius Coruncanius, who was consul B. C. 281, has been handed down to us as the first person who publicly adopted this practice. The transition of the name, from the patron who gave his client the benefit of his opinion and counsel in legal difficulties to the advocate who openly espoused the cause of another in a court of justice, is too obvious to require proof.

The term *Advocatus* was not applied to a pleader in the courts until after the time of Cicero. Its proper signification was that a friend who, by his presence at a trial gave countenance and support to the accused It was always considered a matter of the greatest importance that a party who had to answer a criminal charge should appear with as many friends and partisans as possible. This array answered a double purpose, for by accompanying him they not only acted as what we should call witnesses to character, but by their numbers and influence materially affected the decision of the tribunal. Not unfrequently (when some noble Roman, who had gained popularity in his provincial government, had to defend himself against an accusation), an embassy of the most distinguished citizens of the province was sent to Rome to testify by their presence to his virtues, and deprecate an unfavorable verdict. Thus, when Cicero defended Balbus, he pointed to the deputies from Gades, men of the highest rank and character, who had come to avert, if possible the calamity of a conviction. Although in this point of view the witnesses who were called to speak in favor of the accused might be called *advocati*, the name was not confined to such, but embraced all who rallied round him at the trial.

In the early ages of the republic the litigant parties appeared personally in court, and carried on the cause themselves. They were not allowed to nominate another to act as their attorney in their behalf except in three cases,- *pro populo*—*pro libertate*,—*pro pupillo*,—that is to say, in actions where the whole community was concerned, or where some question of personal liberty or guardianship was involved. The inconvenience, however, of this rule led to the substitution of persons who, under the names of *cognitores* and *procuratores*, performed functions which bear some resemblance to those of attorneys at the present day. The precise distinction between these is not accurately known, nor is it very important. It seems, however, that the *cognitor* acted for and managed the cause of a party resident at Rome, while the *procurator* was appointed in the place of one who was out of Italy, or whose absence from the city was occasioned by some public duty.

Besides the *Patroni Causarum*, or advocates who appeared in courts, there was another important class of lawyers at Rome, called *Juris Consulti*, whom we might not improperly designate as chamber counsel. We have seen that the Jus Civile, properly so called, consisted of the oral or written opinions of lawyers, who, when applied to by parties, expounded the doctrines of the law, and informed their fellow-citizens of their rights and liabilities. Their houses were frequented for this purpose, and some of them had such a reputation that their dwellings were styled the oracles of the state. When it was known that they were willing and competent to deliver opinions on points of law, they were even in public addressed by clients on the subject of their affairs, " *de omni denique aut officio aut negotio* " (*Cic. Brut.* 33), and used sometimes to walk up and down the forum in a most patriarchal fashion, for the express purpose of being consulted on legal difficulties.[1] And under the tuition of these jurisconsults, the young men at Rome prepared themselves for practice in the courts. "They

---

[1] This peripatetic mode of doing business seems still to exist in Scotland, where the advocates pace every morning during term time the Parliament House in Edinburgh, and are there met by their clients.

assembled early in the morning in the atrium, and listened to the advice which was given to those who came to consult the lawyer. This mode of education is the best in all cases where it is practicable" (*Neibuhr, Lect.* ii. 18). Thus Cicero attached himself to Scævola, the greatest lawyer of his day; and, in his own strong language, he tells us, that he hardly ever quitted his side until he had acquired a sufficient amount of legal instruction. And to complete their education they generally took as their model one of the famous advocates of the day, and assiduously attended him whenever he spoke in public, in order that they might become familiar with the proper style of forensic oratory. The introduction to the forum or "calling to the bar," as we may term it, was observed by the Romans as a most important epoch of life. At the age of seventeen the youthful student laid aside his boyish dress (*prætexta*), and assumed the garb of manhood (*toga virilis*). He then proceeded to the forum, attended by a festive company of friends, and was there brought forward by some distinguished citizen, generally of consular rank, and formally introduced as a practitioner in the courts of law. After this he might at once undertake the conduct of causes; and we are told that Cotta publicly accused Carbo in a speech on the very day in which he made his first appearance there. It may give some idea of the interest taken in the ceremony to know that Augustus, when emperor, accepted his thirteenth consulship expressly for the purpose of ushering his two sons, Caius and Lucius, into the forum, and Tiberius returned from a foreign expedition to Rome in order to perform the same office for Drusus Germanicus.

The profession of a jurisconsult was in some families, as for instance that of the Scævolas, hereditary; the members of which, with one exception, that of Quintus Mucius, seem not to have undertaken the conduct of causes in court. They contented themselves with the reputation which they gained as lawyers, to whom their fellow-citizens might resort with confidence for advice, or devoted themselves to the study of law, for the sake of the emoluments they were thereby enabled to acquire; for although there can be no doubt that in the majority of cases their opinions were given gratuitously, as a means of gaining popularity and influence, there seems to have been no law against their being paid by fees, which applied only to advocates; and in this respect they resembled the Rhetoricians of Athens, who, as we have seen, composed speeches for litigant parties, and by that means earned a livelihood. As this knowledge of the jus civile was possessed by few, the adepts in its mysteries seem to have had a sufficiently good opinion of themselves, and to have plumed themselves not a little on their black-letter lore. Cicero, however, ridicules their pretensions, and in his speech in defense of Murena says that three days are sufficient to master this kind of learning. "If, therefore, you put me on my mettle, overwhelmed with business as I am, I will in three days declare myself a jurisconsult." We can easily imagine that such men, either from inability to speak, or disinclination, or want of confidence in their own powers, or dislike of contentious and noisy strife, might decline to practice in the forum. This is what happens in England, where, as a distinct branch of the profession, there are many most able men, who have a large amount of practice at chambers, and yet do not appear in court, and pass their lives immersed in law as conveyancers or special pleaders, without ever arguing a single case. But we are surprised to find such a broad line of distinction as was recognized at Rome between the jurisconsult and the advocate with regard to legal attainments. Not that the latter might not be, and frequently was, an able lawyer, but a knowledge of law was considered a very secondary object with him in comparison with other qualifications. It appears at first sight inexplicable how the Roman advocates should have ventured to undertake causes involving nice and technical questions of law, without having previously prepared themselves by a careful study of its rules and principles, and that, notwithstanding, they should have been able to establish a reputation and attract clients. But a latitude was allowed in those days wholly unknown in the strict and formal system of judicial proceedings in England. Even when the cause depended upon the investigation of abstruse points of law,—on the interpretation of the Twelve Tables, or the construction of a will, — the advocate employed arguments and indulged himself in appeals, addressed, not to the understanding, but to the feelings and passions of the court. A jest supplied the place of an authority, and loose declamatory harangues were sometimes permitted to influence decisions, which ought to have been formed upon the closest and most rigid investigation of legal principles. Rhetoric and logic had not then, as with us, distinct and separate domains. The former constantly invaded the province of the latter, and in cases where we should think it unworthy, as indeed it would be hopeless, to employ any other means for our clients than close and severe argument, the Roman counsel would condescend to the use of the most transparent sophistry, and endeavor, too often successfully, by raillery and wit to obtain judgment in his favor. But we must not forget the difference between the tribunals in the two countries. The Roman judices were, as we have seen, much more like jurymen than judges, and therefore liable to be imposed upon by fallacies, which, if addressed to an English court, would render the counsel who propounded them merely ridiculous.

The neglect of the distinction between the functions of the judge and those of the jury, was a capital defect in the ancient forms of legal procedure. The maxim of the English law, that *ad quæstiones juris respondent judices, ad quæstiones facti juratores*, was unknown to the tribunals of Greece and Rome; and yet it is hardly possible to overrate the advantages that arise from the recognition of this principle. Questions of law and fact are widely different in their nature, and their solution depends upon very different processes of reasoning. To determine the latter requires merely natural intelligence and impartiality of judgment; but the former demand a peculiar kind of knowledge which can only be acquired by previous reading. It may, however, be asserted, that it would be much more safe to allow a man whose mind has been trained and disciplined by legal studies, to determine matters of fact as well as law, than to intrust the latter to the verdict of a jury. The tendency of such a tribunal is to warp the law, and make it bend to what are conceived to be the merits and equity of a case. But the consequence of this must be an uncertain and varying system of decisions, which would confound all legal landmarks, and render it impossible to predicate beforehand what are the rights and liabilities of parties. *Hoc enim si fieret*, says Bacon, *judex prorsus transiret in legislatorem, atque omnia exarbitrio fluerent* (*De Augment. Scient. Aphor.* 44).

No such mischief can arise from perverse verdicts when they are confined to their proper sphere—the investigation of disputed facts. For although they may be erroneous and unjust, they do not furnish precedents for subsequent conclusions, and for this reason,—that no two cases are exactly alike in their circumstances: and therefore the decision arrived at in the one affords no guide to that which ought to be come to in the other. When we have connected together all the links of a chain of evidence, which lead to the result that we must pronounce A. guilty of the crime of murder, this by no means assists us in determining whether B., under different, or even under similar circumstances at another period, has been guilty of a similar crime.

It would be a logical absurdity to suppose that contingent and empirical facts can depend upon fixed principles; and it is necessary, as each problem is presented to us for inquiry, to examine it upon its own independent evidence, without reference to what may be supposed to be analogous instances.

But even in those cases where it was right to work upon the feelings, and invoke the sympathies of the tribunal they addressed, the Roman advocates availed themselves of expedients which would be condemned by our cold notions of correct propriety. The warm sun of the South quickened the sensibilities of both the speaker and his audience, to a degree that enabled him to venture upon the boldest and most startling appeals, without doing violence to decorum.[1] The Romans loved the poetry of action, and the strongest figures of rhetoric were often inadequate to express the intensity of their emotions. Some of the great events of their history are impressed with this character, and thereby invested with a kind of dramatic effect. Thus when Brutus wished to overthrow a dynasty, he bore the bleeding body of Lucretia to the forum, for he knew that the sad spectacle would more effectually rouse his countrymen to revolt, than all the burning eloquence of the tongue. And when, not long afterwards, the Commons were bowed down to the dust beneath the load of debts which they owed their patrician creditors, an old man, who had just escaped from prison into which his creditor had thrown him, in squalid rags, pale and famishing, with haggard beard and hair, appeared sud-

---

[1] Climate is not without its effect upon the gravity of courts of justice. An amusing instance is mentioned in Ford's Handbook of Spain. The jealous Toledo clergy wished to put down the *Bolero* (a favorite Spanish dance) on the pretense of immorality. The dancers were allowed, in their defense, to exhibit a specimen to the court. When they began, the bench and the bar showed symptoms of restlessness, and, at last, casting aside gowns and briefs, they joined, as if tarantula-bitten, in the irresistible capering. Verdict for the defendants, with costs.

denly in the streets of Rome, and cried in agony to the citizens for help. A crowd collected round him; he showed them the bloody marks of his inhuman treatment; he told them that he had fought in eight-and-twenty battles; that his house and farm-yard had been plundered and burnt by the enemy; he had been forced to borrow; usurious interest had increased the debt to many times its original amount; this he could not pay, and his creditor had, as the law allowed, seized him and his two sons, and put them in chains. The people recognized the features of a brave veteran; compassion and indignation caused an uproar through the city, and the excitement thus occasioned did not finally subside, until in the following year the secession of the Commons to the Sacred Hill gained for them the relief which they had so long sought in vain. The bonds of the insolvent debtors were canceled, and those who had become the slaves of their creditors were restored to freedom (*Niebuhr*, i. 529, 540).

Thus, too, Manlius, when impeached before the people, pointed to the Capitol which he had saved, and was with loud acclamations acquitted.

I know not whether we ought to add, as another instance, the memorable deed of Virginius, who plunged a dagger into his daughter's heart, when Appius Claudius had adjudged her as a slave to one of his fawning clients, the perjured minister of his lust; for this was the only mode by which the father could save the maiden from dishonor. But the necessity for such a dreadful act excited the Commons to insurrection, and freed them forever from the tyranny of the Decemvirs. And when Antony wished to excite the feelings of the Roman multitude to the highest pitch of horror and indignation against the murderers of Cæsar, he lifted up the bloody toga, as the body lay upon its bier in the Campus Martius, and pointed to the rents made in it by the daggers of the assassins. Who does not remember the passage in Shakespeare, where the poet, with that intuitive knowledge which enabled him to live in past ages as though they were his own, has seized upon this historical incident, and embalmed it in his own immortal verse?

> " You all do know this mantle: I remember
> The first time ever Cæsar put it on:
> 'Twas on a summer's evening in his tent;
> That day he overcame the Nervii:
> Look! in this place ran Cassius' dagger through;
> See! what a rent the envious Casca made:
> Through this the well-beloved Brutus stabb'd,
> And as he pluck'd the cursed steel away,
> Mark how the blood of Cæsar followed it."

In like manner the advocates at Rome gave effect to their appeals by producing, on fit occasions, the living image of a client's misery, and his claims upon the compassion of the courts. Thus, when Antony was defending against the charge of pecuniary corruption Aquilius, who had successfully conducted the campaign in Sicily against the fugitive slaves, and was unable to disprove or refute the charge, in the midst of his harangue, after appealing in impassioned tones to the services rendered to his country by the brave soldier who stood by his side, he suddenly unloosed the folds of his client's robe and showed to his fellow-citizens, who sat upon his trial, the scars of the wounds which had been received in their behalf. They could not resist the effect of such a sight, and Aquilius was acquitted. A similiar instance is recorded of Hyperides at Athens, who, when Phryne was accused of some act of sacrilege, bared the bosom of the culprit and bade the judges remember that she was a woman. The artifice succeeded, and Phryne was pronounced not guilty. Thus, too, when Galba was impeached before the people for an act of base treachery towards the Lusitanians, and Cato had delivered against him one of his most terrible harangues, feeling that the danger of conviction was imminent, he snatched into his arms the son of Sulpicius Gallus, his relative, then recently dead, whose memory was endeared to his countrymen, and holding him before the assembled multitude commended his own two sons to their protection, as though he were making a hasty will. At the same time he exclaimed, in tears, that he appointed the Roman people guardians of his orphan children. This saved him from destruction, for a verdict of acquittal followed the piteous appeal.

And when Cicero defended Fonteius against the accusations of Induciomarus and the other Gauls, who had come to Rome to impeach him of corrupt conduct during his prætorian government, he pointed to the mother and sister of his client clinging to him in passionate embrace, and reminded the judges that that sister was a Vestal virgin whose chief tie to earth was her brother's existence. "Let it not be said hereafter," he exclaimed, as the affecting scene was acted before their eyes, "that the eternal fire which was preserved by the midnight care and watching of Fonteia was extinguished by the tears of your priestess. A Vestal virgin extends towards you in suppliant prayer those hands, which she has been used to lift up to the immortal gods in your behalf. Beware of the danger and the sin you may incur by rejecting the entreaty of her, whose prayers if the gods were to despise, Rome itself would be in ruins" (*Pro Fonteio*, 17).

It is, however, needless to multiply instances, for such was the ordinary and recognized mode of working upon the feelings of the court.[1] Nor was it confined to defenses only, for similar displays were used on the part of

[1] *Quintilian*, vi. I, mentions one or two cases where this attempt at dramatic effect resulted in ludicrous failure. For instance, when Glyco Spirilion, in the midst of an impassioned appeal, had a boy brought into court all in tears, as though he wept for the loss of his parent, and asked him why he cried so piteously, the urchin, being badly tutored in his part, answered "Because I have just been birched," *ex pædagogo se vellicari respondit.*

the prosecution to excite horror and indignation against crime. Sometimes, if a murder had been committed, a picture representing the foul deed was openly exhibited during the trial, that the eyes of the judges might rest upon the hideous scene, while their ears were listening to the cry for vengeance against the assassin.

This appears to our notions of the functions of a judge most reprehensible, but we must remember that there was at Rome no ulterior party, as with us, who could exercise the prerogative of mercy. The court sat not only as both judge and jury, but it considered itself at liberty to *pardon* as well as to convict. This may explain what otherwise would seem to be a grevious dereliction of duty in the Roman tribunals. For if they had merely to try the simple question of guilt or innocence, that is, if their duty was confined solely to the investigation of the facts alleged to have been commited, it would have been most improper to admit artifices, the object of which was to disable them from coming to a calm and dispassionate conclusion. But this was not so. The judges represented the state against which the offense had been committed, and as such were entitled to remit the punishment awarded by the law. But this being the case, it was thought unnecessary to go through the form of a conviction and a subsequent pardon by the same tribunal, and the shorter process was adopted of bringing in a verdict of acquittal, which by no means necessarily implied what "not guilty" does with us, namely, the innocence of the accused. Unless we adopt some such theory as this, it seems impossible to understand the appeals to the compassion of judges, who were bound by a solemn oath to adjudicate uprightly and truly, for it would have been an insult to ask them to acquit in cases where the charge could not be denied. It would have been tantamount to beseeching them to affirm a lie. Let me, however, fortify this view by quoting the opinion of Niebuhr on the subject. It would be impossible to appeal to a higher authority. He says, "But after all, we must remember that those *i. e.* (the Roman) courts were not juries, whose object is simply to discover whether a person is guilty or not, and where a higher power presides which may step in, either pardoning or mitigating. In those *quæstiones perpetuæ* the judges had stepped into the place of the people, who formerly judged in the popular courts, and they pronounced their sentence in the capacity of sovereign. The people more frequently pardoned than they acquitted, so that pardoning and acquitting coalesced as identical; and as there was no other place in which the pardoning power could manifest itself, it entered into the courts of justice. This is the point of view from which we have to consider the courts of justice and the pleaders for the accused at that time" (*Lectures, Hist. of Rome*, ii. 23).

But besides these startling and dramatic appeals, which must at times have extorted an acquittal, however guilty the criminal may have been, the dress and demeanor of the accused were always carefully adjusted to the exigency of the occasion. Seated near his counsel, with uncombed hair and beard, both suffered to grow to an unusual length, and clothed in a mean and miserable garb, the party who was on his trial implored by tearful looks and mute gestures of despair the compassion of his judges. Nor was he the only suppliant: a host of friends accompanied him who were all dressed in deep mourning to express their sympathy and sorrow,—a custom which led to such abuse, by tending to overawe the judges, and deter them from doing their duty, that a law was passed forbidding any persons so to appear, who were not relatives within a certain degree of the accused.

We must not, however, suppose that a Roman counsel undertook the conduct of a cause, which depended upon the proper solution of some legal difficulty, without endeavoring to make himself acquainted with sufficient law to answer his purpose for the particular occasion. He betook himself, if necessary, to some learned lawyer, a Scævola for instance, or a Sulpicius, and received from him such instruction as the nature of the case required. And those who were interested in the result of the trial took care to supply him with as much learning as they could bring to bear upon the question at issue. In this respect they seem to have acted in a capacity not very dissimilar to that of attorneys in preparing a case for counsel. The difference between the Roman and English advocate is this:—The former (if he was one of that numerous class who trusted to their powers of oratory alone, and neglected the study of law) did not prepare himself by previous training to handle legal questions. He did not go through a course of painful study, in order to make himself master of legal principles and familiar with legal authorities, but trusted to the information imparted to him by others, as each emergency arose. Whereas the latter devotes himself for years to his books; and in the solitude of his chambers, or by careful attendance in the courts, endeavors to imbue his intellect with such a knowledge of law, as to be ready for every demand that may be made upon it, no matter how difficult or sudden, holding with Sir Edward Coke, "this for an undoubted verity, that there is no knowledge, case, or point in law, seems it of never so little account, but will stand the student in stead at one time or other, and therefore in reading nothing to be pretermitted" (*Co. Litt.* 9, a). And yet, notwithstanding this extempore mode of preparing for a case, an attentive perusal of the ancient writers leaves us bewildered at the thought of the temerity of men, who were not afraid to hold themselves out as counsel ready to undertake the cause of others, while they were themselves ignorant of the very rudiments of the law administered in the courts. True it is, that in England there are many who are lawyers only in name; but they are either such as do not affect to practice at all, or such as have at all events attempted to master the principles of law, though their intellect unfits them for its arduous requirements. At Rome, however, an advocate might boast, like Antony, of his ignorance of law, without any loss of employment or reputation. He might, perhaps, like Hipsæus, strenuously exert himself to get his client nonsuited; or, like Octavius, complain of the mistakes in the case of his opponent, as though that were a hardship upon him, not seeing that the effect was to secure a verdict in his own favor. When such suicidal conduct was exhibited, well might Cicero exclaim, "What can be conceived more disgraceful, than that a man, who professes to be able to undertake the causes of his friends, and assist those who are in difficulty, and throw the shield of his protection over the weak, should so blunder in the easiest and most trifling cases, as to appear to some an object of pity, to others of contempt" (*Cic. de Orat.* i. 37)?

It will be interesting to see the kind of cases requiring a more technical knowledge of law, in which these advocates of the olden time used to be engaged. There is little doubt that if there existed such a thing as a volume of reports of cases, such as were decided every day by the ordinary tribunals at Rome, we should obtain a much better knowledge of the manners, customs, and ordinary life of the Romans than we now possess. We should there see the citizen in his private life, buying and selling in the market and on the corn exchange, quarreling with his neighbors for interfering with his windows, refusing to be bound by contracts through fraud or inability to fulfill them, and acting the same drama which is daily exhibited in our courts.

Let us take, for instance, the case of the Roman soldier, who was serving with the army in a distant province when news of his death reached his father at Rome.

"Roland the brave, the brave Roland—
False tidings reach'd his native strand,
That he was slain in fight."

Believing that his son was no more, the latter altered his will, and named therein another as his heir. He died soon after, and when his son returned from the campaign, and made his appearance at home, he found a stranger in possession of his inheritance. He commenced an action in the court of the Centumvirs; and the judges had to determine the question whether a son could be disinherited, without express words to that effect in a will.[1] The opportunity of arguing this point first brought Lord Eldon, then Mr. Scott, into notice (Ackroyd *v.* Smithson, 1 *Bro. Ch. Cas.* 503).

One of the *causes célèbre,* before the time of Cicero, was that of Coponius against Curius, in which Crassus, who affected to despise legal knowledge, was opposed to Scævola, the most learned lawyer of his day in Rome. Coponius, when on his death-bed, thinking that his wife was pregnant, made a will, in which he named as his heir the child to whom he expected she would give birth, provided it were a son; but directed that in case his posthumous son should die before he attained his majority (as we should say), then M. Curius was to be his heir. Coponius died, and his widow proved not to be pregnant.

Upon this M. Coponius, who was the heir at law[2] of

---

[1] *Cic. de Orat.* i. 38. According to the English law, a false reason given for revoking a legacy prevents the revocation from taking effect. Thus, where a man assigns, in his codicil as a reason for revoking the legacies given by his will, that the legatees were dead, which turned out not to be the fact, it was held to be no revocation, the reason being false. Campbell *v.* French, 3 *Ves.* 321. But where a woman, having given by her will £300 to the children of A., left by a codicil to B. the £300 previously designed for A.'s children, on the ground that she "knew not whether any of them were alive, and if they were well provided for;" the revocation was held to be effectual, for the Court would not inquire whether the first-named legatees were well provided for or not. Att. Gen. *v.* Ward, 3 *Ves.* 327.

[2] *Agnatus mortui.* It must be borne in mind that the Roman law made

the deceased, claimed the property of which Curius had taken possession, and brought an action (of ejectment?) in the court of the Centumvirs against Curius, who asserted his right under the will. Scævola was counsel for Coponius, and Crassus for Curius. The plaintiff contended that the words of the will ought to be literally construed, and that it contained a condition precedent which had not been fulfilled. Curius was only to succeed as heir on a certain specified event happening, namely, the death of a posthumous son before attaining his majority; but if no son was born, there was no period at which Curius could take. Scævola further insisted that the defendant had been nominated in the will guardian of the infant, whose birth was expected and presupposed; and that he had, as we should say, a remainder limited, contingent upon the infant's not attaining its majority. But what title had he, if the contingency was rendered impossible by reason of there being no son?

Crassus, on the other hand, ridiculed these legal technicalities, contending that the will ought to be construed *cy pres*, that is, as nearly according to the intention of the testator as possible, and argued that the intention here clearly was to make Curius his heir in case he had no son. He enforced this view of the case with so much wit, that the trial, which promised to be a very dull affair, became lively and amusing; and the result was, that Curius had the verdict in his favor.

The case of Auratas against Gratidian involved the consideration how far the principle of *caveat emptor* applied in a sale of real property. Here Crassus was counsel for the plaintiff, and Antony for the defendant. Gratidian had resold to Auratas some premises which he had originally purchased from him, and which were sub-

no distinction between realty and personalty; and therefore the personal **re**presentative of the deceased was his heir at law.

ject to certain easements[1] in third parties, which fact he did not communicate at the time of the resale. The vendee, therefore, sought to recover damages equal to the amount by which the marketable value of the property was thereby diminished. It would seem, however, from Cicero's account, that Auratas was aware of the existence of these easements when he conveyed the property to Gratidian, and therefore we can hardly imagine on what ground he could expect damages for the concealment of a defect which was notorious to himself. The doctrine of the English law on this subject is expressed in the following maxim :—*Caveat emptor, qui ignorare nondebuit, quod jus alienum emit.* But the application of the rule is by no means easy. If there is no express warranty, the question in each case is, whether one can be implied by law. In a sale of chattels every affirmation made by the seller, at the time of the sale, amounts to a warranty, provided it be so intended. In the case of a sale or lease of houses or lands, there is no implied warranty on the part of the vendor that they are or shall be fit for habitation. Nor is there an implied warranty that a vendor has a good title to the property. A distinction is recognized in the English law between a warranty and a representation. The former becomes part of the contract; the latter is collateral to it, and it frequently is very difficult to determine how far it is binding upon the party making it, so as to give the vendee a right of action if it turns out to be untrue. It is a general rule that *simplex commendatio non obligat;* a vendor has a right to recommend his own wares, and thereby invite custom ;—and in the case, therefore, of a purchase without warranty, a man's own natural sagacity and common sense must be his protection. But if the representation be made with intent to deceive, this amounts to fraud, and gives a purchaser a right of action,

[1] Servitutes. The term in our law most nearly approaching this is *easements;* but it is not quite equivalent.

The liability of a vendor was in another instance sought to be extended beyond what either law or common sense could justify. Bucculeius, a Roman lawyer, who, as Cicero tells us, had a remarkably good opinion of himself, sold a house to Fufius, which commanded a good prospect over the city. By-and-by some buildings were erected in a distant quarter of the town, which interrupted the view from the windows in that direction; and Fufius, imagining that his enjoyment of light was thereby improperly diminished, brought an action, not against the party whose act had caused the annoyance by interfering with his "ancient lights," but against Bucculeius the vendor.

Another interesting question, involving the law of marriage and divorce, is mentioned by Cicero. A citizen of Rome had been resident for a time with his wife in Spain, and having occasion to return to Italy he left her behind him in a state of pregnancy. When he arrived in Rome the faithless husband remained there, and married another lady, without giving to his existing wife that notice of his intention to dissolve the marriage which the law required. Not long afterwards he died intestate, and each of the women whom he had married gave birth to a posthumous son. The question was, which of these two was legitimate, and therefore entitled to succeed as heir to the father's property? And this depended upon whether the contracting a new marriage *ipso facto* dissolved a prior one, without the intervention of any of the formalities of a divorce, and without any notice being given.[1] If so, then, according

---

[1] The ordinary forms of divorce were by *diffarreatio* and *remancipatio;* but in later times it seems that a mere notice of an intention to separate was sufficient. The first instance of divorce at Rome was said to be that by which Sp. Carvilius Ruga put away his wife, B. C. 234, because she had borne him no offspring.—*Aul. Gell.* iv. 3, xvii. 21. The ladies appear to have had a similar privilege; for Cicero mentions Paula Valeria as waiting for the return of her husband from his provincial government, in order to serve him with notice of divorce.—*Ep. ad Fam.* viii. 7.

to the Roman law, the son who was born in Spain would be bastardized; but if not, the second wife was degraded to the condition of a mistress, and her son became illegitimate.

This reminds us of that famous trial of modern times, Dalrymple *v.* Dalrymple (2 *Hagg. Cons. Rep.* 54), in which Lord Stowell delivered one of his most celebrated judgments. The question there, however, was not as to the validity of a prior divorce, but the existence of a prior marriage. Mr. Dalrymple, afterwards Earl of Stair, had, while in Scotland in the year 1804, by *verba de præsenti*, acknowledged a Miss Johanna Gordon as his wife, and she had consented to cohabit with him as such. He afterwards returned to England, which was the place of his birth and domicile, and he there married, in 1808, Miss Laura Manners. Miss Gordon, or, as we ought to call her, Mrs. Dalrymple, instituted a suit for the restitution of conjugal rights, and a counter-suit was also commenced by the second wife. Lord Stowell decided that the first marriage was valid and binding according to the law of Scotland, and therefore must be upheld in the English Consistory Court.

Now for a case in which Marius was judge. Titinius, an inhabitant of Minturnæ, had married a woman named Fannia, of loose character, well knowing her previous reputation; and having afterwards divorced himself from her on the plea of adultery, he refused to give her back her dowry. The cause came before Marius, who privately advised Titinius not to oppose the claim; but finding him obstinate, he gave judgment, imposing a nominal fine on the wife for her incontinence, and compelling the husband to restore her dowry, on the ground that he had married her for the iniquitous purpose of thus getting possession of her property. The fair and frail *Fanny* afterwards showed her gratitude to her judge, by receiving him into her house, after he had, as is well known, been denounced as a public enemy by the senate, and obliged to take refuge in the marshy swamps of Minturnæ. On another occasion, a curious point of law was determined. A man borrowed a horse to ride to Aricia, and having extended his equestrian excursion a short distance beyond the town, he was tried for stealing the horse and convicted.[1]

Quintilian mentions several instances where litigation arose from the ambiguous wording of wills. One was that of a testator, who expressed his wish that a statue should be erected, and used the following language, *poni statuam auream hastam in manu tenentem.* The question here was, whether the statue was to be of gold, or only the spear; and we can well imagine the astute arguments which might be urged in favor of either interpretation. A golden statue would not have been without precedent. Gorgias of Leontini, the famous rhetorician and sophist, so delighted the assembled Greeks at the Pythian games by the brilliancy of his eloquence, that a statue of him in beaten gold was erected in the temple of Apollo. Another instance was the bequest of a Greek who left Πάντα Λέοντι, and both Leon and *Panta*leon claimed the legacy.[2] These are

---

[1] *Val. Max.* viii. 2. "If A. lend B. a horse, and he ride away with him, or if I send goods by a carrier, and he carry them away, it is not larceny; because the original taking was *bonâ fide*, and without fraud."—1 *Hale, P. C.* 504. If, however, the carrier breaks bulk by opening a bale or package, and takes any of the contents, he is guilty of larceny, for by his tortuous act the contract of bailment is determined.—3 *Inst.* 107. An interesting case happened a few years ago. By a treaty between Great Britain and the United States, it was agreed that all persons charged with felony, and escaping across the Canadian frontier, should be mutually given up. A runaway slave, in his flight, seized upon a horse in the American territories, and mounting upon his back, got safe into Canada. He there turned the horse adrift. The Americans demanded him as a *felon* for stealing the horse, and not as a fugitive slave. The case was laid before the English Attorney-General, who was of opinion that no felony had been committed, as the horse had not been taken *animo furandi*. The poor slave, therefore, happily escaped.

[2] We must remember that the old mode of writing this would have been ΠΑΝΤΑΛΗΟΝΤΙ; so that *Pantaloon* had a very fair chance of suc-

instances of what would be called, in the English law, patent ambiguity; and the rule is, that where this occurs on the face of an instrument, no evidence can be adduced to remove the obscurity, and the bequest is held to be void for uncertainty. But if a man leaves property to John Styles, and it is proved that there are two John Styles's, evidence may be admitted to show which of the two the testator meant. For the will itself is unambiguous, and the doubt is only created by the evidence given of the existence of more than one individual of the same name. The rule, therefore, is, that the same means which first raised the doubt may be also employed to remove it. But if there is a patent ambiguity as to the factum of the instrument, parol evidence may be admitted, under some circumstances, to explain it.

There seems to have been no limit to the number of counsel who might be engaged on the same side, although it was not usual to retain more than four. We read, however, that Scaurus was defended by six, and these the most eminent of their day at Rome;—Clodius Pulcher, Marcellus, Callidius, Messala Niger, Hortensius and Cicero. Besides having this formidable array, he spoke also in his own behalf; and, by his earnest appeal to the compassion of the judges, contributed not a little to the favorable result of the trial. When there were several counsel, they divided the task by each taking a separate part of the charge, and speaking upon it, as was done by the managers on the impeachment of Warren Hastings; and the whole case was afterwards summed up by the advocate who was thought likely to do it most effectually. Thus Cicero tells us that this

ceeding. These are cases similar to that leading one, Stradling *v.* Stiles, quoted in Martinus Scriblerus, where a testator bequeathed to a legatee all his black and white horses; and it turned out that he had both black horses and white horses, and also piebald ones. "The debate, therefore, was, whether or no the said Matthew Stradling should have the said **pyed** horses by virtue of the said bequest."

part of the duty, the peroration, generally devolved upon him. He complains, however, in his speech in defense of Murena, of the difficulty he felt in following Hortensius and Crassus, who had preceded him, and by disposing of the separate parts of the accusation exhausted the subject, so that there was little or nothing left to which he could address himself. Pliny has given us an account of the manner in which the different counsel for the prosecution and defense followed each other at the trial of Bassus, who was accused of corruption in the government of Bithynia, during the reign of Nerva, and whom he and others defended before the senate. Pomponius Rufus first stated the case against him, and Theophanes followed on the same side. Pliny then rose on behalf of the accused, and spoke for five hours, when he was succeeded by Lucius Albinus, who was retained along with him. Hercanius Pollio spoke next for the prosecution, and Theophanes also a second time, when it became so late that lights were brought in. Next day Titius, Homulo, and Fronto addressed the court for the defense, and afterwards the evidence was taken. On another occasion Pliny and Cornelius Tacitus were retained by the province of Africa to impeach Marius Priscus in the senate of various "high crimes and misdemeanors" in his proconsular government. The Emperor, who happened that year to be consul himself, presided in the senate; and Pliny describes the interest which the trial excited, and how crowded the house was, it being the month of January, when the attendance of senators was always greatest. He rose in considerable agitation and anxiety to press the charge against the accused, but spoke at great length, and with so much energy, that the emperor more than once beckoned to a freedman of Pliny who stood near him, and told him to urge the latter to use less exertion, lest he should injure himself. On the next day Salvius Liberalis spoke for the defense, and he was immediately answered by

Tacitus. Fronto Catius then followed on behalf of Marius, and thus concluded the speeches. Marius was convicted, and Pliny and Tacitus received a vote of thanks from the senate, for the satisfactory manner in which they had conducted the case for the prosecution.

Cicero, however, strongly condemned the practice of allowing several counsel to speak upon the same side, *quo nihil est vitiosius*. For it seems they frequently made separate set speeches, without having been present at the argument which they had to answer, and wearied the court by going over the same ground which had been occupied by those who had preceded them;—a fault which it is much more easy to censure than to avoid. The time which the speaker might occupy was formerly unlimited; but Pompey, in his third consulship, introduced the clepsydra or water-glass, by which the pleaders were obliged to measure the duration of their speeches. It seems that the presiding magistrate determined beforehand the quantity of time or water which each side might consume at a trial, and clepsydræ of various sizes were used according as much or little time was allowed.

We are surprised to find that in causes of trivial importance it was not unusual for advocates to sit when they addressed the court; and Quintilian bestows a few hints upon those who adopted this mode of delivering their speeches.

It is curious and interesting to trace the similarity in matters of every-day practice between ancient and modern times, and not unfrequently we seem, while studying the classic authors, to be reading what might have happened yesterday. Nothing tends so forcibly as this to make us realize the past, and live as it were among the people of remote antiquity. An instance of this occurs in the speech of Cicero in defense of Cluentius. A counsel frequently has to determine at a trial whether he will take a legal and technical objection on behalf of his client, or whether he will waive any such advantage, and stand wholly upon what are called the merits of the case. He is often expressly instructed not to avail himself of a defense which the strict rules of law would afford, but boldly grapple with the facts, and let the issue of the cause be determined solely with reference to them. In some cases it is obvious that this is the only course which can with propriety be adopted, as for instance, in trials for libel where character is at stake, and where the only anxiety is to disprove a calumnious imputation. It would be to no purpose that a man should bring an action of slander against another, for saying of him that he had been guilty of acts of gross immorality, and obtain a verdict, not by disproving the plea alleging the truth of the charge, but by insisting upon some technical objection. This would no more establish his reputation than if, after conviction for felony, he were to succeed in arresting judgment on account of some flaw in the indictment. But not unfrequently cases occur where the wishes of the client and the advice of his counsel are opposed to each other in this respect, and the latter is unwilling to peril the chances of a favorable verdict by consenting to forego an advantage which the law affords. Let us see what was the practice of Cicero.

Cluentius was accused of having poisoned his stepfather Oppianicus, and also of having conspired, on a former occasion, to procure his condemnation at a trial, by bribing the judges. These two charges were mixed up together, for the ancient Romans knew nothing of the precision of our indictments; and a court was constituted to try Cluentius, to which jurisdiction was given by a law that applied to the offense of such a conspiracy, only when committed by those who had held a public office, or were members of the senate. Now Cluentius did not come within either of these definitions, and therefore was, on that ground, entitled to an acquittal on the charge of conspiracy. But this would not have relieved him from the odium attaching to the charge, and he therefore refused to avail himself of the legal defense. Cicero, who was his counsel, gives the following account of his consultation with the client (*Pro Cluentio*, c. 52). " When the conduct of this case was offered to me, being well acquainted with the laws, with which I ought to be conversant and familiar, I immediately said to Cluentius, that he was safe from a conviction on so much of the charge as related to the conspiracy, although persons of my own rank might be found guilty of it. But he immediately began to pray and beseech me not to defend him by taking the point of law. When I had reasoned with him at some length, he induced me to adopt his view: for he declared with tears that he was not more anxious to retain his civic rights than his reputation and character. I therefore complied with his request, but for this reason (but I by no means ought to do so on all occasions), because I saw that, without resorting to the legal objection, there was a complete defense upon the merits. I perceived that my client would come off with more honor if I defended him as I have done, though there would be less trouble and difficulty if I took the objection of which he was unwilling that I should avail myself; for if my only object had been to get the verdict in this case, I should have contented myself with simply citing the law, and immediately have sat down." He then, however, grapples with the argument of Attius, the counsel on the other side, that it would be a disgraceful incongruity that a senator should be amendable to the particular law in question, but not one of the equestrian order like Cluentius. "Admitting it were so," he says, (*Ibid.* c. 53) " you must allow that it would be much more disgraceful not to abide by the law, for this is the support of the rank which we enjoy in the commonwealth, this the foundation of liberty, this the fountain of equity. The mind, the soul, the will, the counsels of the state consist in the laws. As bodies can not use their limbs and sinews without a soul, so is the state powerless without the law. The ministers of the law are the magistrates, the interpreters of the law the judges, and to this end are we all the servants of the law, that we may thereby be free."

Another instance may be taken from Cicero's advice as to the mode of dealing with a witness. He quite understood the danger of putting too many questions in cross-examination, which often has the effect of rivetting the unfavorable impression already produced by the examination-in-chief. The following passage from his speech in defense of Fonteius contains hints which might be useful for Nisi Prius practice at the present day. "It is my duty as counsel to put a question or two, and that briefly, to a witness when examining to any particular fact; and often to abstain from putting any questions at all, lest I should give an adverse witness an opportunity of damaging my case, or seem to put leading questions to a willing one" (*Pro Fonteio.* c. 6).

It would excite no little laughter now-a-days to see an advocate setting out for Westminster Hall attended by a long train of clients and admiring friends, and escorted to his home after the labors of the day amidst their congratulations and applause. Yet this was the ordinary case at Rome, where, as it was the usual custom to appear in public with a crowd of parasites and retainers, such marks of popularity occasioned no surprise. But even in cold and decorous England one instance at least of this enthusiasm has been known. After the trials of Hardy, Horne Tooke, and Thelwall, and their triumphant acquittals through the splendid advocacy of Erskine, his horses were taken from his carriage, and he was drawn home by the mob with tumultuous cheers.

FORUM—POMPEII.

CHAPTER V.

SOME ACCOUNT OF THE ADVOCATES OF ROME DURING THE REPUBLIC.

IN inquiring into the history of Advocacy at Rome, we need not ascend higher than the time of Marc Cato, the censor. Previously to him, no name adorns her forensic annals; and oratory was scarcely known. A peculiar kind of public speaking had indeed been cultivated there from the earliest times of the commonwealth,—that of funeral orations; some of which, like that pronounced by the great Fabius over his son, and that by Q. Metellus over his father, were read and admired at Rome in the days of the Cæsars.[1] But we must not be deluded by a name, or imagine that if time had spared to us these *oraisons funèbres* of the ancient Romans, we should have found in them anything to compare with the speech of Pericles, as given by Thucydides, or the eloquent harangues of Bossuet.

We hear of a few men whose memory was cherished by their countrymen as having been the orators of bygone days; but their speeches were not those of advocates addressing legal tribunals, but appeals to the multitude; and of many of these Cicero admits that there was no authentic tradition that they possessed any of

---

[1] *Plin. Hist. Nat.* vii. 43, 44. With the exception of a fragment of the speech delivered by Metellus, which may still be read in Pliny, no specimen of this more early kind of Roman oratory remains.

the charms of eloquence, his expression being "*tantum-modo conjecturâ ducor ad suspicandum*" (*Brut.* 14). Such were Menenius the dictator, to whom was attributed that famous apologue which, according to popular belief, had the effect of quelling the insurrection of the commons when they had quitted Rome, and taken their stand on the Sacred Hill, and Fabricius, and Popilius, and Curius Dentatus, and Fabius Maximus, and Appius Claudius.

The first whose reputation for eloquence rested upon positive testimony was Cornelius Cethegus, consul in the second Punic war, nearly a century and a half before the consulship of Cicero. Of him the poet Ennius sang as "the flower of all the people," and "the orator with the silver tongue" (*Cic. Brut.* 15). But no fragment of his speeches was preserved, even in the time of Cicero, and the verses of Ennius were then the only record of his fame. The rigid simplicity of legal forms among the Romans in the early ages of the republic afforded little scope for the efforts of an advocate, for actions were then determined with all the strictness which characterizes the system of special pleading in the English law.

We are so much in the habit of regarding Cato as the stern moralist and censor of Rome, that we are at first surprised when we discover that he was one of her most gifted advocates. If we may credit the testimony of antiquity, he was an eloquent orator, a profound lawyer, and a great writer. We think of him only as the living type of the old Roman severity of manners, struggling alone against the tide of innovation, and fearing not to attack the noblest and most powerful citizens if they yielded to the corruption of the times. In this spirit of inflexible virtue he denounced Minucius the consul, and robbed him of his anticipated triumph; and Veturius, whom he deprived of his Equestrian rank; and Galba, against whom, for a base and perfidious act of treachery towards the Lusitanians, many thousands of whom he massacred after betraying them into a pretended negotiation for peace, he launched the terrors of his invective when bending under the weight of fourscore years. We can scarcely believe that he was one of the most accomplished men of letters of whom Rome can boast, when we recollect his hostility to the introduction of Greek philosophy. Greece, however, had her revenge; and in his old age Cato betook himself to the study of her language and literature, which he had before affected to despise. I say affected, for we may well believe that his contempt was not genuine. It was because he dreaded the effect which the degraded and effeminate manners of the Greeks in his day might have upon his countrymen, that he opposed all intercourse between them; and not because he was insensible to the advantages which a Roman would obtain from an acquaintance with the language in which Thucydides and Plato wrote, and Pericles and Demosthenes spoke. The orations which Cato at various times delivered were very numerous; and Cicero says that more than one hundred and fifty of his speeches were extant in his day; but the study of them was then entirely neglected, although he remarks that they were well worthy of diligent perusal. They chiefly related to public affairs; but Cato sometimes defended, though he was more generally known as the accuser of his fellow-citizens.

The great age to which he lived enabled him to witness the rising reputation of the two illustrious friends, Scipio the younger, and Lælius. The conqueror of Carthage and Numantia was numbered among the most celebrated orators of Rome; and Cicero speaks of him and Lælius as *in primis eloquentes* (*Brut.* 21). We know, however, the names of no private causes in which he was engaged. Those of which we find mention in the classic writers were all of a public nature. Such were his five orations in his own defense, when accused before the people by Asellus the tribune; his speeches for the temple of Castor against the agrarian law of Tiberius Gracchus, and against the proposed Papirian law. To these may be added his accusations of Sulpicius Galba and Lucius Cotta.

C. Lælius, surnamed "the wise," for the forbearance he displayed as tribune when he abandoned his proposal of an agrarian law, because he saw that its discussion would convulse the state, was distinguished for his mild and gentle eloquence (*Brut.* 21). But he was also a gallant soldier and successful general, and when, after filling the office of prætor, he obtained as his province Western Spain (the modern Portugal), he crushed the hostile attempts of Viriathus the leader of the Lusitanians. One of his most famous speeches was that *De Collegiis*, which he delivered against a proposed law for taking the power of electing members of the College of Priests from that body, and vesting it in the people. His eloquence prevailed, and the mode of election remained unaltered, until it was changed many years afterwards by the Domitian law. We know the names of very few of the causes which he undertook, but Cicero mentions one interesting trial in which he was engaged, arising out of the following circumstances. In the lonely pine forests that skirted the southern extremity of the Apennine range some atrocious murders had been committed, and suspicion fell upon the members of a company who farmed the public revenues arising from that district. The senate ordered the consuls to investigate the matter, and the suspected parties were put upon their trial. They engaged Lælius as their counsel, and he spoke the first day well and ably in their behalf. The court, however, was not yet satisfied as to their innocence or guilt, and the consuls adjourned the inquiry. When, after an interval of a few days, it was resumed, Lælius spoke with still greater force and eloquence, but with no decisive result, and the case was again adjourned.

Lælius was escorted home by his grateful clients, who thanked him for his exertions, and expressed concern lest he should be exhausted by his efforts. He told them that he had done his best, but advised them to apply to Galba to continue the defense, since he thought him better fitted than himself to conduct such a case, as his style of speaking was more earnest and impassioned. They went therefore to Galba, who, after some hesitation and diffidence, consented to be their advocate. He had only one day to prepare, and he devoted it to the task; shutting himself up with his amanuensis in an inner room in his house, where, with all the vehemence of his nature, and as though he were actually in court, he dictated his thoughts aloud. He did not quit the apartment until summoned next day to the court, where the consuls were already seated, and it was remarked that he left his house with the look and appearance of a man who had just delivered a great speech, and not merely prepared one. He rose to plead for the accused, and by the power and pathos of his eloquence, he gained a verdict of acquittal that very day, and satisfied not only the court, but all who heard him, of the innocence of his clients.

Servius Sulpicius Galba was by no means a learned lawyer, but Cicero speaks of him as an orator in high terms. He says, that he alone among his contemporaries was pre-eminent for eloquence, *inter tot æquales unus excellens*. He first among the Latins studied speaking as an art, and employed the artifices of rhetoric to work upon the minds of his audience. But with all this, his speeches seemed to the taste of the next generation bald and antiquated in style, so that they soon disappeared and were wholly lost.

We can hardly number the Gracchi in the list of Roman advocates, though the fiery eloquence of Caius placed him high among the orators of the republic. But it was chiefly in the turbulent assemblies of the people that his voice was heard, denouncing his political adversaries as the enemies of the state; and of the numerous speeches attributed to him, we only find one in which he seems to have undertaken the defense of a party on his trial. He is known to us rather as the democratic leader of the commons, who lost his life in a popular tumult, which the aristocratic party charged him with exciting. But we must receive with the greatest caution the account of his character which we find in the patrician writers. They have represented him as a demagogue whose very name was a watchword of sedition, and have described his efforts to obtain the passing of the agrarian law as an attempt at confiscation of property. But justice has at last been done to his memory; for it is now universally admitted that the bill for an agrarian law was nothing more than a most righteous proposal, that the Plebs should be allowed to participate in the enjoyment of the demesne lands of the state, from which it was unfairly excluded; and Niebuhr has, in a very remarkable chapter of his Lectures on the History of Rome, vindicated the character of Caius Gracchus from the calumny which so long obscured it, and shown that, so far from being a factious demagogue, he was a virtuous and upright citizen. "There are two classes of men, the one consisting of those who are sincere and open, and seek and love the beautiful and sublime, who delight in eminent men, and see in them the glory of their age and nation; the other comprising those who think only of themselves, are envious, jealous, and sometimes very unhappy creatures, without having a distinct will of their own: they can not bear to see great men in the enjoyment of general esteem. It was these latter, a set of men more fatal to mankind than original sin, that rose against Caius Gracchus. He was too spotless, too pure, and too glorious, not to be an offense to many; for every one was reminded by his example of what he ought to be: It was the greatness of Gracchus which determined them to bring him down "(*Lect. Hist. of Rome*, i. 350).

It would be to little purpose to dwell upon the names of the less celebrated advocates who flourished in the period that intervened before Antony appeared, and we may dismiss them with a brief and passing notice. Among them were Lepidus Porcina, an orator of no mean repute, who first among the Latins attained that gentleness of style which Cicero says was characteristic of the Greeks; and Caius Carbo, the volatile and fickle leader of the popular party, who, however, successfully defended Opimius, when called upon to answer for the death of the younger Gracchus. Public trials were then becoming more frequent, on account of the law brought forward by Piso the tribune, which provided for the impeachment of those Roman officers who improperly received money in their provincial governments. Æmilius Scaurus, another advocate well known in his day, was the scion of a noble house, but so fallen in fortunes that his father was a charcoal-seller, as Statius, an opponent, once ungenerously reminded him, by quoting, though hardly applicable to an Æmilius, however lowly in estate, the lines —

"St, tacete:—quid hoc clamoris? quibus nec mater, nec pater,
Tantâ confidentiâ estis? auferte enim istam superbiam."

Which we may thus render:—

"Whence this clamor? why this bother?
Father hast thou none, nor mother;
Meek and humble should'st thou be,
Born without a pedigree."

He deserves a more ample biography; but here we need only mention, that he gained popularity among his fellow citizens by his opinions as a lawyer, and by this means climbed to the highest honors in the state. In the courts he spoke with such an air of serious dignity, that it was said of him that he seemed rather to be giving solemn testimony as a witness than advocating the cause of a client.

Rutilius Rufus enjoyed a higher reputation as a jurist than a speaker. He had studied law under Publius Nucius Scævola, and was much resorted to by clients for his legal knowledge. He was one of those characters who win the love and admiration of their countrymen. Cicero calls him a model of spotless innocence, and Velleius Paterculus says that he was the most excellent person, not only of his own, but of any age. In the consciousness of his own integrity, he condemned the practice of appealing to the compassion of the court on a trial, and said that even death was to be preferred to the humiliating scene which Galba had gone through. Nor did his practice differ from his precept, for when he was unjustly accused of illegally receiving money as a magistrate, and had to defend himself against the unscrupulous attacks of Apicius, who conducted the prosecution, he disdained to assume the attitude of a suppliant, and pleaded his cause with the simple and unadorned majesty of truth. He was assisted at his trial by his nephew Cotta, and Q. Mucius Scævola; but he would not suffer them to adopt a more impassioned style of defense. Rutilius was condemned to banishment, and Cicero says that this was the cause of his conviction. "So great a man was thus lost to the state, while his cause was pleaded as though it were being tried in the Utopian republic of Plato. No groans or cries of grief were heard from any of his counsel, no complaint or sorrow was expressed, not even a foot was stamped in energy, and no appeal was made to the pity of his countrymen" (*De Orat.* i. 53).

We must pass over the names of Caius Galba, the heir of many hopes, who was condemned to an untimely death on a charge of participation in the Jugurthine conspiracy; and Fimbria, a tolerable lawyer, but bitter and malevolent speaker; and Calvinius, who would have gained a higher reputation as an advocate, had he not been a martyr to the gout, which prevented him from practicing much in the courts; and Curio and Catullus, and the two Memmii, that we may devote more space to the memory of those whose celebrity has survived the lapse of ages.

In the foremost rank of these stands Mark Antony, grandfather of the Triumvir, who was born B. C. 143. At the age of twenty-nine, he was called upon to answer the charge of having dishonored a vestal virgin, but he defended himself successfully and was acquitted. He appeared first as a public prosecutor against Papirius Carbo, whose camp had been taken by the Cimbri, and who was put upon his trial as a traitor to the republic. Carbo did not venture to abide the result, but destroyed himself by poison. Antony filled successively the chief public offices, as tribune, ædile, prætor, and consul, and while discharging the duties of censor, was accused by A. Duronius, who had an old grudge against him as the cause of his expulsion from the senate, for proposing the repeal of a sumptuary law. The result is not known with certainty, but we may presume that he was acquitted. During the miserable civil war that raged between Marius and Sylla, he adhered to the party of the latter, and when Marius returned to Rome, while Sylla was carrying on the contest with Mithridates in Greece, Antony, who had concealed himself, was betrayed by a slave to the ruthless tyrant, now master of the lives and fortunes of his fellow-citizens, and he was put to death. Even at the last, the magic voice of the great orator had nearly saved him, and the incident may be told in the touching language of a still greater master of eloquence, our own Jeremy Taylor. "But so," he says, "a Roman gentleman kept off a whole band of soldiers who were sent to murder him, and his eloquence was stronger than their anger or design; but suddenly a rude trooper rushed upon him, who neither had nor would hear him speak, and he thrust his spear into that throat, whose music had charmed all his fellows into peace and gentleness."[1] His head was struck off and exposed to public view on the Rostra, where he had so often stood, "to wield the fierce democracy" of Rome with the power of his persuasive tongue.

Although his reputation as an advocate was so great, and the cases in which he was engaged were numerous, we know the names of only two private causes which he undertook, one of which was that in which he was counsel for Gratidian, as has been already mentioned, and the other, in which he appeared for the brothers Cossi, and was opposed by Curio. But of the particulars of this trial we have no information whatever. We have seen with what art he procured the acquittal of Aquilius, but his defense of Norbanus was a greater triumph. The case was this:—Norbanus, while tribune, had impeached Servilius Cæpio for having, like Carbo, stained by his cowardice the honor of the Roman arms in a conflict with the Cimbri, and, although the senate and the patricians exerted all their influence to save him, and the colleagues of Norbanus tried to interpose their veto and prevent the trial, he sternly persisted in the charge, and Cæpio was driven into banishment. For this he was accused of treason against the state, and the prosecution was conducted by Sulpicius Rufus, one of the most celebrated advocates of that day. But Antony rescued his client from the impending danger of a conviction, and Cicero has recorded with what dexterity and skill he conducted the defense (*De Orat*. ii. 48).

He had few accomplishments of learning, and what seems strange to our modern notions, was not only ignorant of the law, but gloried in his ignorance. Cicero represents him as contending that the study of law was almost useless to an advocate, and we have no reason to

---

[1] Sermon on the Deceitfulness of the Heart.

doubt that his practice accorded with his opinion. He wrote a meager treatise on the art of speaking, of which two sentences only have been preserved; one of these was, that "he had seen many good speakers, but never yet an eloquent one." This is frequently quoted by Cicero, and we may well believe, not without a secret feeling of self-complacency at the thought that he himself had realized what Antony had looked for in vain.[1]

The illustrious rival of Antony in the forum was Lucius Licinius Crassus, who was born B. C. 140, and was therefore three years his junior. He, like Antony, filled the different offices of state, and in all of them except the censorship, by a happy coincidence, had Quintus Mucius Scævola, one of the greatest of Roman lawyers, as his colleague. We are therefore surprised to find that when, after a successful campaign in Gaul, he claimed the honor of a triumph, Scævola, by his consular authority, interposed and prevented it; though this ungracious act does not seem to have impaired their friendship. He and Scævola together proposed and carried the Licinian law, to prevent any one from assuming, without strict title, the rights and privileges of a Roman citizen. This impolitic law exasperated the Italian allies, and conduced not a little to the irritation and discontent which burst forth in what was called the Italian war. He signalized his censorship, in conjunction with Domitius Ahenobarbus, by a decree which banished for a time all the professors of rhetoric from Rome. After he had laid down the office of censor, he was about to withdraw for a time from public affairs to

[1] Antony is said never to have published any of his speeches, and for this he assigns a curious and unsatisfactory reason. He said that he avoided doing so, in order that if his words should at any time be inconveniently quoted against him, he might deny that he had used them. To say nothing of the loose morality of this, its absurdity is exposed by Cicero, who asks whether men can not remember what we do or say, even though we do not leave a written record of our opinions.—*Pro Cluentio*, c. 50.

recruit his health, which had suffered from his exertions, when he died suddenly at the age of forty-nine.

The manner of his death reminds us of the last scene of the great Chatham. Philippus the consul had made a fierce attack upon the senate in one of his mob harangues, and this had been noticed in that assembly by Drusus, who brought forward a motion on the subject. Crassus rose to support it, and, on this occasion, surpassed himself. He spoke with vehement energy in defense of the authority of the senate, which he asserted had never been wanting in duty to the state, and, in answer to a threat of Philippus, exclaimed, "If you wish to coerce Crassus into silence, this tongue of mine must first be cut out; and even if that were torn off, my free spirit with its very breath would denounce your licentiousness." While speaking, he was seized with a pain in his side; a cold sweat and shivering came over him, and he went home in a raging fever, which carried him off at the end of a week (*Cic. de Orat.* iii. 1.)

Beginning at an early age, Crassus had always what we should call a large share of practice at the Roman bar. Cicero represents him as apologizing for not coming up to his own standard of legal accomplishments, on the ground of his not having sufficient leisure for study: *Cui disciplina fuerit forum, magister usus, et leges, et instituta populi Romani, mosque majorum,* (*Ibid.* 20),—so that he seems to furnish an instance of that *præpropera praxis* against which Coke so cautiously, though in most cases so unnecessarily, warns the student. But not one of the speeches of Crassus has been preserved, and we can judge of him only by the panegyrics of his countrymen. By them he was always spoken of in terms of the highest praise. We grieve to think that we must apply to so many forensic triumphs, not only of Crassus, but Antony, Hortensius, Cotta, and others, the words of Hooker, and say of their charms of eloquence, what he applied to unwritten discourses from the pulpit, that "they spend their life in their birth, and may have public audience but once."[1]

The character which Cicero gives of his eloquence suggests a comparison between him and Canning, and reminds us of the style of the most brilliant of modern orators. He says that Crassus was a most weighty and impressive speaker, but he enlivened the seriousness of his subject by sparkling and polished wit; his diction was almost fastidiously correct, and he had a marvelous power of opening and explaining questions. He was fertile in arguments, and apt in illustrations, which he employed with equal success in discussing a dry point of law, or taking a more extended view of the merits of a case. He did not use much action, nor modulate the tones of his voice, but poured forth a stream of deep impassioned eloquence, over which the light flashes of his wit played like sunbeams on the surface. For quick and ready answer in debate he was unrivaled, and in the opinion of Cicero his style of speaking was admirably adapted for popular assemblies, while that of Antony was better suited to the courts.

At the age of twenty-one Crassus pleaded his first cause, in which he appeared as the public prosecutor of C. Carbo, and procured his condemnation. At seven-and-twenty he defended Licinia, a vestal, tried on the following charge:—Æmilia, the chief of the vestal virgins, had broken her vows with Betucius Barrus, a Roman knight, and her example had been followed by two frail sisters, Marcia and Licinia, who found lovers in two friends of Barrus. The College of Priests instituted an inquiry, and the result was that Æmilia was found guilty; but Marcia and Licinia were acquitted. Sextus

---

[1] The whole of the fragments of speeches delivered by the Roman orators, which have come down to us, have been collected by Meyer in a single octavo volume. They embrace a period of more than 700 years, from Appius Claudius Cæcus, B. C. 350, to Q. Aurelius Symmachus, A. D. 410, and 158 names are included in the list.

Peducæus, however, an officious tribune of the commons, would not let the matter drop; and he so bitterly assailed L. Metellus, the Pontifex Maximus, with taunts and reproaches, that the latter, in order to relieve himself and the sacred college from the scandal of having improperly acquitted the fair vestals, demanded an investigation:—L. Cassius, whose well-known severity had procured for him the title of *scopulus reorum*, or "the hanging judge,"[1] was appointed the commissioner to conduct it. We know not whether Marcia was defended; but Licinia had Crassus for her counsel. The proofs, however, were too strong for the eloquence of her advocate, and the hapless girl was convicted; and both she and Marcia were condemned to the fearful death which the laws of Rome adjudged against a fallen vestal.[2] They suffered like Constance de Beverley in "Marmion:"—

> "Yet well the luckless wretch might shriek,
> Well might her paleness terror speak:
> For there were seen in that dark wall,
> Two niches narrow, deep, and tall,
> Who enters at such griesly door,
> Shall ne'er, I ween, find exit more."

Of the private cases in which he was engaged none was more celebrated than that which has been already quoted, the case of Coponius against Curius. This raised his reputation to the highest pitch, and it was said of him and Scævola who opposed him, that Crassus had

---

[1] One of our judges, Sir Francis Page, earned for himself the unenviable *sobriquet* of "hanging Page." He lived in the reigns of the first two Georges.

[2] The punishment of a vestal who violated her vow was frightful. She was stripped of her sacred robes, and after being scourged, was dressed like a corpse, and borne in a close litter to a place called the *Campus sceleratus*, near the Colline gate. Here there yawned for her reception a vault containing a couch, a lamp, and a small table with some food. She was then compelled to descend to her living tomb, over which earth was thrown, until it reached the level of the rest of the ground, and she was left to perish. This horrible kind of death was known to the old French law, and was called *enfouissement*.

therein shown himself the most learned of orators, and Scævola the most eloquent of lawyers. Cicero speaks of this effort in enthusiastic terms, and declares that he would rather have delivered that one speech of Crassus than have enjoyed two triumphs for capturing castles of the enemy. The question was simply one of construction of the words of a will, and nothing can more strongly illustrate the difference between the Roman mode of procedure and our own. It has been mentioned that the distinction between law and fact, and the separation of the province of the judge from that of the jnry, was to the Romans practically unknown. In our courts the interpretation of written documents rests wholly with the judge, who, by long previous training and habit, is proof against the sophistry and fallacies which are too often mistaken for argument by a jury. It must, however, be borne in mind, that the Roman judges were in the nature of jurymen, taken indeed from the upper classes, but still not qualified by any course of legal study to decide correctly upon the questions of law which came before them. What more unpromising subject for raillery and jest at the English bar can be conceived than an argument in a will cause? And yet Crassus seems to have succeeded in getting judgment for the plaintiff solely by the dexterous use of this light kind of artillery. Scævola insisted upon the literal construction of the will, and pointed out the danger of departing from the plain words of written documents, in order to indulge in plausible conjectures as to what the writer may possibly have meant. This doctrine has always been rigidly upheld and acted upon in England; and although it can not be denied that sometimes, in consequence, the real intentions of parties have been frustrated, and the law has become the instrument of wrong, the rule upon the whole works well, and promotes the ends of justice. Crassus, however, knew that no such doctrine prevailed in the legal tribunals at

Rome, and he therefore made an *ad captandum* speech, in which he ridiculed the nice technicalities of Scævola, and amused the court with anecdotes and jokes. He showed that the generality of men do not express themselves with the precision of lawyers, and that what they write must not be taken *au pied de lettre*. If wills were to be construed so strictly, he said, every testator ought to have a Scævola at his side, and what captious wire-drawing and hair-splitting of words there would be if courts looked only at what was actually written, and did not consider the wishes and intentions of the writer. A fine share of practice Scævola would have if no one dared to make a will which was not technically correct! By this style of argument Crassus had the laugh on his side, and the result was, as we have seen, that his client was successful.

We know the names of several other causes in which he was engaged, but it is useless to mention them when all that have survived are a few sentences, which have lost their force from the absence of the context; or jests, which after the lapse of nineteen centuries, seem, like most of the Roman witticisms, wonderfully deficient in point. Cicero has preserved one spirited passage from the speech in which Crassus supported the bill brought forward by Servilius Cæpio, for transferring the judicial authority from the equestrian order to the senate. Addressing the assembled multitude of Roman citizens, he exclaimed, "Save us from our misery; snatch us from the jaws of those whose ferocity can not be satiated with our blood; let us not be the servants of any master but yourselves; you, whom it is our duty to serve, and whom we *can* serve without dishonor" (*De Orat.* i. 52).

Crassus and Antony, as is well known, are the chief speakers in the famous dialogue De Oratore. The scene is laid at Tusculum, in the villa of Crassus, to which he is represented by Cicero as having retired for a few days, in order to recruit his health and spirits, both of which had suffered in the violent political contests which were then agitating Rome. Thither had come to enjoy the society of Crassus, his father-in-law, Quintus Mucius Scævola, the great lawyer, and Antony, his rival, but at the same time most intimate friend; and Caius Cotta, and Publius Sulpicius, who both in early youth gave bright promise of future eminence. The first day was devoted to politics, the state of which at Rome, while the attacks of the consul Philippus were directed against the authority of the senate, caused apprehension in the minds of the three elder Romans, who, being themselves senators, felt for the dignity of their order. The next day, at the suggestion of Scævola, they seated themselves under the shade of a wide-spreading tree, and the conversation was directed by Crassus to the subject of eloquence. It would lead us beyond the limits of our present inquiry to attempt anything like an analysis of the dialogue which is then supposed to have taken place. Nor could an epitome of the contents of these delightful books give any just or adequate idea of their excellence. They must be perused in the original to be appreciated. We shall then have some notion of the genius of Cicero, whose works are "a library of eloquence and reason," and of the unrivaled charm of his style, which, like the wand of an enchanter, converts whatever it touches into gold.

He mentions an anecdote of Crassus and Hortensius which redounds little to the credit of these two distinguished Romans. Minucius Basilus had died while in Greece, possessed of considerable wealth; and a forged will was produced at Rome by some parties, who, in order to protect their own knavery, had inserted the names of Crassus and Hortensius, both then in the zenith of their fame, as co-heirs with themselves of the deceased. And Cicero says that although they suspected the fraud they did not scruple to avail themselves of the forgery. Such conduct seems to us incredible in men of the position and character of the two great orators; but it is one of the many proofs how little heathen morality can be depended upon, " and even as they did not like to retain God in their knowledge, God gave them over to a reprobate mind to do those things which are not convenient."

Sulpicius is a name illustrious among Roman lawyers from the reputation gained by two members of that family, Publius and Servius. The former was the less celebrated of the two, but his career was cut short by a premature death in the convulsion of civil war. He espoused the side of Marius, and when Sylla, who had been compelled by the outbreak of an insurrection to abandon Rome, returned from Nola with his legions and took forcible possession of the city, Sulpicius was with many others proscribed and perished in his attempt to escape. The great cause in which he distinguished himself, was that of Norbanus, whom, at the age of thirty, he defended, and was, as has been noticed, opposed by Antony. Cicero says that he was of all the advocates of his time the one who might most justly be called " a grand and tragic orator." His style was lofty and impassioned, his action graceful and easy, his voice sweet and powerful, his language nervous and spirited. But although he was much engaged in the conduct of causes, he left no records of his eloquence behind him, as he never committed any of his speeches to writing, and, indeed, frankly confessed that he was unable to compose.

We now come to the name of Servius Sulpicius, which is so associated in our minds with that of Cicero—

" The Roman friend of Rome's least mortal mind."

His celebrated and beautiful letter to Tully, and affectionate attempt to assuage the grief of the afflicted father weeping for the loss of his daughter, powerfully excites our sympathies even at this distance of time. But who can read it without feeling how poor and vain were the

AN OLD ROMAN TOMB.

topics of consolation which pagan philosophy could supply to soothe a mourner's sorrow when compared with the hope full of immortality that bids the Christian look beyond the grave? What are general reflections upon the desolation of cities once flourishing in all the pomp and pride of power, but now laid waste in ruinous heaps, in comparison with those few simple words, so full of the deepest meaning, "I heard a voice from heaven saying unto me, 'Write, blessed are the dead which die in the Lord;'" and the calm assurance we have concerning them who are asleep, so that we "sorrow not even as others which have no hope?"

But to turn from this digression, and pursue no further the train of thought which the name of Servius Sulpicius has awakened. He stands with Mucius Scævola at the head of the Roman jurists in the time of the republic; and it was to a rebuke from the latter that he owed his fame; for having occasion to apply to that great legal authority for advice in a cause in which he was engaged, he showed himself so unable to understand the learning of the black-letter lawyer, that Scævola was provoked to exclaim, "It is disgraceful to a man who professes to be an advocate, to be ignorant of law" (*Pomponius de Origine Juris. Dig.* I. ii. § 43). Stung by this reproach, Servius from that day devoted himself to the study of the *jus civile* with such ardor and success, that his reputation as a jurist became greater than that of Scævola himself. Cicero indeed says, that no one of his countrymen was to be compared with him in legal attainments. But although he is lavish in praise of his learning as a lawyer, he speaks slightingly of him as an orator. Not so, however, Quintilian and Pomponius, the latter of whom places him in the first rank as an advocate. We may easily imagine that, in comparison with his profound learning, the graces of his eloquence were but lightly appreciated. Having opposed L. Murena unsuccessfully as a candidate for the consulship, he accused his competitor of bribery and corruption; but Murena was defended by Cicero, and acquitted.

In his speech on that occasion, Cicero wittily contrasts the qualifications of Sulpicius, the peaceful civilian, for the honor to which he aspired, with those of Murena, who had served with distinction as a soldier under his own father, in the war against Mithridates in Asia Minor. "Can there be a doubt," he says, that to obtain the office of consul, a military is much more useful than a legal reputation? You steal hours from sleep, in order to write opinions for your clients; he, that he may arrive early with his army at the place to which he is marching; you are awakened by the crowing of the cock, he by the clang of trumpets. You draw pleadings on paper, he draws up troops on the battle-field; you take care that verdicts, he, that cities and camps, are not lost; he knows how hostile squadrons are repelled, you, when actions of trespass lie;[1] he is versed in the arts of enlarging boundaries, you, in preserving land-marks. In good truth (to speak my real opinion), martial renown carries the day against all competitors."

Sulpicius, thus disappointed, gave up public life for a time, and devoted himself for the next two years to the assiduous practice of his profession, pleading in the courts, and giving opinions to clients who consulted him on points of law. He died while absent from Rome on an embassy to Antony, the triumvir, who was then in arms at Mutina, and Cicero proposed that a brazen tab-

---

[1] "Tu, ut aquæ pulviæ arceantur;" literally, "how rain-water is kept off." The right to let rain-water run upon a neighbor's roof, was an important easement or *servitus* at Rome, called *stillicidium ;* and where this was improperly exercised, an action, such as we should call "trespass," or "trespass upon the case" according to the circumstances, would lie. It has been held in our Courts that, if a man builds a house so near that of another that it shoots water upon the latter, the person injured may enter upon the owner's soil and pull it down. R. v. Rosewell, 2 *Salk*, 459. But there is an important proviso to be borne in mind, namely, that no person is in the house at the time. See Perry v. Fitzhowe, 8 *Q. B.* 776.

let should be erected to his memory in the Rostra, an honor which, according to former precedents, had been bestowed only upon those who had met with violent deaths, while clothed with the sacred office of ambassador. His speech on the occasion forms the ninth Philippic, and may be considered as a funeral oration pronounced by him over his departed friend. He there utters that noble eulogium upon the Roman advocate: "He did not consider himself a lawyer rather than a servant of justice, and his constant endeavor was to temper the severity of law, by reference to principles of equity. He had less pleasure in advising that actions should be brought, than in removing all cause for litigation." The statue was decreed, and existed at the time when Pomponius wrote.

Among those of lesser note was Publius Antistius—*rabula sane probabilis*—as Cicero calls him, in terms of equivocal praise. Like the briefless of the present day, he never opened his lips in court for many years, and was treated with some ridicule by his legal brethren. At last, however, he was intrusted with an important cause, and acquitted himself better than Sulpicius, who was with him. After this the tide of success began to flow, and he was constantly employed, being retained in all the great trials. He was quick of apprehension, diligent in composition, had a strong memory, and was a fluent and ready speaker; but he had a bad voice and awkward delivery. Cicero says that he owed his practice to the absence of competitors. During the period that followed the dismal times of Marius, Cinna, and Sylla, the forum was destitute of first-rate advocates; for, as Cicero says, "As soon as ever the first note of civil war is heard, our profession becomes mute" (*Pro Murena*, 10), and Antistius had only to cope with Carbo and Pomponius, to both of whom he was superior. *Au royaume des aveugles les borgnes sont rois.*

We may now rapidly pass over a crowd of names of

which all we know is that Cicero has recorded them in his account of the Roman orators, but contemptuously dismissed them as scarcely worthy of his notice. Such was Arrius, the smooth-spoken and wary counsel, who, by his prudent tact as an advocate, rose to honor, and wealth, and influence, without either natural ability or acquired learning; and Titius, who used such mincing and affected action that his name was given to a newly-invented dance at Rome; and Pontidius, who, though not deficient in forensic skill, had so little command over his temper as frequently to come into collision with the judge, *cujus* DELENITOR *debet esse orator*, as Cicero says, with a lively perception of the danger of this kind of folly (1 *Brut.* 70).

Of the more immediate contemporaries of Cicero, no advocate approached him in reputation so nearly as Hortensius; and as his name has been chosen to give the title to the present work, we may indulge in some details of his biography. Unlike the most of those who have passed in review before us, he kept himself aloof from the strife of parties, and preferred the luxurious enjoyments of private life to dangerous eminence as a politician. After acting for a short period as military tribune, he gave up the camp for the court, and was content with the triumphs of the forum, confining himself exclusively to the proper duties of an advocate, in the discharge of which he was inferior only to his great rival. And he spared no pains to attain excellence as a speaker. Cicero says that he knew no one who was animated with greater zeal for his profession; and that, like a statute of Phidias, his genius, when he was still very young, was at once recognized and admired. His memory was prodigious; so that, without taking a single note, he could recollect everything that was said by an opponent; and he had no necessity to write down even the heads of any speech which he intended to deliver. On one occasion he repeated off-hand, for a wager, the names of all the articles which had been sold at an auction, the names of the purchasers, and also the prices. He must have found this an immense advantage when practicing in the courts. He was distinguished for the skillful manner in which he divided the subjects on which he had to speak, and he was quick and ready in resources. His voice also was clear and melodious, one of nature's best gifts to an orator; but his action was studied, and had too much of artificial effect. He seems to have taken great pains with his personal appearance, and to have dressed with all the care of a Roman exquisite, adjusting the folds of his robe in the most graceful manner.

In this respect he was not unlike Lord Chatham, who, when a martyr to the gout, used to arrange his flannels with studious care before he rose to speak in the House of Lords; and Erskine was remarkable for the attention which he paid to such matters. We are told that the habit of the latter was to survey beforehand the court in which he was to speak, in order to select the most appropriate place for himself, and that a particularly neat wig (if there be such a thing), and smart yellow gloves, denoted to the spectators the presence of the matchless advocate.[1] Hortensius took such pains with his action and delivery, that Æsop and Roscius used to attend the courts where he spoke, in order that they might gather useful hints for the stage; and this once provoked Torquatus, his opponent in a cause, to call him Dionysia, a celebrated dancer, the Taglioni of her day at Rome; upon which Hortensius retorted, "Well! I had rather be Dionysia, than a clumsy, clownish bumpkin like you, Torquatus "(*Aul. Gell*). While speaking of his foibles, we may mention that he had an extraordinary

---

[1] We may, however, doubt whether either of these orators would have been willing to imitate the example of Hortensius, who once brought an action of trespass against his colleague in the magistracy for having accidentally run up against him in the street and displaced the folds of his robe.

passion for fish, not as articles of food for the table, but as playthings in his ponds. He had the water sometimes warmed lest they should suffer from cold, and it was said that he once shed tears on the death of a favorite lamprey. Among other pieces of extravagance, he used to *water* his plane-trees with *wine*. But we need not dwell longer upon these harmless follies. A graver charge made against him is that of being privy to the bribery of judges in the courts where he practiced. This, if true, is another of the many proofs of the low standard of Roman morals, but it wants authority to support it.

At nineteen years of age he pleaded his first cause, when he spoke in behalf of the province of Africa, and in the name of the inhabitants besought the senate to order the trial of a Roman governor, whom they accused of malversation and corruption. A few years afterwards, he appeared as counsel for a royal client, Nicomedes, king of Bithynia, who, being expelled by his brother from the throne, implored the assistance of the Roman arms, and Hortensius successfully advocated his prayer in the senate. One of his most celebrated efforts was his defense of Dolabella, Cn. F., who was accused by Julius Cæsar of extortion and corruption. He acted as junior on this occasion to Cotta, but so far eclipsed him, that he appeared to be really the leader at the trial. The fault of Cotta was want of fire and energy. He was too languid for the sharp conflict of the bar. " For the crowd and bustle of the forum require a speaker, energetic, spirited, alert, and powerful in voice " (*Cic. Brut.* 92). Their efforts were successful, and Dolabella was acquitted.

In the great case against Verres, which, of all the trials of antiquity, bears the nearest resemblance to the impeachment of Warren Hastings, Cicero appeared for the prosecution, and Hortensius for the defense. His speech, now unhappily lost, existed in the time of Quintilian, from whom we learn that it would not bear comparison with that of his opponent; but at the outset of the case, Cicero paid the highest compliment to his eloquence and skill. A preliminary question had arisen as to who ought to conduct the prosecution, and Q. Cæcilius had the temerity to claim that right, as having been quæstor of the province of Sicily more recently than Cicero, and therefore entitled to appear for the inhabitants in preference to him. But Cicero effectually disposed of his pretensions in a speech, which, for cutting sarcasm and irony, has never been surpassed. It suited his purpose to exaggerate the merits of Hortensius, in order to contrast them more strongly with the defects of Cæcilius. And what more ludicrous effect of the disparity between them can be imagined, than a confused and erroneous suspicion produced in the mind of the prosecuting counsel by the speech of his opponent, that the client, whom that opponent defends is innocent? Yet, this is what Cicero suggests. Addressing Cæcilius, he says, *Ipse profecto metuere incipies ne innocenti periculum facesseris.* Of the very few good jokes ever perpetrated by Cicero—and his frequent attempts deserved a better fate—one of the best was made at the expense of Hortensius, at this trial. The latter was known (in violation of the Cincian law, which required the services of advocates at Rome to be gratuitous) to have received as a present from his client a valuable image of the Sphinx, one of the spoils of his Sicilian government. While Cicero was examining a witness, Hortensius said, "You speak riddles. I can not understand you." "Well!" rejoined Cicero, "that is odd; for you have a Sphinx at home to solve them.

In other causes Hortensius was more fortunate in having Cicero as his colleague. They were associated in the defense of C. Rabinius, who was charged with having caused the death of a tribune of the commons; and Licinius Murena and Publius Sylla, who were both at different times accused of bribery and corruption in canvassing for the consulship. had these illustrious orators for their counsel. But the results were different: Murena was acquitted and retained his office, Sylla was convicted and deprived of it. Together also they defended L. Flaccus, who was charged with maladministration in the province of Asia Minor, of which he had been for three years governor; and L. Sextus, accused of tumultuary violence in a riot occasioned by the Clodian faction; and Scaurus, impeached on the charge of bribery and extortion; and Milo when put upon his trial for the murder of Clodius.

Hortensius died at the commencement of the civil war between Cæsar and Pompey; and Cicero, in his Dialogue *De Claris Oratoribus*, bestowed a generous tribute of praise upon his friend. "When," he says, "after quitting Cilicia, I had come to Rhodes, and received there the news of the death of Hortensius, it was obvious to all how deeply I was afflicted. . . . My sorrow was increased by the reflection, that at a time when so few wise and good citizens were left, we had to mourn the loss of the authority and good sense of so distinguished a man, who had been intimately associated with me through life, and who died at a period when the state most needed him; and I grieved because there was taken away from me, not, as many thought, a rival who stood in the way of my reputation, but a partner and companion in a glorious calling. For if we are told that, in a lighter species of art, noble-minded poets have mourned for the death of poets who were their contemporaries, with what feelings ought I to have borne his loss with whom it was more honorable to contend, than to be without a competitor at all; especially as his career was never embarrassed by me, nor mine by him, but, on the contrary, each was assisted by the other, with mutual help, advice, and encouragement. But since he, with that good fortune which he always enjoyed, has departed from us at a time more favorable for himself than his countrymen, and has died when it was easier if he still lived to deplore the condition of the republic than to render it any service; and since life was spared him so long as it was permitted to dwell with virtue and happiness in the state :—let us bewail, if so it must be, our own misfortune and loss, and consider his death an occasion rather for congratulating him than condoling with ourselves, so that whenever our thoughts turn to the memory of a man so illustrious and blest, we may show that we have more regard for him than for ourselves. For if we grieve because we can no longer enjoy his society, that is our calamity, which we ought to bear without giving way to excessive sorrow, lest we should seem to regard his death not as the bereavement of a friend, but the loss of some private advantage of our own. But if we mourn as though some evil has happened to himself, we show that we are not sufficiently thankful for his good fortune."

It would be unfair to omit all mention of Hortensia, the daughter of this brilliant orator, for she seems to have inherited the mantle of her father's eloquence; and we are told by Valerius Maximus (*Lib.* viii. c. 3), that when the triumvirs, Octavius, Lepidus, and Antony, had imposed a tax upon the Roman matrons, and the advocates of the day were craven enough to decline the perilous task of speaking on their behalf against the obnoxious law, Hortensia came forward as the champion of her sex, and made such an effective speech, that the greatest part of the tax was remitted. Quintilian says of this accomplished lady, that her speech was well worthy of perusal, without taking into account the sex of the speaker.

And honorable mention ought also to be made of another Roman lady, Amæsia Sentia, who defended herself before the prætor in an action which had been brought against her. A great crowd had been attracted to the court by the novelty of the spectacle; and she pleaded her own cause with such vigor and address, that she received at once an almost unanimous judgment in her favor. The spirit which she displayed on this occasion gained her the name of Androgyne. But we can not applaud the conduct of Afrania, the wife of Licinius Buccio, a senator, who was a most quarrelsome and litigious dame, and who, getting perpetually into legal scrapes, used, out of sheer impudence, to advocate her own case; and as her voice was by no means melodious, it was compared to the yelping of a dog: so that to be called an Afrania was a reproach among the women of Rome.

If the nature of this work required that I should criticise in detail the genius of Cicero, I might well shrink from the attempt; and I should act not unwisely in imitating the Grecian painter, who, having chosen as the subject of his picture the sacrifice of Iphigenia, employed the resources of his art on the other figures of the group, but concealed the countenance of Agamemnon in the folds of his robe, and left to the imagination to conceive what he dared not venture to portray. But the scope of the present essay is not so ambitious. It is not Cicero as a statesmen, saluted by the title of *Pater Patriæ* for his successful efforts against the enemies of the republic; or as a philosopher, discussing amidst the shades of Tusculum the immortality of the soul, and inquiring into the grounds and principles of moral duty; but Cicero as an advocate, sole " monarch of the forum," and leader of the Roman bar, whom we have to consider.

And Cicero was proud of his vocation. He applied himself to it with untiring assiduity, and had a lofty idea of its requirements. " I," he said, when contending with Cæcilius for the right of conducting the prosecution against Verres, " who, as all are aware, have had such practice in the forum and in trials, that none or few of the same age as myself have been engaged in more causes, and who devote all the time which I can spare from the service of my friends, to the studies and labors of my profession, in order that I may be better prepared and readier for practice at the bar; I, notwithstanding this,—so may the gods be merciful to me!—declare, that whenever I think of the moment when I shall have to rise and speak in defense of a client, am not only disturbed in mind, but tremble in every limb of my body" (*In Cæcil. Divinatio*, 13). If such was the avowal of Cicero, what must at times be the feelings of less gifted advocates, when called upon to defend liberty or life, where the result is so often determined by the manner in which they acquit themselves of their task?

When raised to the highest offices in the state, Cicero gratefully acknowledged that he owed his elevation "after much toil and many perils," to his success at the bar as an advocate, and he has left us an interesting account of the mode in which he prepared and trained himself for the arduous struggles of the forum and the courts. We there see an illustrious example of genius submitting to the severest toil, in order to attain that excellence which nothing but toil and labor can bestow. He had too exalted an opinion of the qualifications necessary for an orator, to be content with the ample gifts with which nature had provided him; and by painful study, and assiduous practice, and diligent observation of the best models, he strove to realize the idea which his mind had formed of a great speaker and great advocate. But let us listen to his own instructive narrative. Crassus was dead;—Cotta an exile from Rome, and Hortensius in the zenith of his fame,—when the youthful Tully first entered that arena where he was destined so soon to carry off the palm from all competitors. Not long before this, there had been a period of much public excitement and agitation at Rome, and all who were candidates for the high honors of the state were compelled to court the favors of the sovereign people by animated harangues, which they almost daily addressed to assembled crowds. Such were Metellus Celer, and Varius, and Carbo, and Pomponius, and Caius Julius, who from the Rostra declaimed to the populace. Below them stood a youth of spare and meager frame, whose long thin neck was eagerly stretched forward, as he endeavored to catch every word that fell from the speaker (*Brut.* 91). Who would have recognized in his pale consumptive figure the future orator of Rome? Yet that was Cicero, whose health was then weak and delicate, and who constantly attended these meetings, attracted by the spell of that eloquence of which he was one day to be himself such a mighty master. But he was no mere idle spectator. He read hard, and devoted a part of each day to writing, that he might accustom himself to accurate and rapid composition.

The advantage of this habit to a speaker was strongly felt by him. He says that by writing on a subject we pay more than ordinary attention to it, and thus many things present themselves to the mind which we should otherwise let slip. Besides this the most appropriate words and sentences occur to us while we bestow careful attention upon our style, and we learn to arrange our thoughts in the best order. A habit is thus engendered of employing always the most apt and striking language, and a speaker who has been accustomed to make use of his pen will, when he is obliged to utter anything extempore, be able to do it with the same correctness and grace as if it had been previously composed. The impetus given will in fact continue. Cicero illustrates this by the elegant simile of a vessel retaining her onward way after the rowers have ceased their strokes, from the mere impulse previously communicated. These are valuable hints from such a teacher and would be acted upon much more generally if it were not for the reason which he himself suggests—the disinclination which men feel to undertake the labor of such a course of preparation.

He studied civil law under the able guidance of Q. Mucius Scævola, whose house was thronged by clients who resorted to the great jurist for advice in legal difficulties. At the same time he refreshed and enlarged his mind by attending the lectures on philosophy which were given by Philo, the leader of the new academy, who had been driven from Athens by the war which Sylla carried on against Mithridates in Greece. And in order to prepare himself for practice at the bar he received instruction from Molo the Rhodian, once a distinguished advocate, but now teacher of the art of oratory at Rome. During this period legal proceedings were almost at a stand-still, while armed factions were contending for the mastery, but calmer times succeeded, and for three years the city enjoyed a hollow, but undisturbed tranquillity. Many, however, of Rome's most eloquent sons—Sulpicius, Catullus, Antony, and Julius—had perished in the civil war, and their place was ill supplied by such speakers as Antistius, Piso, Pomponius, and Carbo, who now enjoyed, after Hortensius, the chief practice in the courts. Cicero tells us that he devoted himself during these three years night and day to the most severe and unremitting study. Burke spent a similar period of his life in desultory reading, and he afterwards complained that he had lost so much time, though we may believe that those years contributed largely to build up the fabric of his vast and miscellaneous knowledge. Cicero, however, kept one object steadily in view, and directed all his energies to the cultivation of eloquence, the absorbing passion of his life. Diodorus the Stoic taught him logic, and he daily declaimed in the presence of some friend, sometimes in his native language, but more frequently in Greek, with which tongue he was perfectly familiar, and which enabled him to transfer some of its rich luxuriance to the more unadorned and meager Latin.

Such was the training by which Cicero sought to qualify himself for success in his career, and he might justly say that when he commenced practice he required little instruction from experience, but was already equal to the conduct of the greatest causes.

It was his favorite theory that no limits could be assigned to the knowledge necessary for an *orator*. According to his own magnificent conception of his office. "I will pronounce him to be a complete and perfect orator who can speak on all subjects with variety and fullness" (*De Orat*. i. 13.) This of course, even in the time of Cicero, was impossible, and now that the empire of science and art has been so immeasurably extended, the mere attempt to grasp at universal knowledge would only render the sciolist ridiculous. The days of admirable Crichtons have gone by, and a man must think himself happy if he can, by severe and patient application, make himself master of only a small domain in that ample territory. But yet in a modified sense it may be truly said that there is no part of knowledge of which an advocate can with safety be wholly ignorant. For it is hardly possible to name a subject which may not fall within the province of judicial inquiry in a court of law. Can Theology refuse to stoop and enter within the temple of Themis? Have we not seen, in the case of Dame Hewley's charity, the sublime mystery of the doctrine of the Trinity brought into discussion, and the question of the right to a most valuable bequest determined by a critical examination of passages in the New Testament? And very recently, during the argument for and against the validity of a marriage with a deceased wife's sister, the most copious learning was brought to bear upon the interpretation of a difficult verse in Leviticus. When cause was shown against the application for a mandamus to be directed to the Archbishop of Canterbury, in order that he might be compelled to receive the objections that were offered against the confirmation of a bishop-elect, what a vast range of topics was embraced, drawn from some of the most obscure depths of ecclesiastical history! Can literature " spread her light wings and fly " at the sight of those gloomy portals? In cases connected with copyright there is no branch of the *belles lettres*, Poetry, Music, History, which may not require the aid of the advocate to explore its merits and vindicate its rights. How infinitely varied are the questions which arise in dealing with the law of libel! If the defendent justifies the accusation he has made by pleading that it is true, on what a wide sea of investigation may it not be necessary to embark! The party attacked may be a divine, or a physician, or a soldier, and the inquiry at the trial will demand an acquaintance with the kind of knowledge peculiar to each profession (*Cic. de Orat.* i. 14).

What shall we say of cases relating to the infringement of patents, which involve the discussion of intricate problems in mechanics, and even, with all the aid which specifications and models, and diagrams can afford, tax the powers of the understanding to the uttermost? *Illustrare autem oratione si quis istas ipsas artes velit, ad oratoris ei confugiendum est facultatem* (*Cic. de Orat.* i. 14). And in trials for sedition and high treason, how indispensable for the due performance of the advocate's task is a memory well furnished with constitutional lore!

But it is needless to multiply instances of the demands which may be made upon his acquirements. " What treasures of science," says D'Aguesseau, " what variety of erudition, what sagacity of discernment, what delicacy of taste, is it not necessary to combine in order to excel at the bar! Whoever shall venture to set limits to the knowledge of the advocate has never conceived a perfect idea of the vast extent of his profession." *Quicquid agunt homines* is its motto, and expresses the measure of its requirements. It thus, however, possesses the peculiar advantage, that almost every kind of study may be made available for its use, and, with reference to the healthy tone of intellect which it demands and produces, we may apply to it what Barrow says of the calling of the scholar: "By virtue of improvement therein, we can see with our own eyes, and guide ourselves by our own reasons, not being led blindfold about, or depending precariously on the conduct of others in matters of highest concern to us; we are exempted from giddy credulity, from wavering levity, from fond admiration of persons and things, being able to distinguish of th'ngs, and to settle our judgments about them, and to get an intimate acquaintance with them, assuring to us their true nature and worth."

But how is this multifarious knowledge to be acquired? The process of attaining it is much less difficult than at first sight appears. Cicero himself furnishes us with the key by which the storehouse is to be unlocked:— *Ipsi omnia, quorum negotium est, consulta ad nos et exquisita deferunt* (*De Orat.* i. 58). In every cause which he undertakes, the advocate has at his command the services of those who are interested in the result, and who procure for him information from every available source. Those who have devoted years of toil and study to some particular department of art or science, exhaust, as it were, their treasures before him; and transfuse into him, for the time, the knowledge which they possess. It is his duty to employ skillfully the materials which are provided for his use, and weave them into a plain and perspicuous statement, so that they may be presented to the minds of the court or jury in a clear and intelligible form. If the most ingenious mechanician, unaccustomed to the art of speaking, were to rise in a court of law to assert or deny the infringement of a patent, the chances are that he would not succeed in making himself understood. And this is one of the many reasons why, independently of legal mysteries, it is necessary that "masters of the art of tongue-fence" should exist in every civilized community.

In considering the orations of Cicero we are struck with the disproportion between the number of those in which he was the accuser, as compared with those which he delivered on behalf of the accused. Of the twenty-four speeches now extant, in which he appeared as an advocate, only three were spoken by him against individuals charged with offenses.[1] The natural kindness of his heart and gentleness of his disposition made him averse to the conduct of criminal prosecutions. "For," he says, "it seems to be the part of a harsh character, or rather of one who is scarcely a man, to bring the lives of many into jeopardy" (*De Offic.* ii. 14). And he felt that it was an invidious and odious task thus to employ the powers of his eloquence. How gracefully, in his speech for Murena, he repels the charge of inconsistency, that he who had shown himself, as consul, such an uncompromising enemy of Catiline, should, while invested with the same office, defend a man accused of bribery and corruption. "But if, at a time when the safety of the commonwealth required sternness and severity, I did violence to my nature, and in my hostility obeyed the necessity of the case rather than my own wishes,—surely now, when every motive urges me to show compassion and kindness, I ought gladly to give way to the promptings of my nature and my usual feelings" (*Pro Murena*, 3).

The first great trial in which he was engaged was that in which he defended Sextius Roscius on a charge of murder; and he tells us, with pardonable pride, that after he had spoken on that occasion, no case seemed

---

[1] In this enumeration, the set of orations against Verres is reckoned as one speech, and those against Catiline and Antony are not included, for they were spoken by Cicero, as a statesman, in the senate.

too important to be intrusted to his care. The trial arose out of the following circumstances:—

Sextius Roscius, an inhabitant of the municipal town of Ameria, where he had considerable property and was much respected, while making a short stay at Rome, was murdered one night near the Palatine baths as he was returning from a party of friends. The news of his death was brought by a freedman of Titus Roscius at daybreak next morning to Ameria, a distance of fifty-six miles. This T. Roscius, surnamed Magnus, as well as another member of the same family surnamed Capito, were both natives of Ameria, and enemies of Sextius. The latter left a son whose life had hitherto been passed in the country, where he attended to the cultivation of his father's estate, to which he was entitled to succeed at the death of the latter. But the Roscii were determined to deprive him of his inheritance, and they induced Chrysogonus, one of Sylla's freedmen, and high in his favor, to assert that Sextius had died in debt to him. Under pretense of liquidating this, the property was seized and sold at a price miserably below its value, and Capito and Chrysogonus became the purchasers. The former bought for himself three of the most flourishing farms, and took possession of the rest of the estate and effects, under pretense of holding them for Chrysogonus. Not content with this, the two Roscii instigated Erucius to accuse the destitute son of having been the assassin of the father; and Cicero had to defend him against the charge.

The trial is a proof of the corrupt state of society at Rome. There is no doubt that young Roscius was in the most imminent danger of a conviction, and that Cicero trembled for the result. And yet no charge was ever more groundless, or supported in a court of justice by more feeble evidence. This consisted almost entirely in an attempt to show that the father disliked his son, of which the only proof was that he kept him in the country, and that he once had the intention of disinheriting him. That such a case, so bare of even a presumption against the accused, should have occupied a criminal tribunal for a considerable time with a doubtful result, was an outrage against common sense; and can only be explained by considering the deplorable condition of the republic, when causes were decided, not according to their merits, but under the influence of bribery or fear. Sylla was all-powerful in the state;—Chrysogonus was his favorite, and Cicero knew that these were arguments against his client which would go far to supply the place of facts. He made a masterly and conclusive speech; but much more elaborate than, according to our notions of criminal jurisprudence, the case seemed to require, for not a tittle of evidence was adduced to connect the son with the murder. He was at Ameria at the time; he had neither friends nor influence at Rome; not a shadow of proof was given that he had ever seen or communicated with the assassins; nay, it was unknown who the actual assassins were. All the presumptions of guilt pointed towards the Roscii, Capito, and Magnus, especially the latter, whose freedman had brought the first intelligence so rapidly to Ameria, and whose previous character and conduct subsequently to the murder, justified the darkest suspicions. Under these circumstances, we should imagine that the duty of the counsel for the accused would be simply to stand on the defensive, and challenge the other side to the proof of the indictment. Unless it could be shown that young Roscius was present at, or privy to the murder, there was an end to the case, and he might at once demand an acquittal. But Cicero did not venture upon such a course before the tribunal which he was addressing. He enters most minutely into the whole case, examines every possible view in which it can be presented, carefully balances the presumptions of guilt as they apply to the one party or the other, deprecates the idea of giving offense to Erucius or Chrysogonus, and artfully appeals to the compassion, and fears, and justice of the court.

Alluding to the dreadful fate which impended over his client, if he should be found guilty,[1] Cicero uttered that striking passage which he afterwards condemned as the effusion of a youthful fancy. "May we not say that our forefathers wished to deprive a parricide of the common elements, from whom they suddenly removed the sky, the sun, and land, and sea? They would not cast out his body to the beasts, lest even the ferocity of brutes should be increased by preying upon a corpse contaminated by such a crime; they would not throw it naked into the river, lest, by being carried into the sea, it might defile the very water by which all other things, when polluted, are supposed to be cleansed. In short, there is nothing so vile or common that they allowed such criminals to participate in it. For what is so universal as air for the living, earth for the dead, the sea for those who are floating in the waves, the shore for the drowning? They so live, as long as they do exist, that they are unable to draw breath from the air; they so die that the earth does not touch their bones; they are so tossed in the waves that they are never washed by them; they are so at last cast away, that not even when dead do they find rest upon the rocks."

Niebuhr says of his conduct on this occasion, "His defense of Roscius of Ameria, whom Chrysogonus wanted to get rid of, excited the greatest admiration of his talents, together with the highest esteem for his own personal character. It was an act of true heroism for a young man like Cicero, and still more so, if we consider his family connection with Marius. Cicero saved his client, but his friends advised him to quit Rome

---

[1] The punishment adjudged against a parricide by the Roman law, was to be sewn up in a sack, with a dog, an ape, a cock, and a viper, and to be thrown into the river.

that Chrysogonus might forget him " (*Lectures Hist. Rome*, ii. 29).

Cicero, however, gives a different reason for his departure from Rome. He says, that after two years' practice at the bar, the state of his health was very critical. He was accustomed while speaking to raise his voice to the highest pitch, and use vehement action in delivery; under which the feeble powers of his body broke down, so that his friends became seriously alarmed for his life, and the physicians recommended him to give up pleading in the courts altogether. But this was more than Cicero could bear. He determined to run any risk rather than abandon the career in which he felt himself predestined to succeed.

In one of his earliest causes Cicero was counsel for another and a greater Roscius, the celebrated actor. The speech that we have is imperfect, and the case was not very interesting, but it may be shortly stated as illustrating the rights of parties and forms of legal precedence at Rome.

C. Fannius Chærea had given up one of his slaves, named Panurgus, to Roscius, on the terms that the latter was to instruct him in acting, and they were afterwards to share between them whatever he gained by his art. Panurgus received the requisite instruction and went upon the stage, but was not long afterwards killed (how, does not appear) by a man named Q. Flavius. Roscius brought an action for this against the latter, and the management of the case was committed to Fannius.[1]

---

[1] It has been laid down that, according to the English law, if a man beats the servant of another to such a degree that he dies, the master loses his right of action, and can only proceed by indictment. See *Yelverton*, 89; 2 *Roll's Abr.* 568. This may be on the ground that the private right of action is merged (as it is termed) in the felony, and consequently the rule should, perhaps, be confined to such cases. With regard to an action by the representatives of a party killed, it may be mentioned that formerly the maxim was, *actio personalis moritur cum personâ*, and the relatives of the deceased, whose death might have been occasioned by the negligence of

Before, however, it was tried, Roscius compromised the matter, but only so far as regarded his own moiety, as he alleged, and Flavius gave up a farm to him in satisfaction of damages. Several years had elapsed, when Fannius applied to the prætor for an order that the accounts between him and Roscius might be settled by arbitation. Calpurnius Piso was appointed arbitrator. He did not make a formal award, but recommended that Roscius should pay to Fannius 10,000 sesterces (about £90) for the trouble and expense which the latter had incurred in conducting the action against Flavius, and that Fannius should enter into an engagement to pay over to Roscius the half of whatever he recovered from Flavius. Fannius agreed to this, and then brought an action on his own account against Flavius for the loss he had sustained by the death of Panurgus, and got a verdict for 100,000 sesterces (£900). Half of this, according to the agreement, ought to have been paid over to Roscius; but Fannius not only retained it, but commenced an action against Roscius for a moiety of the value of the farm which the latter had obtained from Flavius, on the pretext that Roscius had settled the former action and obtained the farm on the partnership account.

Cicero maintained that his client did not owe Fannius a farthing. So confident was he of the strength of his case, that he offered to consent to a verdict against him, provided the plaintiff could show that the debt now claimed was entered in his ledger. He was willing to allow the entries of the plaintiff to be evidence in his

another party, could obtain no pecuniary compensation for their loss. But this has been remedied by the statute, 9 and 10 *Vict.* c. 93, entitled " An Act for compensating the families of persons killed by accidents," which provides that an action may be brought in the name of the executor or administrator for the benefit of the " wife, husband, parent, and child " of the person whose death shall have been caused by such wrongful act or neglect, as would (if death had not ensued) have entitled the deceased to recover damages on account thereof.

own favor; and in tendering such an issue, we may be very sure that Cicero had good information that he might do so with safety. But he made a distinction between the ledger (*tabulæ* or *codex*) and the day-book, or mere memorandum of accounts (*adversaria*). Fannius wished to put the latter in evidence, but Cicero objected, and said that he could not admit loose papers, full of erasures and interlineations, in which, no doubt, Fannius had inserted the debt when he determined to make his unjust claim. He seized the opportunity of praising the skill and virtues of his client, whose name as an actor has become so world-famous. "Has Roscius defrauded his partner? Can such an imputation rest upon one who has in him (I say it boldly) more honesty than he has art, more truth than accomplishments, whom the Roman people consider to be a better man than he is an actor; who, though admirably fitted for the stage on account of his skill in his profession, yet is most worthy of being a senator on account of his modesty and decorum?" And again: "The other side contend that Panurgus was the property of Fannius; but I say that he belonged wholly to Roscius. For what was the property of Fannius? The body of his slave. What of Roscius? The instruction he received. The part that belonged to Fannius was not worth six pounds, that which belonged to Roscius was worth more than four times as much. For no one valued him for his bodily frame, but for his skill as a comic actor. His mere limbs could not earn more than twelve pence at a time: but by the instruction which my client imparted to him he used to gain not less than twenty-four pounds a day. For what were the qualifications of Panurgus, and what support did he bring with him to back him upon the stage? The friends and admirers of Roscius patronized him because he had been his pupil;—all who had heard of Roscius thought that Panurgus, coming from him, must be perfectly accomplished in his art. This is the way with the vulgar, they are guided little by truth, but much by opinion. Few took the trouble to observe what skill Panurgus really had, but all asked where he had been taught. They thought that nothing awkward and clumsy could be produced by such a master. If he had come from Statilius, even though he surpassed Roscius himself, none would have tolerated him, for no one would believe that, as a virtuous son may be born to a wicked father, so a good comedian can proceed from the school of a villainously bad actor. Because he came from Roscius he seemed to have more skill than he really possessed."

The defense of Cluentius discloses a melancholy tale of wickedness; and Sassia, the mother of his client, might almost contest the palm of pre-eminence in guilt with Lucrece di Borgia. Not long after her husband's death her daughter married her first cousin Aurius Melinus, for whom the mother soon conceived an adulterous passion. She employed all her arts to alienate his affection from his wife, and at last succeeded in inducing him to divorce her. She then flew to the arms of her son-in-law, and openly married him. But where can more withering language be found than that by which Cicero brands her infamy? "That nuptial couch which two years before she had spread for her daughter on her marriage, she bids him adorn and prepare in the same house for herself, while her daughter is turned away as an outcast. The mother-in-law weds her son-in-law with no religious ceremonies, with none to give the bride away, amidst the dark and gloomy forebodings of all." By and by, however, Melinus, having incurred the enmity of Oppianicus, against whom there was the strongest suspicion that he had poisoned his own wife and brother, and procured the murder of a near relative of Melinus, was, through the interest of Oppianicus with the tyrant Sylla, included in one of his lists of proscription and put to death. This murder of her husband attracted the love of Sassia; and Oppianicus being equally smitten, paid his addresses to her, and offered her marriage. She at first refused, on the ground that he had three sons alive, and she did not wish to be incumbered with such a family. Oppianicus understood the hint, and in the course of a few days caused two of them to be murdered. The scruples of Sassia were now removed, and she married Oppianicus, wooed and won, as Cicero says, not by nuptial presents, but the death of murdered children: *non nuptialibus donis, sed filiorum funeribus delinita:*

> "The funeral-baked meats,
> Did coldly furnish forth the marriage tables."

The career of Oppianicus was one of the most abandoned villainy, and having unsuccessfully attempted to take off Cluentius by poison, he was put upon his trial for this crime, and being convicted was sentenced to banishment. He had endeavored to bribe his judges, and for that purpose had distributed among some of them a large sum of money, which they took, but, notwithstanding, pronounced a verdict of guilty. For this offense they were afterwards put upon their trial and convicted. Oppianicus died in exile five years after his condemnation; and three years after his death Sassia bestowed her daughter in marriage upon his son by a former wife, and urged him to accuse her own son Cluentius of having caused her deceased husband Oppianicus to be poisoned. It was on this occasion that Cicero defended Cluentius; and his speech is one of his most elaborate and successful efforts.

I hardly know where we could find a better description of the duties which devolve upon a jury than is contained in the following passage:—"I can not doubt, gentlemen, that if you were to sit on the trial of a man who was beyond the reach of the statute under which he was indicted, although his character might be odious, and himself personally obnoxious to you, and you might feel very reluctant to pronounce a verdict of acquittal, you would, notwithstanding, acquit him, and respect your oath rather than gratify your dislike. For it is the duty of every intelligent juryman to consider that the functions with which he is invested by the state are limited by the extent of his commission: and he must remember that not merely power has been delegated to him, but trust reposed in him. It may be his duty to acquit one whom he detests, or convict another against whom he has no feeling of enmity. He ought ever to consider, not his own wishes, but the obligation which the law and his oath impose. He should carefully attend to the particular statute on which the indictment is framed, the kind of person accused, and the nature of the offense charged. And in addition to all this, a wise and honest citizen, when he enters that jury box,[1] ought to remember that he does not sit there alone, and may not act simply as he pleases; but that he takes with him as his assessors the Law itself, and the restraints of religion, equity, and honor, and must put away passion, hatred, envy, fear, and all private likings and dislikings. He ought to give the greatest weight to the authority of conscience, which we have received from the immortal gods,—which never can be separated from us, and which, i. it bears witness throughout our whole life to the purity of our thoughts and actions, will enable

---

[1] *Cum illam judicandi causâ tabellam sumpserit.* The Roman judices on a trial were each provided with three tablets, one of which was marked with the letter A for *Absolvo*, "not guilty," the second with C for *Condemno*, "guilty," and the third with N. L. for *Non liquet*, "not proven." One of these tablets was placed by each Judex in a box (*cista*) when he gave his verdict, and the result depended upon which letter had the majority. Lord Bacon throws the weigh of his authority in favor of allowing a verdict of "not proven," such as exists in Scotland. *In curiis censoriis calculum tertium dato ut judicibus non imponatur necessitas, aut absolvendi aut condemnandi ; sed etiam ut* Non liquere *pronuntiare possint.—De Augm. Scient. Aph.* 40. Sir Walter Scott, however, called this "a bastard verdict."

us to live free from fear and in the practice of every virtue."

With this we may compare the address to a juryman by Bishop Sanderson in one of his assize sermons:—"If thou comest hither to serve for the king upon the grand inquest, or between party and party, in any cause whatsoever (like those *selecti judices* among the Romans whom the prætor for the year being was to nominate, and upon that oath out of the most able and serviceable men in his judgment, both for estate, understanding, and integrity); or to serve upon the *tales*, perhaps at thine own suit, to get something toward bearing charges for thy journey; or yoked with a crafty or a willful foreman that is made beforehand, and a mess of tame after-men withal, that dare not think of being wiser than their leader, or unwilling to stickle against a major part, whether they go right or wrong; or resolved already upon the verdict, no matter what the evidence be;—consider what is the weight and religion of an oath. Remember that he sinneth not less that sinneth with company. Whatsoever the rest do, resolve thou to do no otherwise than God shall put into thy heart, and as the evidence shall lead thee. The third rule in that text must be thy rule, 'Thou shalt not follow a multitude to do evil.' They are silly that, in point either of religion or justice, would teach us to measure either truth or right by multitudes."

Where all the speeches are so admirable, it is difficult to make a selection in order to exhibit the peculiar excellence of Cicero, but I think that his defense of L. Licinius Murena may be cited as one of the most pleasing specimens of his style.

Towards the close of his own memorable consulship, Murena and Silanus were, after a severe contest in the comitia centuriata, chosen as consuls for the ensuing year. One of the competitors was Servius Sulpicius, the well-known lawyer, who, immediately after his defeat accused Murena of having employed bribery and corruption to carry his election. This had been made illegal by the Calpurnian law, which punished the offense by merely disqualifying for public office the party who was guilty of it; but during that very year Cicero had himself procured the passing of a law which inflicted the additional punishment of exile for ten years. The prosecution was conducted by Servius Sulpicius, assisted by three *subscriptores*, as they were called, who " were with him in the case," M. Cato, Cn. Postumius, and a son of Sulpicius. On the other side, for the defense, were Hortensius, Crassus, and Cicero, three of the most brilliant names at the Roman bar. We must call to mind the circumstances of the time, and the position and character of the parties at the trial, in order to appreciate the admirable speech which Cicero delivered on this occasion. That which we possess is unfortunately imperfect, but enough has been left to justify the praise of Manutius, who calls it *jucunda in primis oratio*.

The state of Rome was full of alarm. The conspiracy of Catiline, who had himself stood for the consulship, had just exploded, and this daring and reckless leader, after being denounced by Cicero in the senate, had quitted the capital with his followers, and was then in open arms against the republic. The trial took place early in December, and in the following month the new consuls would enter upon their office. Sulpicius, the defeated candidate, was a lawyer; Murena, the successful one, a soldier; Cato, who took part in the prosecution, had recently been elected one of the tribunes of the commons, and he was a follower of the cold and stern philosophy of the Stoics. Cicero spoke last, after the charge against his client had been investigated and repelled by Hortensius and Crassus.

He begins by saying a few words about himself—no ungrateful subject with Cicero—for Cato had commented with some severity upon the fact that he, a consul, the professed enemy of corruption and author of a severe enactment against it, now appeared as counsel for Murena, who was accused of violating that very law. But what, asks Tully, was more natural than that a consul should be defended by a consul? If those who were just returned from a long and perilous voyage are ready to assist with their experience and advice the mariners who are about to tempt the same seas, and to point out to them the rocks and shoals from which they themselves have only just escaped, with what feelings ought he, who after a stormy consulship had now caught sight of land, to regard the man who had to face such a political tempest as he saw lowering before him? It would, indeed, be inconsistent to be the author of the law against bribery, and then in pleading for another to assert that it is no offense. Where, however, is the inconsistency when the defense consists in a denial that any bribery was committed at all?

But Sulpicius complained that Cicero had violated their ancient friendship in undertaking the cause of Murena. Of this the jury shall themselves decide. True it was that in the contest for the consulship he had supported Sulpicius, and done for him all that lay in his power as a friend and partisan. But that time has now gone by. The state of things is different. Under the obligation of friendship for Sulpicius he had opposed Murena as a candidate for civic honors, but he was under no obligation to endanger his safety. The principle can never be admitted that we may not defend even our enemies against the accusations of our friends. "As for me," exclaimed Cicero, "it is no longer an open question whether I may refuse the aid of my services in averting danger from the accused. For since I have reaped such a harvest from my profession as no one previously has done, I should be acting a mean and ungrateful part if I were now to relinquish those exertions by which I obtained its rewards." If friendship for Sulpicius were a sufficient reason for declining to defend Murena, the same might apply to Hortensius, and Crassus, and others, the consequence of which would be that a consul-elect might be unable to find a counsel to undertake his cause in a state where the wisdom of their ancestors had provided that not even the lowest citizen should be without an advocate.

The plan of attack had been first to throw aspersions upon Murena's character; next to contrast his claims to the honor of the consulship with those of his opponent; and lastly to establish the charges of bribery. Cicero therefore follows the same order, and, in a brief review of his client's life, shows that he had honorably won laurels in the campaign against Mithridates, and contributed some spoils of the enemy to his own father's triumph. But Cato pretended that he was corrupted by the effeminate manners of the East, and said that Murena was "a dancer!" "Nay, but Cato, a man of your authority ought not to pick up nicknames in the street, or use the scurrilous language of buffoons. You ought not lightly to call the consul of the Roman people a dancer, but consider what other faults such a character must have to whom that epithet can be justly applied."

But to come to the question of comparative merit—Sulpicius was of the patrician, Murena of the plebeian order. If, however, it is to be said that no one is a man of good family unless he is a patrician, it is a dangerous doctrine, and perhaps may lead to a second secession of the plebeians to the Aventine Hill. "And, after all, Sulpicius, your lineage, though noble, is better known to antiquarians and bookworms than to the electors of Rome, for your father was only a knight, and your grandfather possessed no remarkable eminence. The knowledge, therefore, of your nobility must be derived, not from the lips of your contemporaries, but from musty annals. . . . . . But after I had in my own case broken down those barriers of rank, so that the path to the consulship for the future, as it had been in days of yore with our ancestors, was as much open to merit as to nobility, I little thought that when a consul-elect, born of an old and distinguished race, was defended by the son of a mere Roman knight, himself a consul, his accusers would venture to speak of upstart families." Adverting now to the personal qualifications of the two candidates, Cicero playfully rallies Sulpicius upon his profession as a lawyer, and contrasts its obscure drudgery with the dashing exploits of Murena as lieutenant of Lucullus in Asia Minor. We have already seen, in the passage previously quoted, with what spirit he draws the comparison between them, and he pursues it at considerable length, greatly to the disadvantage of his "learned friend." He seizes also the opportunity of pointing out the superiority of eloquence over case-law, and shows how often legal opinions and decisions are upset by a clever speech from an advocate, adding, with affected modesty, "I would say less in its praise if I were a proficient in the art : as it is, I speak not of myself, but of those who are or have been eminent as orators." To show how necessary it was that a Roman consul should possess that qualification, especially in perilous times, he says, "The faculty of speaking is a great and dignified attribute, and one which has often turned the scale in an election for the consulship ; great, indeed, to be able by means of persuasive eloquence to sway the senate, the people, and the courts. A consul is required who can, if need be, restrain by his oratory the mad violence of the tribunes, and wield the fierce democracy and resist corruption. Think it not strange then if, on account of having this gift, men, even though not in the ranks of nobility, have often obtained the consulship, especially since it is one which conciliates the warmest favor, the strongest friendships, the most ardent support. But in your profession, Sulpicius, there is nothing of all this."

Cicero then alludes to other reasons which accounted for the greater popularity of his client, his good fortune in having obtained as prætor the office of administering civil justice, whereas his rival, as has been already mentioned, had to discharge the odious duty of conducting criminal inquiries against those who embezzled the public moneys. Besides this, Sulpicius seemed to have made up his mind from the first that he must be defeated in the contest, and while engaged in his canvass to have determined upon the prosecution of his competitor. But that is not the way, cried Cicero, to succeed. "I like a candidate for office, especially such an office as the consulship, to go forth to the forum and the *Campus Martius* full of hope, and spirit, and resources. I disapprove of the getting up of a case against an opponent— the sure herald of defeat. I like not solicitude about evidence rather than about votes; threats rather than flattery; virtuous indignation rather than courteous salutations; especially since the fashion now is for the electors, generally, to call upon the candidates at their houses, and judge by the countenance of each how far he feels confident, and what are his chances of success.

"'Do you see,' says one, 'him there with the downcast and gloomy look? He is dispirited; he has lost all heart, and thrown up the cards.' Then this rumor begins to be whispered about—'Are you aware that so and so meditates a prosecution, is getting up a case, and looking out for evidence against his rivals? I'll vote for some one else, since he shows the white feather, and despairs of success.' The most intimate friends of candidates of this kind are disheartened, and lose all zeal, and either abandon a cause which seems as good as lost, or reserve all their support and influence for the subsequent trial which is to take place.

But, moreover, Murena had ingratiated himself with the populace by giving a series of public shows and games, and the great orator and philosopher is not ashamed to confess that he could take pleasure in such things. "But if I, who am debarred by my occupation from all kinds of amusement, and can find recreation even in business itself, am notwithstanding delighted and attracted by shows, why should we be surprised at this in the ignorant multitude?"

Cicero then proceeds to answer in detail the charges of bribery which had been dwelt upon by Postumius and the younger Sulpicius, but this part of his speech is unfortunately lost, and we come next to his reply to Cato, who seems to have summed up the case on the part of the prosecution. How artfully he warns the court against the danger of being overawed by that illustrious name, and quotes examples to show that in former times the overweening power of the accusers had proved the safety of the accused. Thus Cotta had been rescued by a verdict of acquittal from the attack made upon him by Scipio Africanus, and Galba from the charge brought against him when the great Cato was the prosecutor, and this was the reason: "In this commonwealth excessive influence in accusers has always been resisted by the people at large, and by wise men, and by far-seeing judges provident of the future." But now he must have a hit at the Stoic philosophy, upon which he throws the blame of Cato's apparent severity, and this is, perhaps, the cleverest part of his speech. In some portions we might almost fancy we were reading the defense of a member of parliament whose seat was contested before an election Committee of the House of Commons, on a petition containing allegations of bribery and treating. Here, however, we have not space for more than a mere outline.

Cato, as a disciple of that rigid school which held all offenses to be equally criminal, and regarded the man who unnecessarily twisted a cock's neck as equally guilty with one who strangled his own father, had professed to be shocked at the idea that Murena had employed solicitation, and the usual electioneering arts, in his canvass. Crowds had gone out to meet him on his return to Rome while he was a candidate for the consulship." "Well, there was nothing extraordinary in this. The wonder would have been if they had stayed away. 'But a band of partisans followed him in procession through the streets.' What then? Prove that they were bribed to do it, and I admit that it was an offense. Without this what have you to find fault with? 'What need is there,' he asks, 'of processions?' Do you ask me what need there is of that which has always been a custom among us? The lower classes have only this one opportunity of our election contests for earning gratitude or conferring obligation. Do not, therefore, deprive them, Cato, of the power to do us this service. Allow those who hope for everything from us to have something which they can give us in return. They can not plead for us in the courts, or give bail for us, or invite us to their houses. All this they ask at our hands, and they think that these benefits can not be repaid by them in any other way than by displaying their zeal as partisans. 'But shows were publicly exhibited, and dinner invitations were promiscuously given.' Now, although in fact this was not done by Murena at all, but only by his friends according to usual custom, yet, I can not help recollecting how many votes we lost owing to inquiries which these things occasioned in the senate.

"Cato, however, joins issue with me like a stern and Stoic philosopher. He denies the proposition that it is right that good will should be conciliated by good dinners. He denies that in the choice of magistrates the judgment should be seduced by pleasure. Therefore, if any candidate with a view to his return invites an elector to supper, he shall be condemned as a violator of the law. 'Would you, forsooth,' says he, 'aim at power and office, and aspire to guide the helm of the state, by fostering the sensual appetites of men, and corrupting their minds? Are you asking for some vicious indulgence from a band of effeminate youths, or the empire of the world from the Roman people?' This is a solemn way of putting it, indeed, but such language is opposed to our habits and customs, and the very constitution itself."

But as he approaches the close of his oration Cicero adopts a more serious tone, and eloquently describes the dangers which threatened the commonwealth from the attacks of Catiline. To the jury he addresses the favorite formula of a distinguished advocate of our own time. "Gentlemen, you are none of you safe!" *Mihi credite, judices, in hâc causâ non solum de L. Murenæ, verùm etiam de vestrâ salute senteniam feretis.* And he finally appeals to their compassion to save his client from the ruin with which an adverse verdict would overwhelm him.

We have already seen, in noticing the life of Hortensius, that the defense of Murena was successful. How far it *ought* to have been so, it is impossible for us now to judge, as we know not by what evidence the specific charges against him were supported, nor how they were disproved. That part of Cicero's speech which professed to grapple with them in detail is lost, but if what remains is submitted to a logical test it will be found to have little real relevancy to the issue which the court had to try. The chief weapon which he uses is the *argumentum ad personam*, which, though galling to an adversary, ought to have availed his client little before an intelligent and honest tribunal. To banter Sulpicius upon "quirks and quillets" of the law, and Cato upon the absurdities of a paradoxical philosophy, was not, according to our notions, the way to establish the innocence of his client; but it was an effectual mode of *prejudicing* the minds of the jury, and the advocate knew well that if he could succeed in doing this he was tolerably sure of a verdict of acquittal. The reason why such verdicts were frequently given at Rome contrary to the evidence has been previously explained, and it was of the utmost consequence to work upon the feelings, and enlist the sympathies of the judices on the side of the accused. Hence it was that we find so many piteous appeals to their compassion, and such affecting pictures drawn of the misery which a conviction would produce. But this is a dangerous ground to take in an English court of justice; it seems to imply that there is no defense upon the merits, and of the counsel who resorts to it may be said, what Cicero applies to a desponding candidate— *jacet, diffidit, abjecit hastas.* The jury are sworn to make a *true* deliverance, and to address their passions alone is equivalent to asking them to violate their oaths.

Perhaps there is no speech of Cicero in which he exhibited his consummate skill as an advocate more conspicuously than when he appeared on behalf of Ligarius, and invoked the mercy and compassion of Julius Cæsar, who, having vanquished Pompey at Pharsalia, and being freed from all further opposition by the death of his great rival, was now the supreme dictator at Rome. The circumstances of the case were shortly these: Ligarius had accompanied, as lieutenant, Considius to his proconsular government in Africa, and made himself so popular in the province that when Considius quitted it, in order to gratify the inhabitants, he left Ligarius governor in his stead. During his command the civil war broke out between Cæsar and Pompey, the latter of whom, as is well known, was supported by the senate, and looked upon as the general of the republic. The province warmly espoused the cause of Pompey, and wished Ligarius to raise troops and declare himself a partisan of that side. He, however, refused to take any part in the struggle, and the Africans, unable to control their zeal, chose as their leader Attius Varus, who had lately come to Utica as prætor of the province. Ligarius did not quit

Africa, but withdrawing for a time from public affairs remained quietly a spectator of events. In the meantime Tubero had been sent by the senate to assume the government, but on his arrival he found it in the hands of Varus, and as the Africans refused to recognize his authority he betook himself to the camp of Pompey, and bore arms against Cæsar at the battle of Pharsalia. He experienced the clemency of the conqueror, and was permitted to reside in Rome undisturbed, but resenting his treatment in Africa as an insult, and imagining that Ligarius was responsible for it, he had the effrontery to instigate his son, who seems himself to have fought at Pharsalia on the same side as his father, to accuse Ligarius of having been while in Africa a partisan of Pompey.

To understand the full force of Cicero's defense, we must remember that he, too, had espoused the side of Pompey and the republic, and it was therefore a matter of no little delicacy to have to advocate the cause of a person upon a charge which applied equally to himself, but the mode in which he performed the task is a masterpiece of art. He cites his own pardon as a proof of the native goodness and mercy of Cæsar, which emboldens him to make the appeal on behalf of his client, and he overwhelms the accuser with shame for attempting to intercept that bounty towards another which had been bestowed so largely upon himself. Never was flattery more dexterously applied to conciliate a judge than on this occasion; and it was no more than was necessary, for the trial took place, not before one of the ordinary tribunals, but before the dictator himself in the forum, sitting both as party against whom the offense was committed, and as judge.[1] Here I can select only

---

[1] No orator has surpassed St. Paul in fervid eloquence, or in knowledge of the topics most likely to influence the tribunal which he was addressing. "But when Paul perceived that the one part were Sadducees, and the other Pharisees, he cried out in the council, 'Men and brethren, I am a Pharisee, the son of a Pharisee; of the hope and resurrection of the dead I am called in question.' And when he had so said, there arose a dissension between

a few extracts, but the whole speech, which is one of the shortest delivered by Cicero, well deserves and repays perusal.

Addressing Tubero he asks, "Who then is it who thinks it is a crime that Ligarius was in Africa? He forsooth, who both wished to be himself in that same Africa, and complains that he was prevented by Ligarius, and beyond all doubt took up arms against Cæsar in the field. For how was your sword employed, Tubero, in the battle of Pharsalia? At whose side was its point aimed? What was the meaning of your armor? What was your intention? Against whom were your eyes, your hands directed? What was your object and desire? But I restrain myself, I press the matter too closely, the young man seems to tremble.[1] I will speak again of myself; I, too, was in arms on the same side."

We are reminded of the scene where Pitt, the great commoner, suddenly apostrophized Murray (afterwards Lord Mansfield) in debate: "I must now address a few words to Mr. Solicitor; they shall be few, but shall be daggers." Murray was agitated, the look was continued; the agitation increased: "Judge Festus trembles," exclaimed Pitt, in a tone of thunder: "he shall hear me some other day."[1]

See now with what skill Cicero avails himself of the argument that Cæsar had been already merciful, and with what tact and delicacy he touches upon the dangerous subject of the comparative merits of the two sides in the civil war.

---

the Pharisees and the Sadducees; and the multitude was divided." And with what admirable art he appealed to the governor, Agrippa, as though it were impossible for him to doubt the truth of the prophecies! "King Agrippa, believest thou the prophets? I *know* that thou believest." Longinus said of St. Paul, that, in dogmatic assertion, he was the first of orators, πρῶτόν φημι προϊστάμενον δόγματος ἀναποδείκτου.—*Fragm.* The passage, however, is, by some scholars, supposed to be spurious.

[1] *Butler's Reminiscences*, i. 145. Such is the anecdote; but it was **Felix**, and not Festus, who trembled before St. Paul.

"Let us be called not criminal, but unhappy, although with Cæsar as our conqueror we can not be so. But I speak not of us who survive, but of those who have perished. Let us allow that they were blinded by zeal, and anger, and obstinacy; but suffer the memory of Cneius Pompey, and many others, to be free from the charge of crime, madness, and parricide. When did any one hear you, Cæsar, accuse them thus? With what other object did you take up arms, than to repel injury and insult from yourself? What else did your victorious legions accomplish than the preservation of their own rights and your dignity? What! when you showed yourself desirous of peace, was it with the wicked or with the virtuous that you wished to be reconciled?

"For my own part, Cæsar, I confess that I should not deem my obligations to you by any means so great if I thought that, though I was spared by you, I was looked upon as a criminal. For how could you have deserved well of the state if you had wished that so many criminals should preserve their privileges and rank? No; you regarded what happened in the light at first of a secession from your party—not a declaration of war; not an armed conflict, but a political strife; both parties desiring the safety of the republic, but led by different opinions and attachments to take different views of the common weal. The rank and reputation of the two leaders were almost on a par, not perhaps so their respective followers; the cause of each was then doubtful, for on either side there was something to approve; now, however, that one certainly must be deemed the best which even the gods have aided. And since your clemency has been proved and experienced, who would not rejoice at a victory which has cost the life of none except those who fell in battle?" And again, how artfully he appeals to the mercy of the dictator in the following passage: "All that I have said I have addressed to your humanity, your clemency, your compassion. I have pleaded many causes, Cæsar, and some even with you as my coadjutor while you paved the way to your future honors by practice in the forum, but never did I adopt this tone for my client, 'Pardon him, judges; he has erred; he is guilty; he did it unwittingly, if ever again '—— That is the language to be addressed to a parent; but to a court of justice, this: " He did not do it; he never contemplated the act; the witnesses are forsworn; the charge is false.' Tell me, Cæsar, that you are sitting as a judge to try Ligarius on the question of fact, and ask me in whose garrison he was found.—I am at once silent. I care not to plead in excuse that which might perhaps avail, even with a judge.' 'He went there as lieutenant before the war. He was left in the province during the continuance of peace. He was taken by surprise when war broke out; he showed no animosity while it lasted—even then he was in his heart, and in his wishes, on your side.' Such would be the line of defense before a judge, but I am speaking to a parent: ' I have sinned; I have acted unadvisedly; I am sorry for my fault; I throw myself upon your mercy; I ask pardon for my offense; I pray you to forgive me.' If no one has obtained forgiveness from you, it is presumption in me to ask it; but if very many have, then do you who have encouraged hope likewise bestow favor."

We see that Cicero alludes to the time when Julius Cæsar was engaged, like himself, as an advocate at the Roman bar, and there is but little doubt that he would have been celebrated as one of the greatest speakers of whom Rome could boast if he had not chosen rather to be her greatest general, and preferred the laurel of the conqueror to the peaceful triumphs of the orator. Quintilian tells us that if he had devoted himself to the forum, he alone would have been named as the rival of Cicero, and that the energy and vehemence of his style corresponded with his character, so that he seemed to speak in the same spirit as that which animated him while carrying on war. Tacitus also says that " Cæsar the dictator was on a par with the greatest orators" (*Ann.* xiii. 3). And he was distinguished by a remarkable elegance and propriety of expression, to which he always paid particular attention. How interesting it would have been to read some of his orations if time had spared them, but none exist, and we know only the names of a few of which incidental mention is made by other writers. These consist of three speeches against Dolabella, who was accused of pecuniary corruption, and three against Domitius and Memmius. He appeared also on behalf of some of the provincial dependencies of the state, speaking on one occasion for the Greeks, and on another for the Bithynians, who, according to the usual custom, sought redress for their grievances by committing their causes into the hands of some powerful advocate at Rome.

We may close the list of orators in the time of the republic with the names of Junius Brutus, Cælius Rufus, Licinius Calvus, Asinius Pollio, and Messala Corvinus, of whom Rufus and Corvinus, or, as he is usually called, Messala, attained considerable eminence in the Forum. They were men of very different characters, the former being as conspicuous for his vices as the latter was distinguished by his virtues. Rufus was defended by Cicero when brought to trial on the charge of having suborned the slaves of a Roman matron, named Clodia, a woman of no good repute, to poison their mistress, and the speech of the advocate reveals a corrupt condition of morals at Rome. Society must have been in a vicious state when a counsel could thus address a grave court of judicature: *Verum si quis est, qui etiam meretriciis amoribus interdictum juventuti putet, est ille quidem valde severus; negare non possum: sed abhorret non modo ab hujus sæculi licentiâ, verum etiam a majorum consuetudine, atque concessis.*

CHAPTER VI.

THE BAR UNDER THE EMPIRE AND IN THE MIDDLE AGES.

THE palmy days of forensic oratory at Rome passed away with the republic. And this is no more than might be expected; for eloquence withers under the cold shade of arbitrary and irresponsible power, and without free institutions few if any opportunities can exist for exercising that godlike gift, except in opposing some act of tyranny at the peril of fortune and of life. And it would be absurd to suppose that a profession would be embraced for such a purpose, and that the advocates of imperial Rome would devote themselves to martyrdom in the hopeless cause of liberty. The fate of Cremutius Cordus, in the reign of Tiberius, was a sufficient warning of the danger incurred by even alluding in terms of praise to the patriots of the republic; for he was accused of the crime of having eulogized Brutus, and designated Cassius as "the last of the Romans," and feeling that the charge was of too heinous a nature to admit any chance of escape,—after a spirited speech, he starved himself to death, and his book was ordered by the senate to be publicly burnt.

With the exception of Quintilian and the younger Pliny, our minds are familiar with the names of none of the advocates who flourished during the five centuries that intervened between Augustus and Justinian; and the former are known to us as writers rather than speakers, for neither of them was remarkable for any high order of eloquence. In the dialogue, *De Causis corruptæ Eloquentiæ,* which was written little more than a century after the death of Cicero, Tacitus feelingly laments that oratory was extinct. "Often," he says, "have you asked me, Justus Fabius, why, when former ages were so distinguished by the genius and renown of orators, our own age, destitute and bereft of glory, scarce retains the very name. For we style none such now except the ancients; but the speakers of the present day are called pleaders, and advocates, and barristers, and anything rather than orators." He proceeds afterwards to investigate the causes of the decline of eloquence, and draws a comparison between the mode of education in former days and that pursued in his own time; dwelling with just severity upon the pernicious custom which had crept in of mothers abandoning the care and nurture of their offspring to servants, instead of like the noble matrons of old, such as Cornelia and Aurelia, watching over and superintending their education themselves. The consequence was, that those who were destined for the bar were trained up in no habits or study, and took no pains to qualify themselves, by laborious preparation, for their profession; but deemed it sufficient to pick up in the schools of rhetoricians meretricious and tinsel ornaments of style. Thus they were accustomed to deliver "miserable show speeches," as Niebuhr calls them, and furnished with such commonplaces as their stock in trade, they retailed them in the courts, under the delusive notion that their empty declamation was eloquence. Tacitus complains strongly of their ignorance of law, which they affected to despise, as a branch of knowledge by no means necessary for them to acquire. If, indeed, we may implicitly trust the accounts which have been left us of the state of the Roman bar at different periods under the Cæsars, we shall have a very low opinion of it. But it is necessary to bear in mind the proneness of every writer to depreciate the merits of his own times, and exalt those of the past. Hesiod, one of the earliest of profane authors, laments that his lot was cast in an iron age, and sighs for that golden period which tradition represented, and his imagination pictured, as one of happiness and virtue.

> O that my lot had not been cast on earth
> In this fifth age of man! would I had died
> Before, for now an iron race succeeds![1]

And from the time when Hesiod wrote, to the present day, each generation has made the same complaint. Is it not characteristic of every kind of literature, whether it be that of the historian, the poet, or the divine, to look back upon the past, and contrast it with the present, always to the disadvantage of the latter? Each speaks of himself as Milton did:—

> . . . . though fall'n on evil days,
> On evil days though fall'n, and evil tongues.

Is it not true that, in the words of Tacitus, "*Vitio malignitatis humanæ vetera semper in laude, præsentia in fastidio esse?*" A more charitable reason, however, may be given than that "malignity" by which he accounts for it. Man sees and feels all the misery of the present, but the past is softened in the dim distance, and the cry of *its* agony is no longer heard across the waste of centuries.

After making due allowance for the exaggerations of satire, it is evident, from a well-known passage in Juvenal, that the bar in his time, at Rome, was by no means in a satisfactory or prosperous state. The poor counsel had no chance against the rich, and in the des-

---

[1] *Opp. et Dies*, 174. The Hindus call the present period Cali Yaga, or evil age.

perate struggle to keep up appearances, and get business, many a briefless barrister was ruined.

> Sic Pedo conturbat, Matho deficit ; exitus hic est
> Tongilli.

Gay clothes and jeweled fingers, a long train of attendants, and a great show of expense, were necessary to attract clients—

> ———— purpura vendit
> Causidicum, vendunt amethystina.

And those who wished to secure a livelihood by the practice of their profession are recommended by the poet to abandon Rome, and betake themselves to Africa or Gaul.

The following is the picture drawn by him of their condition in his time, and it must be admitted that it is by no means flattering (*Sat.* vii. 106-214).

> Say now what honors advocates attend,
> Whose shelves beneath a load of volumes bend ;
> Their voice stentorian in the courts we hear,
> But chiefly when some creditor is near :
> A show of business eager to display,
> Their lungs like panting bellows work away.
> Alas ! a hundred lawyers scarce can gain,
> What one successful jockey will obtain.—
> The court has met : with pale and careworn face
> You rise to plead some hapless client's case,
> And crack your voice ; for what ? When all is o'er,
> To see a bunch of laurel on your door.
> This is the meed of eloquence ; to dine
> On dried-up hams, and cabbage, and sour wine :
> If by good luck four briefs you chance to hold,
> And your eye glistens at the sight of gold ;
> Think not to pocket all the hard-won fee,
> For the attorney claims his share with thee.[1]
> Large sums Æmilius can command, 'tis true,
> Although a far worse advocate than you ;
> But then his steeds of bronze and brazen car
> The rich Æmilius to the world declare ;
> While lance in hand he rides a sculptur'd knight,
> And seems a warrior charging in the fight.

[1] " Inde cadunt partes ex fœdere pragmaticorum."

Pliny the younger frequently speaks of the changed state of the forum in his day, and of the unworthy arts which were resorted to to gain a reputation and attract clients. "You are right in your conjecture," he says, addressing his friend Maximus (*Epist.* ii. 14); "I am tired to death of causes in the centumviral courts, which give me practice rather than pleasure, for they are for the most part trifling and trumpery. A case seldom occurs distinguished either by the rank of the parties, or the importance of the matter in dispute. Besides, there are very few counsel with whom it is at all agreeable to be engaged. The rest are generally obscure young men with plenty of effrontery, who go there to make declamatory speeches with such rashness and want of modesty, that my friend Attilius seems to have said, with great truth, that boys at the bar begin with causes in those courts, just as they did with Homer at school." He then adverts to the dignified proceedings of former days, and contrasts with them the indecent practice of his own time, when advocates were in the habit of hiring *claqueurs* to attend upon them, and applaud their speeches in court. "If," he continues, "you chance to pass through the hall, and wish to know how each counsel acquits himself, you have no occasion to listen to what he says. You may rest assured that he is the worst speaker who has the loudest applause." Pliny goes on to state, on the authority of Quintilian, that Largius Licinius first introduced this contemptible custom. "Once, when Domitius Afer was pleading a cause before the centumvirs, he suddenly heard, in the adjoining court, a loud and unusual shouting, and for a few moments he stopped. When the noice ceased he went on, but soon there was another shout of applause and he again paused. After he had resumed his argument he was again interrupted, and he then asked who was speaking in the other court. He was told that it was Licinius; upon which he said, addressing the judges,

This is a death-blow to the profession.'" It seems that the precedent thus set was soon improved upon, and all sorts of cries to denote approbation or disapprobation of the speeches of counsel resounded in the courts: the favorite sign of the latter being a kind of Irish howl or yell, *ululatus*, which Pliny says is the only word he can find to express it.

As might be expected, the conventional rules which are known by the name of the etiquette of the profession had no place at the Roman bar. In England it would be deemed a most improper act for any counsel to make interest for the employment of another with him in a cause, for with such a selection he ought not, in the most distant way, to interfere. Otherwise it is obvious that an odious system of favoritism would prevail, which would be ruinous to the independence of the members. But, in amusing contrast to this, we know how anxiously and earnestly Pliny used to recommend a junior. Writing to his friend Triarius, he says, "You ask me to undertake without a fee a cause in which you are interested, and which, you tell me, is a good one, and will make a noise in the world. Well, I will do so, but not gratuitously. 'How is this?' you will exclaim. 'Is it possible that *you* can talk in this mercenary manner? Very possible: for I intend to demand a remuneration which will be more to my credit than if I pleaded without a fee. I beg as a favor, and indeed make it a stipulation, that Cremutius Ruso shall be retained along with me. This is my usual custom, and what I have frequently done in the case of several distinguished young men; for it is my particular delight to give deserving youths opportunities at the bar, and to point them out for future eminence. Pray, now oblige me by this favor, before Ruso opens his lips in court; for when he has spoken, you will thank me for having selected him. I engage for him that he will fully satisfy your anxiety, my own hopes, and the importance of the cause. He has excellent capacity, and will soon be able to bring forward others, if in the meantime he gets a helping hand from us; for no barrister's abilities are so well known and recognized beforehand that he can rise in his profession, unless he has the opportunity of holding a brief, and is backed by some friend who will speak well of him and recommend him." There is, no doubt, much truth in this; but now-a-days Ruso would have to wait in vain for such a letter in his favor from a Queen's counsel.

It would be easy to give a numerous catalogue of advocates who practiced in the courts under the empire, and of whom scattered notices are to be found in the ancient writers. But to what purpose would it be to chronicle names which evoke no reminiscences in our minds, and which we know only by some passing and casual remark of the authors who have recorded them? Who now remembers Marcellus Eprius and Crispus Vibius, the favorites of Vespasian, whose reputation in their day was so great, that Tacitus declares it had spread to the remotest corners of the earth, and who, by the exercise of their profession, reaped such an abundant harvest of wealth and honors (*De Orat. Dial.* 8)? In vain should we mention the name of Æmilius, the leader of the bar at Rome, who, as we have seen, forgetting the peaceful nature of his vocation, gratified his vanity by placing in his house a statue of himself as a warrior on horseback, brandishing a lance. And in vain should we speak of the exuberant fullness of Sulla, the vigor of Africanus, the precocious excellence of Domitius Afer, cut off by an early death, the stentorian voice of Trachallus, and the elegance of Julius Secundus (*Quintil.* x. I. xii. 10).

Of Quintilian, whose interesting and instructive work *De Institutione Oratoria* has become the text-book of all who wish to study advocacy as an art, very little is known beyond what is supplied by the few incidental allusions to himself which occur in that treatise. But these are sufficient to inspire us not only with admiration of his genius, but love for his amiable character. One of the most affecting passages in all the remains of classical antiquity is that, at the opening of the sixth book, in which he bewails the loss of his children and his wife. And if, in the bitterness of his soul he murmurs against the Divine will, we must remember that he had not been taught the lesson, that " whom the Lord loveth he chasteneth, and scourgeth every son whom he receiveth ;" nor that the Being, whose hand had smitten him, " doth not afflict willingly, nor grieve the children of men."[1] He had fondly hoped that his eldest son, whose youthful genius gave promise of future eminence, would, in after years, read and profit by his father's labors, and, animated by that hope, he had devoted himself untiringly to his task. "But him," he says, "of whom I had conceived the highest expectations, and in whom I placed the only hope of my old age, I lost by a second bereavement.

'The shaft flew twice, and twice my peace was slain.'

"What can I do now? or for what object can I believe that my existence is prolonged, since Heaven thus frowns upon me? For it so happened, that when I began to write the treatise 'On the Causes of the Decline of Eloquence,' I was stricken by a similar blow. My best

---

[1] Mabillon, in his *Iter Italicum*, p. 79, gives the following epitaph found in Rome:—

Procope . Manus . Lebo . Contra .
Deum . Qui . Me . Innocentem . Sustulit . Quæ . Vixit . Annos . XX.

Compare now the sentiment here expressed with that contained in a fragment of a Christian epitaph found in the Catacombs:—

Qui Dedit et Abstulit
Omini Benedic . .
Qui Bixit Ann . .
Pace Cons . . .

See Maitland's *Church in the Catacombs*, pp. 13, 14.

course then would have been to cast upon the funeral pile, whose flames were about to consume my own flesh and blood, my luckless work and all my literary labors, and not weary, with fresh attempts, a life that so unnaturally survived. For what affectionate parent could forgive me if I were able to continue my studies, and would not detest my stoicism if I, who am the survivor of all who are dear to me, could find any other use for my voice than to upbraid the gods? Shall I assert that no providence orders things below? If I can not say this, looking merely at myself- (and yet my only fault is that I continue to exist),—I might on account of those innocents consigned to an untimely grave. Their mother had been snatched away from me before, after giving birth to two sons, and when she had not yet completed her nineteenth year, but she in her death, though it was to me a most sad bereavement, might be considered happy—that single affliction had so crushed me that it was out of the power of fortune ever to render *me* so. For not only because she was adorned with every virtue of her sex did her death plunge me into inconsolable sorrow, but owing to her youthful years, especially when compared with mine, I might mourn over her as though I had lost a child. Still, however, I found comfort in my surviving children, though she, cruel in her wish that I should continue to live, escaped by a hasty flight the most agonizing sorrow. My youngest son, when he had completed his fifth year, was the first of my two darlings that died. I have no wish to magnify my misfortunes, nor increase my cause for sorrow, and, O, that I had the means of assuaging it. But how can I disguise from myself the sweetness of his countenance, the charm of his prattle, the sparkles of his wit, the calmness and (what I know will scarcely be believed) the depth of his mind, such as would have won my affection, even if he had been the child of another? But by the treachery of Fortune, that she might wound me more deeply, it so happened that he was fonder of me than any one, and preferred me to his nurses, to his grandmother who brought him up, and, in short, to all who generally win the affections at that early age." The mourning father then goes on to describe the death, after an illness of eight months, of his eldest son, the young Quintilian, when he had entered his tenth year, and he lingers, with all a parent's love over the memory of his engaging disposition and rare acquirements.

Ammianus Marcellinus, the historian, who flourished in the fourth century after Christ, draws such a lamentable picture of the ignorance, rapacity, and meaness of the lawyers and advocates of Rome, and the provinces, when he wrote (*Lib.* xxx. c. 4), that it is difficult to believe that it is not a caricature, like that by which Swift indulged his spleen against the profession in the account which he makes Gulliver give of it in describing his voyage to the Houyhnhnms. Even Gibbon admits the "extravagant satire" of the passage; and it is impossible to believe that if it truly represented the actions and characters of Roman advocates, their rights and privileges would have been so fully acknowledged, and so reverently cared for as they were by the later Roman emperors. That this was so, we have incontestible proof in the language which we find applied to them in the code of Justinian.

In one of the imperial edicts, the following honorable testimony is borne to the value of their office. "Praiseworthy and necessary for human life is advocacy, which ought to be remunerated by the highest rewards" (*Cod.* ii. *tit.* viii. 23). It would be tedious to enumerate all the regulations which occur with reference to this subject, for many of the distinctions and honors accorded to the *Togatorum consortium*, or members of the bar, have now lost their meaning, and being founded on the peculiar state of society and usages which then existed, would be hardly intelligible without a lengthened explanation. It will be sufficient to state, generally, that, among other privileges, they were exempted from many offices and burdens which other citizens had to bear ; and after they had ceased to exercise their profession, they were admitted to the order of Counts (*comites*) of the first rank, and numbered among the *clarissimi* of the state. It is well known that under the Roman law the power of a father over his children, until they were legally emancipated from his control, was almost absolute. And whatever a son might gain by his own exertions, so long as he remained unemancipated, became the property of his father. An exception, however, occurred in the case of those who were engaged in military service. They were permitted to acquire property, which was exclusively their own, and which they could bequeath by will. This was known by the name of *peculium castrense*. And the same privilege was conceded to advocates, who might retain whatever they earned in the exercise of their profession, *veluti peculium castrense ad exemplum militum*,—even while they remained subject to the parental authority in other respects.

By another imperial ordinance, addressed by the Emperors Valentinian, Valens, and Gratian, A. D. 370, to Olybrius, the prefect of Rome, care was taken to prevent an undue preponderance of counsel on either side at a trial of a cause. It was declared to be the duty of the presiding judge to see that a fair distribution of the leading advocates was made, so that they might not all be engaged for the same client. And if it appeared that a party had retained so many counsel on his side, that his adversary was unable to obtain proper legal assistance, this was to be taken as a proof that his cause was unjust, and he was to be reprimanded and punished by the judge. It seems, therefore, that "muffling" retainers were by this equitable law prevented, and the contest between the parties rendered as fair as an equality of weapons could make it. And if any advocate was assigned by the judge to either party, and declined the task, on insufficient grounds, he was to be disbarred forever (*Cod.* ii. vi. 7).

The nearest approach to Queen's Counsel under the Roman Empire consisted in the *advocati fisci* of whom such frequent mention is made in the code of Justinian, and who seem to have been 'first appointed in the reign of Hadrian. Their office was to attend to all cases in which the interests of the crown were concerned. and except in some peculiar instances they were not allowed to undertake private causes. Even after they had ceased to hold office they could not, without a special license from the emperor (*auctoribus nobis*), appear against the crown. They were, however, allowed even while in office to do so in causes in which they themselves, or their children, or parents, or wards, were parties.

The body of advocates was, in the time of Constantine, divided into two classes, called statuti and supernumerarii. The former were those who belonged to a particular corps, and confined their practice to a particular forum, the numbers attending which, were limited by law. Thus, in the court of the perfect of the city at Constantinople, eighty were allowed to practice, in Alexandria fifty, and in other places different numbers. The supernumerarii were those who were attached to no particular bar, and supplied such vacancies as occurred among the statuti. By a special edict, however, preference was to be given in such cases to the sons of advocates, who were to be admitted without payment of fees, provided that they displayed a sufficient knowledge of law.

It seems that an express law was necessary to prevent the fair sex from attempting *pendre la parole* in the courts of law; for Ulpian, in his treatise *ad Edictum*, tells us that the prætor prohibited them from pleading the causes of others, "that they might not intermeddle in such matters, contrary to the modesty befitting their sex, nor engage in employments proper to men." The occasion of passing this edict is said to have been the conduct of a virago named Carfania, a most troublesome and ill-conditioned lady (*improbissima fœmina*), who caused the magistrates a great deal of annoyance by her importunity in court. An exception, however, was made in favor of women whose fathers were prevented from conducting their own suits, owing to sickness or infirmity, and who could not get any one else to plead for them. But as a general rule, those who were unable to retain counsel to defend them, either on account of the overweening influence of their opponents, or any other valid cause, as well as those who were incapacitated from appearing in their own behalf, by reason of being blind or deaf, had counsel assigned them by the prætor himself, who announced his benevolent intention in the words SI NON HABEBUNT ADVOCATUM, EGO DABO.

When Valens was emperor, and extortion and plunder were the order of the day, a new species of abuse prevailed; for both judges and counsel are said to have taken bribes to effect the removal of causes, where the parties had not much power or influence, from the civil courts to military tribunals. It would seem, however, that for some reason or other, which it is not easy to explain, litigants themselves were in the habit of thus changing the jurisdiction, and at last the emperor Arcadius was obliged to put a stop to the practice, by a royal constitution or ordinance. This enacted that whoever, without a license from the emperor, in contempt of the ordinary courts, transferred a civil cause to a military court, should, in addition to other penalties, undergo the sentence of banishment: and his counsel who assisted him in thus removing the case (quære, by *certiorari?*) was to be fined ten pounds of gold. And Valentinian passed a law, that if an advocate practiced before any other than the ordinary tribunals, he was to be deprived of his office, or, as we should say, disbarred.

When causes were once decided, they were not allowed to be reheard on the ground that the trial had proceeded in the absence of counsel; but if it could be satisfactorily proved that an advocate had betrayed his trust, he was to be punished, and the cause might be heard afresh. Such an application, however, was made at the peril of the party; for if he failed to establish the fact of the misconduct of his counsel, he was to be convicted of calumny, and the previous judgment was to stand.

Another salutary edict was directed against scurrility and abuse in the conduct of a cause. Advocates were told to confine themselves to the merits of the case, and not indulge in open invective, or covert sarcasm, against their opponents.

Under the early Christian emperors, the proverb *nemo causidicus nisi clericus* did not apply, for Justinian strictly prohibited any one in holy orders from pleading in the courts, whatever might be the nature of the cause; whether it was one in which he was personally interested, or in which his church or monastery was a party. Nor was he allowed to become bail for any one engaged in a lawsuit to secure his appearance, or otherwise; and the reasons assigned were, that no pecuniary loss might fall upon the church, and that her ministers might not be hindered from the due discharge of their sacred functions.

At a later period there was some difference of opinion as to the propriety of allowing advocates to be ordained after they had quitted their profession. The custom varied in different churches. In those of Rome and Spain it appears that the prohibition existed, for Innocent, bishop of Rome, in a letter to the council of Toledo, complains that many who, after having received the grace of baptism, had followed the profession of ad vocates, being unable to resist the attraction of fees, had afterwards been admitted to the priesthood. He therefore proposed a canon, that no one who had after baptism pleaded causes in the courts, should be received into holy orders. But this was by no means the universal rule.

During the long night of darkness which overspread the face of Europe after the sun of the Roman empire had set, and while, amidst the ruins of ancient institutions, feudalism was preparing to emerge, and effect so remarkable a change in the laws and incidents of property and personal rights, we can not expect to find that advocates enjoyed any repute, or left many traces of their existence behind them. The languages of Western Europe were then in a state of transition, and unfitted for any efforts of the speaker beyond the ordinary purposes of daily life. But that advocates existed among the various nations which usurped the dominion of ancient Rome, we know from several incidental notices contained in their laws. Thus, among the Lombards, one of these provided that if perchance any one, owing to his simpleness, knew not how to plead his own cause, he was to commence his suit, and if the king or judge saw that he had right on his side, he was then to appoint him a man to undertake his cause; and Heineccius tells us that advocates were throughout the German tribes allowed to plead, after permission had in each case been first obtained from the judge, to which Hachenberg adds that they were enjoined to conduct their cases in plain and unadorned language, without any tedious circumlocution. The name by which they were generally distinguished was not very complimentary, for they were called clamatores, or *clamourers*, by which appellation they are frequently referred to in the capitularies of Charlemagne.

When the successful issue of the first crusade, A. D. 1099, had placed Godfrey, Duke of Bouillon, or Boulogne, on the throne of Jerusalem, one of his first cares was to cause a code of laws to be compiled for his new kingdom, which were taken from the various feudal customs and usages that prevailed in the countries of Western Europe. At the same time he established two secular courts of justice, one called *La Haute Cour*, the High Court, of which he himself, as suzerain, was the chief justiciary; and the other *La Cour des Bourgeois,* or court of the commonalty, called also the Viscount's court, presided over by one of his feudal lords who bore that title. The judges of the High Court were the chevaliers who held by tenure of knights' service, or perhaps only those who held *in capite,* as we are told that it consisted of those who had done homage to the sovereign as their liege lord; and the judges of the court of commonalty were *bourgeois* of the city, or townsfolk, " the most upright and wise to be found therein." But in neither the High Court nor the Court of the Bourgeois did the sovereign or the viscount take any part in the judgment pronounced. The office of each seems to have been simply to preside over the proceedings, and give proper directions for the conduct of the suit. In this respect there is a striking similarity between their functions and those of the archon at Athens and prætor at Rome, as we have already seen. In the High Court were to be adjudged exclusively the causes of all the great feudatories of the kingdom, and in the Court of the Bourgeois, as its name imports, justice was to be administered to the commonalty.

The code of laws thus compiled consisted of two collections, both called assizes; the one intended for the Haute Cour, and the other for the Cour des Bourgeois. When completed they were placed in a casket and deposited in the treasury of the Church of the Holy Sepulchre at Jerusalem, whence they derived their name of *Lettres du Sépulcre.* The city, however, was taken by Saladin, on the 2nd of October, 1187, and in the confusion that followed, the celebrated volume or volumes disappeared, and they were never afterwards recovered. But though the original copy of these assizes or laws had thus perished, the system established by them remained, and portions must have existed in different writings independently of what was preserved by memory and tradition. A collection of them was accordingly made, or, as we may say, edited, by Jean D'Ibelin, who lived in the early part of the thirteenth century, under the titles of " Assizes de la Haute Cour, Livre de Jean D'Ibelin," and " Livre des Assizes de la Cour des Bourgeois," and this is, perhaps, the oldest treatise on feudal law extant in the world. It contains much curious and interesting matter, and to the legal antiquary is a mine of valuable learning, where we find the germ of many of the laws and customs which have been interwoven into our own system, and become part of our common law. This might be expected when we recollect the sources from which the compilation of the Assizes de Jerusalem was taken, and the work proves how much of our jurisprudence we owe to our Norman forefathers. It is a common mistake to suppose that they introduced only the peculiarities of the feudal system, and that all our most valued institutions are derived from the Saxons. This is not the place for entering upon so wide a field of inquiry, for we must confine ourselves to such parts of the venerable code as relate more immediately to the subject of the present work; and they possess additional interest when we consider that we there find regulations not then for the first time devised and put in force, but such as prevailed throughout Christendom, and were transplanted to the East;—and which, were it not for this collection of Assizes, would in all probability have been buried and lost in the night of ages.

As an illustration of the above remarks, let us transcribe from the *Abrégé du Livere des Assizes* the law which lays down the rule to be observed in a case of murder, where we shall see the court sitting as a coroner's jury, and the custom of "viewing the body," in full force as at the present day. It is so far relevant to the subject of the present work, that we find that the advocate plays an important in the proceedings.

The chapter is entitled, *La Clamour de Murtre e Homecide.* "If the murdered man has wife, or relative, he or she ought to speak to the court thus:—'Sire, I pray you that you would give me such and such an advocate for my counsel, in order that I may make and pursue my claim;' and the president ought immediately to choose an advocate to be of counsel to the person who has made the request. And afterwards the advocate ought to listen and pay attention to what his client wishes to say and do. And then the advocate ought to come with that person into the presence of the viscount or the bailiff and the court, and speak thus on his or her behalf. If the person be a widow, he ought to request that one of the jury (*i.e.*, member of the court, *juré*) should be added as counsel, and the president ought to assign whomsoever it pleaseth him to ask for. The advocate is then to consult with the jury, and they are then to take their seats, and the advocate proceeds thus :— 'Sire, such and such a person, who is here present, prays and requests you to bring the court with you, and come and see the body of her husband' (or her brother, as the case may be), 'which lies dead outside.' And the viscount or the bailiff ought forthwith to conduct the court, and go to view the body, and the blows upon it. And the court ought carefully to observe how many blows it has, and also to notice what blow produced death. And when they have carefully viewed the body, they ought to return to their seats, and the advocate must follow and address them thus:—" The speech, however, is too long to insert, and it will be sufficient to mention that the pleader therein accuses the suspected person with having "wickedly, disloyally, feloniously, and outrageously" committed the murder, and prays the court that he may be pursued and taken wherever he may be found, and that justice may be done upon him. The court then is to promise to aid the petitioner in her search after the murderer; and if she hears any news of him, she is to advise the court thereof. "And afterwards the advocate is to say, 'Sire, what do you order her to do?' and the president shall say, 'Let her do that which seemeth her good;' and then the advocate shall rejoin,—'Sire, may it please you to order that the house of the malefactor be sealed up, for if his house and goods are under your seal, and the malefactor know thereof, it may be that he will come into your power.'"

One of the chapters in the *Livre de Jean D'Ibelin* is headed, *De quel Maniere doit estre le Plaideor*, and points out his character and duty. "The pleader ought to be true and constant (*loial et estable*); he ought to advise well and faithfully all those of either sex to whom he is assigned of counsel, and to plead for them faithfully in the best way he can against all men. And neither for love of him against whom he pleads, nor for hate of him to whom he is given as counsel, nor for any fear of shame or loss, nor for any gift or promise made to him, is he to hold back from giving good and true advice to him or her to whom the president of the court (*le seigneur*) has assigned him as counsel; and if he acts otherwise, he is convicted of disloyalty." He was also to keep inviolate the confidence placed in him by his client and in court he was to exert himself to speak in the most effective manner possible.

Another chapter is entitled, "*Coment l'on deit plaider*

It should be observed that the word *plaideer* or *plaider* in these assizes is used with reference to a party to a suit, as well as to his counsel. A person who had a cause in court was said *plaider*. In the Pandects we find the word *postulare* similarly applied in both senses.

en la Haute Cour du Royaume de Jerusalem, ou en celle de Chipre," and directions are given to the advocate to plead with wisdom, honesty, and courtesy, " *sagement et leiaument, et corteisement.*" By honest or *loyal* pleading is meant " that he should not plead wrongfully against right, wittingly, nor plead falsely, nor offer any false proofs, nor wittingly take away the right from him against whom he pleads." Moreover, " it becometh him who is a good and subtle pleader to have naturally good sense, and to have his wits about him ; and he must not be hesitating nor bashful (*ne esbay*), nor hasty, nor careless; and he must take care that while he is pleading, he does not allow either his hearing or his thoughts to have their attention diverted; and he must guard against too much anger or emotion in speaking, which are apt to cause a man to talk nonsense, and take from him his wit and knowledge." But with great *naiveté* it is added, that in truth, the qualifications of a good pleader are innumerable, and the more a man knows the better pleader he will be.

Whoever had a cause depending in the High Court, might demand of the seigneur, or president, to assign to him as counsel the best pleader of the court, and that whether the party applying " were himself an advocate or not," in order that in the former case he might have the assistance of further counsel, " *car il n'est nul si sage plaideor qui ne puisse bien et souvent estre averti el plait de ce qui bon li est par un autre plaideor o lui : que deus plaideors sevent plus et veent plus cler et el plait, et faillent meins que un,*" " because there is no pleader so skillful that he may not often be usefully advised in his pleading by another counsel along with him ; since two pleaders know more, and see more clearly the cause, and make fewer mistakes than one." After giving many sage reasons why advocates or pleaders should be employed, the chapter concludes by saying, " And for these reasons, and several others which would be too long to repeat, every one who wishes to plead in the High Court, ought to demand of the seigneur a counsel, before he brings his cause before it." These passages prove that one of the duties of the president was to assign counsel to parties; and we learn also that he was bound to appoint any advocate whom the suitor might name, always excepting such as were specially retained by himself; for there seem to have been some, who having done homage to the sovereign, acted as it were in the capacity of king's counsel, and their services were at his exclusive command.

But in the Haute Cour it was not necessary for a party to choose a pleader; he might appear in person. In the Cour des Bourgeois it was different: he was there obliged to have an advocate. The reason of this distinction seems to have been, that the law was supposed to be known by the nobles, who alone could bring forward their causes in the former, and they were familiar with the French language, in which the proceedings were carried on: whereas the commonalty were for the most part ignorant both of the law and the language of their court of justice.

The above regulations apply to the advocates who practiced in the Haute Cour; but the *Livre des Assises de la Cour des Bourgeois* was not less careful or particular in providing for the duties of the *avant-parliers*, or pleaders in the lower courts. It enumerates those who are not permitted to discharge the functions of advocates, such as serfs and minors, the deaf and the blind, and also women (*Chaps.* 17, 18, 19). An exception, however, was made in favor of the latter, if a father was prevented by sickness from attending, in which case, the daughter might plead his cause in court, just as we have seen it was permitted by the Roman law. A chapter of the *Abrégé du Livre des Assises* contains some useful hints and good advice, which may be studied with advantage by the *avant-parlier* of the present day (*Chap.* 12). *Et sachés que ceste gent doivent estre ehleus à gent bien parlans, et de belle loquence, et sachant des assises, et usages et bones coustumes qui se doivent uzer en la dite cour ; a ce que par lor bien parler el monstrant les raizons de la bone gent chascun puisse et doye parvenir tost en son droit et en sa raizon.* They were told also to remember what St. Augustin said, namely that, "in order that their discourse may have dignity and beauty, there are three things necessary to them ; first, it must please ; secondly, it must convince ; thirdly, it must persuade. For the first effect, the pleaders must speak gracefully ; for the second, plainly ; for the third, with great ardor and fervency ; and, whenever the court so ordains, they are to take oath that they will preserve the rights and prerogatives of the king, and the honor of the viscount and the court ; and that they will, to the best of their knowledge, give good and true advice to all to whom they shall be assigned as counsel, or who shall require their services ; and that they will keep secret the secrets of the court and of those for whom they act as counsel ;" and they were to have a fee (*selaire*) in proportion to the assistance which they rendered,—*selonc les convenances que il font à la gent.*

CHAPTER VII.

THE NOBLESSE DE LA ROBE.

NOWHERE has the profession of the law achieved for itself a prouder position than in France in former times. Beside her mailed chivalry stood an order of men known as the *noblesse de la robe*, whose only patent of nobility was admission on the roll of advocates, and from whose ranks were taken the magistrates who, as members of the parliament of Paris, represented the feudal court and council of the ancient kings. Two individuals of that order attained each a rare distinction; the one Ives de Kaermartin, who lived in the reign of Philip the Fair, being canonized as a saint:—the other, Gui Foucault, after gaining celebrity as an advocate, was advanced to the triple crown as Pope Clement IV. Illustrious as are the names of many who have adorned the judgment seat in England, none stand higher than those of l'Hopital, le Tellier, and D'Aguesseau, each of whom held the office of Chancellor of France, and was the ornament of the century in which he lived; and of those who did not rise to such lofty pre-eminence in their profession, many were distinguished for their profound learning, their varied accomplishments, and their powerful eloquence. In times of tyranny and licentiousness, under the despotic sway of Louis XI., Francis I. and Louis XIV., and amidst the disgraceful vices of the regency of the Duke of Orleans, it is refreshing to see with what an even hand justice was generally administered in the courts, and with what boldness and fidelity the advocates of France discharged their duties.

From the earliest times Gaul has been famous as a nursery of lawyers, and Juvenal tells us that to her we are under obligations for instruction in eloquence.

> Gallia causidicos docuit facunda Britannos.

Schools for the instruction of students in the art of rhetoric were established, and obtained considerable eminence in various parts of France.

We shall have occasion to notice, in the present chapter, with what care royal ordinances were framed to regulate the duties and preserve the privileges of the order of advocates; and they proved themselves well worthy of the support and countenance of the Crown; for, on many occasions, as, for instance, in the struggle to establish the validity of the Salic law in 1317, they rendered it most important services; and to them the Gallican church owed its successful resistance to the arrogant pretensions and usurpations of the Papal See. It is well known how, commencing with Gregory VII., the proud and politic Hildebrand, the Popes gradually asserted, as God's vicegerents upon earth, their right to collation and investitude in the case of all spiritual dignities and benefices throughout Christendom. At the same time they claimed for the revenue of the church exemption from taxes, and denied the authority of the secular arm over the clergy, reserving to themselves and their own officers exclusive jurisdiction wherever ecclesiastical causes or persons were concerned. This doctrine rendered the law impotent against crimes, no matter how atrocious, when committed by a priest, and the most monstrous abuses were the consequence. In England, the prevalence of these led to the Constitutions of Clarendon in 1164, which the firmness of Henry II. forced upon the church, and thus laid the foundation of the mortal enmity which existed between that monarch and Thomas à Becket. The object of these Constitutions was to make the clergy amendable to the law, by providing that clerks accused of any crime should be tried in the King's courts; and that all suits and actions, concerning advowsons and presentations, should be determined according to the common law. They further enacted that the revenues of Episcopal sees should, during vacancies, belong to the Crown, and that every bishop elect should do homage to the Crown for his temporalities.

But the pretensions of the popes went much further than a claim to have cognizance in matters of a spiritual nature. Taking as their authority the text of Scripture "Know ye not that we shall judge angels? how much more things that pertain to this life?" they assumed a right to interfere in the temporal affairs of kingdoms to an extent which is scarcely credible. In the bull of excommunication against Henry IV., emperor of Germany, which Gregory VII. addressed to the prelates throughout Europe, he said, "Most holy fathers and princes, let the whole world understand and know that if ye have power on earth to bind and to loose, ye have power also on earth to take away from, or grant to any one, according to his deserts, empires, kingdoms, principalities, dukedoms, marquisates, earldoms, and in short the possessions of all men."

These extravagant claims of the Holy See terrified the laity, who, however, in that unlettered age, hardly knew how to defeat pretensions that were founded on the misapplication of Scripture, and urged with all the perverse ingenuity of canonists and casuists. At the time when they were asserted most confidently, the throne of France was occupied by Saint Louis, whose life shines like a star in the midst of a dark and vicious age. But the very excellence of his character constituted in this instance the danger. He was, as his name implies, eminently devout, and therefore trembled at the thought of opposition to the Roman Pontiff. But he was at the same time unwilling to surrender the independence of his crown, and the liberties of his kingdom to a foreign potentate; and he anxiously looked round for assistance. The great feudatories of France, with their armed retainers, were here powerless, for they could not contend in controversy with Italian clerks, and the question was to be decided by a war not of the sword, but of argument and opinion.

The clergy, as such, did not venture to come into conflict with their spiritual Head; nor did they care to contradict pretensions, which, though in some respects inconvenient to themselves, yet exalted the power and increased the authority of the church. But although it is true that in that age a large proportion of lawyers were also clerks, yet the habits of their profession rendered them far more fearless and independent than the cowled monks, or parochial clergy, who devoted themselves exclusively to the spiritual duties of their calling. And in this dilemma the council of the king turned to the advocates for help, and called upon them to rally round the throne, and refute the arguments by which the aggressions of the pope were supported.

They were not appealed to in vain. Nobly did they acquit themselves of the task, and in a vast number of writings which issued from their pens, they boldly grappled with the claims advanced by the Holy See, and demonstrated their fallacy. In many of their positions they seem to have anticipated the Reformation. They formally denied that Jesus Christ had constituted St. Peter his Vicar-General upon earth, so as to give him power to govern kingdoms, and dispose of crowns; or that any authority had been delegated to St. Peter different from or exceeding that of the other apostles. They asserted that Jesus Christ had given to his apostles the keys of the kingdom of heaven only, and not temporal jurisdiction. That the pope and the clergy had nothing to do with questions of peace or war; but must seek to influence princes and potentates by prayers, remonstrances, and exhortations. That the pope was not the bishop of the bishops, but that all were equally with him the vicars of Christ upon earth. That St. Peter had been nothing more than the head of the apostolic college, *primus inter pares*—as the dean is the head of a chapter; but his teaching was neither more pure nor of greater authority than that of St. John, St. Philip, or St. Bartholomew. They also firmly denied the right of the pope to interfere with appointments to spiritual benefices in the realm of France, and maintained that all ecclesiastical as well as lay possessions were liable to taxation for the common exigencies of the kingdom.

This spirited attack upon the ultramontane doctrines, which was led by the advocates, soon awakened the secular clergy also to resistance: and the consequence was, that the Church of Rome deemed it prudent not to attempt any longer at that time to enforce its arrogant pretensions in France. It fulminated no thunders against Saint Louis, but desisted for some years from its encroachments upon the authority of the crown in that kingdom. The pious monarch rejoiced in his peaceful triumph, and evinced the utmost gratitude towards that body of men to whom he was so much indebted for the result.

Soon afterwards, in 1268, was issued the royal ordinance, so well known under the name of the Pragmatic Sanction, whereby the king guaranteed the independence of all sees and spiritual benefices within the realm against interference on the part of Rome; and forbade any contributions to be raised or levied for the use of the papal See, without the express permission of the king, and the consent of the church in the kingdom. It concluded by approving and confirming in the fullest manner all " the liberties, franchises, immunities, prerogatives, rights, and privileges" of the Gallican church.

During the reign of Philip the Fair, in 1300, the Vatican made another attempt to subvert these liberties and rights, and Pope Boniface VIII. sent Bernard de Saisset, bishop of Pamiers, into France, to assert there the supremacy of the papal See over the Crown itself, under pain of excommunication and interdict. Philip, however, nothing daunted by the threat, ordered the arrest of the prelate; and Boniface immediately issued a series of bulls against the king, in which he declared that temporal sovereigns had no power over ecclesiastics, and prohibited the clergy from paying taxes or granting subsidies to the crown, without express permission from the Pope. One short missive, or "little bull" as it was called, was addressed personally to the king, and in was the following terms:—

"Boniface, Bishop, Servant of the servants of God, to Philip, king of the French:

"Fear the Lord, and keep his commandments. We wish you to know that you are subjected to us in spiritual and temporal things; that the collation to benefices and prebends does not belong to you in any manner; and that if you have the custody of livings while they are vacant, it is only to preserve the fruits for the future incumbents.

"If you have bestowed any benefices, we declare your collation to be null both in fact and law. We revoke everything of the kind that has taken place, and those who hold a contrary opinion are declared heretics."

Philip applied to his chancellor, Pierre Flotte, to compose an answer to this, and he devolved the task upon a young advocate, named Pierre de Cugnières, upon whose spirit and intelligence he knew he could rely. The reply was as laconic as the bull; and when we remember that it was written at the beginning of the fourteenth century, when the court of Rome was in the zenith of its power, we can not but admire the boldness and wit of the performance. It ran thus:—

"Philip, by the grace of God king of the French, to Boniface, pretended Pope, little or no greeting:

"Let your great Stupidity know (*sciat tua maxima Fatuitas*) that we are not subject to any one in temporal matters; that the collation to vacant benefices and sees belongs to us in right of our crown; that the revenues during each vacancy are ours; that the presentations which we have made, and shall make, are valid both for the past and the future; that we will support to the utmost of our power those whom we have presented, and whom we shall present, and that those who hold a contrary opinion shall be deemed fools and idiots."[1]

Other lawyers also came to the rescue, and one of them, Pierre du Bois, "*avocat du Roi à Coutances*," wrote what he called a *Consultation*, in which he fairly took the "bull" by the horns, and declared that the pope thereby had become, and ought to be reputed, a heretic, unless he publicly repented and gave satisfaction to the king for the affront which he had put upon him.

The reign of Philip the Fair presents the most important epoch in the history of the bar of France, for then, for the first time, the parliament became stationary at Paris. It is difficult to come to any accurate conclusion respecting the composition and functions of this body in very early times, but from the time of Pepin, in 757, the chief judicial tribunal in France seems to have been the *cour royale*, or assembly of the great barons of the kingdom, who sat in council with their sovereign. In it alone could the tenants *in capite*, who held directly from the crown, be tried, and it was used as a court of appeal from inferior jurisdictions. These latter were very numerous, and known by various names, such as *bailliages*, *sénéchaussées*, *vicomtés*, *prévotés*, *vigueries*, *grueries*, *chatellenies*, besides the ecclesiastical tribunals. The *cour royale* had no fixed place of meeting, but, like

---

[1] *Preuves des Libertés de l'Eglise Gallicaine,* p. 103, quoted by Fournel, tom. i. p. 132.

our own *aula regia*, the origin of the three common-law courts was ambulatory, and followed the sovereign wherever he happened to be at the time when it was summoned. Fournel says that special commissions were from time to time appointed, which were composed of members of the great council and dispatched into the provinces to hold a kind of assize court, entertain appeals, and reform abuses in the administration of justice. These he calls parliaments, but the name seems to have been unknown in France until the reign of St. Louis, and the first mention of it occurs in some letters patent re-establishing the *bailliage* of St. Jangon en Mâconnair, in 1258. The law that was administered consisted of the feudal, canon, and civil law, and in proportion as the two latter prevailed it became necessary to secure the assistance of the clergy, who alone, in those times, were competent to undertake the study of them. In fact, it may be said that the only lawyers in France, as elsewhere, were then the clergy, and the maxim of *nullus causidicus nisi clericus* might be applied with literal truth. Thus it was that *gens de loi* gained admission to the parliament, in order that they might explain the law and customs of the kingdom to the ignorant warriors who composed the court. But for some time they had no voice in the decisions of the tribunal, but sat merely as assessors, and were known by the name of *rapporteurs*, to distinguish them from the *conseillers jugeurs*. This distinction was, however, afterwards abolished in the reign of Philip of Valois, and the *gens de loi*, by a natural and obvious transition, assumed the place which had been occupied by the *gens d'épée;* for the feudal barons had little taste for the tedious technicalities of litigation, and as causes became more numerous and complicated, they gradually absented themselves from the court where the duties they had to perform were of such an irksome character, so that in process of time the learned clerks had to transact the whole of the judicial business. We shall see that they afterwards succeeded in placing themselves more upon a par with the proud chivalry which affected to despise them, by being admitted to the dignity of knighthood as *chevaliers es lois.*

Whatever may have been the origin of the term parliament, it was certainly applied to the sittings of the *cour royale* before the reign of Philip the Fair; and in the ordinance which he issued in 1302, and to which is attributed its stationary character for the future, he declared his will and pleasure that there should be two parliaments, *duo parliamenta*, held every year at Paris. These were to sit for two months at a time, and to be convened on the octaves of Easter and All Saints.

At each session the parliament consisted of four chambers; the principal of which was the chamber of pleas, known afterwards as the *grand' chambre.* Besides this, there were two chambers of inquiry, one *des enquetes*, and another of requests. The president of the *grand' chambre* was called the premier, and there were two others who supplied his place during any temporary absence, and who as well as himself were, in consequence of a peculiar kind of cap which they wore, known by the name of *présidents à mortier.* The three upper chambers had each a president, who was distinguished from those above mentioned, by being called *président* AU *parlement* instead of *président* DU *parlement.* The court of the *grand' chambre* consisted of two prelates, two peers, thirteen clerks, and the same number of laymen.

Not many years afterwards, in 1319, Philip issued an ordinance which declared that there should be no more prelates in parliament; and the reason assigned was, that their attention might not be withdrawn from the management of their spiritualities, and because the king wished to have in his parliament men who could sit there without interruption, and were not busied with other grave occupations. Bernardi says that this edict had no effect, on account of the necessity felt of having the aid of the superior intelligence of the clergy; but I apprehend that he is mistaken in supposing that it was intended to exclude them. The words used in the ordinance are, *il n'y aura nulz prélats au parlement*, and it might well be that the attendance of these high dignitaries of the church was dispensed with, while that of simple clerks was retained. Indeed, we know from an ordinance of the following year, 1320, that the latter still continued members of the court, for the number was then fixed at twenty, of whom eight were to be clerks, and twelve laymen.

The members of the parliament were called *conseillers*, and from very early times they attained the dignity by the election of the court, confirmed by the approval of the crown, being chosen chiefly, if not exclusively, out of the body of advocates, both lay and clerical, who practiced at the bar. We read in an ordinance of Charles VII., in 1446, *Pour ce qu'aulcunes desdictes ordonnances anciennes font mention d'eslire officiers conseillers en nostredictè court de parlement ès lieux et sieges d'icelle, quand ils vacqueront, ordonnons que pour mieux et plus seurement y pourvoir doresnavant . . . . l'election soit faicte par forme de scrutin en nostredicte court,* &c., and the chambers of the parliament were to select two or three persons, who were most fit and competent for the office when any vacancy occurred, and to certify to the sovereign which one of these they deemed best qualified to succeed, in order that he might appoint him in conformity with their choice, if he approved of it. *Afin que puissions avoir advis à pourveoir à icelui office, ainsi que verrons qu' à faire sera.*

Such is an outline of the origin and constitution of that parliament which afterwards attained such dignity and distinction, and of which King John, who was taken prisoner by Edward, the Black Prince, in one of his ordinances says, "It is the supreme and capital court of justice in France; it directs the administration of the law, and represents in the eyes of people the greatness of the royal majesty." And in another ordinance the same monarch directs, that the members of the high court of parliament should be taken as the guides and models of all other magistrates. The place of its sittings was the ancient palace of the Merovingian kings, so well known in later times as the Palais de Justice, which was given up to its use by Philip the Fair. There is a magnificent hall, richly gilt, and adorned with the fantastic forms of the arabesque style of architecture, upon which the rays of light fell softened through windows of colored glass, the high court of justice was held. Sometimes the king himself sat there on his royal couch, *lit royal*, surrounded on each side by the judges, *conseillers*, who sat upon an elevated bench covered with tapestry, on which were woven the lilies of France. Below this was another bench hung with the same kind of tapestry, which was reserved for the different officers of the court, and also as a seat of honor for the senior advocates, *anciens avocats*. In front were the benches which were occupied by the younger advocates, attorneys, and persons interested in the cause that was going on. The hall was filled with a numerous crowd, who delighted to listen to the eloquence of the bar;[1] and not unfrequently personages of the highest rank came from distant countries to Paris, merely to be present at the sittings of that august assembly, whose renown was spread throughout Europe; just as strangers flocked from all parts of Greece to hear Demosthenes. In the letters patent, dated the 16th of February, 1417, which Isabella,

---

[1] *Fournel*, tom. i. 263, mentions a circumstance of this kind in one of the tales of the thirteenth century, called "The Scarlet Mantle," when a Vavassour is represented as leaving his old castle and *his young wife* to go to Senlis, in order to listen to pleadings in court. The exact meaning of the term Vavassour has puzzled legal antiquaries. Chaucer says of his Frankelein,

"A shereve hadde he ben and a contour,
Was no wher swiche a worthy Vavassour."

the wife of the imbecile monarch Charles VI., issued for the purpose of creating a parliament at Troyes, in opposition to that which sat in Paris, then in the hands of her enemies, she thus speaks of the glory of the parliament in former times. " Then justice in full equity was promptly administered by the peers of France and royal councilors, appointed as members of the chief and sovereign court of the realm, rendering to each his own, exalting the good and punishing the bad according to their deserts, without sparing any;—of which the fame was so great and glorious throughout the whole world, that nations and provinces, as well those that bordered upon the kingdom as those that were far distant, oftentimes resorted thither, some to contemplate that administration of justice which they deemed rather a miracle than within the reach of human hopes; others to submit themselves to its decisions in order to have right done them, and an end put to their serious disputes and high quarrels, and there they found at all times equity, justice, and faithful judgment."

We have noticed that the proceedings of the parliament were sometimes graced by the presence of royalty. This was owing to a peculiar reason. Philip of Valois, in 1318, had issued an ordinance whereby it was provided that causes of a certain class and description should be pleaded before the king himself; and these were therefore entered upon the " king's list," *le role du roi*, and reserved until it suited his pleasure to attend. This, however, became the source of a great abuse, for men of influence and rank about the court, against whom actions were brought, no matter of what kind or for what amount, assumed the privilege of making them " remanets" for the king, and their example was soon followed by others in the most trumpery causes, so that the reserved list was crowded with entries, and fell so much into arrear as to amount almost to a denial of justice. To remedy this, Charles V., in 1370, addressed letters to the parliament, in which he pointed out the mischiefs that arose from the practice, and ordered the court, notwithstanding any royal mandates which had been obtained by suitors to the contrary, to proceed to try, and give judgment in, all causes where delay was neither reasonable nor just; and he announced that it was not his intention for the future to hear such trifling cases argued in his presence, or allow them to be reserved. It is doubtful whether the object of the ordinance of Philip was to assert the prerogative of the crown to decide as a judge upon causes heard in its presence, or merely to give more imposing effect to the proceedings. It has been thought not improbable that, in very early times in England, the king himself used to be present in court, and tried cases between party and party. Hawkins, in his Pleas of the Crown, says (book ii. ch. 1), "And it is said by Sir Edward Coke, that the king has committed and distributed all his power of judicature to several courts of justice; and though it may be argued, with the highest probability, both from the nature of the thing, and the constant tenor of our ancient records and histories since the conquest, and also from the form of all process in the King's Bench and Chancery, which is always made returnable before the king himself, that in old time our kings in person often determined causes between party and party, proper for those courts; yet at this day, by the long, constant, and uninterrupted usage of many ages, our kings seem to have delegated their whole judicial power to the judges of their several courts, which, by the same immemorial usage, have gained a known and stated jurisdiction, regulated by certain and established rules, which our kings themselves can not alter without an act of parliament.

"Yet it seems that the king himself can not sit in judgment upon any indictment, because he is one of the parties to the suit; and, therefore, where it is said in some of our ancient histories, that our kings have sometimes sat in person with the justices at the arraignment of great offenders, probably it ought not to be intended that they came as judges, but as spectators only, for the greater solemnity of the proceeding."

As a proof of the strict severity with which any malpractices on the part of the members of the court of parliament, in France, were punished, we read that in 1348 one of the judges, named Alain de Ourdery, *Chevalier Conseiller du Roy* was hanged by order of the parliament, for having falsified some depositions in a case which came before him. And another signal instance of the same impartial justice occurred in 1496, when Claude de Chamvreux, a clerk and councilor, was convicted of having made a false report regarding some matters which had been referred to him. An attempt was made by the Church to save her son, and the bishop of Paris claimed cognizance of the case. But the parliament stood firm, and refused to allow the guilty judge thus to escape. He was deprived of his office, and openly stripped of his scarlet gown and furred cap; and then, with naked feet and bare head, and holding in his hand a lighted torch, he fell upon his knees upon the floor, and begged aloud for mercy from God, and the king, and justice, and the parties whom he had injured. The report which he had falsified was then torn to pieces by an officer of the court; and the culprit was conducted to the quadrangle of the Palais de Justice, and, being consigned over to the public executioner, was forced to mount upon a cart, and conducted to the pillory, where he stood for three hours. He was afterwards branded on the forehead by a hot iron with a *fleur de lis*, and banished forever from the realm.

In this country, during the reign of Edward I., Sir Thomas Wayland, Chief Justice of the Common Pleas, was attainted of felony for taking bribes;—his lands and goods were forfeited, and he was banished the realm:

and in that of Edward III., Sir William Thorpe, Chief Justice of the King's Bench, having been convicted of receiving five bribes, which amounted to one hundred pounds, was sentenced to be hanged, and all his lands and goods were forfeited.[1]

We have so far considered the parliament as a court of justice, which was its peculiar and appropriate function; for if at any time it seemed to assume actively a political character, this was only on special occasions, when state questions were referred to it by the crown, that the king might have the benefit of its advice and support. It would be difficult to define its jurisdiction and office better than by quoting the words which De la Vacquerie, the chief president, addressed, in 1485, to the Duke of Orleans, who wished to make the parliament the instrument of his revolutionary views during the reign of Charles VIII. With lofty dignity the president repelled the seditious overtures of the prince. "As for the court of parliament," he said, "it has been constituted by the king for the administration of justice, and not for matters of war or finance, nor to deal with the acts and government of the king or great princes. And the members of the court of parliament are clerks and men of letters, whose office it is to bestow their time and attention upon judicial questions; and whenever it shall please the crown to command their services further, the court will obey, for it keeps its eye fixed upon the king alone, who is its head, and under whom it is; and, therefore, as to making remonstrances to the crown, or meddling with other business, without the good pleasure and express commandment of the king, it is a thing it ought not to do."

[1] The entry of the judgment against him in the roll gives the following reason for this severity. *Quia prædictus Willielmus Thorpe qui sacramentum domini regis erga populum suum habuit ad custodiendum, fregit malitiose, false et rebelliter, quantum in ipso fuit.* The last trial for judicial corruption was that of Lord Chancellor Macclesfield, in 1725, who was fined in the sum of £30,000, and ordered to be imprisoned in the Tower until it was paid.

We see here the distinction accurately drawn between what we may call the ordinary and extraordinary duties of the parliament. It sat in its permanent form as a court of justice; but the sovereign might refer to it matters of state policy, the consideration of which it could not refuse to entertain; and in this respect it acted as a sort of privy council.

But besides these rarer occasions on which it stepped beyond its legitimate province, the parliament had a political aspect in one very important part of its constitution. This consisted in its office of registering the edicts of the sovereign, without which they had not the force and validity of law. Before the reign of St. Louis, the royal ordinances were intrusted to the keeping of the chancellor, and were by him communicated to the bailiffs, seneschals, and provosts throughout the kingdom, who proclaimed them in their different courts, and in the market-places. That monarch was the first who sent his edicts to the parliament, and other inferior courts of judicature, in order that they might be registered in their records; and after the parliament became stationary at Paris, registration by it was necessary to give legal effect to the ordinances of the crown. And although French history furnishes us with few instances where registration was refused in opposition to the mandate of the sovereign, yet cases did occur which proved that it was no mere idle ceremony, but an integral and essential part of the legislative authority. Indeed, an ordinance of Charles V., in 1359, provides that the parliament was to pay no regard to any letters or orders from the king, if they were contrary to the fundamental laws of the realm. And the sanction of the parliament was thought to be a matter of so much importance by foreign states, that they frequently made it a condition that the treaties which they entered into with the crown of France should be registered by the parliament, in order that a kind of national recognition might be thus secured. At one very critical period the firmness of the parliament in refusing to register a royal edict, preserved the kingdom from humiliating subjection to the papal see. I allude to the attempt made by the Pope, in the reign of Louis XI., to procure the revocation of the Pragmatic Sanction, which was justly considered the charter of the liberties of the Gallican church. The king basely consented to betray those liberties, and in 1463 he issued an ordinance in which he styled the Pragmatic Sanction by the most opprobrious names, stating that it had its birth in times of sedition and schism, and he utterly revoked and annulled it. The parliament, however, refused to register this ordinance, and its resistance was supported by the public voice. The pope attached little value to the revocation, until it was formally registered, and a pressing deputation was sent from Rome to insist upon this being done. In the meantime, however, the king, seeing the temper of the nation, was not sorry to find an excuse for retracing his steps, and took no measures to overcome the obstinacy of the parliament. The consequence was, that the act of revocation became a dead letter, and the palladium of the Gallican church was preserved.

The refusal of the parliament of Paris to register an edict which imposed an additional duty on stamps, and another for a more equal imposition of the land-tax, may be said to have been one of the proximate causes of the first French Revolution. For, although these decrees were arbitrarily registered in a *lit de justice*, and the refractory parliament was exiled to Troyes, yet the dissatisfaction thereby occasioned made the demand for the convocation of the States General more imperious throughout the nation. It must, however, be mentioned that, in this instance, the parliament did not stand firm, but consented to a kind of compromise which the minister Brienne proposed, in order to get rid of the dilemma. The two edicts passed in the *lit de justice* were withdrawn, and that which imposed an equable land-tax was registered by the parliament without further. opposition.

Before quitting this part of the subject, it is right to notice that other parliaments were established as courts of justice, at various times, in different parts of the kingdom. This became necessary, in order to relieve the parliament of Paris from the great influx of appeals, and also to diminish the expense to suitors, who were often obliged to come from a great distance to the capital, to prosecute their suits. Such was the origin of the parliaments of Bordeaux for Aquitaine, Dijon for Burgundy, Rennes for Britanny, Rouen for Normandy, Toulouse for Languedoc, Pau for Bearn and Navarre, Aix for Provence, Dole for Franche-Comté, Grenoble for Dauphiny, and Metz for Lorraine. And it is important to notice that these were within their separate jurisdictions sovereign and independent courts, and no ordinance emanating from the crown had the force of law within a particular district, until it had been registered by *its* parliament; so, that sometimes, a single province was excepted from the operation of what was elsewhere the general law of the land. An instance of this occurred so late as 1747, when the parliament of Aix refused to register a royal edict relating to trust estates.

The storm of the Revolution swept away these ancient institutions; although, or perhaps because, they formed the surest guaranty for the preservation of rational liberty. Their requiem was sung by Burke in the following just and eloquent panegyric: " They composed permanent bodies politic, constituted to resist arbitrary innovation ; and from that corporate constitution, and from most of their forms, they were well calculated to afford both certainty and stability to the laws. They had been a safe asylum to secure these laws in all the revolutions of humor and opinion. They had saved that sacred deposit of the country during the reigns of arbitrary princes and the struggles of arbitrary factions. They kept alive the memory and record of the constitution. They were the great security to private property, which might be said (when personal liberty had no existence) to be in fact as well guarded in France as in any other country." [1]

The sale of judicial offices was introduced in the reign of Louis XII., but only two instances are recorded of its occurrence during the lifetime of that monarch. It was under his successor, Francis I., that the pernicious system came into full operation, and the opposition of the parliament was vain. A long prescription had established the right of advocates to be nominated to vacancies that happened in that body; but a distinction was now attempted to be drawn between a vacancy caused by a resignation of office into the hands of the king, and one occasioned by death, and it was contended that in the former case, the right of election (as previously explained) on the part of the parliament did not apply. The parliament was indignant at this encroachment upon its privileges, and, in 1521, it made an order that in future every one who was nominated by the king to the office of counselor should be minutely and strictly examined as to the mode in which he had obtained the appointment, and inquiry was to made into the truth of the facts connected with it. Shortly afterwards an opportunity occurred of testing the sincerity of these resolutions, for three appointments by the crown having taken place, the parliament discovered that the nominees had each paid a large sum of money for the place, and it refused to admit them as members of the court.

But the necessities of the king, lavish in expenditure,

---

[1] *Reflections on the French Rev.*, v. 367. "The lawyers in France have displayed more just and manly sentiments of government, and have made a nobler struggle against despotic power, than any set of men in the kingdom."—MOORE'S *Travels in France*, i. 102.

and addicted to pleasure, compelled him to persevere in this mode of replenishing his empty coffers; and during the reign of his son, Henry II., it became a common practice to dispose of judicial offices in the different parliaments of the kingdom to the highest bidder, for which purpose a *bureau* was opened, and a regular tariff of prices was established. This continued until the year 1771, when the system was put an end to by a royal edict, passed at the time when the parliament, so well known as the *parliament Maupeou*, was constituted.

It is needless to dwell upon the evils of such a practice. They are too obvious to require comment. " It has been strongly remarked, that there is no rule better established (it should be added, in law and reason, for unfortunately it is often otherwise in practice), respecting the disposition of every office in which the public are concerned, than this *Detur digniori*. On principles of public policy, no money consideration ought to influence the appointment of such offices. It was observed of old that the sale of offices accomplished the ruin of the Roman empire. *Nullâ aliâ re magis Romana Respublica interiit quam quod magistratus officia venalia erant.*" [1]

The virtuous Chancellor l'Hopital feelingly deplored the consequences of this system. " Associated," said he, "with a few upright men whom cruel death has spared, we support, as best we may, the ancient splendor of the magistracy. How its lustre is dimmed! How it is debased since access to it has been thrown open to all the world; and we have seen enter into it a crowd of young

---

[1] Story's *Equity Jurisprudence*, § 295. "Therefore, by the law of England (12 *Rich. II.* c. 2), it is further provided that no officer or minister of the king shall be ordained or made for any gift or brocage, favor or affection; nor that any which pursueth by him or any other, privily or openly, to be in any manner of office, shall be put in the same office, or in any other; but that all such officers shall be made of the best and most lawful men, and sufficient: a law worthy to be written in letters of gold, but more worthy to be put in due execution."—*Coke Litt.* 234 a.

men without talent and without industry, who are ignorant of the first elements of law, and whose title consists in the money they have paid! In the distribution of offices of trust, regard is no longer had to merit. Virtue is forced to give way to wealth, and yet it is when vices multiply, that virtue, in order to repress them, ought to be invested with power and authority."[1]

Louis Hutin asceded the throne in 1314, and reigned only eighteen months; but in that brief period he effected some judicial reforms, and to him has been attributed the origin of the *grands jours*, or assizes, which afterwards formed a not unimportant part of the system of judicature in France. For, in order to correct abuses in the administration of justice throughout the kingdom, he appointed a commission of inquiry, *commission inquisitoriale*, which was every three years to make a tour in the provinces, and was armed with full power to redress grievances and punish such members of the inferior courts as had been guilty of corruption or any other malversation of duty. But we have seen that commissions similar to these used to issue in still earlier times, when, as yet, the name of parliament was un-

---

[1] *Epistol.* i. p. 15. See Bernardi, *Histoire du Droit Public*, 451–457.

With reference to the sale of the judicial office in France, Alison, in his *History of Europe*, vol. i. p. 178, says, "Though the system may appear strange to English ideas, yet a little reflection must show, as Burke has observed, that it was admirably fitted both to confer independence and insure respectability." And he gives, as a reference, Burke's works, v. (vi. is printed by mistake) 367. But this remark is hardly borne out by the cautious language of the philosophic orator, who says, " They (the parliaments) possessed one fundamental excellence: they were independent. *The most doubtful circumstance attendant on their office, that of its being vendible*, contributed, however, to this independency of character. They held for life. Indeed, they may be said to have held by inheritance." On the other hand, it is well to bear in mind the warning which the premier, President Guillard, gave to Francis I. "Croyez que ceux qui auront si cher acheté la justice la vendront, et ne sera cautelle ni malice qu'ils ne trouvent."—MABLY, *Observ. sur l'Hist. de France*, tom. iii. p. 131.

known, and the *cour royale* or *conseil souverain* formed the supreme court of justice in the kingdom.

It has been mentioned that Saint Louis felt grateful to the advocates for the part they had taken in his struggle with the pope; and in the earliest French code that was ever framed,—his *Etablissements*, in 1270, *faits par grand conseil de sages hommes et de bons clercs*,—the object of which was to collect and systematize the scattered laws of the kingdom,[1] one chapter was devoted to a consideration of the rights and duties of that body. They were therein enjoined to present no cause to the court which was not just and loyal, and to practice courtesy and forbearance towards their opponents while refuting their arguments, without using words of contumely or abuse. They were also forbidden to make any bargains with their clients respecting their fees during the conduct of a cause,—*et il ne doit fere nul marché a celui pourqui il plaide, plet pendent.*

Saint Louis died in 1270, very soon after the compilation of this work, and he was succeeded by his son, Philip the Bold, who, in 1274, issued a royal ordinance which applied exclusively to advocates. By this they were obliged, under pain of being disbarred, to take an oath upon the Holy Gospels that they would, both in their oral pleadings and their opinions upon cases submitted to them, discharge their duty with care, diligence, and fidelity; and would support causes only so long as they believed them to be just, but abandon them when they discovered that they were not. The amount of their fees was to be regulated by the importance of the cause and the ability of the advocate (just as it is practically with us at present); but it was, in no case, to exceed thirty *livres tournois.*

[1] These *Etablissements* were divided into two books—the one containing 168 articles, and the other 40,—and consisted of portions of the Roman law, canons, councils, decretals, customs of the realm and Royal ordinances. They are collected in an immense work, called *Ordonnances du Louvre*. On the subject of the ordinances, see Bernardi, *Histoire du Droit*, 369.

It would be tedious and not very useful to follow in chronological order the numerous edicts issued by the French kings to regulate the conduct and practice of advocates. Their frequency proves the high importance attached to the due exercise of the duties of their office; and sometimes they speak in tones of grave reproach when they notice abuses that had crept in and called for reformation. I propose only to give a general view of their position in France during the middle ages, and a brief account of some of the peculiarities of customs and manners connected with the subject, in the time that intervened between the accession of St. Louis to the throne and the beginning of the seventeenth century, a period of more than 340 years. It is obvious that many changes must have taken place in that interval, and that what was true of a particular date might not apply to an epoch removed from it only a few years. But, separated as we are from those ages by so great a distance, it is not material that we should assign every peculiar usage to its precise year, especially as there prevailed throughout this period a general similarity of customs and habits, so that an anachronism is not likely to lead into any serious error.

When we speak of the *noblesse de la robe*, the term is not used in a figurative and merely complimentary sense, for the bar in France constituted a lesser order of nobility, and was recognized as such from the commencement of the fourteenth century. We have seen that, by the Roman law, advocates who had discharged the duties of their office with fidelity, were, after they had ceased to practice in the courts, deemed worthy of being held in special honor, and were numbered among the counts (*comites*), and most illustrious (*elarissimi*) of the empire. Before the reign of Philip the Bold, the only nobility in France consisted of the great feudal lords, who held fiefs directly from the crown, and it was said that these must have remained in the family for three generations before the tenant was ennobled. But in 1288 Philip the Bold granted letters patent of nobility to Raoul, goldsmith to the king, and this precedent was afterwards made use of as a mode of replenishing the royal exchequer, by the sale of *lettres d'anoblissment* to individuals; just as our own James I. compelled persons to be knighted, and created the order of the baronetage, for the sole purpose of filling his coffers. Philip the Fair seems to have been the first French monarch who bestowed knighthood upon some of the most distinguished advocates of his time. They were styled by various titles, such as *chevaliers ès loix, chevaliers de justice, chevaliers de lettres et de sciences*, and *chevaliers clercs*, and this, in all probability, suggested the idea of claiming for the whole body the honor of nobility; which, though an usurpation at first, was gradually acquiesced in as a right, and about the middle of the fourteenth century we find them in full possession of the privileges which belonged to an order of the noblesse. Bartolus, who was born in 1300, and died in 1350, and whose authority as a jurist was, for a long period unrivalled in Italy and France, where he was styled "the mirror and lamp of law," goes so far as to say,[1] that after ten years of practice in his profession, the *docteur en droit*, or advocate, became *ipso facto* a chevalier or knight.

But this seems to be a mistake, and the better opinion is, that at the end of that period the learned civilian was considered to be qualified to receive the honor of knighthood, which was bestowed upon him, if at all, by the sovereign in person, or by some ancient *chevalier ès*

---

[1] *Ad lib.* i. *Cod de professoribus.* Bartolus was also celebrated for his munificence;—and we are told of the gorgeous trappings of his horse, and his liberality in scattering money to the populace as he rode along the streets of Bologna. To this Bishop Hall alludes in the following lines from his *Virgidemiæ, or Satires:*—

"While father Bartoll on his foot cloth rode,
Upon high pavement gaily silver-strowed."

lois deputed for that purpose. The candidate for the honor thus addressed the king, or chevalier, from whose hands he was about to receive his spurs: " I pray thee, then, most excellent father, that thou wouldst cause me to wear first a sword, next a baldric, next golden spurs, and lastly a golden collar and a ring, which are all the insignia of a knight. And I declare that I may not use them in profane occupations, but in maintaining the rights of the church and the Christian faith, and in the service of learning in which I have been for a long time enrolled a soldier" (Fournel, *Histoire*, i. 274, 275).

About the same period it became usual to speak of the advocates who attended the court of parliament as an ORDER; a name which they retained until the Revolution of 1789.[1] Before any one was admitted as a member of it, or allowed to enroll his name upon the list, or *tableau*, which was kept by the parliament, he was formally presented by some advocate of long standing, as with us one of the benchers of the inns of court performs that office, and obliged to take an "oath of advocacy," *serment d'advocacerie*. But the court was expressly forbidden to administer this oath, unless it was satisfied by a previous examination, that the candidate for admission was competent to discharge the duties of the office, " in order that people might not be deceived and betrayed into placing their affairs in the hands of an advocate who could do nothing in a cause, being misled by the oath which he had taken in open court, and his seeming sufficiency." Nor even then was the admission

---

[1] Fournel notices the mistake of Voltaire in his *"Histoire du Parlement,"* where the latter says that advocates assumed the dignity of an order about the year 1730; and he shows that they had been already in possession of that style or title for 400 years previously.—Tom. i. 277, 278. Voltaire had a spite against the bar in consequence of a libel which appeared against him in 1739, which purported to be written by an *avocat*. He says, however, in a letter which he addressed to the *bâtonnier* of the order on the subject, that he repented every day of his life that he had not embraced that profession.—*Ib.*

complete. The candidate after taking this oath became an *avocat écoutant,* and entered upon a noviciate for several years of study and attendance on the court, before his name was actually inscribed upon the roll of advocates. He thus became a duly qualified member of the order, and subject to its rules and discipline. Among many other prohibitions, we find the following:—

1. He was not to undertake just and unjust causes alike without distinction, nor maintain such as he undertook, with trickery, fallacies, and misquotations of authorities.

2. He was not in his pleadings to indulge in abuse of the opposite party or his counsel.

3. He was not to compromise the interests of his clients, by absence from court when the cause in which he was retained was called on.

4. He was not to violate the respect due to the court, by either improper expressions, or unbecoming gestures.

5. He was not to exhibit a sordid avidity of gain, by putting too high a price upon his services.

6. He was not to make any bargain with his client for a share in the fruits of the judgment he might recover.

7. He was not to lead a dissipated life, or one contrary to the modesty and gravity of his calling.

8. He was not, under pain of being disbarred, to refuse his services to the indigent and oppressed.[1]

Throughout these rules we see that the analogy of the order of knighthood is preserved, and the last breathes

---

[1] These regulations, and many other curious particulars connected with this part of the subject, are to be found in a venerable work written in 1360, called *Somme rurale, au le grand Coutumier général de pratique, civil et canon,* by Jean Bouteiller, *conseiller en la cour de parlement.* The *Somme rurale,* however, was a misnomer, as the book had as little to do with agriculture as Miss Edgeworth's *Irish Bulls* with Hibernian cattle. It has been supposed that Bouteiller called his work *rurale* because he composed it during vacation time in the country, on the same principle that induced Horne Tooke to entitle his etymological work, *Diversions of Purley.*

the very spirit of chivalry. Purity of life and disinterested zeal in the cause of the poor and friendless were enjoined upon the chevalier and advocate alike; and doubtless the resemblance between the two professions, of which the latter was thus reminded, had a powerful effect in producing a tone of high-minded feeling which ought ever to be the characteristic of the bar. But sometimes this resemblance was carried further than was either safe or agreeable, and the advocate had to perform a warlike office, not in a figurative, but a literal sense. I allude to the appeal or wager of battel, whereby the sword was made the arbiter of disputes, and sanguinary duels were solemnly sanctioned by courts of law.

The prevalence of these judicial combats throughout Europe, forms one of the most remarkable features of the middle ages. It was a direct appeal to the God of battles, and the favorite ordeal by which his judgment was invoked. Meyer thinks that the origin of the custom may be traced to the ancient Germans, who, as Tacitus informs us, when they were at war with a neighboring tribe, made capture of one of the enemy, and compelled him to fight with a champion of their own, each being armed with his native weapons; and the issue of the contest was deemed prophetic of the result of the war. It was somewhat after this fashion that the contest between the Saxon and the Gael, as described in the "Lady of the Lake," was to be determined—

> Who spills the foremost foeman's life
> His party conquers in the strife."

But, however it may have arisen, it was a practice too well suited to the rude ignorance and chivalrous spirit of the middle ages not to find general acceptance. Even those who discerned the fallacy of such attempts to force, as it were, the Almighty to declare on which side the right lay, hardly ventured to discourage them, and Luitprand, king of the Lombards, in one of his edicts, while he disapproved of them, declared that he felt himself constrained to allow them: "We are uncertain," he says, " respecting the judgment of God, and we have heard that many by means of the combat lose their cause; but, on account of the custom of our nation of the Lombards, we can not abrogate the law itself." St. Louis, in his *Etablissements*, endeavored to limit the frequency of these duels, but they were retained in a variety of cases where written or oral evidence could not be supplied. The appeal to arms was open to all, and was resorted to in civil as well as in criminal trials. The weapons which might be used were regulated according to the rank and degree of the combatants. Thus the noble entered the lists on horseback with lance, sword, dagger, and shield; the squire fought on foot with only a sword and buckler; and the churls settled their legal differences with cudgels or knives. Those whose age, sex, or calling, such as infants, women, and ecclesiastics, prevented them from engaging in personal conflict, provided themselves with paid champions, who, besides the risk of being slain, had an additional motive for vanquishing their opponents, for if they were forced to yield, the penalty was the loss of a hand.[1]

Perhaps the two most remarkable instances of judicial combat upon record are the following, which took place in Spain in the eleventh century:—Alphonso, king of Leon and Castile, in the year 1038, meditated the introduction of the Roman law into his dominions; but being uncertain whether this or the customary law, which had hitherto prevailed, was the best, he appointed two champions to determine the question with their swords in actual conflict; and the result was that the

---

[1] Sometimes, however, the clergy did not consider themselves as protected "by their cloth." Thus we read that Austregisile, archbishop of Bourges, who was accused of fraud, obeyed the order of his sovereign to clear his character in the lists. Luckily for him the horse of his adversary fell and killed his rider.—MEYER, *Orig. Inst. Jud.* l. ii. c. 7.

chevalier who represented the civil law was beaten. During the reign of the same monarch, the question was agitated whether the Musarabic or Roman liturgy and ritual should be used in the Spanish churches; and the decision was referred, as in the former case, to the sword. Two knights in complete armor entered the lists, and John Ruys de Matanca, the champion of the Musarabic, *i. e.* Gothic, ritual was victorious. The queen and archbishop of Toledo, however, were dissatisfied with the result, and they had influence sufficient to have the matter submitted to a different kind of ordeal. A large fire was kindled, and a copy of each liturgy was thrown into it. The Musarabic (perhaps being bound in some species of asbestos) stood the test, and remained unscathed, while the rival volume perished in the flames. But it is not easy to convince an opponent in a theological controversy, and because it was discovered, or asserted, that the ashes of the latter had curled to the top of the flames and leaped out of them, the victory was claimed for the Roman ritual. The result was that both liturgies were sanctioned; but as the Roman was chiefly favored, it gradually superseded its competitor.

This barbarous usage continued until a comparatively late period, and even in the Papal States was only formally prohibited and abolished in the year 1505. The last judicial combat in France, was that between Jarnac and La Chatiegnerail, which was formally adjudged by the parliament of Paris to take place during the reign of Henry II. in the middle of the sixteenth century. To the disgrace of England the "wager of battle," as I shall have occasion in the next chapter more particularly to mention, might have been demanded in a court of law not more than thirty years ago.

The duty of the advocate in France, whose client wished to challenge his adversary, was to apply to the court for what may be called a rule *nisi*, and the counsel for the opposite party showed cause against it. The judges then determined whether the combat should be allowed or not. Beaumanoir, an old French author, who lived in the latter part of the thirteenth century, has left us a graphic account of the manner in which the proceedings took place; and it will be interesting to quote a few passages from his work.[1]

The counsel for the appellant, having *par les plus belles paroles et mieux ordonnées qu'il pouvoit*, stated the case of his client, called upon his opponent to confess or deny the charge against him; saying, that if it was denied, his client was ready to prove it by witnesses or otherwise. He then added, "but he will prove it in his own person, or by his champion, in the lists like a gentleman, on horseback, with arms and all other things suitable in wager of battle, and in such case in manner conformable to his rank, and here he offers his gage." At these words, like a fearless cavalier, he threw a glove down upon the floor. Upon this the counsel on the other side rose, and after having argued vigorously against the motion for a duel, he concluded by stoutly declaring that if the court should decide in favor of a single combat, "my client denies what is alleged against him; and says, on the contrary, that he who has authorized the charge to be brought forward, LIES, and this he is ready to maintain either in person or by champion, and thereto he pledges his gage."

The appellee then stepped forward himself, and, after a short address to the court, in which he said that the plaintiff lied like a villain, *sauf l'honneur de la cour*, and that he himself adopted all that his advocate had stated in his behalf, and was ready to fight if the court should so determine—he threw down his glove also beside the other.

But the learned counsel who thus acted as the chal-

[1] It is called *Le livre des Coutumes et Usages de Beauvoisins, selon ce que il corroit au temps que ce livre futs fait, c'est à savoir, l'An de l'Incarnation de notre Seigneur*, 1283.

lenger had need of his all acumen, while he offered the duello. For if, by unapt terms, he identified himself with his client, as is done in the present day, and did not make it sufficiently appear that he challenged in the name of another by procuration, the defendant might treat the appeal to arms as made by the advocate on his own account as well as by the client, and force the former to engage with him in single combat. We may well imagine how careful the gentlemen of the long robe were in the choice of their expressions with such a catastrophe before them, and how diligently they studied the law of principal and agent to see what words they ought to use to save themselves from personal liability.[1] This mischance had well nigh happened to Hugh de Fabrefort, one of the most celebrated advocates of the fourteenth century, who, when counsel for Armand de Montaign against Aymeric de Dunefort, incautiously declared that he would prove his assertion by his body on the field of battle, *sans dire expressement que la preuve s'en feroit par le combat de sa partie;* and, being taken at his word, he had great difficulty in escaping an encounter, which caused no little merriment to the audience.

But, *place aux Dames.*—A curious instance of a lady availing herself, in 1540, of the right to appear by champion in a "breach of promise of marriage" case, is mentioned in the memoirs of the Maréchal de Vielleville. The husband of Philippe de Montespedon having died in Piedmont without issue, she was left a young, rich,

[1] In our courts of law nice and difficult questions often arise as to whether an agent has, by the language of an instrument which he has signed, rendered himself personally liable. If the old French custom, as narrated in the text, existed among us, there is little doubt that no point of law would be more accurately known, or more familiar to counsel than this. The most amusing instance of identification with a client occurred in the case of a counsel for a female prisoner, who was convicted on a capital charge, and on her being asked what she had to say why sentence of death should not be passed upon her, he rose and said, "If you please, my lord, *we are with child.*" He was, however, wrong in point of law—for pregnancy is no plea in arrest of judgment, but only in stay of execution.

and beautiful widow, and was sought in marriage by several noble suitors. Among these was the Marquis de Saluces, to whose attentions she seemed to listen favorably, and she permitted him to accompany her from Turin to Paris. It turned out, however, that the sly dame merely wished to have the advantage of his escort on the journey; and when she arrived at its termination, she cavalierly dismissed him, saying, "Adieu, sir! your lodging is at the hostel des Ursins, and mine at the hostel Saint Denis, close to that of the Augustines." The marquis still persisted in his suit; but as Philippe continued obdurate, he asserted that she had made him a formal promise of marriage, and cited her to appear before the court of parliament. She came there, attended by a numerous company of friends, and having been desired by the president to hold up her hand, she was asked whether she had ever promised marriage to the marquis, who was then present in court. She answered upon her honor that she had not; and when the court proceeded to press her with further questions, she exclaimed with passionate warmth, "Gentlemen, I never was in a court of justice before; and this makes me fear that I may not answer properly. But to put a stop to all captious cavilling and word-catching, I swear in the face of this assembly to God and the king,—to God under pain of eternal damnation to my soul; and to the king under the penalty of loss of honor and life,— that I have never given pledge or promise of marriage to the Marquis de Saluces, and, what is more, that I never thought of such a thing in my life. And if there is any one who will assert the contrary, here is my chevalier whom I offer to maintain my words, which he knows are entirely true, and uttered by the lips of a lady of honor, if ever there was one. And this I do, trusting in God and my good right, that he will prove the plaintiff to be (begging the pardon of the court) a villainous liar."

This spirited defiance caused no little sensation in the audience; and the president told the registrar that he might put up his papers, for Madame la Maréchale had taken another and much shorter road towards settling the dispute. Then, addressing the marquis, he asked, " Well, sir, what say you to this challenge?" But the love, as well as the valor of the latter, was fast oozing away; and the craven knight answered by a very decided negative: " I want not," said he, " to take a wife by force; and if she does not wish to have me, I do not wish to have her." And so, making a low obeisance to the court, he prudently retired, and the fair Philippe heard no more of his pretensions to her hand.

Besides the *avocats écoutants*, or students, there were two other classes, called the *plaidants* and the *consultants*, the former consisting of those who pleaded in the courts, and the latter of members of older standing who had withdrawn from the strife of tongues, and employed themselves as chamber counsel in giving opinions.

With regard to the *plaidants* we are told by Beaumanoir that in his time their speeches possessed, at all events the rare merit of brevity. " 'Tis a good custom," he says, "which advocates have of compressing their pleadings into as few words as possible. For the memory of man easily retains a few words, which are much more agreeable to the judges who have to listen to them; and it is a great hindrance to judges to hear long speeches which have nothing to do with the question in dispute."[1] But a century later we find serious complaints made against them for tedious prolixity in the written papers used in a cause, and an ordinance of Charles VI., in 1413, animadverted strongly upon this abuse. It says that "advocates as well as attorneys in all the courts of the kingdom are accustomed to extort from our poor subjects too great fees and profits which they have not earned, in the matter of

[1] Cited by M. Berryer, in his *Modèles de l'Eloq. Judiciaire.*

written proceedings, which they make longer and more prolix than necessity requires, and we forbid the aforesaid advocates and attorneys, on the oaths they have sworn, and under pain of exemplary punishment, to take any other fees than such as are moderate, or to use prolixity in their writings; but they must make them as short as the case will allow. And, if it is found that they do the contrary, we strictly enjoin upon the members of our present and future parliaments, and upon all to whom it may appertain, to punish and correct the aforesaid persons rigorously, and in such a manner that it may serve as a warning to all others." A similar injunction is contained in a famous ordinance of Charles VII., in 1454, which was issued on the subject of "law reform," *sur la réformation de la justice*, and in which are found many interesting particulars connected with the constitution of the parliament and its duties, as well as regulations respecting the conduct of advocates. Several articles prohibit verbiage, and lengthy and tedious repetitions in the written papers of a cause, and then follows one directed specially against prolixity in the speeches of counsel, who are commanded, on the oaths they have taken, to be brief in their statements, and especially in cases of appeal. And it seems that, in their zeal for their respective clients, the advocates were too apt to forget good manners; for the ordinance goes on to notice, that " they are accustomed in their pleadings to use harsh and opprobrious language towards the opposite side, which serves no good purpose, but is a practice contrary to reason and all proper decency, to the great scandal of justice," and they are forbidden in future to engage in the unseemly strife of mutual abuse in any manner or degree, or to say anything which tends to vilify another, and is not necessary for establishing the facts of the cause in which they are engaged.

In earlier times it had been thought necessary to provide against a much more serious offense; for, in 1291, we find an ordinance which bids advocates beware of palming off falsely-cited customs upon the court. The temptation to do this arose from the infinite variety of local usages, which prevailed and had the force of law in the different provinces of France. When causes, therefore, were appealed, it became a matter of necessity to ascertain accurately what was the *lex loci* by which the particular case ought to be governed, and an opportunity was afforded to a dishonest counsel of misstating the custom for the purpose of getting judgment in his favor.[1] But, notwithstanding this, we know from various circumstances that the trust reposed in the honor and integrity of the law was great; and as an instance of this, it may be mentioned that, in the reign of Charles VI., when an action was brought by the prior of the church of Notre Dame des Champs against an advocate named M. Clement de Reillac, to recover some papers which had been intrusted to him, the simple assertion of the latter that he had restored them was held sufficient proof of the fact. This, however, may per-

[1] Caveant advocati ne circa consuetudines mendaces reperiantur. I hardly know whether the following can be considered as any very blameable instance of the citation of a "false custom." In the small town or village of Billi Billois, in France, one of the peasants married a woman, who greatly to his surprise and discomfort, presented him with a fine child at the end of four months after their wedding. He immediately went to consult a lawyer, who, however, had been apprised previously by the frail dame, or her gallant, of the intended application. When the good man came, the advocate took down from his shelves a venerable-looking folio, and after carefully turning over the leaves, read with great gravity the following lines:—

"Dans le Billi Billois,
Une femme, au bout de quatre mois,
Accouche pour la première fois."

"In the town of Billi Billois, 'tis said,
When fully four months are gone and sped,
A new-married wife is brought to bed."

"Oh!" said the husband, "it's the custom of the place, is it? that makes all the difference"—and he went home contentedly to his wife.

haps not have been in reality so great a departure from the ordinary rules of evidence as at first sight it appears; for in some cases a party accused of a crime was allowed to deny the charge upon oath, and if he was confirmed by others who swore that they believed in his veracity, he was acquitted. The number of these *conjurateurs* or *compurgateurs*, as they were called, varied according to the nature of the offense, but usually they were not less than three, and sometimes even sixty were required. This explains the old forms of expression,—*jurer de la tierce main, de la cinquième main, de la dixième main,* &c. Our own law in former times afforded an exact parallel to this in civil cases; for until a comparatively recent period, a defendant in an action of debt, or detinue, or account, was permitted to "wage his law," that is, deny upon oath that he owed the money, or detained the goods; and if a sufficient number of compurgators could be found who would swear that they believed in their consciences that he spoke the truth, he defeated the plaintiff's claim. The number required was at least eleven, and they were said to be sworn *de credulitate*, as he himself was *de fidelitate*.[1]

When the Papal see was transferred to Avignon, in the reign of Philip the Fair, many of the Italian jurists accompanied the court, and established themselves there. Being in point of learning and legal dexterity superior to the French lawyers of that period, the latter were not unwilling to adopt them as guides and authorities for the forms of judicial procedure and practice; and a variety of treatises were written on those subjects, which show how entirely the profession of the law was at that time in the hands of ecclesiastics. Instruction was conveyed under the form of trials, in which the different parties were characters taken from the Bible. the most holy names were introduced as those of plaintiffs and defendants; and Moses, Abraham, Isaac, Jacob,

[1] See a full account of this in *Blackstone's Comm.*, iii. 341-348.

Solomon, Isaiah, Jeremiah, St. John the Baptist, the Virgin Mary, and many others, figured as advocates, witnesses, and officers of the court. To give an idea of the style and titles of these ancient "text books," I will mention two that appeared in the fourteenth century; one of which, attributed to the famous Bartolus, was called *Processus Satanæ contra D. Virginem coram judice Jesu;* and the other, *Processus Luciferi contra Jesum coram judice Salomone,* which was written by Jacques Palladino, better known as Teramo, the name of the town where he was born.

These remind us of Bishop Sherlock's *Trial of the Witnesses,* where the credibility of the account of our Saviour's resurrection is submitted to a jury, and the arguments on both sides are presented under the form of speeches of counsel engaged in a trial for perjury. The following is the conclusion of this curious specimen of episcopal reasoning:—

"*Judge.*—What say you? Are the Apostles guilty of giving false evidence in the case of the resurrection of Jesus, or not guilty?

"*Foreman.*—Not guilty.

"*Judge.*—Very well; and now, gentlemen, I resign my commission, and am your humble servant." The company then rose up, and were beginning to pay their compliments to the judge and the counsel, but were interrupted by a gentleman who went up to the judge and offered him a fee. "What is this?" says the Judge. "A fee, sir," said the gentleman. "A fee to a judge is a bribe," said the Judge. "True, sir," said the gentleman; "but you have resigned your commission, and will not be the first judge who has come from the bench to the bar without any diminution of honor.[1] Now,

---

[1] This is correctly stated by the bishop, for in old times, in England, it was not an unfrequent custom for men, who had sat as judges, when arbitrarily deprived of their office by the king, to practice again as advocates in the court over which they had presided.

Lazarus's case is to come on next, and this fee is to retain you on his side."

Nor was the fondness for the form of imaginary trials confined merely to authors who were anxious to convey under that guise legal information. It assumed sometimes a practical shape, and we read of cases where animals were tried and convicted in due form of law. Thus, in 1314, a bull, having killed a man by tossing him with his horns, was brought before the judges in the province of Valois, and indicted as a criminal, and after several witnesses had given evidence, it was condemned to be hanged. This sentence was confirmed by an order of the parliament and carried into effect. And we are told that an unfortunate pig, which chanced to kill a child in Burgundy, was in like manner solemnly tried in court, and suffered the same punishment.[1]

Owing also to a laudable desire to make the study of the law more palatable to the public, and to entice them to acquire some knowledge of its principles and the forms of legal procedure, attractive titles were given to books which treated of such dry subjects. Thus, about the year 1500, a work was published which was likely to arrest the attention of the gay gallants of the age. It was written by Martial d'Auvergne, and called "Declarations, Proceedings, and Decrees of Love, pronounced in the Court and at the Bar of Cupid, in the case of different Disputes heard before that Magistrate." When opened, it proved to be a very learned treatise upon law, but applied to fictitious amusing cases, as the following headings of some of the "decrees" sufficiently indicate :—

---

[1] *Fournel*, t. i. 119, 289. By the old law of France, if a vicious animal killed a person, and it was proved that its owner knew of its propensity to attack people, and suffered it to go at large, he was hanged, and the animal also. This was making a more formidable use of the *scienter* than is known to the English law. I think I have read somewhere of a trial in this country, where the dog of a sheep-stealer was sentenced to be hanged as well as its master.

5th. Process between two lovers wooing the same lady.

18th. Concerning a kiss taken by force by a lover, against which the lady appealed.

20th. An action brought by a lover against his mistress, to compel her to take down a cage containing a quail, which kept up a continual noise whenever it saw him at the door of the lady.

It is curious and not uninstructive, as illustrating the manners of the age, to see how carefully effect both of person and manner in advocates was studied in those days. In the *Stylus Parlamenti*, which has been already mentioned, there is a chapter *De modo, gestu et habitu quem habere debet advocatus curiæ parlamenti;* and some of the rules must, I fear, have borne hard upon not a few of the practitioners. An advocate was required to be of an imposing presence and a well-proportioned figure, so as to make a favorable impression upon the court and the audience. He was to have an open, cheerful, and smiling countenance, which would be of itself a letter of recommendation. He was to avoid all appearance of assurance or presumption, and, on the contrary, conciliate good will by a modest and unassuming demeanor. His attitude, when addressing the judges, was to be respectful, and his costume ought to display neither dandyism nor negligence. While speaking, he was neither to twist nor bite his lips. His voice was not to be too loud, nor was he, on the other hand, to mumble his words. His action, while speaking, was to be appropriate to his subject, and the motion of his limbs was to be duly regulated. Excellent rules, but very unnecessary;—for we may be tolerably sure that they had little or no influence upon those for whose benefit they were designed. No man can be tutored into grace. The debonair advocate owed his advantages of face and form to nature, and laughed at the idea of acquiring them by art; and the awkward and the ugly are destined to be so from their birth, in spite of all that study and practice can accomplish.

Those who wish to glean some knowledge of the advocates who flourished in France in the earliest periods of which any notice has come down to us, may consult the *Dialogue des Avocats*, written by Loisel, himself a distinguished lawyer, soon after the disturbance which the attempt to enforce the ordinance of Blois, in 1602, (of which we shall have occasion hereafter to speak) had occasioned among the Parisian advocates. But there is not much to interest the general reader in his quaint narrative. A crowd of names is placed before us, and the notices of each are chiefly confined to an account of the qualities for which they were distinguished in their profession. It would be to little purpose to attempt to arrest the attention of the present generation by the names of Jean Filleal, Jean de Rumilly, Gilles de Noir, Roual d'Ulmones, Jean le Coq dit Galli, Jean de Neuilly, Roual d'Amiens, Denys de Mauray, Pierre l'Orfèvre, Jean Conard, Jean Perrier, Roual Pimont, Martin Doublé, Oudard Bertine, and Jean de la Rivière, " tous fameux avocats de leur temps;" or to enumerate the various excellencies of the contemporaries of Pasquier and Pithou, to whom Loisel in his Dialogue, like Cicero in his Brutus, has paid the tribute of affectionate remembrance. Let us, however, make honorable mention of Matthieu Chartrier, who put into the poor-box every month 100 francs out of the fees that he received; and Guy Coquille, Sieur de Romenay, who gave in charity a tithe of his professional income, *décimoit son gain mis en bourse pour les pauvres honteux;* and Manquin, who bestowed upon the poor the fees he gained upon Saints' days and Sundays.

The speeches of the advocates of the sixteenth, and the early part of the seventeenth century in France, are generally disfigured by an inordinate display of classical learning, and are often in many parts mere centos of quotations from Greek and Latin authors. M. Berryer says that they exhibit " an amalgam of paganism and Christianity, where Jupiter, Minerva, and all the fabled gods of antiquity are found by the side of our Saviour and the saints: a luxuriant profusion of undigested knowledge which borrows from all ages since the creation of the world :—a rage for historical allusions which confounds in the same page the names of persons the most opposite, who are amazed to find themselves in company together. You meet in the same passage with Ammian Marcellinus, Homer, Plutarch, and St. Chrysostom, Darius and Charlemagne ; by and by, a few Hebrew words, then verses in Greek, Latin, and French, and all with reference perhaps to a suit for a divorce by a husband against his wife " (*Mod. d'El. Jud.*)

The truth is, that when, after the siege and capture of Constantinople by the Turks, in the middle of the fifteenth century, the remains of the classic writers had been scattered over Western Europe, and these had not long afterwards become, by means of printing, accessible to the public, they were read with a zeal and avidity of which we can hardly at the present day form a conception. The minds of men had been so long starved upon the dry husks of the schoolmen and their barren subtleties, that when the rich banquet of ancient learning was placed within their reach, they devoured it with famished appetites ;—

"Greedily they ingorged without restraint,"

devoting day and night to the study of the Greek and Latin writers, and by this means that ponderous erudition was acquired which makes us think with wonder upon the names of Casaubon, Scaliger, Gronovius, Salmasius, and Magliabecchi. Hence it is that the writings of this period present such a strange array of far-fetched allusions and learned quotations ; and the speeches of the French advocates were in this respect quite in accordance with the taste and fashion of the time. Their fondness for the display of multifarious learning is amusingly satirized by Racine in his comedy of *Les Plaideurs*, where Petit Jean and L'Intimé appear as advocates for and against the canine prisoner who is accused of having stolen and devoured a capon. This is the commencement of Petit Jean's speech for the prosecution:

>Messieurs, quand je regarde avec exactitude
>L'inconstance du monde et sa vicissitude ;
>Lorsque je vois parmi tant d'hommes différents,
>Pas une étoile fixe, et tant d'astres errants,
>Quand je vois les Césars, quand je vois leur fortune ;
>Quand je vois le soleil, et quand je vois la lune ;
>Quand je vois les états des Babiboniens
>Transférés des serpens aux Nacédoniens ;
>Quand je vois les Lorrians, de l'état dépotique,
>Passer au démocrite, et puis au monarchique ;
>Quand je vois le Japon . . . . .

But he is surpassed by the counsel for the defense.

>*L'Intimé.*
>   Avant la naissance du monde—
>
>*Dandin.*
>
>Avocat, ah ! passons au déluge.
>
>   *L'Intimé.*
>   Avant donc,
>La naissance du monde, et sa création,
>Le monde, l'univers tout, la nature entière
>Etait ensevelie au fond de la matière,
>Les éléments, le feu, l'air, et la terre, et l'eau,
>Enfoncés, entassés, ne faisaient qu'un monceau,
>Une confusion, une masse sans forme,
>Un désordre, un chaos, une cohue énorme
>Unus erat toto naturæ vultus in orbe,
>Quem Græci dixere Chaos, rudis indigestaque moles.[1]

[1] Martial ridicules the same practice in a Roman lawyer, named **Postumus**, the cause of action being "trover," for the "conversion" of **three kids**.

>   Tu Cannas, Mithridaticumque bellum,
>   Et perjuria Punici furoris,
>   Et Sullas, Mariosque, Muciosque
>   Magnâ voce sonas, manuque totâ.—
>   Jam dic, Postume, de tribus capellis.

As an example of the mode in which they availed themselves of classical illustration, let us take the commencement of a speech delivered by Anne Robert,[1] in the year 1599, as counsel for Henri Bellenger and his wife, who having been falsely charged with the crime of murder, and put to the torture, sought to recover damages against their accuser. "The ancient poets, gentlemen, having discoursed of several combats which took place at the memorable siege of Troy, narrate that Telephus, the son of Hercules, having in an encounter with Achilles been grievously wounded by his lance, and seeing that the pain of his wound increased, for which he could find no remedy, went to consult the oracle of Apollo, which answered that nothing could cure or relieve him except the same spear of Achilles, by which he had been wounded:—that spear, called Pelios from Mount Pelion, from the top of which Chiron had taken it to give it to Achilles." He then shows that in like manner his clients looked for redress from that tribunal which had previously condemned them.

But now and then the genius of eloquence burst the bonds of pedantry, and we meet with passages in the speeches of counsel for their clients, which have all the fire and spirit of the ancient orators, and are disencumbered of the load of learning which generally oppresses them. Such was the address of Févret to the parliament of Dijon on a remarkable occasion.

One morning, in the spring of the year 1625, a soldier observed a crow attempting to drag a small bundle of linen away from the foot of a wall which was close to the residence of the parents of a young girl named

[1] The reader must not suppose that *ladies* were in those days members of the French bar. The name of "Anne" in France is not exclusively appropriated to the fair sex. And in this country, when Queen Anne stood godmother to the third son of the Duke of Hamilton, she gave him her own name without any addition, and Lord *Anne* Hamilton afterwards obtained a commission in the Guards. Anne, Duke de Montmorenci, is another instance of this feminine appellation.

Helen Gillet. He went up and found that it contained the body of a new-born infant, and the linen was marked with the initials H. G. This directed suspicion upon Helen, who was tried on the charge of murder; and although the evidence was very vague and unsatisfactory, she was condemned to death by the parliament of Dijon.

The execution was ordered to take place on the 13th of May, 1625—the day before the marriage was celebrated between Charles I. of England and Henrietta Maria of France. We are told that on the appointed morning the executioner confessed himself and received the sacrament, and that when he arrived at the scaffold he exhibited the most lively signs of intense mental anguish. He wrung his hands and raised them to heaven —and falling on his knees, prayed for pardon from the culprit, and begged the blessings of the assistant priests. He cried out that he wished he were in the place of her who was about to receive from him the mortal stroke. At last, when the head of the miserable girl was laid upon the block, he raised the axe, but, missing his blow, only wounded her left shoulder. The force of the stroke was such that she fell at full length on the floor of the scaffold. The headsman, horror-stricken himself, called aloud to the populace to kill him, and stones were thrown at him from all sides. His wife, however, who was by his side, darted forward, and seizing Helen, placed her head once more upon the block, and the executioner struck again, but again missed his blow. The rage of the multitude now knew no bounds, and the executioner in terror fled for safety to a small chapel which stood near the foot of the scaffold. His wife then snatched a cord, and twisting it round the neck of the prisoner tried to strangle her; but volleys of stones flew from the crowd, and the female fiend drew out a pair of long, sharp scissors, with which she stabbed her victim in the face and neck, and different parts of the body, and would soon have dispatched her had not the populace rushed upon the scaffold, and in a transport of rage killed both her and her husband upon the spot. Helen Gillet was immediately taken to a surgeon, and he succeeded in restoring her to life and consciousness, The inhabitants of Dijon then presented a petition to the king, and prayed him to grant her his royal pardon. The prayer was successful, and it was on the occasion of presenting for registration the instrument which annulled the conviction, that Févret made such an eloquent appeal to the court which had formally pronounced the sentence of condemnation. We can, however, afford space for only a few passages.

"The unhappy girl who now presents herself before you is amazed to find herself alive. Her eyes, confounded by the remembrance of events which appear to her like a dream, wander restlessly over the assembly gathered in this hall, from which she went forth to ascend the scaffold which never yields back its victims. But by God's special grace she has been restored :—a marvelous resurrection brings her again before you, and she comes to supplicate your compassion, and entreat you not to be more cruel to her than that death which has spared her.

"She never beheld Justice except when clothed in the garb of severe majesty. She never looked upon her face except when it frowned in anger. She never saw her except when armed with the sword with which she strikes. But to-day, O blessed change! all is different. She see that hand disarmed, and those arms stretched out towards her to offer succor and protection to the criminal, become a suppliant. You behold a few days ago this poor girl with her face covered with shame, and her spirit bowed beneath the misery of her hapless doom, walk with firm step to meet death in order to appease offended justice. Now she throws herself prostrate at your feet, and humbles herself before that sword which, like the point of the lance of old, can heal the wounds which it has made. Here is an instance of escape from death more marvelous than any. Here the sword has struck, the cord has done its office, the point of the scissors has pierced; and yet, in spite of her tender years, the weakness of her sex,—in the midst of the horrors of an execution, in the dreadful terrors of death, gashed with ten gaping wounds, this young female was unable to die. What am I saying? She wished to die, but death has been deaf to her voice. What an astounding fact, that a feeble child should have wrestled in close embrace with that mighty giant on the field of his triumphs, in the place of his most bloody deeds, armed only with the trust which she had in God! She has been victorious over shame and fear, the headsman, the sword, the cord, the dagger, and death!"

As a curious specimen of the twilight state of intelligence in the human mind at that period in France, let us take one of the pleadings of Julien Peleus, who, under the reigns of Henry III. and Henry IV. gained the highest reputation as a learned lawyer, and was a great favorite with both those monarchs. But he did not confine himself to black-letter lore; he wrote history, and even attempted poetry. As is always the case with eminent men, he did not escape the attacks of the envious and the malevolent; but he cared little for their spite, and in the preface to one of his works he thus vigorously throws down the gauntlet of defiance. "I protest before heaven and earth, that the sneers, the gibes, and the calumnies of those malignant creatures are my titles of honor, and I am content to believe that my labors are not useless, since that brood of vipers is so envenomed with lies against me." The cause to which I allude was certainly a grave one; and in a form somewhat more suited to the genius of the present age, it has been the subject of a solemn decision in the Courts of Westminster. The question was, whether a tenant was justified in quitting a house and rescinding the contract of letting, on the ground that it is haunted by evil spirits.¹ Jean la Tapy had hired a house at Bordeaux from Robert de Vigne, but after inhabiting it for a short time, he found, like John Wesley, that he had evil spirits for his fellow-lodgers. They appeared sometimes in the shape of infants, sometimes in horrible forms, and terrified the inmates,—displacing the furniture, rattling and making all kinds of uncouth noises in the rooms, and tumbling the family topsy-turvy out of their beds. This was not to be endured, and Jean having quitted the premises in a fright, brought an action against his landlord to have the contract rescinded (we should say, filed a bill to have the lease delivered up to be canceled), and to recover the rent which he had already paid in advance. The trial took place before the seneschal of Guyenne, and judgment was given against the defendant, who then appealed to the parliament of Bordeaux. Here Peleus was counsel for the appelant, and his argument presents an amusing mixture of pedantry, credulity and good sense. The following are a few extracts:—He begins by a general denial, and contends

---

¹ I refer to the case of Smith v. Marrable, 11 *Mees. & W.* 5, which was an action of *assumpsit* for use and occupation;—plea, *non-assumpsit*. The plaintiff had let a furnished house to the defendant for a few weeks; but on the day after taking possession with his family, they found that it was invested with nocturnal dæmons—*Anglicé*, bugs. They accordingly quitted it before the expiration of the first week, and the action was brought to recover the rent that was claimed for the whole time agreed upon. Lord Abinger, Chief Baron, in summing up the case to the jury, told them that if they believed the defendant left the plaintiff's house on account of the nuisance occasioned by the vermin being so intolerable as to render it impossible that he could live in it with any reasonable comfort, they ought to find a verdict for the defendant. The jury did so, and a new trial was moved for on the ground of misdirection; but the court upheld the ruling of Lord Abinger. The doctrine, however, laid down in this case, must be received with great caution, as the reader may satisfy himself if he will consult the subsequent cases of Sutton v. Temple, 12 *Mees. & W.* 52; Hart v. Windsor, *Id.* 68; Surplice v. Farnsworth, 7 *Mann & Gr.* 576. It was an important ingredient in Smith v. Marrable that the contract of letting there was for a *ready-furnished* house, though this distinction may not appear obvious to those who are not lawyers.

that, according to the opinion of some philosophers, such apparitions were nothing more than the good or evil desires of the soul, suggesting good or evil thoughts. "Nor is it any objection," he says, "to this theory, that they appear to us in our dreams in different shapes, and throw us into such affright as to deprive us of our breath, and take away the power of speech, of which we have, no doubt, sufficient experience; for these illusions so deceive us that we seem to see what we do not see, and hear what we do not hear. In short, the philosophers say that they are all a vain imagination, proceeding from a superfluity of humors and fullness of blood, which collect round the heart and oppress the stomach. But to go deeper into the matter, and admitting the existence of these spirits—they must be either good or evil. If good, the tenant has no reason to complain, but ought rather to esteem himself fortunate in having met with a house which angels have chosen for their habitation. But if evil, and as formidable as the respondent alleges, that is no legitimate ground for abandoning the premises. If that were so, the regions of the north would be depopulated, considering the numbers of specters which are said to be there. But, in fact, the tenant criminates himself, and proves that he is deficient both in faith and courage, since these spirits always avoid those houses which are inhabited by brave men, and attack only cowards. The virtuous man, firm and intrepid, so far from being disturbed by such a trifle, would not, even *si fractus illabatur orbis* — if the world were in ruins around him, be moved from his serenity."

Peleus then cites a crowd of examples, drawn from Greek and Roman history, to prove that courage and virtue have at all times sufficed to put to flight apparitions of this nature. He next shows that we may fairly believe that, since the advent of our Saviour, they no longer frequent the houses of Christians, but are banished to remote deserts, to await the end of all things; and he then reverts to the idea that we ought rather to refer such visions to some internal cause connected with bodily derangement, since those are chiefly troubled with them who are most full of food and wine, and suffer from indigestion and crudity of stomach. Thus the ancient bacchantes and priestesses of Cybele fancied that they were inspired by divinity, when, in reality, they were only tipsy with the fumes of wine. That our senses deceive us may be proved by many instances. Thus apples look larger when plunged in water—towers which are square look round at a distance; and why may we not believe that the ears of the respondent, who heard such strange noises and sounds all over the house, were imperfect, having the passages too narrow, or, perhaps, altogether closed by some catarrhic humor or affection? This is said to have happened to a philosopher, who had such a singing in his ears that he fancied he always heard instruments of music, and used to dance to the sound, and measure his steps in tune.

Hitherto Peleus has been, as it were, traversing the fact; he now begins in the language of pleading to confess and avoid. Whatever be the nature of the spirits that haunt the house, the tenant ought first to have applied all the remedies in his power, before, by quitting the premises, he gave them a bad name. "God and nature have given us plenty of means to get rid of such intruders. Why did he not use laurel, or rue, or salt thrown upon charcoal, or lapwing feathers, or that excellent mixture of the herb *areolus vetulus* with rhubarb and white wine? Why did he not hang up before his front door leather made from hyena skin; or the gall of a dog, which is held to be of such marvelous efficacy in driving away demons?

"Or if these remedies were not at hand, or disliked by him, why did he not apply to his bishop or his priest.

APPARITIONS.

who have others of sovereign virtue, such as adjurations, purifications, exorcisms, consecrated oil, incense, and holy water? St. Chrysostom holds that devils can not infest a room where there is a volume of the Scriptures. If then such remedies might be had, the tenant ought to have remained. Hercules, after a long struggle, rendered Nereus and Proteus obedient to his will. All actions are measured by the result. If the heel of Achilles (that is to say his constancy and firmness) had not been vulnerable, he would have been immortal!"

"Wherefore," says the wily advocate at the close of his speech, "I conclude that these spirits or dæmons have no bodily existence, and that at all events they are not of sufficient importance to justify the breaking of a contract agreed upon between the parties. ' The old jurists seem to have settled this question, since they have nowhere (in treating of the relations of landlord and tenant) made mention of such spirits or apparitions, though in their time they were more common than at present. And even if the fact be as alleged by the respondent, he might have been delivered from the annoyance by the use of the numerous remedies which nature and mother Church supply, if he had exerted proper diligence:—and therefore, since the tenant convicts himself of a distempered brain, of cowardice, impiety, and neglect of his proper duties, the appellant prays the court to amend the judgment of the seneschal, and declare it to be erroneous, and decree the appeal, and condemn the respondent to pay the penalties contained in the lease."

An order of the court was thereupon made on the 21st of March, 1595, by M. de Nesmond, second president of the parliament of Bordeaux, in the name of himself and colleagues, all dressed in their scarlet robes (*en robbes rouges*), and by it they deputed commissioners to inspect the premises and adjoining houses, in order that they might have ocular evidence as to the fact of the apparitions. The result was that a new trial was granted, "because the doubt was founded on the question of the apparition of spirits and dæmons; and it became necessary to discuss it more at length, and bring forward all the reasons that might be alleged as well on the one side as on the other, in order to make the truth appear (*donner le jour à la vérité*)."

The names of the most distinguised advocates in France who flourished in the sixteenth century are those of Lemaitre, Marillac, Chartrier, Brulant, Riant, Rebours, and Boulas; and still more celebrated are those of Séguier and De Thou, the two most eloquent speakers of their day, and l'Hopital, chancellor of France, and Pibrac, his son-in-law, a man of powerful intelligence and vast erudition; and Brisson, president of the parliament of Paris, of whom Henry III. said that no king but himself could boast of so learned a subject, and who met with so tragical a fate, being hanged by the assassins of the League to a beam of the council chamber in the Palais de Justice; and Pithou, the accomplished scholar and divine, De Montholon, De Lizet, Poyet, and Pasquier. How few of even these names awaken any echo in the minds of the present generation! Like the grass, so have they withered. Yet they were men of mark and likelihood in their time;—"famous men—men of renown."

Pasquier, however, demands a brief notice, of whom Southey says that he was "one of the most celebrated advocates, most accomplished scholars, and most learned men of France." He was born at Paris, in 1529, and was called to the bar at the age of twenty. He mentions with pride and pleasure that he attended the first lecture, which the great jurist, Cujas, delivered at the Institute in Toulouse, and he became one of his most diligent pupils. After having practiced at the bar for some time with indifferent success, a severe illness prevented him from following his profession for nearly two years, which he passed in the country. When he returned to Paris to resume his avocations, he says, "I found myself such a stranger, that hardly an attorney recognized me. The little root that I had previously taken was quite withered and dead. I saw several advocates of my own standing getting on before me, though I had previously shot ahead of them. I walked for two months up and down the hall of the Court without having anything to do; and, believe me, it was a heartbreaking business; so that, in disgust, I almost determined to quit the profession altogether." It is amusing for us in the present day, when years must be spent in briefless expectation, to read of Pasquier's patience being exhausted, because, for two months, he was unemployed. He had, however, to pass through a trying period of probation. during which, though without much business in the courts, he gained some éclat by a work entitled *Recherches sur la France*. But it was not until 1564, when he had been at the bar fourteen years—a time almost long enough for even a modern noviciate, that by one of those fortunate events which have so often rescued a lawyer from obscurity, and the forlorn hope of which buoys up many a sinking heart, he was intrusted with a cause of great and grave importance, and emerged at once to fame. A more noble opportunity for the display of his abilities could hardly have occurred. It was the case of the University of Paris against the Society of Jesuits, who claimed to be matriculated and admitted as members of that body; and Pasquier was counsel for the University. This he owed to the friendship (and how could it be more usefully exerted?) of two of its most distinguished professors, Béquin and Levasseur, who had sufficient influence with their colleagues to get him employed in their behalf; and Pasquier justified their confidence by acquitting himself of the task with brilliant success. A few passages may be given from his speech, which will, I think be found interesting.

He begins with an artful allusion to his own profession implying confidence in the justice of his case. " Most earnestly could I wish that we, advocates as we are, were not in the habit of pledging our belief upon the merits of the causes we undertake, except so far as we see that they are consistent with the general good of the community; but, how it is, I know not, the vicious practice has crept in among us, which is even made a merit of by some, of regarding all things with indifference, provided we can succeed in gaining our verdicts." After showing that, in 1554, the Faculty of Theology in Paris had pronounced a decree against the Jesuits, he thus proceeds : " However, I shall never be ashamed of binding my conscience to that of the venerable Faculty, and maintaining with it, that there never was a sect more partial and ambitious, or of which the propositions were of more pernicious consequence than this. Nay, I will be still more bold. For, to say truth, I am of the number of those who, without using circumlocution, call things by their right names, and say of bread that it is bread, and of wine that it is wine. I frankly then assert that this sect is in its principles schismatic, and consequently heretical. It is a heresy built by Ignatius Loyola on ignorance of the antiquities of our church. I will not hesitate to tell you, that he introduced error into the midst of our church as dangerous as that of Martin Luther. The one and the other both appeared in the same century, at an interval of only eight years apart. Both formed these sects, saying that their principles were in accordance with those of our primitive church, in order more easily to attract simple folk as their followers. I am a son of the Roman church, and I wish to live and die in her faith. God grant that I may never stray from her guidance in a single point. Nevertheless, I affirm that Ignatius has not been less a sectarian or disturber of our religion than Luther. I will add that his sect is more to be dreaded than that of the other ; for when timorous consciences hear the name of Luther and Calvin they are on their guard, but they are easily taken by surprise, and imbibe the poison of the Ignatians, since they fancy that *they* are the foremost champions (*protestans*) of our religion against the heretics, although they are, in reality, its chief destroyers. I may aptly compare them to the ivy, which, clinging to an ancient wall, makes a show of supporting it, while it is undermining the foundations and making it totter to its fall." This is bold language in the sixteenth century against those who professed to be, and were, the most devoted soldiers of the papal See. After a vehement attack upon the order, which is well worthy of perusal, Pasquier concludes in a strain of prophetic warning, which, when we consider the subsequent history of the Jesuits, is very remarkable. "If, however, these remonstrances do not move you, we take God to witness, and protest before the world, that we have not been wanting to our duty; in order that, if things take a different course, posterity may at all events know that this age has not been destitute of men who could, as though a glass, descry the coming storm; and we trust that it will be sounded like a trumpet in the ears of our successors, that like as this great university of Paris is the first in all France, nay, in all the universe, so it was never weary, and never will be weary, of combating all kinds of sects and novelties in religion; first, for the honor and glory of God and His church, next for the majesty of our prince, and lastly for the repose and tranquillity of the state."

But Pasquier was not only a lawyer and a man of learning, but a joker of jokes, and the Jekyll of his day. We may easily, therefore, understand his friendship with Montaigne, and his fondness for the essays of that gossiping genius of which he speaks as *n'ayant nul livre entre les mains tant caressé*. It will give us an amusing idea of the manners of the times in which he lived, when we learn that the speeches of Pasquier at the bar (and after the great Jesuit cause he had no lack of retainers) hardly gained him so wide-spread a celebrity as his verses upon a flea!

The story is one of the curiosities of literature, and may here be briefly told. While he was attending the assizes at Poictiers, he called one day upon Madame des Roches and her fair and accomplished daughter, Mademoiselle Catherine, *l'une des plus belles et sages de nostre France*, and in the course of his visit spied a flea which had impertinently hopped upon the bosom of the latter, *parquée au beau milieu de son sein*. A modern barrister would have affected not to see it, but this accorded little with the gallantry of the age or the taste of Pasquier. He made a witty allusion to the position taken up by the intruder, and complimented it *de s'estre mise en si beau jour*, which the young lady answered by a repartee. This led to a *contention mignarde* between them, in which jest succeeded jest, until it was at last agreed that each should compose an epigram on the occasion and send it to the other. This was done, and wonderful was the success of these performances when they were handed about among the bar.[1] *Ces deux jeux poétiques commencèrent à courir par les mains de plusieurs*, and verses in profusion were written on the subject. Even the president of the court, De Harlay, condescended to compliment in an epigram the muse of Pasquier; and the fame of the incident soon spread

---

[1] These poetical effusions are too long to quote *in extenso;* but the following are the concluding lines of Pasquier's performance:—

>Si tu moques les plus belles,
>Si tu as aussi des aisles
>Tout ainsi que Cupidon,
>Je te requiers un seul don
>Pour ma pauvre ame ulcérée
>O Pulce! O ma Cythérée!
>C'est que ma dame par toy
>Se puisse éveiller pour moy
>Que pour moy elle s'éveille
>Et ait la pulce en l'aureille

from Poictiers to Paris, where Pierre de Soulfour, the president of the parliament, and Brisson, the grave and learned Brisson, were both bitten by Mademoiselle Catherine's flea, and composed verses in its honor. Those of the latter, after showing how frogs and mice had been sung by Homer, and Lesbia's sparrow by Catullus, thus proceed :—

> Pictonici at Pulicis longe præclarior est sors,
> Quem fovet in tepido casta puella sinu ;
> Fortunate Pulex nimium, tua si bona noris,
> Alternis vatum nobilitate metris.

And Scaliger employed his erudition on the same interesting theme. In fact, says Titon du Tillet, *tout le Parnasse latin et françois dn royaume voulut prendre part à cette rare découverte.*[1]

Before taking leave of the sixteenth century, let us avail ourselves of a sketch which M. Berryer has drawn in lively colors of one of these advocates of the olden time while engaged in the performance of his daily duties (*Mod. de l'El. Jud.*). We see him, dressed in his robes of black satin, set out at an early hour, on a summer morning, from one of the picturesque houses, with peaked turrets and high gable ends, which rose above the banks of the Seine in old Paris, and hurrying forward to the court, because the clock of the Holy Chapel has just struck six, at which hour the judges are obliged to take their seats, under pain of losing their salary for the day. He is busy in thinking over the cause which he has to plead, and taxes his ingenuity to compress his speech into as brief a compass as possible ; for he remembers that an ordinance of Charles VIII., issued in

[1] The reader will find an account of this curious incident in the third volume of Southey's *Doctor*. Pasquier was so pleased with the idea, that he collected all the verses in a small volume called *La Puce ; ou Jeux Poetiques François et Latins : composez sur la Puce aux Grands Jours de Poictiers, l'an* 1579, *dont Pasquier futle premier motif*. One of the epigrams made on the occasion by Nicholas Rapin was witty at the expense of the lawyers.

> Causidicos habuit vigilantes Curia, namque
> Illis perpetuus tinnit in ore culex.

1493, imposes a fine upon long-winded advocates who weary the court with their prolixity. Look at his countenance. The furred hood which covers his head, and the ample grey cloak, the collar of which hides half his face, can not so far conceal it as to prevent you from seeing an expression of anger there, which no doubt is excited by the recollection of the arguments used by his opponent on the preceding evening. But think not that when he reaches the court and rises to reply, he will retort by any abusive language; for, by another regulation of the same king, counsel are expressly forbidden to use any opprobrious words towards their antagonists. The judges are seated on their chairs; the parties are before them; and now he, whose portrait we are sketching, rises to address the court. He speaks under the solemn sanction of an oath, for he has sworn to undertake only such causes as in his conscience he believes to be just; he has also sworn not to spin out his pleadings by any of the tricks of his profession, but make them as concise as possible. If, in the course of his harangue, he touches on any question which he thinks may possibly affect the interests of the Crown, he suddenly stops and gives formal notice of it to the court. Twelve o'clock strikes just after the cause is over and judgment pronounced, and the court rises. His client has been successful, and he now takes his counsel aside to settle with him the amount of his fees; and it is not without an effort that he grudgingly gives him the sum which the royal ordinance permits him to receive. M. Berryer then follows him to his home, surrounded by his family, where he prepares in the evening his speech for the morrow; or indulges himself, like Pasquier, in sportive toying with the muse, or takes up his pen, like Pithou, to defend the liberties of the Gallican church.

The feeling of hereditary pride which these *gens de robe* took in their vocation was that which Dandin in

Les Plaideurs expresses, when he upbraids his son in the following lines:—

> Ma robe vous fait honte. Un fils de juge! ah, fi!
> Tu fais le gentilhomme: hé! Dandin, mon ami,
> Regarde dans ma chambre et dans ma garde-robe
> Les portraits des Dandins: tous ont porté la robe:
> Et c'est le bon parti. Compare prix pour prix
> Les étrennes d'un bon juge à celles d'un marquis:
> Attends que nous soyons à la fin de décembre.
> Qu'est-ce qu'un gentilhomme? Un pilier d'antichambre.

The reign of Louis XIV. was a brilliant period for the French bar, if we may judge by the reputation and eminence which some of the most gifted advocates attained. Here I can hardly do more than cite their names; for it would require a volume of itself to give biographical sketches of them, and criticise in detail the numerous speeches which have been preserved as monuments of their eloquence and ability. Those who were best known in after times are the two Talons, Omer and Denys, father and son, each advocate-general in the parliament of Paris, and the latter one of its presidents; — of whom Mr. Berryer says with truth, that posterity has placed them both in the rank of the greatest magistrates of France; also Lemaistre, Patru, Fourcroy Erard, Gillet, Pelisson, the steadfast friend and illustrious defender of the fallen minister Fouquet; Lenoble, Terrasson, Nivelle, and D'Aguesseau.

Nivelle was engaged in some of the most celebrated trials of the seventeenth century; but none, perhaps, excited so much public attention and interest as that of which the reader may be not unwilling to peruse a short account, as it is one of the *causes célèbres* of Europe, and Nivelle was counsel for the prisoner.

Who has not heard of the Marchioness de Brinvilliers? In the annals of crime she has gained a terrible name as the Great Poisoner. The story of her life is more like a romance than a reality, and part of her guilt is shrouded in a veil of darkness which, at this distance of time, it is impossible to penetrate. In order to understand the defense attempted by her advocate, let us briefly review the facts with which he had to deal. Marie Marguerite d'Aubray was the daughter of M. d'Aubray, who held the office of *lieutenant civil* at Paris. Her eyes were remarkable for their soft and gentle expression, and she was distinguished by her personal beauty as well as the charms of her conversation, which shone in the brilliant society of Paris in the early part of the reign of Louis XIV. She had two brothers and one sister, and in 1651 was married to the Marquis de Brinvilliers, the possessor of ample wealth, and to whom she brought a fortune of 200,000 livres. No alliance could have been formed under brighter auspices—none ever led to a more deplorable catastrophe. At the end of a year after their marriage the affection of the Marquis for his wife seemed to lessen, and she imagined, perhaps, not without reason, that she was treated with neglect. He was *maitre de camp* in the regiment of Normandy, and while in service had formed an acquaintance with a cavalry officer named Godin, or Sainte-Croix, as he was generally called—the natural son of some man of rank; but the secret of his birth was never divulged. Under the mask of a pleasing exterior he concealed the villany of his character, and being invited by the Marquis to his house he became there a favorite inmate. He watched the conduct of the wedded pair, and soon observed the discontent of the Marchioness. It is needless to detail the arts by which he inspired her with a passion for himself. The result was that the *liaison* became too manifest to escape the eyes of others, although, as is too often the case, the injured party himself, the husband, remained in ignorance of it. M. d'Aubray had been for some time absent, but on his return he was informed of the disgrace which had fallen on his family. The aged father immediately sought his daughter, and on his knees implored her to abandon a connection which was fraught with infamy. She repelled him from her, and retorted by upbraiding him with suffering her to be neglected by her husband. M. d'Aubray then threatened her with the exercise of his magisterial authority, and bade her tremble at the consequence of disobedience. "*Trembler! elle! la Marquis de Brinvilliers! Pauvre pere!*"[1]

Soon afterwards the affairs of the Marquis, who was dissipated and extravagant, fell into disorder, and the Marchioness eagerly seized this opportunity to demand a divorce. But she did not wholly succeed in her object; for the court pronounced judgment in favor of separation of property only, and the marital rights of the husband in other respects remained untouched. She, however, no longed sought to conceal her shame, but lived openly with Sainte-Croix, who had even the effrontery to call himself her husband.

M. d'Aubray had now recourse to summary measures. He obtained a *lettre de cachet*, and Sainte-Croix was arrested and confined in the Bastile. He there found a companion in a fellow-prisoner, named Exili, an Italian, who was an expert chemist, and who instructed Sainte-Croix in the horrible art of preparing secret and deadly poisons. At the expiration of a year both he and Exili were released from prison, and, armed with the terrible power of life and death, he lost no time in renewing his connection with the Marchioness; but his conduct was now marked with more circumspection. How soon, or in what manner, she consented to become his pupil in the infernal trade of murder we know not; but there is every reason to believe that in the hospitals of Paris, which she visited under the pretense of charity, she tried upon the miserable inmates the effect of the poisons with which Sainte-Croix furnished her. And ere long she made an experiment upon the life of a young servant girl, named Françoise Roussel; but the dose was

[1] M. de Berryer.

not sufficiently powerful, and the victim did not die, though her health was ruined forever.

Her next attempt was more successful. While on a visit to her father at his country seat at Offemont, she mixed some poison in his soup, and having offered it to him with her own hand, he took it and died soon after. His death excited no suspicion, and she was now hardened in crime. In order to possess herself of the whole of the fortune of her own family, that she might squander it upon her guilty paramour, she resolved to destroy them all, and she poisoned both her brothers, the younger of whom was a member of the court of parliament at Paris. About the same time she attempted the life of her only sister, but, for some unknown reason, on this occasion she failed. Hitherto her career had been one of triumphant villainy; but retribution was at hand. While engaged in his laboratory on some dangerous experiments with poisons, the glass mask which Sainte-Croix used to wear over his face happened to drop off, and he fell dead on the floor. The commissary of police was sent for, who immediately sealed up his effects; and afterwards, on making an inventory of them, there was found attached to a small casket a slip of paper, on which was written a most urgent request that the person into whose hands it might fall after Sainte-Croix's death would transmit the contents to the Marchioness de Brinvilliers, as they were entirely her property: or would, in case she was not then living, immediately burn the casket and its contents without opening it. The paper concluded with a solemn adjuration addressed to the finder, and was signed "Sainte-Croix." The casket was opened, and was found to contain a number of small packets carefully sealed, and inclosing sublimate—also a square phial filled with a colorless liquid; and twenty-seven pieces of paper on each of which was written "*plusieurs secrets importants.*"[1] It contained likewise

[1] It is curious and interesting to see how completely the chemists of that

several letters from the Marchioness to Sainte-Croix, and it is remarkable that they did not furnish a single hint of the nefarious practices in which they had been engaged, although written apparently in the most unreserved confidence. There was only one allusion to poison, and that certainly had no bearing upon the question of her guilt, for in one of her most impassioned letters she said that she had determined to put an end to her existence, and pretended that she had taken some of the poison which he had given her. This poison she described as Glazer's receipt. Suspicion, however, was excited by the discovery of so many mysterious packets, and by the recollection of the sudden deaths of the three near relatives of the Marchioness. It was also remembered that she had frequently been heard to allude to the means she possessed of getting rid of an enemy, when she used the singular expression—*on lui donne par exemple un coup de pistolet dans un bouillon*—and that when more than usually piqued she used to say, *Je vais prendre mon poison*. When she heard of the death of Sainte-Croix she made the most strenuous efforts to get possession of the casket, but in vain, and soon afterwards she quitted France for England. One of her domestics, named Lachaussée, was then seized, and put to the torture, and he confessed that he had assisted the Marchioness and Sainte-Croix in poisoning her eldest brother. He was condemned to be broken alive upon the wheel; but before his death he retracted so much of his previous

---

day were at fault in attempting to analyze these poisons. In a report which was prepared by those who were appointed to make the requisite experiments they say, "This artificial poison baffles all our researches. It is so disguised that we can not recognize it—so subtle that it mocks the art and skill of practitioners. In water the poison is precipitated without dissolving; if put into the fire it leaves only an acrid substance behind. . . . The poison of Sainte-Croix has been submitted to various tests :—it overcomes the art of physicians, and laughs at all their experience." What a wonderful change has taken place since then? Chemical science can now make the grave reveal its secrets in a way almost miraculous.

confession as implicated his mistress, and declared that she was innocent of the murder.

This was in the year 1673, and, at the instance of the French ambassador, the Marchioness was compelled to quit England. She fled first to Brussels, and afterwards to Liege, where she sought refuge within the walls of a convent. But the avenger of blood was upon her track, and she was not suffered thus to escape. An officer of justice, named Desgrais, was dispatched from Paris to arrest her, and having arrived at Liege and communicated the purpose of his journey to the authorities of the town, he received from them permission to carry her away. But he feared lest, if he attempted force, she might destroy herself; he therefore disguised himself as a French abbé, and, after several visits to the convent, succeeded in making her believe that he was passionately in love with her. She agreed to meet him at an appointed hour outside the town, and when she reached the place she was immediately seized by the guard, whom Desgrais had in attendance, and hurried off to France. During the journey she tried to commit suicide, but was prevented, and was at last safely lodged within the walls of the Conciergerie. Before leaving Liege, Desgrais seized all her papers, and he found underneath her bed in the convent a box, which contained a paper written by her, which purported to be a confession, and in which she admitted to the fullest extent all her guilt. This document commenced with the words, *Je me confesse à Dieu et à vous, mon père.*

Such was the case which Nivelle had to grapple with when he rose to defend the Marchioness de Brinvilliers on her trial before the parliament of Paris. Dark as was the cloud of suspicion which hung over her, it was not improbable that the evidence would prove insufficient for a conviction if the fatal confession could be kept back.[1] This was the damning fact, which, if

---

[1] When Fauntleroy, the banker, was arrested, there was found, in a tin

admitted as evidence, rendered defense hopeless—and to the point, therefore, of its inadmissibility the advocate addressed all his energies. In Roman Catholic countries the secrets of the confessional are held so sacred that no use can be made of them in a court of justice. In England the law seems to be, that a confession to a clergyman is not privileged; nor is one made to a Popish priest. Lord Wynford laid it down, that " the privilege does not apply to clergymen;" but he added a very important distinction, " I, for one, *will never compel a clergyman to disclose* communications made to him by a prisoner; but, if he chooses to disclose them, I shall receive them in evidence " (3 *Carr* and *Payne*, 519). And when it was stated before Lord Kenyon that Mr. Justice Buller had admitted in a capital case the confession of a Roman Catholic made to a Protestant clergyman, upon which the prisoner was convicted and executed, he said, " I should have paused before I admitted the evidence there admitted." He endeavored, however, to support the decision of Mr. Justice Buller, by remarking, " The Popish religion is now unknown to the law of this country, nor was it necessary for the prisoner to make that confession to aid him in his defense " (*Peake*, 79). The reason here alleged, namely, that the state ignores the existence of the Roman Catholic religion, would hardly be advanced at the present day, when such ample recognition has been made of the professors of that faith by various statutes passed during the last fifty years; and probably, when the case arises, a judge may be disposed to act upon the intimation of Lord Wynford as to what his own course would be—namely, not to compel a priest to disclose a

box in an iron safe of the bank, of which the prisoner kept the key, a paper containing a full confession of his guilt. This paper was dated several years prior to his apprehension, and seems to have been written for the purpose of exonerating his partners in case he effected his escape before discovery. But it was, of course, conclusive as to his own guilt. "Quos Deus vult perdere prius dementat."

confession made to him, but to receive it if offered in evidence. Even this would distinguish the privilege of a person in holy orders from that of a counsel or attorney in a very material respect. For, in the latter cases, it is the privilege of the client, who may, if he chooses, prevent communications which he has made to them, acting for him in their professional character, from being disclosed in a court of justice. But it may be laid down as a general rule, that every statement made by a party to any person not being his counsel or attorney is evidence against him; and the only exception to this rule, of which I am aware, is the case where inducements have been held out to a prisoner to criminate himself.

The great object of the counsel for De Brinvilliers was to treat the paper found in the convent as a confession intended for the priest, and entitled, therefore, to the same protection as one actually made to him. And it might certainly with some plausibility be urged, that the outpourings of a soul before its God in the secret solitude of the chamber were not less sacred than if made into the ear of man. But, supposing this line of argument to be successful, it would still be necessary to do away with the presumptions of guilt afforded by the other facts of the case, and Nivelle performed his difficult task with admirable tact and ability. He seized upon the character of Sainte-Croix, and painted it in the darkest colors, in order to preoccupy the minds of the court with the idea of *his* guilt, and thus divert their attention from the evidence that bore against the prisoner. He argued that in order to revenge himself for the imprisonment which he had suffered, Sainte-Croix had resolved to murder the family of M. d'Aubray, and had employed Lachaussée, who, by his own confession, was an accomplice, as the instrument of his crimes. Having enslaved the affections of the Marchioness, he was anxious that she should inherit the whole fortune of the family, for he knew that it would be bestowed upon himself. Her sudden flight after his death might be explained by the state of her pecuniary affairs. She quitted France to escape from her creditors, not because she dreaded the charge of murder. "Crimes of such revolting atrocity as those of which the Marchioness de Brinvilliers is accused, require proofs so much the stronger, and more conclusive, as they are imputed to a person of exalted birth, whom both her education and her wealth protect against suspicion. The greater the crime the clearer ought to be the evidence, the more irreproachable the character of the witnesses. Acts of unheard of wickedness are not lightly undertaken; the cry of conscience is not easily stifled in the breast; the mind shudders with horror, the soul is agonized when it consummates a monstrous crime. The Holy Scriptures well express the nature of the conflict, when they compare to the pangs of travail the effort which must be made to perpetrate a crime—

> Parturiit injustitiam, peperit iniquitatem.

The culpable connection that subsisted between the Marchioness and Sainte-Croix is no proof of her guilt. Are we to suppose, because she indulged in an illicit passion, that she also committed the dreadful acts of which she is accused? Is a first fault a sufficient proof of the existence of a second? Must we not demand other evidence than such presumptions to produce conviction of guilt in the minds of the court?

"Listen to the dying words of Lachaussée. He declared that the Marchioness had no knowledge of the poisonings. Let us give credit to the assertions of a man on the point of death. Then it is that truth irresistibly reveals itself, in the last moments, when he is approaching the awful tribunal of God. Then all the fetters in which fear and hope, and respect for man, and love of life, enchain affrighted truth, are broken asunder, because all human motives vanish like shadows before the overpowering light of divine justice, into the arms of which the dying man is about to fall.

"The letters that passed between Sainte-Croix and the prisoner at the bar are before you, in which they poured out their inmost souls to each other, and yet they do not contain a single allusion to the crimes of which she is accused. Can you believe that this was possible, if she is guilty?"

But now her advocate had to deal with the most difficult part of the case, and get rid as he best might of the effect of her own confession. Only two courses were open to him—first, to contend that the document was not admissible in evidence; and next, that, if received, it ought to be regarded as the raving of insanity, and not the credible statement of a person in possession of her faculties. The latter was, indeed, a hopeless alternative; but the former view was supported by dexterous and able argument. "In that confession," he said, "which commences with the words, 'I confess before Almighty God that I have poisoned my father, my two brothers, and my sister,' one can see only an insensate accusation, which can be of no avail in a court of justice, because the inviolable law of secrecy imposed equally upon the confessor and all who come to a knowledge of the confession, whether it be verbal or written, renders it useless for all the purpose of civil life. This inviolable law was dictated by Jesus Christ, at the same time as the precept commanding us to reveal our sins to a confessor. Without that condition of secrecy, who would dare to avow his faults? It is the necessary accompaniment of the precept. It is evident that Christ, in calling sinners to the tribunal of repentence, in order to show mercy upon them, did not wish to expose them to the danger of losing their honor and their life by the revelation of their sins. How could we reconcile such a catastrophe with the goodness of God, which is manifested in that ordinance? Hence it follows that this law of secrecy extends to confessions which are written as well as to those which are uttered ; and that it has a binding obligation upon confessors, and all those who by any means become cognizant of the confession, because the same motives of secrecy derived from the nature of the sacrament, and the obligation to confess, apply to the one party as well as to the other."

M. Nivelle then proceeds to show that this law of secrecy must have been imposed by Christ himself; and that those who violate it are guilty of the sin of sacrilege. "Those who do so," he continued, "defeat the designs of God, by driving away from the footstool of penitence those who approach it on the faith of secrecy. They terrify all consciences, and repel them from that harbor of safety : and, especially, they banish from it the greatest criminals, that is to say, those who have the greatest need of that healing remedy. They scare away all who, from the weakness of their memory, are obliged to commit their confession to writing, a course often prescribed to them by their spiritual instructor, or suggested by the fervor of their own piety ; and, as a necessary consequence, the deaf and dumb, who have no other means of confession, must be deprived of the assurance of absolution.

"Let me not be told that the paper written by the Marchioness de Brinvilliers was only the memorandum of a confession, and not a real confession itself. It begins with the words, ' I confess myself to God, and to you, my father' (alluding to the priest for whom the confession was designed). It is clear, then, that it is a genuine confession ; but even if not, if it was only the memorandum of an intended confession, it would be equally protected from disclosure. What excuse for their conduct could judges allege who availed themselves of the sacramental confession of an accused person as the means of his conviction ? Will they rely upon their office as magistrates, and as such, the depositaries of human justice, which is an image of that of God himself? Will they plead the interests of the public to which everything ought to give way? Dare they place all these reasons in the balance with a single precept that has emanated from Christ? They find in the name of Christian which they bear, a light which dissipates all these vain clouds of sophistry; for the same title imposes upon them the obligation to prefer the commandments of God to their fortunes, their lives, their honor, the ties of flesh and blood, and to every kind of interest, whether public or private."

After having urged that the mind of the prisoner was in such an unsettled state when the confession was written, that it could not be safely relied upon, M. Nivelle concluded by an artful appeal to the compassion of the court. "Be just, gentlemen, and invoke not against us the proofs which God, and morality, and justice, and your own convictions forbid you to employ. Alas! there still remain too many means for our destruction,—means which we could not hope to repel, if we did not take refuge in your charity, your pity, and your benevolent justice towards a lady of the highest rank, united to a great number of you by the ties of relationship, and whom a single word from your mouth can restore to life and honor, or hurl into the most terrible misfortune, which will involve the members of her numerous family in part of her misery and shame."

Such is an outline of the defense of this great criminal, which was conducted by Nivelle with consummate skill, and in a manner worthy of his high reputation. But against the propriety of one passage we must strongly protest. It is that in which, when speaking of the enormity of the charges against her, he implies his own belief in her innocence. He says, " Puisse ma voix les repousser! puisse-t-elle appeler sur cette tete abandonnée de tous un intéret *dont ma conscience l'a jugée digne.*" This could not be sincere, and was certainly going further than the duty of an advocate required. He was at liberty to present arguments to the court, of the validity of which they were competent to form their own opinion. He was at liberty to contend that certain evidence ought not to be received; but he had no right to pledge himself to a falsehood by professing a conviction which he did not entertain. The facts of the case, however, were too strong to be got over, and the court found the prisoner guilty, and pronounced against her the following dreadful sentence :—

" The court condemns the said d'Aubray de Brinvilliers to make the *amende honorable* before the principal door of the church of Notre Dame, where she shall be placed on a cart with her feet naked, and a cord round her neck, holding in her hands a burning torch of the weight of two pounds; and there being on her knees, she shall say and declare that, out of vengeance and malice aforethought, and in order to possess herself of their property, she caused her father and her two brothers to be poisoned, and attempted the life of her deceased sister, of which crimes she repents and craves pardon of God, the king and justice; after which she is to be taken and conveyed in the said cart to the Place de Grève in this town, in order to have her head struck off on a scaffold, and her body burnt, and the ashes scattered to the winds; but she is first to undergo the torture, both ordinary and extraordinary, in order that she may reveal the names of her accomplices."

The punishment of the torture is said to have been remitted, but the rest of the sentence was immediately carried into execution ; and in the letters of Madame de Sevigné is contained a graphic but flippant narrative of the last moments of the ill-fated Marchioness de Brinvilliers.¹

---

¹ " Enfin c'en est fait, la Brinvilliers est en l'air : son pauvre petit corps a été jeté après l'exécution, dans un grand feu, et ses cendres au vent ; de sort que nous la respirerons." What an extraordinary idea ! Madame de

Of D'Aguesseau it is difficult to speak in terms which will not seem to be those of exaggeration. His name stands in lofty pre-eminence at the head of a long list of illustrious men, who have adorned the judgment-seat in France. Such were La Vacquerie, president of the parliament of Paris under the mean and selfish bigot Louis XI., and Matthieu Molé, who, while holding the same high office in the midst of turbulent factions, and in imminent danger of his life, discharged his duties with such unshaken firmness and indomitable courage as to win the admiration of his enemies, and of whom Cardinal de Retz said, "If it were not a kind of blasphemy to assert that there exists in our age any one more intrepid than the great Gustavus and the prince of Condé, I should say that it is Matthieu Molé, first president." Such, too, were L'Hopital, the wise, and learned, and virtuous judge; and Montesquieu, president of the parliament of Bordeaux; and Le Tellier, over whom Bossuet pronounced one of the most splendid of his funeral orations, in which he mentions that the dying Chancellor, when stretched in extreme old age on a bed of cruel suffering, found consolation in the thought that he had never once given advice against his conscience, nor allowed a single act of injustice to be perpetrated which he had the power of preventing.

But though D'Aguesseau is chiefly known to us as the great Chancellor, the seals of which office he held for thirty-four years, a model of purity and excellence, amidst the corruption which disgraced society in France during the regency of the Duke of Orleans and reign of

Sevigné says that when the prisoner saw the pails of water, which were prepared for the purpose of administering the "question" to her, she said, "They certainly must intend to drown me; for no one can pretend, considering the size of my figure, that I can drink all that." It is almost incredible, but we are told that this atrocious criminal was a popular favorite, and that on the day after her execution a mob assembled in the Place de Grève, and demanded with loud cries the ashes of the Saint who had been sacrificed the evening before.

Louis XV., we must not forget that he was one of the most eloquent advocates and writers whom his country has produced. When, at the age of twenty-three, he made his first appearance as advocate-general, and addressed the court, the charm of his style produced a great sensation, and Denis Talon, who had grown grey at the bar, exclaimed in rapture, " Would that I might finish my career as that young man has commenced his." No one every had a higher view of the dignity of his vocation, or guarded its honor with more jealous care. The discourses which at different times he delivered on the subject are some of the most beautiful compositions in the world ; and it is impossible to read them without being inspired by the enthusiasm of their author. " Think not," said he, addressing himself to the youthful members of the bar, "think not that it is sufficient for you to have united nobleness and purity of motives to greatness of natural talents; and be assured that the most deep-seated, and perhaps most incurable, disease of your profession is the blind temerity with which men venture to engage in it, without having rendered themselves worthy of it by long and laborious preparation. What treasures of science, what variety of erudition, what sagacity of discernment, what delicacy of taste, must be combined in order to attain excellence at the bar ! Whoever ventures to assign limits to the knowledge required in an advocate has never conceived a perfect idea of the vast extent of your profession. Let others study human nature only in detail; the orator is not perfect, if, by the constant study of the most pure morality, he does not understand and penetrate and make himself master of the entire man."

Speaking of the requirements of the French law, he says, " Let the jurisprudence of Rome be for him a second philosophy ; let him throw himself with ardor into the immense sea of the canons: let him have ever before his eyes the authority of the ordinances of our kings, and the wisdom of the oracles of our senates; let him devour the common law, penetrate its spirit, and reconcile its principles; and let each citizen of that large number of small communities which embraces in one single whole such a diversity of laws and customs, be able to believe, when consulting him, that he was born in his own neighborhood, and has studied only the usages of his own province. Let history give him experience, and, if I may so express myself, maturity of age by anticipation; and, after having raised a solid edifice of knowledge out of so many different materials, let him add to it all the ornaments of language, and all the magnificence of art which belongs to his profession. Let the ancient orators impart to him their insinuating beauty, their copiousness, their sublimity: let the historians bestow upon him their simplicity, their method, their variety: let the poets inspire him with the loftiness of their invention, the vivacity of their images, the boldness of their expression, and especially that concealed rhythm, that secret harmony of expression, which, without having the fetters and uniformity of poetry, often preserves all its sweetness and all its grace. Let him add the courtesy of the French to the Attic salt of the Greeks and the refinement of the Romans. Let us, as though he were transformed into one of the ancient orators, recognize in him their genius and character rather than their thoughts and style; and, imitation becoming to him a second nature, let him speak like Cicero, when Cicero imitates Demosthenes; or like Virgil, when, by a noble, but more difficult plagiarism, he does not blush to enrich himself with the spoils of Homer."

One of the most remarkable cases in which D'Aguesseau was engaged as counsel at the bar, was the following: Louis de la Pivardière, a gentleman of a good family but decayed estate, married, in 1687, a widow named De Menon, who possessed a small property near Narbonne. The union was not a happy one; and De la Pivardière began to treat his wife with neglect, who found consolation in the attentions of Charost, the Abbé of Mizeray. The husband frequently absented himself from home, and while at Auxerre on one occasion he met with the daughter of a man who held the office of *huissier* in the town, and fell desperately in love with her. Concealing the fact that he had a wife living, he married this new object of his attachment; and, on the death of the father, which soon happened, he succeeded to the same appointment which the latter had held. For two years De la Pivardière lived in undisturbed union with his Auxerre wife, paying, every six months, a visit to his property at Narbonne, where he drew his rents, and then went away, meeting with no opposition to his departure from his first wife, at whose house, indeed, he generally found the Abbé an inmate on his return. Matters continued in this state until information was given to the lady at Narbonne, that the cause of her husband's frequent absence was the fact of his possessing another wife at Auxerre. Though she had ceased to love him, and in all probability had for a long time herself indulged in an illicit passion, this discovery inflamed her jealousy, and she only waited for his appearance to upbraid him with his infidelity. It happened that he came to Narbonne very soon after his wife had received the intelligence. He arrived at his château on the evening of the festival of Notre-Dame, in August, 1697, and found that a brilliant party had assembled in the salons to do honor to the day. His sudden apparition disconcerted the guests, and his wife received him with such marked coldness and aversion, that the company, who were ignorant of the true cause, could not forbear expressing their surprise. It may be easily imagined that their mirth was effectually damped, and the party soon broke up, leaving the husband and wife to an agreeable tete-à-tete. No sooner had they gone, than she broke out into passionate reproaches, and told him to go to his new wife and ask her, if he wanted an explanation of the reason of her own coldness and displeasure.

After a violent quarrel, De la Pivardière retired to bed, and his wife then locked the door of the apartment where one of the maid servants slept, and removed two of the others and her two youthful children to an apartment at the top of the house which they had not occupied before. During the night a knocking was heard at the gate of the mansion, and when one of the female servants went down to inquire who was there, a man asked whether the Sieur de la Pivardière had arrived, and, being told that he had, he immediately disappeared.

Next day, La Pivardière was not to be found, although his horse and riding apparel remained at the château. Some time elapsed, and still nothing was heard about him, and the remarkable circumstances attending his return sharpened the suspicions of the neighborhood. At last officers of justice arrived at the house to investigate the matter and draw up a *procès verbal*. They found the mattress and bed on which La Pivardière had slept, stained with blood, and in the cellar a deep trench dug about the size of a man's body, although no corpse was there when they examined it. In addition to these and other circumstances, the two maid servants, whom Madame de la Pivardière had placed on the night in question in the attic, deposed positively to the fact of the murder. They declared that their mistress had introduced two valets of the Abbé de Mizeray into the chamber of her husband, and that they had assassinated him. And the daughter of La Pivardière, a girl of the age of nine years, deposed that she heard in the middle of the night the voice of her father crying out, "O my God, have pity on me!" What proof could seem more complete than this? The Abbé was arrested, and the servants were confronted with him; but in his presence they hesitated, faltered, and at last openly retracted and disavowed all that they had previously sworn. No sooner, however, was he removed, than they reiterated their former statement, and, on being again confronted with him, they pertinaciously adhered to it. While matters were in this state, a most unexpected turn was given to the proceedings. It was confidently asserted that La Pivardière was alive, and several witnesses came forward and swore that they had seen him at Châteauroux and at Issoudun, a few days after the time when he was said to have been murdered at Narbonne. Upon this, she who was either his wife or widow, and upon whom such a load of suspicion rested, applied to the court for a warrant of arrest against her husband, that the fact of his existence might be duly proved. Two months elapsed before Pivardière again appeared, but he was then seen at Romorantin, and, being recognized, he was immediately seized and carried to the prison where the two maid servants were confined, in order that he might be identified. They, however, both declared that he was not their missing master, and that they did not know the individual before them. In this perplexity the *procureur du roi* demanded his detention that the mystery might be cleared up; but the authorities refused to interfere, and he went away from the place, leaving the fact of Pivardière's existence enveloped in greater mystery than ever. Not long afterwards, the accused parties were put upon their trial for the supposed murder, and an order was issued for the arrest of the individual who was said to be La Pivardière, wherever he might be found. He did not, however, require to be searched for, but voluntarily came forward, and, appearing before the *procureur* at Romorantin, he declared that he was De la Pivardière, and avowed his double marriage. What follows is singular enough. Instead of being immediately arrested and tried for bigamy, he made a formal demand that his identity should be first established by legal proof in a civil process; and it was in this stage of the affair that D'Aguesseau was employed as counsel; and he had to prove that the person whose suit was before the court was the same De la Pivardière, whose supposed murder was the subject of the criminal trial which was then pending. This he did in a very elaborate argument, in which he commented, with masterly skill, upon the conflict of probabilities and evidence in this extraordinary case. The result was that the identity was established, and the surviving servant, who had given evidence as to the fact of the murder, was condemned to make the *amende honorable*, to be whipped, branded with a *fleur-de-lis*, and banished forever from the place where the parliament was sitting. The accused parties were, of course, set at liberty.[1]

During the eighteenth century, until towards its close, the profession of the law continued to flourish in France, and many eloquent speakers upheld its former reputation; among whom may be specially mentioned: De Sacy, De Mauléon, Séguier, Gerbier, Lally Tollendal, Servan, Portalis, Ducoudray, Saint Amand, Malesherbes, Tronchet, and Desèze. But amidst the wreck of institutions at the time of the Revolution, when the ancient parliaments of the kingdom were swept away, the order of advocates was involved in the general destruction. By a decree of the 2nd of September, 1790, the National Assembly pronounced its doom, and abolished at one swoop all the rights and privileges of the bar. It ordained *que les hommes de loi, ci-devant appélés avocats, ne devant former ni ordre ni corporation, n'auront aucun costume particulier dans leurs fonctions*. Thus, the very name of *avocat* ceased for a time to exist, and those who

---

[1] The most remarkable trial in this country, involving question of indentity of a party, was that of Elizabeth Canning, in 1754, for perjury.— *State Trials*, xix. 283. It excited at the time an extraordinary degree of interest, and the country may be said to have been divided upon the question, whether Mary Squires satisfactorily proved an *alibi* or not. But it is difficult to understand how there could be a doubt in the case; and it says little for the acumen of people in those days that Canning's story of her robbery, and imprisonment for a month in a hayloft, should have found credence in a court of justice.

still followed the profession were styled, in the new and ridiculous nomenclature of the Revolution, *defenseurs officieux*. But no previous study was required to prepare them for the discharge of their duties; no discipline was enforced: there was no longer a bar in France united by a common bond of sympathy, and obedient to the traditionary rules which had been handed down from a remote antiquity. And it may seem strange that this measure not only was not resisted by its members, but even accepted by them with alacrity and joy. The reason of this was, as Fournel informs us, a regard to the dignity of their calling, and a conviction that, under the new order of things, it must be degraded from its ancient position (*Hist. des Avoc.*, tom. ii. 540, *et seq.*). We are told that those who were most distinguished by zeal for their profession, and who attached the most importance to the name of advocate and the honor of their order, were those who declared themselves most strongly in favor of the abolition of their name and privileges. Instead of the old parliaments of France, invested with all their venerable attributes of solemnity and pomp, there were now substituted petty courts of justice, which, it was feared, would be inundated by a new class of practitioners, who, animated by no feeling of *esprit de corps*, or regard for the honor of the profession, would totally change its nature, and prove themselves unworthy of the time-honored name of *avocats*. In a spirit of Spartan self-sacrifice the existing members of the bar said, "Sole depositaries of that noble profession, we will not suffer it to be changed by passing into hands which would stain its honor; let us not have successors unworthy of us: let us ourselves destroy the object of our affections, rather than expose it to outrage and insult." Even if we dissent from the policy of such a resolution, we must admire the feeling which animated those who thus consented to the destruction of their privileges.

The object of the furious zealots of liberty in the

Legislative Assembly and the convention was to proscribe all real freedom of discussion, and to prevent any attempts to rescue the victims of their tyranny from the axe of the guillotine. For they dreaded the fearless efforts of the advocate, who pleaded for the life of his client; and to frustrate this, they decreed the cruel sophism, *La loi donne aux accusés pour défenseurs des jurés patriotes ; elle n'en doit point aux conspirateurs.* As a legitimate consequence of this reasoning was erected that court of assassins, the Revolutionary Tribunal, where Fourquier Tinville acted as public prosecutor, and such infamous wretches as Herman, Coffinhal Dumas, and Leroi *Dix-Aout* sat as judges or jurymen, and the most monstrous mockery of justice took place that has ever shocked the sight of civilized men.

Before this tribunal had been called into existence, the National Convention had consummated its crimes by decreeing the death of Louis. As an act of grace, it allowed him on his trial to be defended by counsel,—and never had advocates a more perilous task to perform than that which at this awful juncture was undertaken by Malesherbes, Tronchet, and Desèze. The first of these had already seen seventy winters, and he might, like Target, unworthy member of the bar, on the plea of age, have declined the tremendous responsibility. But the brave old man would avail himself of no such excuse. He said, "I was twice called to the council of him who was my master, when all the world coveted that honor; and I owe him the same service now when it has become one which many account dangerous."[1]

[1] Malesherbes was not long in following his royal master to the scaffold. He was guillotined on the 22nd of April, 1793, and a monument was afterwards erected to his memory in the hall of the Palais de Justice with the following inscription, which has been attributed to Louis XVIII.:

      Strenue semper fidelis,
          Regi suo
       In solio veritatem,
     Præsidium in carcere,
           Attulit.

The indictment to which Louis was called upon to plead was of enormous length, and the number of documents which his counsel had to peruse, in preparing his defense, was one hundred and sixty-two. For this arduous labor only four days were allowed them, and well might they complain of the cruelty which placed them in a position of such overwhelming difficulty Desèze was the advocate chosen to speak for their royal master, and on the 26th of December, 1792, he appeared with his colleagues at the bar of the Convention, where he pleaded the cause of the discrowned king, for three hours, with the most touching eloquence.

It would be difficult to imagine a more affecting scene than that day presented. The descendant of a line of kings, who, since the time of Hugh Capet, had sat for seven hundred years upon the throne of France, stood, like our own Charles the First, before his subjects to receive the doom of death. For he and his fearless advocates well knew that all defense was vain. It would have been as easy to persuade a troop of wolves to forego their prey, as to appeal with effect to the justice and humanity of that tribunal. The Girondists, indeed, numbered among them men who, like Vergniaud, Roland, Brissot, Barbaroux, Isnard, and Gaudet, were not deaf to the voice of reason, and whose hearts were not steeled against compassion; but, though intrepid on the scaffold, they had no moral courage. They could not cope with the fierce energy of the Mountain, and, to escape the charge of befriending royalty, they were ready to condemn the innocent. And this is the dark blot upon the history of men who might otherwise command our respect for their sincerity, and our pity for their misfortunes. They had not the boldness to act up to their convictions. They wished, and yet they feared, to rescue Louis from death—

> Letting "I dare not," wait upon "I would,"
> Like the poor cat i' the adage ;

and their fate is an awful warning to mankind not to surrender the dictates of conscience to the voice of clamor, and purchase a fleeting popularity at the expense of justice and of truth.

Of his effort on this occasion, Desèze afterwards modestly said, "Compelled as I was to prepare a defense of such importance in four nights, while I employed the day-time with my colleagues in examining the numerous papers which were communicated to us, I need hardly say that it bears marks of the extreme haste in which I was obliged to compose it, and that it presents in some sort, as it were, only results; but I had to fulfill a sacred duty, and I consulted only my devotion, and not my powers." When they withdrew from the hall Louis fell on his neck, and embracing him, said with tears, *Mon pauvre Desèze*. He must have felt himself at that moment well repaid for all his anxieties by such an affecting acknowledgment of his exertions.

The concluding passage of his eloquent speech seems to have fully reached the height of his great argument. "Louis anticipated the wishes of his people by his own sacrifices, and yet it is in the name of that same people that you demand to-day—Citizens! I cannot go on—I pause before History. Remember that she will judge your judgment, and that her voice will be that of ages!" This is the same thought which was so finely expressed by Quintilian respecting Socrates, when he refused to supplicate the judges for his life:—*Posterorum se judiciis reservavit.*

Marie Antoinette, also, did not disdain the aid of counsel, when, for the first time in history, a queen appeared as a criminal before her subjects. Chauveau-Lagarde and Tronçon-Ducoudray were the advocates of this daughter of the Cæsars, whose hair was blanched with sorrow at that memorable hour. Their speeches have not been preserved; but, from the only notice of them that remains, they seemed to have sued for mercy rather than asserted the innocence of their client. We may, however, be sure that nothing they could have said would have equaled her own sublime apostrophe, beside which, the adjuration of Demosthenes, when he swore by the souls of those who fell at Marathon, sinks into insignificance. When the wretch Hebert (originally a ticket-taker at a theater, where he robbed his employers) dared to utter against her that ineffable accusation which fiends would have been ashamed to breathe, she at first made no reply; but when she was again reminded of the charge, she said, *Si je n'ai pas répondu, c'est que la nature se refuse à repondre à une telle imputation faite à une mère.* Here her voice was choked with emotion, but recovering herself, she turned towards the women who thronged the hall, and exclaimed, *J'en appelle au cœur de toutes les mères ici présentes. S'il y en a une qui puisse croire à la possibilité des horreurs qu'on m'impute, qu'elle se lève!*[1] But not one woman rose to answer the electrifying appeal, and if the earth had opened to swallow up that den of murderers it would have seemed only the just retribution of Heaven.

Better days began to dawn upon the bar when the star of Napoleon was in the ascendant. Not that he had any love for the profession, which he disliked for its fearless and independent spirit. When a project had been submitted to him for the restoration of the order without any restrictions upon free liberty of speech, he angrily refused to sanction it, and inveighed against advocates in no measured terms. "The decree," he said, "is absurd; it leaves no handle, no means of acting against them. They are a factious kind of persons—the concoct-

---

[1] *Procès de la Reine, Hist. Parl.* xxix. 358. Thiers, *Rev. Franc.*, v. 388. *Biog. Univer.*, art. M. Antoinette.

As a proof of the calm courage of Marie Antoinette at such a crisis, it may be mentioned that, for several hours during her trial, her fingers played upon the arm of her chair, as though they were touching the keys of a pianoforte. Perhaps her thoughts were straying to the happy days of her earlier youth.

ors of crimes and treasons; as long as I wear a sword at my side I will never sign such a decree; I wish it were the law that the tongue of an advocate might be cut out who uses it against the government."

This burst of passion, however, had no lasting effect; and the first symptom that the good old times of the bar were returning was the restoration of its costume. In 1802 a decree appeared, providing that "the *gens de loi* and the attorneys should wear, in all the courts of justice, a gown made of wool, closed in front, and with wide sleeves; a black cap (*toque noire qui heureusement a remplacé le bonnet carré*); a cravat like that worn by the judges, and hair long or cropped."

In 1804 Napoleon decreed the re-establishment of the order of advocates, "as one of the means most proper to maintain the probity, delicacy, disinterestedness, desire of conciliation, love of truth and justice, an enlightened zeal for the weak and the oppressed, which are the essential foundations of their profession." In 1810 he issued an imperial ordinance containing a number of rules, for the purpose of regulating "that salutary discipline of which advocates showed themselves such jealous guardians in the palmy days of the bar." Among the rights and duties thus prescribed occur the following:—

"We expressly forbid advocates to add their signatures to opinions, pleadings, or writings which are not their own, or which they have not duly considered: we likewise forbid them to make any bargains for their fees, or to compel their clients to recompense them, before the conclusion of a case (*à reconnaitre leurs soins avant les plaidoiries*), under the penalty of a reprimand for the first offense, and expulsion from the bar in case it is repeated.

"Advocates shall have free scope for the exercise of their office in the defense of justice and of truth; at the same time it is our wish that they should abstain from all inventions in their facts, and from other evil practices, as well as from all useless or superfluous speeches.

"We forbid them to indulge in any injurious or offensive personalities against parties to whom they are opposed or their counsel—to assert any fact seriously affecting the honor or reputation of the opposite party, unless the necessity of the case requires it, and they have express written instructions to that effect from their clients, or the attorneys of the latter."

Before we conclude this chapter it may be interesting to see what is the form of procedure which the French code prescribes in criminal trials. On the day fixed for the opening of the assize court, twelve jurymen[1] must take their seats opposite to the accused, and the president is to interrogate him as to his name, age, profession, residence, and place of birth. He must then notify to the counsel of the prisoner that he is *to say nothing contrary to his conscience*, or to the respect due to the laws; and that he ought to express himself with decency and moderation. In the next place, he must, standing up and uncovered, address the jury in the following terms:—"You shall swear and promise, before God and before men, to examine with the most scrupulous attention the charges which shall be preferred against the prisoner (naming him); to betray neither the interests of the accused, nor of society which accuses him; to communicate with no one until after you have given your verdict; to listen neither to hate nor malice, nor fear, nor favor; to decide, after hearing the charges and the defense, according to your conscience and intimate conviction, with the impartiality and firmness which belongs to a man who is just and free." Upon this each of the jury, being separately called on

---

[1] When a trial is likely to last a long time, one or two supplementary jurymen are taken by lot from the jury-panel, who attend to the evidence and supply the place of any juror or jurors who may not have sufficient strength to sit out the trial.—*Code d'Instruction Criminelle*, liv. ii. chap. 5.

by the president, shall raise his hand and say, "I swear."

The officer of the court then reads the commission, or decree of the *cour royale*, remitting the case to the assizes, and also the indictment, *acte d'accusation*. The attorney general then opens the case against the prisoner, and gives in a list of the witnesses who are to be examined— both for the crown and for the prisoner; and their names, professions, and places of residence must be notified twenty-four hours, at least, to the prisoner, before their examination on the part of the crown; and the same notice must be given to the crown on the part of the prisoner. Each witness is sworn to speak without fear or hate, and the truth, and nothing but the truth. After each deposition has been given, the president must ask the witness, if it is of the prisoner at the bar *that he has heard so and so* (*qu'il a entendu parler*). The witness is not to be interrupted; but the accused, or his counsel, may, after he has given evidence, interrogate him through the medium of the president, and say, as well against him as against his testimony, whatever may conduce to the defense. The president may question the witness *and the prisoner* on all points which he deems necessary to the elucidation of the facts of the case. The other judges and the attorney general may do the same, on first obtaining permission from the president; but the prosecutor himself can put such questions only through the medium of the president. When the witnesses for the prosecution have been heard, the prisoner is to bring forward those in his behalf of whom he has previously furnished a list, and who can depose either with reference to the charges mentioned in the indictment, or to his character as a man of honor and probity. But no witness is admissible who is related to the prisoner, in either the directly ascending or descending line, or is his brother or sister, or husband or wife, even after a divorce has been pronounced, nor is an informer to whom the law assigns a reward [1]—(*dénonciateurs dont la dénonciation est récompensée pécuniairement par la loi*). In all these cases, however, the objection may be waived by the crown or the prisoner, where the evidence is offered by the other side. When facts are deposed to, tending to convict the prisoner, it is the duty of the president to call upon him to say whether he admits their truth. When the witnesses have given their evidence, the prosecutor, or his counsel, and the attorney general, are to be heard in support of the indictment; and the prisoner, or his counsel, may then make his defense. Upon this the prosecutor and the attorney general may reply, *but in all cases the prisoner, or his counsel, is to have the last word.*

It is then the duty of the president to sum up; and he informs the jury that if a majority of them think that there exist, in favor of the accused, extenuating circumstances, though they find him guilty, they are to announce their verdict in the following terms: " In the opinion of the majority there are extenuating circumstances in favor of the prisoner." He also informs them that they are to give their votes by ballot (*au scrutin secret*);[2] and

---

[1] It is difficult to understand this; for it may be asked what is the use of an informer, paid by the law, if he may not give evidence in court against the prisoner? But we must remember that in France a written deposition is evidence, even although the party who made it is alive and can be produced at the trial. Not so in England.

[2] This is a humane and important provision. In England the general practice (though not imperative) is, that if the prisoner's counsel calls no witnesses, except to character, there is no reply on the part of the prosecution. But where the prosecution is conducted by the government, as in cases where the law-officers of the crown are employed, they often insist upon a right to reply, whether witnesses are called by the prisoner or not.

[3] The mode in which the jury vote is regulated by a law of the 13th of May, 1836, is as follows:—Each juryman receives in turn from the foreman a slip of paper, marked with the stamp of the court, and containing the words " On my honor and conscience my verdict is . . . . . ." He is then to fill up the blank space with the word Yes! or No! upon a table so arranged that none of his colleagues can see what he writes, and afterwards hand the paper closed up to the foreman, who is to deposit it in a box kept for the purpose. A similar operation must be gone through on

that if the accused is found guilty by a majority of only one vote (*à la simple majorité*), they must state this when they deliver in their verdict. They then retire from the jury-box, and on their return the president asks them for their verdict; upon which the foreman rises, and, placing his hand upon his heart, says, "Upon my honor and conscience, before God and before man, the verdict of the jury is 'Yes! the prisoner is guilty,'—or, 'No! the prisoner is not guilty.'" At the same time he delivers to the president the verdict in writing, signed by himself.

One important difference between our criminal procedure and that of France deserves to be noticed. There, if the court is unanimously of opinion that the jury are mistaken in their verdict, it must not pronounce any judgment, but appoint a new trial to take place at the next assizes, on which none of the former jury may sit. Where the prisoner is found guilty by a majority of one, a new trial must be granted, if a *majority* of the court think it advisable. But there can be no new trial where the prisoner is *acquitted*, whether contrary to the opinion of the court or not. In England, also, the inflexible rule is, that no man can be put in legal jeopardy twice upon the same charge; and if a prisoner, immediately after a verdict of acquittal, were to confess his guilt in open court, or if the verdict were in direct and flagrant opposition to the evidence, he could not be tried again. But, on the other hand, if there are grounds for believing that a verdict of guilty is erroneous, the only course is to respite the sentence, and apply to the Crown for pardon; which has the effect of entirely obliterating all the former

the questions of whether there are extenuating or aggravating circumstances or not; whether the fact admits of legal excuse; and whether the prisoner was competent to distinguish right from wrong when he committed the act. The foreman must then draw out the slips of paper and write down the result, without, however, stating the number of votes on each side, except when there is a majority of only one for a conviction. The slips of paper must then be burnt in the presence of the jury.

proceedings, and, to use the words of Blackstone, "makes the offender a new man."[1]

In order to illustrate the practical working of the French system, perhaps no better instance can be selected than the trial of Madame Lafarge, which, in the month of September, 1840, fixed the attention of Europe upon the assize court of the obscure provincial town of Tulle, in France, and excited a degree of interest almost unparalleled. And now that that interest has died away, and the public no longer listen with eager curiosity for a revelation of the gloomy secrets of the mansion at Glandier, we may find a consideration of the trial not without its use, from the contrast which it presents to our own mode of procedure, and the defects which it glaringly exhibits. But let us first cast a rapid glance at the facts.

Marie Capelle, the heroine of the tragedy, was born at Paris, in 1816, of a good family. Her father was a colonel of artillery, and her uncle, M. de Garat, by whom she was brought up, after the death of both her parents when she was quite a child, was one of the directors of the Bank of France. She thus had access to good society, and, when about twenty years of age, she formed an intimate friendship with Mlle. Nicolai. It is not necessary to detail the incidents of a love adventure, in which she acted as the confidante of her friend, although it was brought prominently forward at the time of her trial. It is sufficient to state that Mlle. Nicolai became the wife of M. de Léotaud; and Marie Capelle, some time afterwards, paid the wedded pair a visit at their country seat. It happened that a female relative of M. de Léotaud was then on the point of being married, and the wedding *trousseau* was in the house, and of course

---

[1] So completely does a pardon of treason or felony extinguish the crime, that when granted to a man, even after conviction or attainder, it will enable him to have an action of slander against another for calling him traitor or felon.—*Hawkins*, P. C. b. 2, c. 37, § 48.

the theme of discussion and admiration among the fair guests who were there assembled. One day Madame de Léotaud brought down her diamonds, that they might be compared with the jewels of the bride, and she afterwards replaced them in her bedroom. Suddenly they disappeared, and, although the most rigid search was made for them, no trace of the lost property could be discovered. Marie Capelle returned to her uncle's house, and remained there until she married M. Lafarge. He was the proprietor of some ironworks at Glandier, in the department of La Corrèze, and had lost his first wife. He was introduced to Marie Capelle through the medium of a matrimonial agent, whose avowed business it was to find partners for those who applied to him. They met; and although, according to her own account in a letter which she wrote at the time to a friend, she saw little to admire in him, she was induced, by his representations of *une belle fortune, un joli château,* within a few days after their first interview to marry him. She thus describes her future husband, in a style truly French, *une assez laide figure, une tournure et des manières très-sauvages, mais de belles dents, un air de bonhomie, une réputation excellente.* The wedding took place at the end of July, 1839, and immediately afterwards the ill-assorted pair set out for Glandier. While on the road they had a quarrel, and Madame Lafarge seems then to have conceived a strong aversion to her husband. When she arrived at Glandier her chagrin was increased by the discovery that the *joli château,* upon which her imagination had dwelt, was an old, dilapidated mansion, situated in a lonely valley, amidst dark and sullen woods. The gloom smote upon the heart of the disconsolate bride, and, hurrying to her chamber, she wrote a most extraordinary letter to M. Lafarge, in which she said that her marriage was intolerable to her, that she already loved another, and that if her husband compelled her to live with him as his wife she would destroy herself; adding, that she had already tried the effects of poison, which had failed, and that all she asked was permission from him to fly from France, and seek a home and an asylum at Smyrna. After, however, this explosion of passionate feeling, she seemed to become more reconciled to her lot, and lived with her husband in terms of amicable, if not affectionate, intercourse. The other inmates of the family were the mother and sister of M. Lafarge. At the end of the year business called him to Paris, and during his absence Madame Lafarge purchased a quantity of arsenic, for the purpose, as she alleged, of destroying the rats which infested the house. One day she proposed to her mother-in-law that, as she was about to send her miniature to her husband, the latter should make a few cakes, and forward them to her son by the same parcel. This was done; and the cakes, when ready, were given to Madame Lafarge to put into the box. It arrived at its destination, but, according to the evidence, when the husband opened it, instead of several small cakes, such as his mother had made, there was one large one, and it was accompanied by a letter from Madame Lafarge, in which she begged him to eat it at a particular hour, saying that she would, at the same time, be similarly employed. After he had eaten the cake, he was seized with violent pain, and this continued with more or less intensity during his journey home, where he arrived on the 5th of January, 1840. It was proved that about this time Madame Lafarge procured some more arsenic, and also some gum-arabic powder, the appearance of which is very similar to that of arsenic. She was in the habit of giving various drinks to her husband during his illness, and into some of these she was observed to put some white powder. On one occasion, after he had tasted an omelette, which she had prepared for him, he cried out that it burned his throat. According to the testimony of some of the witnesses, she seemed anxious to conceal what she was doing when she mixed or stirred any of the drinks which she offered to him. In the meantime the usual medical attendant was treating the disorder as of an inflammatory kind; but the suspicions of the family were now awakened, and on the night of the 12th of January another physician was sent for, to whom their fears were communicated. He thought that the symptoms were those of poison, and immediately administered peroxide of iron; but M. Lafarge rapidly became worse, and on the morning of the 14th he died. An examination of the body took place before its burial, and the medical men declared that they recognized the presence of arsenic in the stomach.

Madame Lafarge was arrested, and while the officers of justice were searching the house at Glandier, the long-missing diamonds of Madame Léotaud were discovered in one of the rooms. Two indictments were preferred against the prisoner, one charging her with the theft of the jewels, and the other with the murder of her husband. The first was tried at Brives, and her counsel made a vigorous but ineffectual attempt to get the case postponed until the more serious charge of murder had been disposed of. When they found that they could not succeed in this, they advised their client to make no defense, and she was found guilty, and sentenced to two years' imprisonment. This judgment was, however, afterwards, on the 3rd of September, set aside by the Court of Tulle, on the ground that the proceedings were irregular, and the reversal was upheld on appeal, by the *Cour de Cassation*, on the 23rd of October.

On the 3rd of September the trial of Madame Lafarge for the murder of her husband commenced at Tulle; and the case for the prosecution was conducted by M. Decoux, the attorney-general. The counsel for the accused were M. Paillet, *bâtonnier* or leader of the bar at Paris, and MM. Lachaud and Bac. The attorney-general opened the case in a speech which, to us who are accustomed to hear the cautious and temperate tone in which the law officers of the crown discharge their duty as prosecutors, seems to denote far too anxious a desire for a conviction. But what shall we think of the following passionate apostrophe to the prisoner, when she was standing at the bar to answer a charge of murder? "Those diamonds," he exclaimed, "those diamonds, Marie Capelle; you have stolen them, I assert it! When you were charged with that crime, what conduct ought you to have observed? You ought to have confessed your guilt, and declared that one day, under the influence of an extraordinary hallucination, you placed your hand upon those ornaments;—that you wished to restore them, but had not the courage to do so. Such a course would have been the avowal of a fault; but in this there was no ignominy. I do not believe that the annals of justice offer us any example of an attempt like that which you have made. I would willingly suppose that you did not conceive it, and that your advisers have led you astray; but I can not believe it—it is impossible.

"Yes! you have defamed Madame de Léotaud.[1] Thus calumny stands by the side of theft. Calumny is also a kind of poisoning, although it kills not the body; yet it poisons the soul."

It is difficult to imagine anything more unfair than this. The only object must have been to prejudice the minds of the jury against the prisoner, and induce them to believe that a woman who could pilfer trinkets would be likely to poison her husband. A most "lame and impotent conclusion," indeed; but one that might most seriously compromise the safety of the accused. It is needless to point out how contrary to every principle of justice it is to mix up charges which are perfectly distinct, and embarrass the prisoner as well as the jury by the

[1] This alludes to the story by which Madame Lafarge sought to explain her possession of the diamonds. She said that Madame de Léotaud had given them to her as a bribe to purchase secrecy with respect to the former amour.

introduction of topics wholly irrelevant to the issue which the latter have to try. In this country such an escapade from a counsel would have drawn down an indignant rebuke from the bench, or rather, we ought to say, it could not have occurred at all.

Not so, however, in France. M. Paillet remonstrated against the course pursued by the attorney-general as illegal, and contrary to the interests of justice, insisting that the affair of the diamonds should be kept separate from the charge of poisoning. This was opposed by M. Decoux; and the court, after having time to consider, decided the point in his favor!

Then commenced the interrogation of the prisoner by the president,—a practice worthy of the dungeons of the Inquisition; for amidst the agitation and alarm of such a crisis, innocence itself may be betrayed into inconsistencies of statements which will seem to be so many indications of guilt. But besides this, *nemo tenetur se ipsum prodere*, and, where the accused party is really criminal, it is merely holding out to him the temptation to utter a series of falsehoods. *We* err, perhaps, in the contrary extreme, and carry our tenderness towards those who are in the grasp of the law to an almost morbid degree. Thus, no confession of guilt by a prisoner beforehand can be received as evidence against him if the most trifling inducement has been held out to him to make the statement, and such a commonplace expression addressed to him as, "You had better tell the truth," would probably exclude the most distinct acknowledgment of his crime.[1] Nay, it is contended that, unless a prisoner is expressly cautioned that what he says will be made use of against him, his voluntary admissions ought not to be received; as though there were any likelihood

---

[1] Not long ago, at a trial at the Central Criminal Court, a policeman was asked whether the prisoner had not made a statement. He answered, "No: he was beginning to do so; *but I knew my duty better*, and I prevented him."

that a man would falsely accuse himself, and as if the object of criminal justice were not the discovery of guilt.

As a specimen of the kind of questions addressed to Madame Lafarge, we may select the following;—

President. " After sending the cake or cakes, and at the time when you presumed that M. Lafarge must have received them, did you not manifest much impatience to receive letters; and did you not say to persons in your company that you dreaded lest you should receive a letter sealed with black?"

Prisoner. "No; I do not believe that I exhibited any such feeling. I was in the habit of frequently receiving letters from Paris, and as I found myself almost solitary at Glandier, I was always impatient to get them."

President. "Did you not observe that M. Lafarge in his last moments, seemed to regard your presence at his bedside with aversion?"

Prisoner. "I perceived plainly enough, a few hours before his death, that he did not look at me with the same interest as formerly; and I attributed this change to some misrepresentation which had been made about me."

One of the witnesses called was M. Massénat, who assisted at the chemical analysis, and he declared his belief in the existence of the arsenic. He added that M. Orfila agreed with him.

M. Paillet. "The letter which M. Orfila wrote to you on the subject, is dated the 31st of July: here is one of the 20th of August, which belies your assertion."

And the letter of this celebrated chemist was actually read, although the author might have been easily summoned from Paris to give his opinion, and the reasons of that opinion, in open court, as was the case at a later period of the trial. No objection, however, was made to its reception as evidence, and it, thereby, appeared that M. Orfila gave a decided negative to the idea that the appearances found in the body of the deceased indicated the presence of arsenic. Upon this the advocate-general applied for a summons to M. Orfila to appear before the court; but the president said that before they could accede to the request a fresh examination of the parts of the body which had been analyzed must be made by other chemists. When this was about to be done, it was found that the different parts had been so carelessly kept, and was so mixed up together, that it was almost impossible to separate or distinguish them. The operation, however, commenced; and in the meantime the examination of witnesses proceeded.

One of the medical witnesses then stated that after they had analyzed the coating of the stomach of the deceased, they obtained a yellowish kind of precipitate, which was placed in a glass tube in order to submit it to the metallic test; but that, "some precautions having been neglected, the tube was broken and the precipitate evaporated. Nevertheless," he added, "notwithstanding this circumstance, the results which we had obtained were sufficient to induce us to come to the conclusion that the spots, which we found in the stomach, had been produced by the poison of arsenic." While M. l'Espinas, one of the physicians, was giving evidence, he stated that when he mentioned to the family his suspicions as to the cause of Lafarge's illness, Madame Bussières, his sister, *exclaimed*, "Ah! the wretch; it is she who has poisoned him!" and that at the same time Mademoiselle Brun, another member of the family, *told* him that she had seen the prisoner take some white powder and put it into a drink; and that, having warned M. Lafarge to be on his guard against his wife, he answered, "It is a miserable business."

Here we see the mischief and danger of hearsay evidence. The exclamation of Madame Bussières was the expression of her opinion on the very question which the jury had to determine, and the court received a statement of what Mademoiselle Brun *had told another that she had seen*, when that lady was herself in attendance to prove upon oath what she had actually witnessed.

Jacques Boutin, the curé of Uzerches, was called to speak to the terms of affectionate intercourse on which the deceased lived with his mother and sister, in order to repel the insinuation that they were the guilty parties. He said, in the course of his evidence, that he had had some conversation with M. Lafarge as his confessor, and, therefore, did not wish to reveal them. The president immediately said that he comprehended and respected his scruples. We have seen that in an English court of justice, the *law* would not regard such a plea of secrecy, although, very probably, the court might, in its discretion, abstain from compelling the witness to divulge what had thus come to his knowledge. The mother of M. Lafarge was next examined at considerable length, and, strange to say, when she was called into the witness-box, M. Paillet, the advocate of the prisoner, who knew that her testimony could not be favorable to his client, and who might have objected to her evidence, merely remarked, " I content myself with bringing before the notice of the court that a formal article of the law, which the president has already read in the course of this trial, forbids the reception of the testimony of the relatives of the accused in the ascending or descending line " (*Code d'Instruct. Crim.*, liv. ii. 322). It seems inexplicable that M. Paillet should have been satisfied with making so faint and feeble a remonstrance when the consequences might be so fatal to the prisoner. After this the attorney-general himself proceeded again to interrogate the prisoner. Let us see the style of questions addressed to a woman on trial for her life.

Attorney-General. " In your own explanation it appears that you spoke of arsenic—of poison. It is with astonishment that one hears such words uttered by the lips of a young female who has received a brilliant education, whose intelligence is far above the common order. It appears that when the sister of Lafarge made an observation to you about it, you said, 'It is a family disease.'"

Prisoner. "I never said so. I may have said in a fit of delirium, perhaps, that I would take poison if I was not allowed to go away."

Now mark the insidious and ensnaring nature of the following question.

Attorney-General. "It is possible that as the letter which you wrote was the result of a fixed determination to escape, *you may have said to yourself,* 'I will try and frighten him,' and, with that intention, you may have said to your sister-in-law,—'You may be the more alarmed since it is a family disease?'"

Prisoner. "But, in the first place, I never had any notion of the disease of which you speak, nor of the words which are attributed to me. All that I remember having said was, 'I wish for a separation.' To which M. Lafarge replied, 'I will never consent to it.'"

Again :—

Attorney-General. "In making your mother-in-law write a letter to her son, you had a project in view in case you should be accused. You wished, supposing that Lafarge should die, to protect yourself by anticipation, by means of that letter, against judicial inquiry. Did you exhibit any fears? Did you speak of a letter sealed with black?"

Prisoner. "I do not recollect it."

Attorney-General. "*But, supposing that you did exhibit those fears, how would you be able to explain them?*"

Prisoner. "I cannot explain a thing which I never did, of which I know nothing."

Attorney-General. "Did you ask how long widows were in the habit of wearing mourning in this part of the country?"

Prisoner. "I have no recollection of doing so."

During this severe cross-examination, for it can be

called by no other name, it was announced that the chemists were ready to make their report, and it may be easily imagined what intense interest was now excited. M. Dubois came forward, and, after a long and minute detail of the processes which he and his colleagues had adopted, he said, " The conclusion at which we have arrived is, that the substances which have been submitted to us *do not contain a single particle of arsenic.*"

This in England would certainly have been tantamount to an acquittal, for it is hardly credible that the prosecution would have insisted upon a third investigation. But the attorney-general was not satisfied, and the court ordered that the corpse of the deceased should be exhumed, and submitted to chemical tests. However much our feelings may be revolted by such a proceeding, it is not easy to say that this course was wrong. The professed object of the inquiry was the discovery of the truth; and the exhumation of the body seemed to furnish the most obvious means of ascertaining it. Two contrary opinions had already been given as to the existence of arsenic, and it was, perhaps, therefore right to resort to an examination of the body as a kind of *experimentum crusis* to determine the fact.

A witness, named Denis Barbier, was next examined, who proved that Madame Lafarge had commissioned him, on more than one occasion, to purchase arsenic for her. He was allowed to state that *he had told his wife* that he was afraid the arsenic was got for the purpose of killing M. Lafarge. He was also asked, by the president, the following question :—" When did you first entertain suspicions of poisoning against the prisoner ? " to which he answered—" When she asked me with such importunity to procure arsenic, and especially when she enjoined secrecy."

In the course of his evidence, Barbier was asked by the advocate-general—

"Have you any cause of complaint against Madame Lafarge?"

Barbier. "No; she never did me anything but kindnesses."

Upon this the attorney-general turned round triumphantly to the prisoner, and said—

"How do you explain, madame, now, the allegation that this witness gives false testimony? Your mother-in-law has deposed, as well as the witness, to the fact that you kept the purchase of arsenic a secret from her. You surely do not accuse the testimony of your mother-in-law. I fancy that you respect it."

Prisoner. "Be it so; I see only that my mother-in-law has repeated the falsehoods of the witness."

President. "Does the prisoner believe that the witness has, in his deposition, followed the suggestions of others?"

Prisoner. "I believe that he simply yields to his old habits, which are little creditable to him."

During the examination of the next witness, Jean Bardon, one of the domestics at Glandier, he was asked—

"Did Denis *tell* you that M. Lafarge had died by poison?"

Bardon. "He said that my master's wife had fed him for fifteen days upon poison. I told him that that was difficult, since only thirteen days elapsed after his return. 'Bah!' he answered, 'she had sent him a poisoned cake two days previously. That made up the fifteen days.'"

With reference to the sending of this cake, the attorney-general, in the course of the trial, said, addressing himself to the jury: "Madame Lafarge has taken care to put out of the way the letter in which she announced to her husband the arrival of the cake, *otherwise we should infallibly have found, written in her own hand, the proof that she had sent him only one cake*—a cake quite different from the smaller ones which she had, in the presence of witnesses, put into the box, after having wrapped them up, as she says, like oranges. But, in default of the letter, we have the answer of M. Lafarge, and doubt is no longer possible."

Now, however, the medical witnesses entered the court, and stated that they had exhumed the body, and had brought away such portions as they deemed necessary for their analyses. The court ordered them to make the investigation in the neighborhood of the hall, but said that it was indispensable, in the first instance, that the prisoner should look at the seals of the packets, and see that they were unbroken. This produced a thrill of horror in the audience, and her attorney was allowed to examine the seals instead of her.

While the chemists were employed on their loathsome task, which rendered the air of the court almost insupportable, several witnesses were examined, one of whom proved that rats infested the house at Glandier; and another, that she saw Madame Lafarge put four small cakes into the box which she sent to her husband. This was an important piece of evidence in favor of the accused, for it went directly to contradict the assertion that she had substituted one large cake for those which had been prepared by her mother-in-law.

As soon as the chemists returned into the court a breathless silence prevailed, and M. Dupuytren read the report which they had prepared. And when he came to the words: "We introduced these precipitates into Marsh's apparatus, and, after making several experiments, we have not obtained a single atom of arsenic"—a burst of applause followed the announcement, which ruffled the temper of the attorney-general, and he exclaimed, in an excited tone,—' Do people think, then, that there remain no more resources for the prosecution? Do they think that we have not yet to fulfill a great and solemn duty?"

M. Dupuytren continued, "However, some of the

experts believed that, while we were using Marsh's apparatus, they detected, for a moment or two, a slight odor of garlic. . . . . We unanimously conclude that there is no arsenic in any of the animal substances submitted to our examination."

This surely ought to have been sufficient. Here was a plain proof that there was no *corpus delicti*, and the prisoner was entitled to an immediate acquittal. We may imagine with what withering eloquence Erskine would have denounced the idea of a fresh attempt to discover traces of poison in a body which had been so minutely and rigorously examined. But the advocate-general called upon the court to require the attendance of some eminent Parisian chemists, in order that there might be a fourth investigation: this request was complied with, and a telegraphic dispatch was transmitted to Paris, ordering MM. Orfila, Bussi, and Ollivier (d'Angers) to come immediately to Tulle. In the meantime Mlle. Brun was examined, and she proved that she saw the prisoner shake some white powder into a cup of *lait de poule*, prepared for her husband, and stir it with her finger, and that on being asked what it was, she answered that it was some orange flower. The witness added, that seeing a little of the white powder on a chair she put it on her tongue, and it produced a pricking sensation, which lasted for an hour.

When M. Orfila and his colleagues arrived they received the portions of the body which had been already analyzed, and immediately commenced their experiments. The result was that on their return to court M. Orfila said, "I will demonstrate that there exists arsenic in the body of Lafarge; that the arsenic does not proceed from the reactives with which we have operated, nor from the earth which surrounded the coffin; that the arsenic extracted by us is no part of that quantity of arsenic which exists naturally in the human body; and, in the last place, I will show that it is not impossible to explain the discrepancy of the results and opinions of the different operators." He declared, therefore, in the name of himself and his colleagues, that there was arsenic in the body of the deceased, *though in the minutest quantity*.[1]

The attorney-general summed up the evidence against the prisoner with more vehemence than he had displayed even in his opening speech; and then M. Paillet rose, and made a feeling and eloquent defence. His concluding words were, "At this last moment, gentlemen, I will only add one word, and it is this, that the condemnation of the innocent is, of all social evils, the most deplorable, because it is the most irreparable. All is doubt in this melancholy transaction, and doubt, in a criminal trial, suffices for the acquittal of the accused. How can we believe that this lady, the depths of whose heart we have sounded—that this lady, who, at the end of the month of December, was conscious of the joys of maternity, could, on the third of January, poison her husband—the father of her child? No; gentlemen, it is impossible. Ah, while you accomplish the fatal mission which is confided to you, beware of adding to the mournful legends of that accursed house of Glandier!"

And here we should suppose that the duties of counsel were at an end, and that nothing remained but the charge of the president to the jury. But, as Sterne says in his Sentimental Journey, "they order this matter better in France;" and, to our utter amazement, up rises the attorney-general, and makes a fierce attack upon the character of the prisoner, accusing her of the robbery of the diamonds! He was followed by M. Bac, the junior counsel for Madame Lafarge, who, at considerable length,

---

[1] The late Sir Astley Cooper assured a friend of mine, that he had taken great pains to satisfy himself, after a careful consideration of the printed report of the trial, as to whether the existence of arsenic as an extraneous poison in the body was proved; and he had come to the conclusion that it was not. See note, *post*, p. 293.

examined the facts connected with the story of the diamonds, and having read several letters to prove that Madame de Léotaud had kept up, after her marriage, a correspondence with her former lover, he asked the jury to infer that she had given the jewels to the prisoner to prevent the disclosure of her frailty. After this extraordinary episode the president summed up the case, and left the following question to the jury: "Is Marie Fortunée Capelle, widow of Pouch Lafarge, guilty of having, in December and January last, caused the death of her husband by means of substances capable of occasioning death, and which, in fact, did occasion it?"

At the end of an hour the jury returned into court and gave in the following written verdict:—

"Yes; by a majority, the accused is Guilty.

"Yes; by a majority, there are extenuating circumstances in favor of the accused."

The judges then retired, and after remaining in deliberation for an hour, resumed their seats and pronounced their sentence, condemning the prisoner to the hulks for life, and to exposure on the pillory in the public square of Tulle.

Thus ended this famous trial; and the question may still be asked—Guilty, or not Guilty? In England, there is little doubt that, upon the evidence, the verdict would have been Not Guilty; in Scotland, it is equally certain that it would have been Not Proven. The amount of arsenic found in the body of the deceased was too infinitesimally small to admit of a safe conclusion that he had died from the effects of poison; especially, when we consider that, if the evidence for the prosecution is relied upon, he must, for many days before his death, have swallowed a large quantity of arsenic: and when we recollect that arsenic enters into the texture of human bones, and that the body, when exhumed, was in a state of extreme decomposition, we see that the risk of an erroneous opinion on the part of the chemists was increased. It is important to bear in mind the fact that the soil of graveyards often contains a compound of arsenic, though generally in an insoluble form. In eight trials on four different soils Orfila found that three of them were arsenical. He used about six pounds of earth in the experiment.[1]

But, yet it is difficult, after a review of the whole case, to resist the conviction that the accused was really guilty. Her previous conduct, and her actions while her husband was laid on the bed of sickness, all seem to point to that conclusion, and our moral sense is by no means shocked by the verdict of the jury. Of the mode in which the trial was conducted, we can hardly speak too strongly in terms of reprobation. Almost every principle of the law of evidence, without reference to our own technical rules, was violated; and we hardly know which most to condemn, the indecent eagerness of the attorney-general for a conviction, the cross-examination of the prisoner herself, or the injustice of the court in permitting, contrary to the remonstrance of her counsel, the affair of the diamonds to be dragged into discussion. Upon the whole, the result is that, however much we may regret that the unbending strictness of the English law sometimes excludes testimony which, perhaps, ought to be admitted, and thereby facil-

---

[1] See Taylor's *Medical Jurisprudence*, p. 83 (third edit.) "If the coffin be cracked or entirely destroyed, so that the earth has become intermixed with the remains, and that which surrounds the coffin yields traces of arsenic, it is evident that no reliance could be placed upon the inference that the arsenic existed in the dead body, unless the poison found in the remains was in extremely large proportion. . . . A difficulty of this kind, cannot, however, *when proper precautions are taken*, often present itself in practice."—*Ib.* It is right to mention that in cases of rapid death from arsenic, even when no traces of the poison can be found in the stomach, or contents of the viscera, it may always be discovered in the tissues.—*Ib.* pp. 81, 82. It is remarkable that Mr. Taylor, in his extremely able work, although he cites several French cases, including that of the Duc de Praslin, does not allude to that of Madame Lafarge.

itates the escape of guilt, a party who is accused in England of a crime of which he is innocent, may congratulate himself that his trial takes place here and not in France.

CHAPTER VIII.

ADVOCACY IN ENGLAND.

AS the object of this work is not to write a history of the bar, but merely to consider the office and functions of a lawyer in his capacity of an advocate, charged with the defense of the rights and interests of his fellow-citizens in courts of justice, it is not necessary to enlarge upon what may be called the archæology of the profession, nor transcribe from ancient writers the curious particulars they record of its state and condition in very early times in England. Nor need we dwell at any length upon the venerable degree and dignity of sergeants-at-law, of whose creation and appointment Fortescue in his work *De Laudibus Legum Angliæ*, and Dugdale in his *Origines*, give such ample details. Great was their state and solemn their inauguration in the olden time. When called to receive their office by the Lord Chancellor, "after that the company is so assembled in their hall, thence cometh down to them the new sergeants: and after that the new sergeants be so come down to the company, then all they standing together, the most ancient of the company rehearseth the manner of learning and study; giving laud and praise to them that have well used them, showing what worship and profit cometh and groweth by reason of the same, in proof whereof those new sergeants, for their cunning, discretion, and wisdom, be called, by the king's highness and his honorable council, to the great promotion and dignity of the office of a sergeant of the law: and then he giveth them a laud and praise for their good conversation, and pain and diligence that they have taken and used in their study, presenting to them the reward of the house, beseeching them to be good and kind to the company" (Dugdale, *Orig. Jurid.* 114). When they had refreshed themselves with "spiced bread, comfits, and other goodly conceits, with hippocrass," the labors of the first day were over. Afterwards they counted upon their writs, a legal mystery which it would not be easy to make very intelligible, and then proceeded to attack a right goodly feast, which Fortescue says "shall continue and last for the space of seven days; and none of those elect persons shall defray the charges growing to him about the costs of this solemnity, with less expenses than four hundred marks." The grandeur of these entertainments in former times was remarkable, and they were generally held in Ely House, where "divers great and solemn feasts," says Stow, "have been kept, especially by the sergeants at the law;" and where royalty did not disdain to appear, accompanied by "all the Lords and Commons of the Parliament." Henry VII. and his queen dined there more than once, and in the twenty-third year of the reign of Henry VIII., he and Queen Catherine honored the newly-created sergeants with their company, " but in two chambers," at a sumptuous repast which lasted for five days. The monarch, however, and his queen were present only on the principal day. "It were tedious to set down the preparation of fish, flesh, and other victuals spent in this feast, and would seem almost incredible: and as to me, it seemeth, wanted little of a feast at a coronation." So says honest Dugdale (*Orig. Jurid.* 128), and agreeing with him, I may spare the reader the enumeration which he gives of the great beefs, fat muttons, porkes, capons, cocks of grouse, pullets, and swans, which were there consumed.[1] When the elevation of these aspirants to the coif was regarded as so important, and attended with such stately ceremony, well might Fortescue exclaim, "Neither is there any man of law, throughout the universal world, which by reason of his office or profession, gaineth so much as one of these sergeants" (*De Laud. Leg. Ang.*).

But "how are the mighty fallen!" The ruthless hand of innovation has swept away their privileges, and they no longer possess now even the monopoly of practice in their own court of Common Pleas, which they enjoyed for upwards of seven hundred years. Firmly, and successfully for a time, was the change resisted when the attempt was made to throw open that court to all advocates, by virtue of a warrant under the sign-manual of the crown; but an Act of Parliament accomplished the same object some years ago, without complaint or even a murmur of opposition.

We know, from several passages in our old writers, that pleaders or advocates existed in this country in very early times. They are said to have been in repute in the reign of William Rufus; and Mathew Paris, the historian, in his *Lives of the Abbots of St. Alban's*, gives us a curious account of the reason why they were temporarily awed into silence at a later period. After stating that the abbey had been much oppressed in the reign of Henry III. by a person who was protected by John Mansel, he goes on to say, "Nor could we obtain any right or redress while the said John was the confidante, and assisted at the councils of the king. Nay, more, the terror and influence of John himself com-

[1] The particulars which Dugdale records of one of these feasts, in 1555, are most inviting, and prove how thoroughly the science of good living was understood by our ancestors. There is one dish, the "chewet pies," which figures very frequently in the bill of fare. One of the ornaments of the table was "a standing dish of wax representing the Court of Common Pleas." It is curious to compare the prices then with those of the present day.

pletely stopped the mouths (*ora penitus obturavit*) of all the judges and pleading advocates (whom we usually call *Countors of the Bench*). So that oftentimes the Lord William, who was then our bursar[1] (a man circumspect and eloquent withal), was obliged to state his complaints himself, in his own person, before the justices, and even before the king and barons (*Barnagium. Ducange, in voc.*). And the justices protested, as they privately whispered into the ear of the said William, that at that time there were two persons who bore rule in the realm,—to wit, Count Richard, and John Mansel, in the face of whom they did not venture to deliver judgment."

We have seen that in France, when judicial combats took, the *gens de loi* were called upon to officiate in the preliminary stage of the proceedings. And in old times in England, the peaceful sergeants had sometimes to act very much in the capacity of seconds to the combatants, as will appear from the following example. It was the case of a writ of right which two demandants brought against Paramour, the tenant of lands in Kent (*Lowe and Kyme* v. *Paramour, Dyer*, 301, a), and occurred in 1571, in the reign of Elizabeth.

"And Paramour chose the trial by battle, and his champion was one George Thorne; and the demandants *e contra*, and their champion was one Henry Nailer, a master of defense. And the court awarded the battle; and the champions were by mainprise, and sworn (quære the form of the oath) to perform the battle at Tothill, in Westminster, on Monday next after the morrow of the Trinity, which was the first day after the utas of the Term, and the same day given to the parties; at which day and place a list was made in an even and level piece of ground, set out square, sixty feet on each side, due east, west, north, and south, and a place or seat for the

---

[1] *Cellarius.* Ducange in his Glossary says that this officer corresponds to the more modern *bursar.* Perhaps *Dominus Wilielmus* would be more correctly translated *Master* than *Lord* William.

judges of the bench was made without and above the lists, and covered with the furniture of the same bench in Westminster Hall; and a bar made there for the sergeants-at-law. And about the tenth hour of the same day, three justices of the bench, Dyer, Weston, and Harper, Welshe being absent on account of sickness, repaired to the place in their robes of scarlet, with the appurtenances and coifs; and the sergeants also. And their public proclamation being three times made with an Oyez, the demandants first were solemnly called, and did not come. After which, the mainpernors of the champions were called to produce the champion of the demandants first, who came into the place, appareled in red sandals over armor of leather, bare-legged from the knee downward, and bare-headed, and bare arms to the elbow, being brought in by the hand of a knight, namely, Sir Jerome Bowes, who carried a red baston of an ell long, tipped and horn, and a yeoman carrying a target made of double leather; and they were brought in at the north side of the lists, and went about the side of the lists until the middest of the lists, and then came towards the bar before the justices with three solemn congies, and there was he made to stand at the south side of the place, being the right side of the court; and after that, the other champion was brought in like manner at the south side of the lists, with like congies, etc., by the hands of Sir Henry Cheney, knight, etc., and was set on the north side of the bar; *and two sergeants being of counsel of each party in the midst between them:* this done, the demandant was solemnly called again, and appeared not, but made default; upon which default, Barham, sergeant for the tenant, prayed the court to record the nonsuit, which was done."

This is said by Blackstone to have been the last trial by battle that was waged in the court of Common Pleas at Westminster; but in the reign of Charles I. another instance occurred in the Court of Pleas at Durham, where

Lilburne, the father of the well-known republican of that name, was the defendant (*Claxton* v. *Lilburn*, 2 *Rushworth's Coll.* 788). A point arose in that case, whether the champions should be permitted to fight, inasmuch as they confessed that they had been hired for money. It was, however, decided by all the judges, that this objection, "coming after the battle gaged, and champions allowed, and sureties given to perform it, ought not to be received."

A curious account is given in the "State Trials" of the proceedings in the Court of Chivalry, on an appeal of high treason, by Donald Lord Rea against David Ramsey, in the same reign; and the dress and appearance of the parties are thus described:—The appellant "was appareled in black velvet, trimmed with silver buttons, his sword in a silver embroidered belt, his order of a Scotch baronet about his neck; and so, with reverence, he entered into his pew: his counsel, Doctor Reeves, standing by. His behavior (like himself, tall, swarthy, black, not comely) very port-like, and of staid countenance. The defendant was alike ushered in by another herald. His sureties were the Lord Roxburgh and Lord Abercorn; and his deport, like himself, stern and brave, a fair, ruddy, yellow-headed bush of hair (so large, and, in those days, unusual, that he was called Ramsey Redhead). His apparel, scarlet, overlaced with silver, the ground hardly discerned, and lined with sky-colored plush, but unarmed, without a sword. After his reverence to the court, he faced the appellant, who alike sterned a countenance at him." His counsel was a Doctor Eden, who agued that his client ought not to be compelled to fight, for certain technical reasons, which he pointed out; but at the same time he added, that Ramsey had told him in private, that though in law he might, yet, in honor and innocency, he would not decline the combat, so that the advocate felt puzzled what to say for him. We are told that both parties were admitted to

APPEAL IN COURT OF CHIVALRY. 301

have common lawyers, but to plead only by civilians; and a Doctor *Duck*, the king's advocate acted as an assessor to the court during the proceedings. The result was, that the lord-constable, taking the appeal in his hands, and folding it up, put it into the glove which the Lord Rea had thrown down in the court for a pawn in that behalf, and held the bill and glove in his right hand, and in his left the answer and glove, or pawn, of David Ramsey; and then, joining the bill and answer, and the gloves, and folding them together, he, with the earl-marshal, solemnly adjudged a duel between the parties " in the name of God, the Father, the Son, and the Holy Ghost, the Holy and most blessed Trinity, who is one and the only God and Judge of battles." The time and place assigned were, " the twelfth day of the month of April next following, between sun and sun, in the fields called Tuttle fields, in or near Westminster, in the presence of our lord the king." It was also decided, in compliance with the prayer of the challenger, that his *counsel* might be received into the lists or field with him " for to counsel him what should be needful," and also (as seems still more needful), that he might have a chirurgeon, with his ointments and instruments, ready to serve him. The king, however, ultimately forbade the duel, being " resolved not to suffer them to fight," on the ground, that he was fully satisfied that Ramsey had committed no such treason as had been imputed to him. And thus ended this great appeal.[1]

In England, as elsewhere on the Continent, the great majority of the lawyers who practiced in the courts were originally shaven clerks; and hence some have derived that indispensable appendage to a barrister's costume,—

[1] Wager of Battle and Trial by Battle were abolished by 59 *Geo.* III., c. 46. The same statute abolished also appeals of murder, in which the same kind of combat took place. Judgment in favor of wager by battle, in an appeal of death, was pronounced by the Court of King's Bench in the year 1818. See Ashford *v.* Thornton, 1 *Barn. & Ald.* iv. 405. This case led to the passing of the above statute.

his wig. For, when the appearance of the clergy as advocates before lay tribunals began to be restrained, as it first was by a constitution of the bishop of Salisbury at the beginning of the reign of Henry III., which provided that advocates in the secular courts should not be clerks or priests unless they undertook their own causes, or those of destitute persons,—it is said that they adopted the wig to conceal the tonsure of their heads, in order that it might not be discovered that they were priests. And in 1259, when William de Bussy, who practiced as an advocate, was called to account for his knavery and mal-practices, he claimed the benefit of his clergy, which, till then, had remained a secret, and to prove that he was in holy orders he wished to untie the fastenings of his coif, whereby his tonsure might appear; but this was not allowed, and an officer of justice seized hold of him, and conveyed him to prison.

It has been already mentioned how little the conduct of advocates in this country has been subjected to any legislative interference; but a statute is still in force, which was passed in the year 1275, in the reign of Edward I., whereby it was provided, "That if any sergeant, countor, or others, do any manner of deceit or collusion in the king's court, or consent unto it, in deceit of the court, or to beguile the court, or the party, and thereof be attained, he shall be imprisoned for a year and a day, and from thenceforth shall not be heard to plead in that court for any man; and if he be no countor he shall be imprisoned in like manner by the space of a year and a day at least; and if the trespass shall require greater punishment it shall be at the king's pleasure."

In that ancient book, the *Mirroir des Justices*, it is laid down[1] that every pleader (or countor, as he is called) on behalf of others ought to have regard to four things. First, that he be a person receivable in judgment; that

[1] Chap. ii. Sect. 5. The *Mirroir* was written by Andrew Horne, who is supposed to have lived in the reign of Edward II.

he be no heretic, excommunicate person, nor criminal, nor a man of religion, nor a woman, nor a beneficed clerk with cure of souls, nor under the age of twenty-one years, nor judge in the same cause, nor attainted of falsity against the right of his office. Secondly, every pleader is to be charged by oath that he will not maintain nor defend what is wrong or false to his knowledge, but will fight (*guerra*) for his client to the utmost of his ability. Thirdly, he is to put in before the court no false delays (dilatory pleas), nor false evidence, nor move nor offer any corruptions, deceits, tricks, or false lies, nor consent to any such, but truly maintain the right of his client, so that it fail not through any folly, negligence, or default in him. Fourthly, in respect of his salary four things are to be considered—the value of the cause; the pains of the sergeant; the worth of the pleader in point of knowledge, eloquence, and gifts; the usage of the court. And a pleader is to be suspended if he be attainted of having received fees from both sides in the same cause, and if he say or do anything in contempt of the court.

Forensic eloquence in this country seems to have been almost unknown until the latter part of the eighteenth century. We read, indeed, of the "silver-tongued" Finch, afterwards Lord Nottingham, who was called in his day the "English Cicero" and the "English Roscius," but no speeches of his have been preserved which justify the epithet; and we search in vain that voluminous and interesting repository of cases, the *State Trials*, where the higher efforts of judicial oratory ought, if anywhere, to be found, for

"Thoughts that breathe, and words that burn,"

in the efforts made by our advocates, in former days, for their clients. We find, indeed, immense learning and research; a wonderful familiarity with precedents, the pole-star of the English lawyer; and sound and logical argument, interrupted, however, too often by puerilities and labored truisms, and conveyed in the stiff and formal periods in which our ancestors used to enunciate their thoughts. And yet, in very early times, we meet with specimens of simple and beautiful English, which show the language was for pathos, and how adapted, therefore, how well fitted for heart-stirring appeals to mercy and compassion. As an instance of this may be selected the confession of Thomas Duke of Gloucester, who, in 1397, in the twenty-first year of the reign of Richard II., was impeached for having levied war against the king, and encroached upon the royal authority. The Duke died in prison before trial, but, previously, made the following confession (*State Trials*, i. 131):

"I, Thomas of Woodstock, the zear[1] of my lord the king 21, be[2] the verture of a commission of my lord the king, the same zear, directed to Wm. Rickhill, justice, the which is comprehended more plainly in the aforesaid commission, knowleche that I was one with sertynge[3] of other men, to assent to the making of a commission, in the which commission I, among others, restrained my lord of his freedom, and took upon me, among others, power regal, truly not knowing me witting, that time that I did against his estate, nor his royaltie, as I did after and do now; and, forasmuch, as I knew afterwards that I had done wrong, and take upon me more than I ought to do, I submitted me to my lord, and cried him mercy and grace, and yet do, as truly and as meekly as any man may, and put me high and low in his mercy and grace, as he hath always been full of mercy and grace to all other. Also, in that time, that I came armed into my lord's presence, and unto his palace, howsoever, that I did it for drede of my life, I knowleche for certain that I did evil, and against his regalitie, and his estate, wherefore, I submit me lowly and meekly to his mercy, and to his grace. Also, in that I took my lord's letters of his

[1] Year.　　　[2] By.　　　[3] Certain.

messages, and opened them against his leave, I knowleche that I did evil, wherefore, I put me lowly in his grace. Also, in that, that I sclaundered my lord, I knowleche that I did evil and wickedly, in that, that I spake to him in slanderous wise, in audience of other folk: bot by the way, that my soul shall too, I meant none evil therein, nevertheless, I wot and knowleche that I did evil and unkindly, wherefore I submit me high and low in his grace. Also, in that I, among other, communed and asked of certain clercs whether that we might give up our homage for drede of our lives or not, and whether that we were assentid thereto for to do it, trewly and by my troth, I ne have now none full mind thereof, but I trowe rather yes than nay, wherefore I submit me high and low ever more in his grace. . . . . . And, therefore, I beseech my liege and sovereign lord the king, that he will of his grace and benignity accept me to his mercy and his grace, as I put my life, my body, and my goods, wholly at his will as lowly, as meekly as any creature can do, or may do to his liege lord; beseeching to his high lordship, that he will, for the passion of him that suffered for all mankind, and the compassion that he had for his mother on the crosse, and the pity he had of Mary Magdalen, that he will vouchsafe for to have compassion and pity, and to accept me to his mercy and to his grace; as he that hath ever been full of mercy and of grace to all his lieges, and to all other that have nought been so nigh unto him as I have been, though I been unworthy."

Sir Thomas Elyot, in his Governor, gives the following explanation of the fact which we are considering:—" But for as much as the tongue, wherein the law is spoken, is barbarous, and the stirring of affections of the mynde in this nature was never used, therefore there lacketh elocution and pronunciation, two of the principal parts of rhetoricke.

> "It was a party-color'd dress,
> Of patch'd and pie-ball'd languages:
> 'Twas English cut on *French* and Latin,
> Like fustian heretofore on satin."

I know no passage in any speech of an advocate, previous to the year 1700, which can be compared with the address of Chief Justice Crewe, in 1626, when the judges were called in to assist the House of Lords in a a claim of peerage (*Jones, Rep.* 96). A question arose upon the death of Henry de Vere, earl of Oxford, without issue, whether Robert de Vere, claiming under an entail as heir-male of the body of Aubrey de Vere, or Lord Willoughby d'Eresby, as heir-general of the deceased earl, was entitled to the earldom. The following is part of "the resolution delivered by Crewe, chief justice, in parliament, concerning the earldom of Oxford; Walter, chief baron, Dodridge and Yelverton, justices; and Trevor, baron, advising with him together thereon:"

"This case stands upon many parts. Subtile disputants may perturb the best judgments. There have been many thick and dark fogs and mists raised in the face of this cause. But *magna est veritas, et prævalet*. Truth lets in the sun to scatter and disperse them.

"Here is represented to your lordships *certamen honoris*, and, as I may well say, *illustris honoris*, illustrious honor. I heard a great peer of this realm and a learned, say, when he lived there was no king in Christendom had such a subject as Oxford. He came in with the Conqueror, earl of Gwynes; shortly after the conquest made great chamberlain of England, above five hundred years ago, by Henry I., the Conqueror's son, brother to Rufus; by Maude the empress, earl of Oxford; confirmed and approved by Henry II. Alberico comiti, so earl before.

"This great honor, this high and noble dignity, hath continued ever since in the remarkable surname of De Vere, by so many ages, descents, and generations, as no other kingdom can produce such a peer in one of the self-same name and title. I find in all this length of time but two attainders of this noble family, and those in stormy and tempestuous times, when the government was unsettled and the kingdom in competition. I have labored to make a covenant with myself that affection may not press upon judgment, for I suppose there is no man that hath any apprehension of gentry or nobleness, but his affection stands to the continuance of so noble a name and house, and would take hold of a twig or a twine thread to uphold it. And yet Time hath its revolutions; there must be a period and an end to all temporal things—*finis rerum*, an end of names, and dignities, and whatsoever is terrene, and why not of De Vere? For where is Bohun? where is Mowbray? where is Mortimer? Nay, which is more and most of all, where is Plantagenet? They are entombed in the urns and sepulchres of mortality. And yet let the name and dignity of De Vere stand so long as it pleaseth God!"

This is a style that soars far beyond the language of forensic speeches, before the magic of Erskine's voice was heard in the courts, and is more like the deep and stately eloquence which we find in the writings of Sir Walter Raleigh, Bacon, Milton, and Sir Thomas Browne. If, however, we wish to know the highest kind of eloquence in this country, in former times, we must turn to our old divines,—to Hall, Taylor, Barrow, and Leighton, in whose works we possess some of the noblest thoughts which have ever been conceived by man, clothed and adorned in a profusion of the richest imagery. It is distressing to compare such compositions with the speeches delivered at the same period, and to observe the vast inferiority of the latter (*Macaulay's Hist. of England*, ii. 177).

But we must remember that from one of the best opportunities that can occur for the display of oratory, advocates, in this country, were debarred until after the Revolution. I allude to speeches in defense of prisoners charged with treason or felony, which, until after that period, they were not permitted, in any such cases, to make.¹

The subject is so interesting that it will justify some detail. It was a settled rule of the common law, that no counsel should be allowed to a prisoner, whether he were a peer or a commoner, upon the question of guilty or not guilty in an indictment for treason or felony,— unless some point of law should arise, *proper to be debated*.² And this, as we shall see, the judges were to decide beforehand, as the cases arose before them ; and too often they refused the assistance prayed for by the hapless prisoner. Thus, when the Duke of Norfolk was indicted for high treason in the reign of Elizabeth, he made a touching appeal to the court for the aid of counsel ; but in vain (A. D. 1571. *State Tr.*, i. 965). " I have," he said, " had very short warning to provide to answer so great a matter ; I have not had fourteen hours in all, both day and night, and now I neither hear the same statute alleged, and yet I am put at once to the whole herd of laws, not knowing which particularly to answer unto. The indictment containeth sundry points and matters to touch me by circumstance, and so to draw me into the matter of treason which are not treasons themselves : therefore, with reverence and humble submission, I am led to think I may have counsel. And this I show, that you may think I move not this suit without any ground. I am hardly handled. I have had short warning, and no books."³ But he was answered by Chief

---

¹ When, therefore, Hallam (*Const. Hist.* iii. 2, 3d edit.), speaking of the reign of Charles II., says, " Though the Bench was frequently subservient, the Bar contained high-spirited advocates, whose firm defense of their clients the judges often reproved, but no longer affected to punish," he must allude to trials other than those of treason or felony.

² The reader may consult the following authorities : Hawkins's *Pleas of the Crown*, Bk. ii. ch. 39 ; Evelyn's *Preface to State Trials*. The learned note to *State Trials*, v. 466. Stephen's *Comm.* iv. 425.

³ The ability with which the Duke of Norfolk defended himself, and the

Justice Dyer, that counsel could not be allowed in point of treason, and his request was refused.

And in that most interesting trial of Colonel Lilburne, the stout-hearted republican soldier, who, after having fought against his king for the parliament, was indicted, as a traitor, for publishing several books, in which he denounced Cromwell's government as tyrannical, usurped, and unlawful, we find that his passionate entreaties and solemn adjurations for the help of counsel had no effect. Over and over again he prayed his judges to assign him counsel, declaring his ignorance of the formalities and niceties of the law, and, therefore, he said, "If you will not assign me counsel to advise and consult with, I am resolved to go no further, though I die for it; and my innocent blood be upon your hands." But not even when he excepted against the matter and form of the indictment, " matter, time, and place," and humbly craved counsel to plead to the errors thereof, was his petition granted; and the trial proceeded, in which the prisoner was left to his unaided efforts (*State Tr.*, iv., 1329). Happily, however, the jury pronounced a verdict of acquittal.

There are few trials more instructive than this. The manly, straightforward bearing of Lilburne, urging an Englishman's right to a fair hearing, and his spirited rebuke to the attorney-general, who forgot the humane maxim of the law, that every man is presumed to be innocent until he is proved to be guilty, make us warmly sympathize with him. And yet the judges who sat upon his trial, Lord Commissioner Keble, and Jermin, justice of the upper bench (those were the times of the Com-

exceptions which he took in point of law to the indictment and evidence drew from Gerard, the attorney-general, who, with the Queen's sergeant and others, conducted the prosecution, the unfeeling remark, " You complained of your close keeping, that you had no books to provide for your answer. It seemeth you have had books and counsel: you allege books and statutes, and Bracton. I am sure the study of such books is not your profession."

monwealth), and others, seem to have been animated by a sincere desire to administer the law, as it then stood, fairly and impartially.

When Sir Henry Vane was indicted for high treason he raised the following most important points of law, and earnestly prayed to have counsel assigned to speak to them (A. D. 1662. *State Tr.*, vi. 153):

"1. Whether the collective body of the parliament can be impeached of high treason? 2. Whether any person acting by authority of parliament can (so long as he acteth by that authority) commit treason? 3. Whether matters acted by that authority can be called in question in an inferior court? 4. Whether a king *de jure*, and out of possession, can have treason committed against him, he not being king *de facto*, and in actual possession? 5. Whether matters done in Southwark, in another county, may be given in evidence to a Middlesex jury?" But the application was refused, and the result of the trial is well known.[1]

In the case of Algernon Sidney we meet with several instances of the harsh and iniquitous severity of the law in those days, with reference to the matter which we are now discussing (A. D. 1683. *State Tr.*, ix. 817). The illustrious prisoner objected, in the course of the proceedings, that the levying of war and conspiring the death of the king were two distinct things, and distinguished by the Statute of Treasons, 25 *Edw. III.*; and that by subsequent statutes it was provided that there must be two witnesses to prove each of those facts; and that in reality only one witness against him, Lord Howard, had spoken either to the levying of war or the conspiracy. He asked, therefore, that he might have counsel to argue the point, but the court decided that it could not be allowed (*State Tr.*, ix. 861, 862). So again, when he contended that conspiring to levy war was not treason, and

---

[1] The same points had been previously decided on the trials of the regicides.

desired to have counsel upon that, his request was denied. And a similar application met with a like result when he raised the objection that some of the jury by whom he was tried were not freeholders of the county in which the venue of the indictment was laid.[1] Many other cases might be quoted to the same effect, such as those of Colledge, "the Protestant joiner" (*Ib.* viii. 550), and Lord Russell (*Ib.* ix. 578), and many others; but those which I have given will be sufficient as examples. It is clear that the judges reserved to themselves the right of determining beforehand whether the objections in point of law *were likely* to be tenable, and if they thought otherwise they, with a most perilous confidence in the correctness of their own opinion, refused to hear the arguments of counsel to the contrary. This is evident from many instances that might be cited, but I will mention only the following. Lord Chief Justice North, on the trial of Colledge, said (*Ib.* viii. 570), "For counsel, you cannot have it unless matter of law arises, and that must be propounded by you; and then if it be a matter debateable the court will assign you counsel, but it must be a matter fit to be argued. For I must tell you a defense in case of high treason ought not to be made by artificial cavils, but by plain fact. If you propose any matter of law the Court will consider of it, and assign you counsel if it be reasonable." And in like manner Jeffreys (then Lord Chief Justice) said to Sidney, "If you assign us any particular point of law, *if the Court think it such a point as may be worth the debating* you shall have counsel" (*State Tr.* ix. 834). But the doctrine was still more

[1] *State Tr.*, ix. 897, 898. It seems that counsel had been assigned to *advise* with Algernon Sidney, although they were not allowed to address the court. When Bamfield, one of these, rose as *Amicus Curiæ*, and suggested in arrest of judgment that there was a material defect in the indictment, the Lord Chief Justice blandly observed, "We have heard of it already: we thank you for your friendship, and are satisfied." He then proceeded to pass sentence of death upon the prisoner.—*Ib.* 901.

plainly avowed by Chief Baron Atkins, at the trial of Lord Preston, in 1691, for he there expressly said, "It is not the doubt of the prisoner, but the doubt of the court, that will occasion the assigning counsel" (*Ib.* xii. 659, 660). Nor was it by any means safe for counsel to volunteer their services, or assist the prisoner at his request without the special permission of the court. Those who did so were severely reprimanded.[1]

Let us now consider what reasons could be offered in defense of a practice so abhorrent to our feelings, and so contrary to the first principles of criminal justice. The rule was bad enough to shock the mind of even such a judge as Jeffreys. "I think it is a hard case," he said, "that a man should have counsel to defend himself for a twopenny trespass, and his witnesses examined upon oath, but if he steal, commit murder, or felony, nay, high treason, where life, estate, honor, and all are concerned, he shall neither have counsel nor his witnesses examined upon oath. But yet, you know as well as I, that the practice of the law is so; and the practice is the law" (Note to *State Tr.* v. 466).

The chief reason assigned for the rule was that the court was counsel for the prisoner; but the accused might not unreasonably except to the discretion of such a counsel in his behalf. Once, a prisoner, when he heard the judge, who was trying him, just after he had given utterance to the above maxim, put a question to the wit-

---

[1] *Solicitor-General.* "I must do my duty. Mr. Williams exceeds his liberty; he informs the prisoner (Algernon Sidney) several things."

Mr. Williams. "I only said if it was a plea, put it in. Mr. Attorney can hear all I say."

"Whereupon *Mr. Williams* was reproved by the Lord Chief Justice."—*State Tr.* ix. 823, and see *Ib.* iv. 1319, vii. 1339.

But in one respect it seems that counsel deserved rebuke, and even Jeffreys was not unjust in administering it. *L. C. J.* "Look you, gentlemen of the jury. There are some gentlemen at the bar, as we are informed, are apt to whisper to the jury. It is no part of their duty; nay, it is against their duty."—*Ib.* ix. 837. What would be thought of such conduct nowadays!

ness directly tending to prove the prisoner's guilt, exclaimed, "Ah! my Lord, if you were my counsel, you would not ask that question."[1]

On another occasion, however, a learned judge was so far misled by this theory, that when upon a trial for the murder of a *male* child, the counsel for the prosecution concluded his case without having asked the sex of the child, he would not allow a witness to be recalled to prove it, but, in consequence of the omission, directed the jury to acquit the prisoner (*Blackst. Com.* v. 355).

In a debate, which took place in the Long Parliament, in November, 1649, Commissioner Whitelocke, one of the keepers of the great seal, said (*Parl. Hist.* iii., 1339), "I confess I can not answer this objection, that for a trespass of sixpence value a man may have a counsellor-at-law to plead for him, but, where his life and posterity are concerned, he is not admitted this privilege and help of lawyers. A law to reform this I think would be just, and give right to the people. What is said in defense, or excuse of this custom, is 'That the judges are of counsel for the prisoners, and are to see that they shall have no wrong.' And are they not to take the same care of all causes that shall be tried before them?"

A striking instance of the violation of this maxim is afforded by the conduct of Jeffreys when he sat on the trial of Alice Lisle, in 1685, who was accused of high treason for having harbored in her house a dissenting minister, named Hicks, knowing him at the time to be a

---

[1] As to the barbarous rule in an earlier period of our history, which prevented a prisoner accused of a capital crime from calling any witnesses to give testimony in his behalf, see *Blackstone*, iv. 359. To the honor of Mary be it told that she changed this inhuman practice, and when she appointed Sir Richard Morgan Chief Justice of the Common Pleas, she enjoined him "that, notwithstanding the old error which did not permit any witness to speak, or any other matter to be heard, in favor of the adversary, her majesty being party; her highness's pleasure was, that whatsoever could be brought in favor of the subject should be admitted to be heard."—*Ib.* and *State Tr.* i. 72. But it was not till the reign of Anne that, in all cases of treason or felony, witnesses for the prisoner could be examined *upon oath*.

traitor.[1] The following language addressed to the prisoner by the brutal judge,—who, in the course of the trial, by browbeating a witness to secure a conviction, "cluttered him out of his senses," and of whom that great magistrate, Sir Michael Foster, with reference to this very trial, pronounced the damning sentence that he was, "perhaps the very worst judge that ever disgraced Westminster Hall,"—must have sounded like bitter irony.

"It is a business that concerns you in point of life and death; all that you have or can value in the world lies at stake, and God forbid that you should be hindered, either in time or anything else, whereby you may defend yourself; but at present it is not your turn to speak, for the forms of law require your accusers first to be heard; and it is absolutely requisite that the usual forms and methods of law be inviolably observed, and be sure it does the prisoner no injury that the law is kept so strictly to; and we have that charity, as well as justice, that it becomes and is not below all courts to have for persons in your condition; and we are obliged to take care that you suffer no detriment or injury by any illegal or irregular proceedings. For though we sit here as judges over you by authority from the king, yet we are accountable, not only to him, but to the King of kings, the great Judge of heaven and earth; and therefore are obliged, both by our oaths, and upon our consciences, to do you

---

[1] *State Tr.* xi. 297. There is some confusion as to the right name of this lady. She is called in the *State Trials* "Lady Alice Lisle." Burnet and Hume call her "Lady Lisle." Macpherson "Mrs. Alice Lisle," Lingard "Alicia Lisle." She was the widow of John Lisle, who had been one of the judges of King Charles I., and her proper appellation therefore was Mrs. Lisle. I have given in the text the name by which she was indicted. There is perhaps no title about which there has been so much inaccuracy, as that of William Lord Russell, who was convicted of high treason in 1683. We find him constantly styled by Lingard and other writers Lord William Russell; but he was the eldest son of the Earl of Bedford, and therefore Lord Russell by courtesy. He was indicted as "William Russell, late of London, Esquire."

justice, and by the Grace of God we shall do it, you may depend upon it" (*State Tr.* xi. 322).

What an affecting comment on these specious promises is contained in the words of the unhappy lady upon the scaffold: "I have been told the court ought to be counsel for the prisoner; instead of which, there was evidence given from thence, which, though it were but hearsay, might possibly affect my jury. My defense was such as might be expected from a weak woman; but such as it was, I did not hear it repeated again to the jury. But I forgive all persons that have done me wrong, and I desire that God will do so likewise!"

Of all the state trials recorded in English history, this is perhaps the one which most excites our indignation, and inspires us with horror at the perpetration of murder committed under the forms of law. There was no proof whatever that the prisoner knew that Hicks, whom she harbored as a non-conformist minister, had been with the rebel army; and the jury said that they were not satisfied that she had notice of that fact, without which she could not be legally convicted. But this was a matter of small account with Jeffreys, who soon disposed of the difficulty by saying, "There is as full proof as proof can be."

It would be difficult to cite an instance where the injustice of the rule, which prevented the advocate of a prisoner charged with felony from speaking in his behalf, was more glaringly exhibited than in the case of Maha Rajah Nundocomar, or Nuncomar, who was tried at Calcutta, in the month of June, 1775, for the forgery of a bond.[1] The jury consisted of Englishmen, inhabitants of Calcutta, and the prisoner was utterly unacquainted with the English language. This was also the case with most of the witnesses for the crown, so that it was necessary to conduct the proceedings through the medium of

---

[1] *State Trials*, xx. 923. For a brilliant sketch of the life of this unfortunate man, see the third vol. of *Macaulay's Essays*

sworn interpreters. Under these circumstances the counsel for the Rajah made the very reasonable request that he should be permitted to address the court in his behalf, but this was refused; and in charging the jury, the chief justice, Sir Elijah Impey, said, " By the laws of England, the counsel for prisoners charged with felony are not allowed to observe on the evidence to the jury, but are to confine themselves to matters of law." He felt, however, what a grievous hardship was thereby inflicted upon a prisoner, in the position of the Maha Rajah, tried by a jury of foreigners, who were ignorant of the language in which he must have spoken if he had addressed them, and he, therefore, added, " But I told them (the counsel) that if they would deliver to me any observations they wished to be made to the jury, I would submit them to you and give them their full force, by which means they will have the same advantage as they would have had in a civil case." But what a mockery was this! A few meager notes, embracing the chief points of defense, such as an advocate would put down on paper to assist his memory while speaking, had been handed to the court, and these were read *verbatim* to the jury by the chief justice, accompanied by a running commentary of his own. And this he called giving the prisoner the same advantage which he would have had if his counsel had been allowed to make an eloquent appeal in his behalf. The result of the trial is well known. Nundocomar was convicted and hanged.

A humane but unsatisfactory view of the subject was taken by Lord Chancellor Nottingham, when addressing the Peers as High Steward, on the trial of Lord Cornwallis : " No other good reason can be given why the law refuses to allow the prisoner at the bar counsel in matters of fact, where life is concerned, excepting this, that the evidence by which he is condemned ought to be so very evident, and so plain, that all the counsel in the world should not be able to answer it " (*State Tr.*, vii. 149).

And Sir John Davys, in the preface to his Reports which has been already quoted, with egregious fallacy, abets the practice on the ground that our law doth abhor the defense and maintenance of bad causes more than any other law in the world. "And this is one cause," he says, "among others, why our law doth not allow counsel unto such as are indicted of treason, murder, rape, or other capital crimes : so as never any professor of the law of England hath been known to defend (for the matter of fact) any traitor, murderer, ravisher, or thief, being indicted and prosecuted at the suit of the king."

'Turpe reos emptâ miseros defendere lingua'

saith the poet ; and therefore it is an honor unto our law that it doth not suffer the professors thereof to dishonor themselves (as the advocates and orators in other countries do) by defending such offenders." As if the guilt or innocence of the accused could depend upon the enormity of the charge ! and as if the maxim of our law were to be reversed, and every man upon his trial were to be presumed guilty until he could prove himself to be innocent !

In a book of great authority on all matters relating to our criminal jurisprudence, it is asserted that where a party accused of a crime is innocent, it is better that he should conduct his own defense. "If it be considered that generally every one of common understanding may as properly speak to a matter of fact as if he were the best lawyer, and that it requires no manner of skill to make a plain and honest defense, which in cases of this kind is always the best, the simplicity and innocence, artless and ingenuous behavior of one whose conscience acquits him, having something in it more moving and convincing than the highest eloquence of persons speaking in a cause not their own."

But this is not true. For though sometimes the simple language of innocence has more effect than the most elaborate oration, how often must the awful circumstances of a trial for life and death incapacitate a prisoner for the task of addressing the tribunal which is to pronounce his doom! If mere appeals to the compassion of the judge or jury were likely to prevail, then, indeed, the tears and misery of the accused might plead more eloquently and more successfully than all the efforts of the most skillful advocate. But hard facts must be grappled with—decrepancies in testimony pointed out—circumstantial evidence explained away, which, however guiltless the prisoner may be, often throw such a dark cloud of suspicion over him, that nothing but the most strenuous exertions of a calm and piercing intellect can remove it. How often, in our state trials, must the heart of the accused have sunk within him, his tongue have cloven to his mouth, and words have failed him, when he saw before him the fatal axe which he knew was ready, as the swift instrument of death, if he failed to secure a verdict of acquittal![1]

But even under the iniquitous system which confined the exertions of advocates in cases of treason or felony to arguments on points of law, opportunities were sometimes given where they could show their independent and fearless spirit. Thus when Hale appeared as counsel for Lord Craven, and the attorney-general of the day threatened him for daring to take the side against the government, he nobly answered, "I am pleading in defense of laws which you are bound to maintain: I am doing justice to my client, and am not to be intimidated."

The attempt to remedy this crying evil by a legislative enactment was long and obstinately resisted, and it was not until 1695, that a statute was passed, 7 Will. III. c. 3, entitled "An Act for regulating of Trials in Cases of Treason and Misprison of Treason," which provided,

[1] The axe was always placed beside or before the prisoner at his trial, when the charge was one of high treason.

among other things, that any person accused and indicted, arraigned or tried for high treason, whereby any corruption of blood may be made to any such offender or his heirs, or for misprision of such treason, " shall be received and admitted to make his full defense by counsel learned in the law ; and in case any person so accused or indicted shall desire counsel, the court before whom he shall be tried, or some judge of that court, shall immediately, upon his request, assign to him such and so many counsel, not exceeding two, as he shall desire, to whom such counsel shall have free access at all seasonable hours ; " but it was expressly declared by section 12 that the statute should not extend to any impeachment or other proceedings in parliament, nor to any indictment of high treason for counterfeiting the great or privy seal, or coin of the realm. It was during the debate that arose upon this bill that Lord Ashley, afterwards Earl of Shaftesbury, rose to speak in its behalf, but was so embarrassed as to be unable to proceed, and he became suddenly silent. With admirable presence of mind, however, he recovered himself, and converted his confusion into one of the strongest arguments in favor of the bill. " If, sir," said he, addressing the Speaker, " I, who rise only to give my opinion on the bill now depending, am so confounded that I am unable to express the least of what I proposed to say, what must the condition of that man be, who, without any assistance, is pleading for his life, and under apprehension of being deprived of it?"

The act was appointed to take effect from the 25th of March, 1696 ; and, monstrous as it may seem, it is nevertheless a fact, that when Sir William Parkyn was tried for high treason, on the 24th of that month, after the statute had been passed, and the very day before it was to come into operation, he in vain prayed that counsel might be allowed him, on the ground that the preamble of the act was declaratory of the common law, inasmuch as it said that there was nothing more just or reasonable. "My Lord," said he, addressing Lord Chief Justice Holt, "it wants but one day."—HOLT. "That is as much as if it were a much longer time, for we are to proceed according to what the law is, and not what it will be." He then asked that his trial might be put off for a single day, in which case he would have been entitled, as of right, to that which he now prayed for as a favor; but his application was refused.[1] When we read of such things our feelings ought to be those of deep thankfulness that the judges of the present day are, in point of humanity, so very different from their predecessors.

The first instance on record in which we find counsel assigned under this act, is on the trial of Rookwood and others, on which occasion Sir Bartholomew Shower and Mr. Phipps defended the prisoners; and it is curious to see in what deprecatory terms they separated themselves from their clients. "My Lord," said Sir Bartholomew, addressing Chief Justice Holt, "we are assigned of counsel in pursuance of an act of parliament, and we hope that nothing which we shall say in defense of our clients shall be imputed to ourselves. I thought it would have been a reflection upon the government and your lordship's justice, if, being assigned, we should have refused to appear: it would have been a publication to the world that we distrusted your candor towards us in our future practice upon other occasions. . . . . We

---

[1] *State Tr.*, xiii. 72. Formerly if a bill was brought into parliament at the close of the session, and passed on the last day, which made an act previously innocent criminal and even capital, and if no day was fixed for the commencement of its operation, it was considered to have been passed on the first day of the session; and the consequence was, that all who had in the meantime been doing what at the time was perfectly legal, were liable to suffer the punishment created by the statute.— *Coke's 4th Inst.* 25; 4 *Term Rep.* 660. The flagrant injustice of this caused the passing of an act, the 33 *Geo.* III., c. 13, whereby it was provided that when no time is specified in any particular act of parliament for its commencement, the clerk of the parliament shall indorse upon it the day on which it receives the royal assent, and that day shall be the date of its commencement.

come not here to countenance the practices for which the prisoners stand accused, nor the principles upon which such practices may be presumed to be founded; for we known of none, either religious or civil, that can warrant or excuse them."—A cold exordium for the speech of an advocate!

In 1747 the provisions of the statute of William III. regarding the assignment of counsel were extended to parliamentary impeachments in cases of high treason, and misprision of treason; but still in no trials for felony, and those cases of inferior treason which concerned the coin of the realm, and the seals, whether the offense were clergyable or not, was a prisoner allowed counsel to plead his cause before a jury. For this Sir Michael Foster could find no better reasons to adduce than the following:—" I know many things have been thrown out upon this subject, and inconveniences, some real and some imaginary, have been suggested by popular writers, who seem to have attended singly to those on one side of the question; but it is impossible, in a state of imperfection, to keep clear of all inconveniences, though wisdom will always direct us to the course which is subject to the fewest and the least; and this is the utmost that human wisdom can do." The necessity for resorting to such an argument as this in defense of the anomaly, was in fact to pronounce its condemnation.

It was, however, reserved for our own times to see this remnant of barbarism swept away; and it was at last, by the 6 and 7 William IV. c. 114, enacted, that all persons tried for felony should be admitted to make their defense by counsel or attorney. The preamble of this statute announces that great principle of criminal jurisprudence, which sophistry had so long resisted, namely, " that it is just and reasonable that persons accused of offenses against the law should be enabled to make their full answer and defense to all that is alleged against them."

We have thus far been dealing with examples of one

only of the many grievous imperfections of our criminal jurisprudence in former times; but the truth is, that up to the period of the revolution of 1688 our criminal trials are a disgrace to the national annals. It has been truly said of them by a modern writer, well qualified to form an opinion, "it would be difficult to name a trial not marked by some violation of the first principles of criminal justice." They were in fact judicial murders. It is shocking to think how many lives were sacrificed upon evidence which would not now suffice to convict a boy of stealing apples from an orchard; and to remember that there was a time in England when the vaguest and loosest statement made by an informer, who might be a bitter personal enemy of the accused, was received as evidence against the prisoner upon a charge of high treason, although the witness was not confronted with him at the trial, and no opportunity was afforded of sifting the truth or falsehood of the testimony.

The danger of such a mode of obtaining a conviction cannot be exaggerated. Our feelings recoil with horror at the thought that the passionate entreaties of men on trial for their lives to have their accusers brought before them, face to face, should have been rejected by the judges.

The Duke of Norfolk, when arraigned in 1571, earnestly begged that the bishop of Ross, whose examination was about to be read against him, might personally come forward and give evidence. He said, "All these prove not that I dealt in the matter of the marriage with the Scottish queen, in any respect of her claim to the crown of England. If the bishop of Ross, or any other, can say otherwise, let them be brought before me, face to face. I have often so desired it, but I could not obtain it" (*State Trials*, i. 985). And his application was made in vain. In like manner the unfortunate Sir Walter Raleigh, on his trial in 1603, when the evidence of Lord Cobham, which had been taken behind his back, was read against him in court, said, "The proof of the common law is by witness and jury: let Cobham be here; let him speak it. Call my accuser before my face, and I have done" (*Ib.* ii. 15). And again, "I beseech you, my lords, let Cobham be sent for; charge him upon his soul, on his allegiance to the king; if he affirm it, I am guilty." But what was the miserable answer of the Lord Chief Justice Popham? "This thing cannot be granted, for then a number of treasons should flourish; the accuser may be drawn by practice while he is in person" (*Ib.* 18). Again the unhappy prisoner pleaded for this bare act of common justice, but in vain, saying, "Indeed where the accuser is not to be had conveniently I agree with you, but here my accuser may; he is alive, and in the house. Susanna had been condemned if Daniel had not cried out, 'Will you condemn an innocent Israelite without examination or knowledge of the truth?' Remember it is absolutely the commandment of God: If a false witness rise up, you shall cause him to be brought before the judges; if he be found false, he shall have the punishment which the accused should have had."

But in no instances perhaps have the rules of evidence been more flagrantly violated in this country than on trials for witchcraft. The proceedings against reputed witches form one of the most melancholy chapters in the annals of human credulity and folly. The life of no old woman in the villages of England or Scotland were safe until the beginning of the last century, if any of her neighbors quarreled with her, and chose to gratify her malice by calling her a witch, for,—independently of the summary process of throwing her into a pond to see whether she could swim, to which the common people imagined that they had a legal right to resort, until 1712, when Chief Justice Parker, afterwards Lord Macclesfield, announced from the bench that if any person died in consequence of such ill usage all concerned in inflicting it would be guilty of murder,—our courts of justice were converted into charnel-houses for the destruction of these miserable victims of ignorance and superstition. Let me give one or two examples of the kind of evidence deemed sufficient in former times to justify a conviction on a charge of witchcraft, the punishment that followed being in all cases death.

In the case of the Essex witches, who were tried in the reign of Charles I., the following is the testimony of Sir Thomas Bowes, knight, " which he spake upon the bench concerning Anne West," she being then at the bar upon her trial.

That a very honest man of Mannintree, *whom he knew would not speake an untruth, affirmed unto him* that very early one morning, as he passed by the said Anne West's dore, about foure a clock, it being a moonlight night, and perceiving her dore to be open so early in the morning, looked into the house, and presently there came three or four little things, in the shape of black rabbits, leaping and skipping about him, who, having a good stick in his hand, struck at them, thinking to kill them, but could not," and so forth (*State Trials*, iv. 857).

And the great name of Sir Matthew Hale is tarnished by his having suffered a conviction to take place in a trial for witchcraft, where the bystanders, whose intelligence ought not to have been superior to that of the learned judge, declared themselves satisfied of the absurdity of the charge. Two women, named Rose Cullender and Amy Duny, were indicted before him, in 1665, for bewitching several persons, and especially three children; and during the trial some experiments were made upon the children, who pretended to fall into epileptic fits, by making the prisoners touch them; " and it was observed that when they were in the midst of their fits, to all men's apprehension wholly deprived of all sense and understanding, closing their fists in such a manner as that the strongest man in the court could not force them open, yet by the least touch of one of these supposed witches, Rose Cullender by name, they would suddenly shriek out by opening their hands, which accident would not happen by the touch of any other person." But, as the narrative proceeds,—"There was an ingenious person that objected there might be a great fallacy in this experiment, and there ought not to be any stress put upon this to convict the parties, for the children might counterfeit this their distemper, and perceiving what was done to them they might in such manner suddenly alter the motion and gesture of their bodies, on purpose to induce persons to believe that they were not natural, but wrought strangely by the touch of the prisoners.

"Wherefore, to avoid this scruple, it was privately desired by the judge that the Lord Cornwallis, Sir Edmund Bacon, and Mr. Sergeant Keeling, and some other gentlemen there in the court, would attend one of the distempered persons in the farther part of the hall, while she was in her fits, and then to send for one of the witches, to try what would then happen, which they did accordingly, and Amy Duny was conveyed from the bar and brought to the maid; they put an apron before her eyes, and then one other person touched her hand, which produced the same effect as the touch of the witch did in the court. Whereupon the gentlemen returned, openly protesting that they did believe the whole transaction of this business was a mere imposture. This put the court and all persons into a stand."

The difficulty, however, was got over by the ingenuity of a Mr. Pacy, who " did declare that possibly the maid might be deceived by a suspicion that the witch touched her when she did not." And the result was, that Sir Matthew Hale having summed up, and told the jury that he made no doubt at all that there were such creatures as witches, the prisoners were found guilty and executed.[1]

[1] *State Trials*, vi. 687. In the preface to this trial will be found some

But enough has been said to show how much alloy was mixed up with the "wisdom of our ancestors" in criminal proceedings, and to make us thankful that we live at a time when the law is administered with more enlightened humanity; and the retrospect in which we have been engaged is not merely interesting as a record of the opinions and practice of our forefathers in matters affecting the lives of their fellow-creatures, but is also fruitful in lessons to ourselves. Nothing is more difficult than to shake off the prejudices which inveterate usage has rooted in our minds. We are too apt to accept as right a system to which we have been habituated, and to fancy that there must be some sound, though hidden and recondite reason for rules which, however anomalous, have been sanctioned by time. And no doubt the presumption always is in favor of the continuance of things that can plead for themselves a long prescription. The very essence of the validity of custom when challenged in our courts of law is that it must be reasonable, and where it has lasted for centuries it is no violent supposition to assume that it was right and proper in its origin. But this may be carried too far where the principle is allowed to stand in the way of real improvement. Thus when, in the year 1731, Sir George Saville brought a bill into the House of Commons to abolish the law Latin in our pleadings, and enact that all legal proceedings should be in the English language, it was opposed by arguments which appear strange to us at the present day, but which

curious particulars on this painful subject. And see the trial of the three Devon witches in 1682. *Ib.* viii. 1018. Selden, in his Table-talk, gives the following extraordinary reason for sacrificing the lives of persons as witches —even on the hypothesis that the crime of witchcraft is impossible:

"The law against witches does not prove that there be any; but it punishes the malice of those people that use such means to take away men's lives. If one should profess by turning his hat thrice and crying *buz*, he could take away a man's life (though in truth he could do no such thing), yet this were a just law made by the state, that whosoever should turn his hat thrice and cry *buz*, with an intention to take away a man's life, should be punished with death."

were doubtless at the time thought to have considerable weight. It was said that if the language and methods of pleading should be changed it would necessarily produce such a confusion that it would cost many years of painful and troublesome application before the new forms could be settled in a certain and regular course of proceedings, so that the making of those alterations would occasion greater delay of justice, give more room to dangerous frauds, render the prosecution of the rights of the subject more difficult and expensive, the recovery of small debts more impracticable, and the number of attorneys more excessive than heretofore.[1]

When the bill was in the House of Lords, Lord Raymond, then chief justice, opposed it, saying that if it passed, the law must likewise be translated into Welsh, since many in Wales understood not English. The Duke of Argyle happily retorted that our prayers were in our native tongue, that they might be intelligible, and why should not the laws wherein our lives and properties are concerned be so for the same reason? He added, "that he was glad to see that the noble lord, perhaps as wise and learned as any that ever sat in that House, had nothing more to offer against the bill than a joke."

But although in capital cases advocates were not allowed to speak in defense of prisoners, great occasions sometimes occurred which afforded scope and opportunity for the highest eloquence, though we look for its display in vain. Such was the trial of the seven Bishops in the reign of James II., than which we can hardly conceive a more august spectacle. Indicted for a conspiracy

[1] *Parl. Hist.* viii. 858. From the time of the Conquest to the reign of Edward III., Norman French was the only language used in our courts. But by the statute 36 *Edward III.* c. 15, the preamble of which stated qe les gentz qe pledent ou sont empledez en les courtz le roi et les courtz dautres nont entendement ne conissance de ce qest dit pour eulx, ne contre eulx, par lour sergeantz et autres pledours,—it was enacted that all pleas in the courts shall be pleaded, debated, and judged in the English tongue, and shall be entered and enrolled in Latin.

of which the overt act was the composing and publishing a libel, which consisted of a petition written and presented by them to the king, these venerable fathers of the church were committed to the Tower, and thence brought before the Court of King's Bench, to be tried by a jury (*State Tr.* xii. 183). They were defended by a strong array of counsel—Sir Robert Sawyer, Pemberton, Finch, Levinz, Pollexfen, and Somers. But their speeches, even upon the merits, were dry and technical, and by no means worthy of the dignity of the occasion.

And what an opportunity that was for the display of the most impassioned oratory! Cicero himself never had a nobler theme on which to pour forth the riches of his eloquence. There stood then at the bar to answer the accusation of having written and uttered a "false, mischievous, and seditious libel"[1] against their sovereign,—Sancroft, the Primate of England, a mild and learned prelate, who at a later period called upon his friends to rejoice with him on his deprivation for not falsifying his oath to the monarch who had persecuted him, "for now," he said, "I live again;" and Ken, whose sweet and simple hymns have been and still are echoed by the voice of thousands throughout the land; and Lloyd, whose laborious pen supplied Bishop Burnet with a great part of the materials for his *History of the Reformation*; and four others of less note—but all men of unblemished character, and unshaken courage in the defense of what they believed to be the cause of truth. And the time chosen for this attack upon the right of the subject to address a respectful remonstrance to the crown, and for branding with the charge of disloyalty the Church of England, which, in the language of the

---

[1] The words of the criminal information were "illicitè, malitiosè, seditiosè, et scandalosè, quoddam, falsum, fictum, perniciosum et seditiosum libellum in scriptis de eodem domino Rege et Regali Declaratione et ordine prædictis (prætextu petitionis) fabricaverunt . . . . . . et publicaverunt."

petition itself, is "both in her principles and in her constant practice unquestionably loyal,"—was when the king was without disguise attempting to impose upon his people a creed which their ancestors had abjured, and which in the preceding century had lighted up the fires of Smithfield and Oxford to destroy such men as Bradford, Ridley, Latimer, and Cranmer. They

> display'd
> Truth's golden colors; nothing could invade
> Their heaven-fill'd thoughts but heaven, in whose just cause
> They liv'd, though murder'd by papistic laws.—*Quarles*.

Wonderful indeed was the sight witnessed on that day in Westminster Hall. Within those old walls have taken place many trials of thrilling and historic interest. There has stood the Duke of Norfolk to answer the charge of asserting the right of Mary Queen of Scots to the throne of England; and the Earl of Strafford, accused of high treason against the sovereign whom he served too faithfully; and Warren Hastings, around whose impeachment was thrown the gorgeous splendor of eastern imagery, evoked by the spell of eloquence from the lips of Sheridan and Burke. But no occasion has been more solemn —none more affecting—than that in which those seven Bishops, "amidst a very great auditory," braved the anger of a bigoted monarch, and the still more dangerous servility of judges, overawed by the doctrine of passive obedience to kingly power;[1] and when they preferred the loss of dignity, and wealth, and station, to the violation of their consciences. Truly it was, in the words of Sir Robert Wright, the Lord Chief Justice, " a case of great concern to the king and the government on the one side, and to my Lords the Bishops on the other," and it ought to be carefully studied by all who wish to know the prog-

---

[1] The animus of the court appears from the following brief colloquy:—

Sergeant Pemberton.—"My Lord, this is very unusual to stay thus for evidence."

L. C. J.—"It is so; but I am sure you ought not to have any favor."— *State Tr.* xii. 354.

ress that has been made in a knowledge of the true principles of the constitution, and the improvement that has taken place in the conduct of trials in courts of justice. While Sir Robert Sawyer was addressing the jury for the defense, he said that the clause in the royal declaration which suspended the execution of all penal laws was of the most dismal consequence that could be. Upon this the Lord Chief Justice, speaking aside, said, "I must not suffer this; they intend to dispute the king's power of suspending laws."

Mr. Justice Powell. "My Lord, they must necessarily fall upon that point; for if the king hath no such power (*as clearly he hath not in my judgment*), the natural consequence will be that this petition is no diminution of the king's regal power, and so not seditious or libelous."

Lord Chief Justice. "Brother, I know you are full of that doctrine; but, however, my Lords the Bishops shall have no occasion to say that I deny to hear their counsel. Brother, you shall have your will for once. I will hear them; let them talk till they are weary."

Mr. Justice Powell. "I desire no greater liberty to be granted them than what in justice the court ought to grant, that is to hear them in defense of their clients."[1]

The defense, however, was poor and spiritless. The best speech was that of Somers, who had been retained at the pressing instance of old Pollexfen—for he "would not be himself retained without him, representing him as the man who would take most pains, and go deepest into all that depended on precedents and records." The conclusion of his address, which was very brief, is distinguished by its terse and nervous force. "My Lord, as to all the matters of fact alleged in the petition—that

---

[1] The conduct of Mr. Justice Powell throughout the whole trial was beyond all praise. With reference to the true view of the law in the case, and the contrast he presented to his learned brethren, it might be said of him, as of Abdiel, that there was

"Amongst the faithless, faithful only he."

they are perfectly true, we have shown by the Journals of both Houses. In every instance which the petitioners mention, this power of dispensation was considered in parliament, and, on debate, declared to be contrary to law. They could have no design to diminish the prerogative, because the king has no such prerogative. Seditious, my Lord, the petition could not be, nor could it possibly stir up sedition in the minds of the people, because it was presented to the king in private and alone. False it could not be, for the matter of it must be seen to be strictly true. There could be nothing of malice, for the occasion, instead of being sought, was forced upon them. A libel it could not be, for the intent of the defendants was innocent, and they kept strictly within the bounds set by the law, which gives the subject leave to apply to his prince by petition when he is aggrieved." The acquittal which followed was chiefly ascribed to this speech of Somers, " the effect of which upon the jury was greatly heightened by the modesty and grace with which it was delivered. He now and ever merited the praise that 'his pleading at the bar was masculine and persuasive, free from everything trivial or affected'" (*Lord Campbell's Lives of the Lord Chancellors*, iv. 88).

To commemorate the trial, medals of the bishops were struck, with the motto " Wisdom hath built her a house, and chosen her seven pillars." On the reverse side was represented a church undermined by two Jesuits with a pickaxe and shovel, and a hand pointing out of a cloud, with the motto " The gates of hell shall not prevail against it" (*Luttrell's MS.*, cited 12 *State Tr.* 184).

It must indeed be admitted that eloquence has always been rare among the advocates of England, and it may be interesting to consider whether there have been causes to account for this. Perhaps one reason is the excessive degree of technicality which formerly pervaded every part and parcel of the English law. Of all the systems that ever were invented to cramp and confine the intellect, that of special pleading seems to have been the most admirably adapted to attain that end. We need not deny that its principles were based in rigid logic; but the development of those principles produced such a luxuriant crop of artificial and wiredrawn distinctions, that the most subtle intellect found it difficult to understand them. It was a miserable exercise of perverted ingenuity to make plain statements unintelligible by involved verbiage, and, while affecting to exclude all ambiguity of expression, to ransack the English language for expletives and synonyms, the result of which was a mass of obscure phraseology, such as even a tutored intellect could hardly comprehend. That a certain kind of astuteness was required for these feats wordy legerdemain is true, but it is the least enviable of mental gifts, and it is distressing to think how constantly the rights of parties depended upon the degree of skill with which English lawyers were able to make themselves familiar with the rules and jargon of such a system.[1] Let me, however, not be misunderstood. In protesting against the abuse of a system, which, when rightly understood and kept within due limits, was a most efficacious means of promoting the ends of justice, I would avail myself of the words of Lord Mansfield, who, while he censures what was evil, does not forget to praise what was good. "The substantial rules of pleading," he says, "are founded in strong sense and in the soundest and closest logic, and so appear, when well understood

---

[1] *History of the Common Law*, i. 303. On one occasion where an obviously sham and tricky plea had been placed upon the record, Lord Mansfield said that if such an instance occurred again he would ask the name of the pleader who had drawn it. He did not explain what consequences would follow; and perhaps the intimation was something like the awful threat of "naming a member in his place," by the Speaker of the House of Commons. Sir Fletcher Norton, when Speaker, was once asked what would be the result of such a proceeding,—upon which he answered with solemn gravity, "Heaven only knows, sir!"

and explained, though by being misunderstood and misapplied, they are often made use of as instruments of chicane " (*Robinson* v. *Raley*, 1 *Burr.* 319).

But whatever might be the defects or merits of the system, a knowledge of special pleading, was formerly indispensable to an English advocate; and what old Rastell says in the following passage was strictly true:—

"This book entituled a collection of entrees, contayneth the forme and maner of good pleading, which is a great part of the cunning of the law of England, as the Right worshipfull and great learned man Syr Thomas Litleton, knight, sometime one of the Justices of the Common place, in his third book of Tenures, in in the chapter of confirmation, saith to his sonne" (*Rastell's Entries*, written in 1564).

Moreover, besides its technicalities, the English law is little favorable to the cultivation of oratory, owing to its enormous and unwieldy mass. This tends to suffocate the fire of genius, and deaden the imagination, which shrinks back in affright from the aspect of the thousand volumes in which are enshrined the mysteries of our jurisprudence. The *immensus aliarum super alias acervatarum legum cumulus* continues yearly to increase, and threatens to render the study of law a hopeless task. Each session of parliament gives birth to a bulky volume of statutes to swell the numerous progeny of legislation. And what shall be said of our reports? When we speak of the common law as unwritten, we amuse ourselves with a fiction; for although it is said to reside *in gremio judicum*, and to be handed down traditionally from generation to generation, we know that for the last five centuries it has existed in written and printed records with which we must make ourselves familiar in order to undertand it.[1] To use the words of Roger North, "the

---

[1] The oldest reports extant in the English law are the *Year Books*, which were written in law French (a strange and uncouth *patois*), and extend from the beginning of Edward II., in 1307, to the latter end of the reign of

gross of law lecture lies in them:" and if in his time he could speak of the "reports of cases now almost innumerable," when the number did not amount to fifty volumes, what would he think of them at the present day when they cannot be estimated at less than several hundred?[1]

The common law may be compared to a plant whose seed is in itself, and, if we may judge from the number of reports which annually issue from the press, it germinates with appalling fecundity. The decisions of the judges, like the *responsa prudentum* amongst the Romans, profess to be merely its exposition—they are declaratory, not enacting—but they do in fact constitute the common law, and every judgment of a court of competent jurisdiction becomes a precedent not to be departed from, unless it be overruled by a court of higher authority.[2] Thus the common law is like the banyan tree—

> "Branching so broad and long, that in the ground
> The bended twigs take root, and daughters grow
> About the mother tree."

The effect of this system upon eloquence has been well discussed by the historian Hume, in the following passage, taken from one of his essays (*Essays*, vol. i. 96):

"It may be said that in ancient times, during the flourishing period of Greek and Roman learning, the municipal laws in every state were but few and simple,

Henry VIII., in 1547. They were first printed in the reign of James I. They contain decisions of the courts collected by four reporters, who were specially appointed to this office, and received a yearly stipend from the crown. In order to ensure accuracy, these learned personages used to meet and confer together, collating their notes of cases.

[1] It has been calculated that in 600 volumes of Law Reports there are not less than 240,000 *points*, *i.e.*, rules or principles of law.—See HOFFMAN'S *Course of Legal Study*, *Pref*.

[2] Bacon uses a striking metaphor to express the respect with which judgments of courts of law, even when overruled, should be treated. *Judicia enim reddita, si forte rescindi necesse est saltem sepeliuntor cum honore.*—*Tractat. de Just., Aphor.* 95. The whole of this TRACTATUS DE JUSTITIA, by Lord Bacon, is full of the profoundest wisdom.

and the decision of causes was, in a great measure, left to the equity and common sense of the judges. The study of the laws was not then a laborious occupation, requiring the drudgery of a whole life to finish it, and incompatible with every other study or profession. The great statesmen and generals among the Romans were all lawyers, and Cicero, to show the facility of acquiring this science, declares that, in the midst of all his occupations, he would undertake, in a few days, to make himself a complete civilian. Now, where a pleader addresses himself to the equity of his judges, he has much more room to display his eloquence than where he must draw his arguments from strict laws, statutes, and precedents. In the former case many circumstances must be taken in; many personal considerations regarded; and even favor and inclination, which it belongs to the orator, by his art and eloquence, to conciliate, may be disguised under the appearance of equity. But how shall a modern lawyer have leisure to quit his toilsome occupations, in order to gather the flowers of Parnassus? or what opportunity shall he have of displaying them, amidst the rigid and subtle arguments, objections and replies, which he is obliged to make use of? The greatest genius, and greatest orator, who should pretend to plead before the chancellor, after a month's study of the laws, would only labor to make himself ridiculous."

Perhaps, however, the chief reason of the absence of eloquence is a neglect of the means to acquire the habit of graceful and fluent elocution. It is indeed extraordinary that so little pains should be taken by men to qualify themselves for success in speaking. We seem to think that eloquence, the most godlike of gifts, must spring into being, like Minerva from the head of Jove, at once, in full and perfect panoply, and that it requires no preparation, or discipline, or study beforehand. We either despise or dread the *infinitus labor et quotidiana meditatio*, of which Tacitus speaks. Indeed it is supposed to detract somewhat from the merit of a speaker, if it is known that he has meditated deeply upon his subject, and committed to writing the periods to which he afterwards gives utterance. And yet why should we imagine that the art of oratory is exempt from the necessity of toil, any more than painting or sculpture, or poetry or music? No one expects excellence in these, except from men who have devoted themselves with untiring assiduity to a study of the principles of their art. Or if a heaven-born genius appears once in a century, which seems to know them by intuition, and to be able to dispense with the necessity of labor, the rest of mankind never dream that the great primeval law is abrogated on their behalf, and that they can gain the prize of victory without patient preparation for the conflict. We know that the orators of Greece and Rome were not ashamed to confess that the midnight oil was consumed over their speeches; and not one of those that we possess was delivered extempore. It does not appear to have occurred to them that such a feat deserved any peculiar praise, and if they did not always escape failure, they at least took every precaution to avoid it. They were fully impressed with the truth of the maxim, *magnus dicendi labor, magna res, magna dignitas, summa autem gratia* (*Cic. pro Murena*, 13), and the pains taken by Demosthenes to overcome a natural defect were only one instance of the zeal with which they aimed at perfection. In order to render their speaking more attractive they diligently availed themselves of all the extrinsic aids which can be supplied by propriety of gesture and modulation of voice. In some cases they carried this to a degree of refinement unworthy perhaps of a masculine eloquence. Thus, we are told that the younger Gracchus, when he harangued the populace, used to employ a skillful flute-player to stand behind him in a position where he could not be observed, and, by the tones of the instrument, regulate the proper pitch of his voice.¹ On this Cicero justly remarks that we may leave the flute-player at home, but carry with us to the Forum the lesson conveyed by the anecdote.

Perhaps, also, another reason is to be found in the few opportunities for speaking which occur to an advocate in the long and dreary interval, during which the best years of his life are consumed in inaction through absence of employment; and when he is fortunate enough to hold a brief, he sits behind the sevenfold shield of a Queen's Counsel, and it is not often that he has the opportunity of doing more than examining a witness called to prove a "notice to produce."

In one of his beautiful discourses, D'Aguesseau, while he mourns over the decline of eloquence at the French bar, boldly investigates the cause (Des Causes de la Décadence de l'Eloquence); and the following are some of the reasons which he adduces:—" If we look at the prodigious number of new members who every year hasten to enroll themselves in your order, one would say that there is no profession in which it is more easy to excel. Nature accords to all men the gift of speech, and all men easily persuade themselves that she has given them at the same time the power of speaking well. *The bar has become the profession of those who have it not;* and eloquence, which had the right to choose with an absolute authority those who are worthy of her in the other professions, is, on the contrary, obliged to content herself with men whom those professions have disdained to receive.

" How often we see those who have to struggle during their whole life against a nature barren and thankless, who have no greater enemy to combat than themselves, nor any prejudice more difficult to efface in the minds of others than that inspired by their external appear-

---

¹ *Cic. de Orat.* iii. 60, 61 ; and see *Aul. Gell.* i. c. 11. Lord Mansfield is said to have been able, by his agreeable mode of reading, to render even a statute interesting.—*Hoffman,* ii. 602.

ance! Still, if they labored earnestly to remove it, they would be only praiseworthy, when by painful toil they had been able to triumph over nature, and convict her of injustice. But in them indolence is added to a want of natural talents—and flatters their deficiencies instead of correcting them—so that we see them frequently, even in the flower of their youth, insipid readers and tedious reciters of their compositions, depriving the orator of all life and spirit, and taking from him the aid of memory and graces of delivery. And what must be the impression produced by an eloquence, cold, languishing, inanimate, which, in that state of death to which it is reduced, preserves only the shadow, or, if we may venture to use the expression, the skeleton, of true eloquence? How worthy of such a result are the motives which attract to the bar a great number of speakers, whom it seems that nature had condemned to perpetual silence! It is not the desire of devoting themselves wholly to the services of the public in a glorious profession; of being the organ and the voice of those whom their weakness hinders from making themselves heard; of imitating the office of the angels whom the Scriptures represent to us as standing round the throne of God, offering the incense and sacrifices of men; and of bearing like them the vows and the prayers of the people to the feet of those whom the same Scriptures call the gods of the earth. Motives so pure and so elevated hardly affect us any longer at all. At the present day men sacrifice only to self-interest. It is that which almost always opens the door of access to your order, as well as to the other employments in the state; and the most liberal and noble of all the professions becomes the most servile and the most mercenary."

The privilege accorded to advocates, while commenting upon the conduct of parties in any case in which they are engaged as counsel, is very great.[1] The extent

---

[1] Let, however, parties beware how they retaliate, at all events against a

of this privilege has indeed been asserted by judges in startling terms; and it has been laid down formerly "that if a counsel speaks scandalous words against one in defending his client's cause, an action lies not against him for so doing, for it is his duty to speak for his client, and it shall be intended to be spoken according to his client's instructions" (*Wood* v. *Gunston, Styles,* 462). But Lord Ellenborough repudiated this notion, and exposed its injustice; "For," he said, "if an action be brought against a counsel, then according to that case he is justified, because it will be intended that he spoke by the information of his client; and if an action be brought against the client, he may justify by showing that he gave no such information to his counsel. So that, if that case were law, an injured party would be without remedy. There must be some limit laid down" (*Hodgson* v. *Scarlett,* 1 *Barn. and Ald.* 238). The occasion on which the Chief Justice uttered these words was in an action brought by an attorney named Hodgson against the late Lord Abinger, then Mr. Scarlett, who had, at the trial of a cause in which Mr. Hodgson acted as attorney for the plaintiff, described him in his address to the jury as "a fraudulent and wicked attorney." The court however decided that the action was not maintainable, and it may be interesting to see the grounds on which it came to that conclusion. In delivering judgment, Lord Ellenborough said, "A counsel intrusted with the interests of others, and speaking from their information, for the sake of public convenience, is privileged in commenting fairly and *bonâ fide* on the circumstances of the case, and in making observations on the parties concerned, and their instruments or agents in bringing the

member of the Northern circuit. "Si home dit al un Counceller del ley en le North, Thou art a daffa-down dilly, Action gist, ove averrment que les parols signifie que il est un, Ambedexter, Mich. 10 Car. B. R. En Peare's case, dit d'estre adjudge en scaccario, et agree per curiam."—*Rolle's Abridg.* 55.

the cause into court. Now the plaintiff in this case was not merely the attorney, but was mixed up in the concoction of the antecedent facts out of which the original cause arose; he was cognizant of all the circumstances, and knew that the plaintiff had no ground of action in that case, in consequence of having already received more than the amount demandable by him. It was in commenting on this conduct that the words were used by the defendant. He had a right so to comment, for the plaintiff was mixed up with the circumstances of the case, and was the agent and instrument in the transaction. The defendant then says that he is a fraudulent and wicked attorney. These were words not used at random and unnecessary, but were a comment upon the plaintiff's conduct as attorney. Perhaps they were too strong: it may have been too much to say, that he was guilty of fraud as between man and man, and of wickedness *in foro divino*. The expression, in the exercise of a candor fit to be adopted, might have been spared. But still a counsel might *bonâ fide* think such an expression justifiable under the circumstances. . . . . It appears to me that the words spoken were uttered in the original cause, and were relevant and pertinent to it, and consequently that this action is not maintainable."[1]

It will be observed that the two grounds here alleged to justify and excuse an advocate when reflecting upon the conduct of others, are, that the information should be given by his client, and that it should be relevant to the cause. And this was decided so long ago as the

[1] In a subsequent case, *Flint* v. *Pike*, 4 *Barn. and Cress.* 478, Mr. Justice Bayley expressed himself with less caution, and said, "The speech of a counsel is privileged by the occasion on which it is spoken; he is at liberty to make strong, even calumnious observations against the party, the witnesses, and the attorney in the cause. The law presumes that he acts in discharge of his duty, and in pursuance of his instructions, and allows him this privilege, because it is for the advantage of the administration of justice that he should have free liberty of speech."

reign of James I., in the case of *Brooke* v. *Sir Henry Montague*,[1] where it was resolved by the court that "a counsellor in law retained hath a privilege to enforce anything which is informed him by his client, and to give it in evidence, it being pertinent to the matter in question, and not to examine whether it be true or false; but it is at the peril of him who informs it; for a counsellor is at his peril to give in evidence that which his client informs him, being pertinent in the matter in question, otherwise action upon the case lies against him by his client, as Popham said;[2] but if he give in evidence anything not material to the issue which is scandalous, he ought to aver it to be true, otherwise he is punishable; for it shall be contended as spoken maliciously and without cause; which is a good ground for an action."

But the privilege is strictly confined to the utterance of the words complained of in a court of justice. If the counsel who has spoken them, or anyone else, afterwards publishes or repeats them, he renders himself liable to an action at the suit of the party aggrieved. The same

---

[1] *Cro. Jac.* 90. Sir Henry Montague pleaded that he had spoken the words complained of as *consiliarius et peritus in lege*. He was afterwards chief justice of the King's Bench, succeeding Sir Edward Coke. "Coke (then attorney-general) cited a case where Parson Prick, in a sermon, recited a story out of Fox's Martyrology, that one Greenwood, being a perjured person, and a great persecutor, had great plagues inflicted upon him, and was killed by the hand of God. Whereas, in truth, he never was so plagued, and was himself present at that sermon; and he thereupon brought his action upon the case for calling him a perjured person, and the defendant pleaded Not guilty. And this matter being disclosed upon the evidence, Wray, chief justice, delivered the law to the jury, that it being delivered but as a story, and not with any malice or intention to slander any, he was not guilty of the words maliciously; and so was found not guilty.—*Ib.*

[2] The contrary, however, has been expressly decided, on the ground that the law looks upon the services of a counsel as given *gratuitously*, so that he is not answerable for any neglect or default in the conduct of a cause. But Popham seems to have been right according to the law in very old times; for we read in *Rolle's Abridgment*, p. 91.—*Si jeo retaine luy d'estre de mon counsel al* Guildhall, *en* London, *al certen jour, sil ne vient al jour per que mou cause* perish, *Action de Deceit gist vers luy.*"—20 *Hen.* 6, 34.

distinction applies in the case of speeches made by members in parliament. Slanderous matter may there be uttered with impunity; but whoever prints and circulates a report of what has been said does so at his peril, unless under the provisions of a recent act it be published by the order or authority of either house of parliament. And it has happened that a peer and a commoner have each been indicted, and found guilty of a libel in sending for publication to the newspapers a copy of a speech delivered by him in his place in parliament (*Rex* v. *Lord Abingdon*, 1 *Esp.* 226. *Rex* v. *Creevey*, 1 *Maule and Sel.* 273). With regard to the speeches of counsel, it has been expressly decided that though anyone is "at liberty to publish a history of the trial, that is of the facts of the case, and of the law of the case as applied to those facts, he is not at liberty to publish observations made by counsel injurious to the character of individuals" (*Flint* v. *Pike*, 4 *Barn. and Cress.* 480). And certainly it would seem to be more reasonable to curtail the license which is permitted to advocates than to extend it beyond what the necessity of the case requires, by allowing others to spread abroad the defamatory expressions without being liable for any consequences if they prove to be untrue.

One of the most remarkable instances on record where the degree of impunity to which counsel are entitled in the exercise of their profession came in question, occurred in the trial of John Cook, one of the regicides. He had acted as solicitor-general for the Commonwealth, during that solemn mockery of justice, when John Bradshaw, sergeant-at-law, sat as judge upon his king; and in that capacity he had prayed that speedy judgment might be pronounced against Charles I., whom he styled "the prisoner at the bar." When tried for high treason, he adroitly attempted to excuse himself on the ground that he had no participation in the king's death—not having formed part of the court which condemned him, and having merely discharged, *for his fee*, the duty of a counsel. And to get rid of the objection that he had demanded the judgment of the court which tried the king, he had recourse to the quibble, that his words ought to be taken *in mitiore sensu*, and that it should be presumed that perhaps he meant a judgment of acquittal! This is his argument, " My lord, when judgment is demanded, is it not twofold, of acquittal or condemnation? If those that then were intrusted with the power of judicature, if they did not know any law to proceed by to take away his majesty, then I demanded their judgment, it doth not appear to be my judgment; and I refer it to the learned counsel, that counsel many times at the assizes and other courts have been sorry that the verdict have been given for their clients, when they have known the right lay on the other side, and so I might in this" (*State Trials*, v. 1094). And with reference to his acts being only those of an advocate, and therefore innocent, he said, " My lord, I humbly answer this, to that which seems to be the most material part in the indictment, that we did assume a power; my lords, I did not assume a power. I hope it will not be said that the counsel had any power: *eloquentia* in the counsel, *judicium* in the judges, and *veritas* in the witnesses, 25th of Acts, Tertullus, that eloquent orator, accused Paul; Paul answered for himself, and it is said, ' Festus being willing to do the Jews a courtesy, he left Paul bound;' it was not the counsel that left him bound: his majesty was never a prisoner to me, and I never laid any hands upon him; if any witnesses have spoke of any irreverence, I must appeal to God in that I did not in the least manner carry myself undutifully to his majesty, though one of the witnesses was pleased to say that I said these words: ' That there is a charge against the prisoner at the "bar;"' it was not said the 'prisoner at the bar;' there was not one disrespective word from me. There is in a case in the third institute of my Lord

Coke: it is to this purpose, that one wilfully and knowingly forswore himself: the case was put to inveigle the court; and though the court does injustice upon a false oath, it is not injustice at all in the witness, it is perjury in him; if there can be no injustice in a witness, much less a counsellor can be said to have his hand in the death of any, because he has no power at all. This must needs follow, that if it shall be conceived to be treason for a counsellor to plead against his majesty, then it will be felony to plead against any man that is condemned unjustly for felony. The counsellor is to make the best of his client's cause, then to leave it to the court." And again, " I must leave it to your consciences, whether you believe that I had a hand in the king's death, when I did write, but only that which others did dictate to me, and when I spoke only for my fee."

Sir Orlando Bridgman, however, the Lord Chief Baron, in summing up the case to the jury, disposed of this ingenious defense by thus addressing the prisoner (*State Trials*, v. 1110):—" Counsel cannot be heard against the king; you undertake to be counsel against the king in his own person and in the highest crime; if the counsel at the bar in behalf of his client should speak treason, he went beyond his sphere; but you did not only speak (but acted) treason. You said you used not a disrespective word to the king; truly, for that you hear what the witnesses have said: you pressed upon him; you called it a delay; you termed him not the king, but the prisoner at the bar, at every word. You say you did not assume an authority; it is an assumption of authority if you countenance or allow of their authority."

Cook was found guilty, and when brought up for judgment he made a last desperate effort to get off by the same plea. Being asked what he had to say why the court should not pronounce judgment upon him to die, according to law, he urged two objections to the indictment, which were overruled, and he then said,

"I say it was professionately."

Lord Chief Baron. — "That hath been overruled already; we have delivered our opinions; the profession of a lawyer will not excuse them or any of them from treason, and this hath been overruled, and is overruled again."

So Cook suffered the death of a traitor, and was hanged.

In this country the distinction between the office of the advocate and that of the attorney is carefully observed. Each has his separate and appropriate sphere of duty, and it cannot, I think, be denied that there is a great advantage in such a division of labor. We may be sure that the work of each is better done by being thus apportioned, and all who are conversant with the progress of a lawsuit must see that the interests of the client are much better consulted by the employment of distinct parties, the one as his solicitor, and the other as his counsel, than if an attempt were made to blend their duties together and devolve them both upon the same individual. Indeed, with a system so full of technicalities and nice and subtle distinctions as the English law, it seems impossible to do this without the almost certain result of failure. To conduct a cause safely through all the "depths and shoals" which imperil it, from the first issuing of the writ of summons until the jury have pronounced their verdict, is no easy task. Writs must be duly served, pleadings correctly drawn, evidence accurately sifted, witnesses carefully examined, notices properly given, before the case makes its appearance in court; and *then*, even although all the previous preparation is complete, then *ibi omnis effusus labor*, unless there be an advocate competent to overcome the difficulties which a watchful and wary adversary will interpose at every step in the progress of the trial, and to impress upon the minds of the twelve " gentlemen " the conviction that a harder case was never brought into court if he is retained for the defendant, nor a more just one if he happens to be for the plaintiff. Few things are more embarrassing than a multiplicity of details, and to these the attorney has to direct special attention ; but, if in addition to his multifarious and important labors were superadded that of pleading the cause of his client in court, the inevitable consequence would be confusion and waste of time. Our system is too precise and technical to admit of such a combination. The delivery of a speech is often the least and easiest part of the duty of an advocate. His ingenuity and skill are far more severely taxed in what are called questions of evidence, which demand all the acumen of his intellect.[1]

Our system of judicial inquiry exacts a strictness and severity of proof unknown to other countries. The rules according to which it is conducted are so complex and numerous, and the distinctions arising out of them so subtle and minute, that, whatever may be the attention and care with which the *theory* of the law of evidence, as administered in the English courts, is studied, practice alone can give the requisite facility and dexterity in dealing with them. *L'usage fait tout*, and to this subject may be especially applied the passage from Quintilian, *plusque, si separes, usus sine doctrinâ quam citra usum doctrinâ valent* (*Quintil. Inst. Orat.* xii. 6). And these rules are adhered to with inflexible uniformity, whatever consequences may result in particular cases from their application. The fact may be as notorious as the noon-day sun, but the judge and the jury must be presumed to be ignorant of it unless it can be established by technical and formal proof. The reception of a document in evidence upon which the whole case turns, may depend upon the absence of an attesting witness who can-

---

[1] *Maximus tamen patrouis circa testimonia sudor est.* — *Quintil. Inst. Orat.* v. 7.

not be found, although there are in court a hundred persons who could prove the genuineness of the disputed handwriting. It is a maxim with English lawyers, that "hard cases make bad law;" and when a canon of evidence is once established, it is never departed from on account of any supposed injustice it may work, or prejudice it may cause, to the real merits of the question in issue. But then the general rules are subject to large exceptions, and not the least difficult part of the task imposed upon an advocate is to understand clearly, and to recognize promptly, what cases fall within the rule, and what within the exception; for he has to argue at the trial of a cause points of evidence on the instant as they arise, while dealing with the arrangement of entangled and complicated facts, and in the presence of an opponent, ready to expose every fallacy, and take advantage of every slip. In no department of an advocate's duty are quickness, and judgment, and tact, more necessary, or more severely tested. Let us try this by an example.

Is a witness giving evidence of a contract, which, if proved, would be fatal to the cause? He must be stopped and examined as to whether it was reduced into writing or not. If the answer is in the affirmative, the instrument must be produced: and the witness is told to say nothing of its contents. But the counsel on the other side is not to be so foiled. He asks the witness as to the cause of the absence of the document, and is informed that it is lost. Here then, it appears, that secondary, and therefore oral evidence, may be admitted. But not yet. How does the witness know that it is lost? What degree of search has been made for it? Was it stamped when he last saw it in existence? Or perhaps the missing document is in the possession of his own client, and this fact is proved by the witness. The party is therefore called upon by the other side to produce it, and thus supply the primary evidence which his counsel insists upon as alone admissible. But the latter can still throw the ægis of his dexterity before his client. No notice has been given to produce the document, and though it may be at the moment in the pocket of his attorney in court, it cannot be read without his consent

But it would lead us too much into technical detail to attempt to illustrate the difficulties which beset the conduct of a cause at *nisi prius*, owing to the nicety of the distinctions upon which questions of evidence depend. A bare enumeration of some of them will suggest to the recollection of the lawyer the many pitfalls that lie hidden beneath the surface. How far is the statement of a deceased person admissible when it has been made against his interest? or in the course of his proper duty and employment? What kind of hearsay evidence is admissible in questions relating to pedigree? When may it be received, not as the narrative of a fact, but as explanatory of its nature? When may a letter be read without producing that to which it is an answer? Of what documents may copies be admitted without producing or proving the loss of the originals? In what mode are judicial proceedings to be proved? How far are the judgments of inferior or foreign courts binding upon parties by way of estoppel? In what cases may a witness be asked to give his opinion, as, for instance, in an action upon a policy of insurance, whether the concealment of a material fact from an underwriter would be likely to affect the premium required as varying the contemplated risk?

I have said that no mere knowledge of the theory of evidence will enable a man to handle it with dexterity in court. To give a counsel, who had never been trained by practice as a junior, a difficult cause involving many disputed points of evidence to conduct alone, would be like placing a man at the helm of a vessel in a storm, who had only studied the rules of navigation; or throwing a person into deep water, who, like Benjamin Franklin, had learnt to swim only upon a table. A question is often innocently asked by a young and inexperienced counsel to which mother wit and common sense would perhaps suggest no objection. But it is objected to nevertheless. What is its fault? Is it in too leading a form?[1] Is it asking for an opinion instead of a fact? Does it refer to mere hearsay? or to *res inter alios acta?* Is it inadmissible as asking for a statement which is no part of the *res gestæ?* or does it refer to the contents of a written instrument? or does the question tend to impeach the credit of his own witness? or is it irrelevant to the issue between the parties? or does it refer to something which has not been alluded to in the cross-examination? Nothing is easier in theory than to understand, after a little consideration, the reasonableness of objections to these questions; but nothing is more difficult in practice than to avoid putting them. Such instances might be multiplied to an almost unlimited extent; but enough has been said to show the nature of the difficulties which render the task of an English advocate in protecting the interests of his client before a jury so different from what it is in any of the other countries of Europe.

It would open too wide a field of discussion, and one hardly falling within the scope of this treatise, to inquire whether the tendency of our canons of evidence is to advance or defeat the ends of justice. It has been often contended that *all evidence*, without exception, ought to be laid before the jury, leaving them to judge of the degree of credibility that ought to be attached to it.

---

[1] With regard to leading questions it would be useful for the objector to remember the following remark of Lord Ellenborough: " I wish that objections to questions as leading might be a little better considered before they are made. It is necessary to a certain extent to lead the mind of the witness to the subject of inquiry. If questions are asked to which the answer yes or no would be conclusive, they would certainly be objectionable; but, in general, no objections are more frivolous."—*Nicholls* v. *Dowding*, 1 *Stark*, 81.

For my own part, I believe that this would work injustice.

The minds of those who have not been trained and disciplined by habits of legal investigation are too apt to be prejudiced by statements which ought really to have no weight at all, and if hearsay evidence were admitted,—to take a single example,—the result, in many cases, would be that mistaken verdicts would be given, either on account of the misreport of words spoken by third parties, or the undue bias which would be communicated by the reception as evidence of their expressed but unfounded opinions. The exclusion of testimony of this kind is very different from the refusal to allow persons to appear as witnesses who have an interest, however remote, in the issue of the trial, and it has been most wisely provided by a recent statute[1] that in such cases they shall be permitted to give evidence, and no objection can be taken to its admissibility, but only to its credibility.

But there is another and an important reason why the functions of the advocate and the attorney should be kept separate. It is one of the most salutary rules of the profession, that a counsel shall not in any way, nor under any pretence, ask for practice. Although he plies for hire, he may not solicit custom. This may appear to be anomalous, but it is founded upon the same principle as that which forbids him to claim his fee as a debt, and in theory treats that as a mere honorary gratuity, which constitutes in fact his means of livelihood. He must not apply to others to make trial of the powers of his intellect, but wait until his merits are discovered and appreciated. Perhaps it cannot be said that this rule is as strictly observed as it ought to be, but it is obvious that if the professions of counsel and attorney were merged into one, it would no longer exist at all. The client in general knows little of the capacity of coun-

---

[1] 6 and 7 *Vict.* c. 85, generally known as Lord Denman's Act.

sel, and the responsibility of selection falls upon his attorney; but if there were no distinction between the two departments, and each might fulfill the duties of the other, it is obvious that, in the generality of cases, the advocate in court would be the same party as the attorney "upon the record." In the United States, however, in all the courts, with the exception of the Supreme Court at Washington, the same person can be admitted to the degree of attorney and counsel, and exercise the powers and functions of each. In the Supreme Court this was first prohibited in 1790, and although afterwards, in 1801, the court declared that counsellors might be admitted as attorneys on taking the usual oaths, this did not imply that they could in that case continue to act as counsellors. They must make their election between the two degrees.[1]

[1] *Kent's Commentaries on American Law*, i. 307. In a very recent case, *ex parte Evans*, 9 *Q. B.* 279, where an application was made to the Court of Queen's Bench for a *certiorari* to bring up an order made by Justices at Quarter Sessions, to the effect that exclusive audience should be granted to barristers when four were present,—that the same might be quashed,—the Court refused the motion. Lord Denman, C. J., said, "It is an important rule that in this, as in other respects, all Courts should have power to regulate their own practice. . . . . It is reasonable that, for the purposes of a Court, there should be privileged orders." And see *Collier* v. *Hicks*, 2 *Barn. and Ad.* 663.

CHAPTER IX.

THE HONORARIUM.

FROM the very earliest times, in every country where advocacy has been known, it has been the custom to look upon the exertions of the advocate as given gratuitously, and the reward which the client bestows as purely honorary, in discharge not of legal obligation, but a mere debt of gratitude. There can be little doubt that this notion has been encouraged and kept up from a jealous apprehension lest the profession should degenerate into a mean and mercenary calling. For there is one peculiarity which distinguishes it from all others, and that is the disfavor with which men regard a presumed readiness to espouse and support by argument either side of a question. This is a circumstance so repugnant to the ordinary sense of duty, and apparently so subversive of the distinction between right and wrong, that there has been always felt an unwillingness to admit that a man is entitled to barter the powers of his intellect for money indifferently in the cause of virtue and of vice.

As regards the origin of the theory of gratuitous service, it is not difficult to account for it if we consider how advocacy at first came to be employed. It was the help which was afforded by the strong to the weak, the succor of protection to the oppressed, yielded by the sentiment of pity which prompts us to assist those who are in distress. In its most primitive form, to plead the cause of another in a court of justice was nothing more than an intercession on behalf of a friend or neighbor, and in such a case the mind revolts at the idea of a pecuniary reward. So long, therefore, as such continued to be the conception of the character of an advocate, who can wonder that it was thought disgraceful for him to accept money or reward? In that point of view every one must feel the truth of the line—

Turpe reos emptâ miseros defendere linguâ.

The account which we have already given of the origin of the name applied to advocates at Rome sufficiently explains why the assistance rendered to suitors in courts of law was in the early ages of the Republic gratuitous. The patron defended his client there without fee or reward, for it was a part of the general system of protection which he was bound by the nature of the tie between them to afford. But as actions multiplied, and a knowledge of legal rights and liabilities became more difficult, more time and study were required to qualify a citizen to undertake the cause of another; and the natural and inevitable consequence was that those who more peculiarly applied themselves to the acquisition of the necessary learning employed it as a means of obtaining money. This, however, was deemed an abuse, and the scandal thereby occasioned led to the passing of the famous Cincian law. It was brought forward in the shape of a *plebiscitum* A. U. 549, by the tribune M. Cincius Alimentus, and was entitled *De Donis et Muneribus*. The only provision which concerns the present subject is that which Tacitus[1] has recorded, *ne quis ob causam orandam pecuniam donumve accipiat*.

That this was effectual we have no reason to doubt, for from the date of its passing until the end of the Republic

---

[1] *Ann.* xi. 5. See on this subject *Brummeri Commentarius ad Legem Cinciam*. (Lutet. Paris, 1768.)

we find hardly any complaints of its evasion; and during those two centuries there were ample reasons why the orators of Rome should lend the aid of their services as advocates without receiving any pecuniary compensation.

No calling or profession offered such opportunities for distinction. In a city where the people bestowed the high offices of state, success in the conduct of causes was a sure and rapid means of advancement. Ambition could choose no better road. The Forum was in fact the Parliament of Rome, the arena of intellectual conflict, where the great triumphs of eloquence were achieved. Perhaps, too, the orators of those days knew something of the feeling which has animated so many illustrious writers, and which is well expressed in the following words of Lord Chancellor Camden :—" It was not for gain that Bacon, Newton, Milton, and Locke, instructed and delighted the world. When the bookseller offered Milton five pounds for his 'Paradise Lost' he did not reject it, and commit his poems to the flames, nor did he accept the miserable pittance as the reward of his labor. He knew that the real price of his work was immortality, and that posterity would pay it."

But even if this were not so, and the advocate required the stimulus of the hope of present reward, he found substantial inducements to exercise his calling. The prætor looked forward to the consulship, and how could he better secure popular favor than by watching for an opportunity to accuse some great criminal against the state, and display the powers of his eloquence and his zeal for his country amidst the assembled crowd in the Forum? Or it might be that he was called upon to undertake the defence of the accused; and here, too, he would have ample opportunity to ingratiate himself with his fellow-citizens, even while he threw the mantle of his protection round the client who was charged with some offense against the majesty of Rome. Thus we can well imagine how an advocate like Lucius Philippus, when he was a candidate for the office of tribune or consul, might avail himself of the opportunities afforded by a cause to ingratiate himself with the sovereign people:—how he might launch out into praise of liberty, and denounce the oppressions of the rich and noble—topics always grateful to the ears of the multitude, who chafe under the inequality of condition which separates them from the other classes.

But further, the advocates in the times of the Republic were generally men of distinguished rank, or members of wealthy families, who might fairly look forward to political power as the prize of their ambition. To such men it was of no moment to receive from their clients pecuniary rewards which their fortune could dispense with. Their great object was popularity among their fellow-citizens, whose suffrages they were so anxious to obtain; and there was no more efficient mode of securing this than the offer of gratuitous services in the courts of law. We may illustrate this view by what has happened in the case of members of the House of Commons in this country. Formerly, attendance there was looked upon as a burden, entailing expense on the representative, and compensated by no accession of dignity or influence. For, under the Plantagenets and the Tudors, what scope was afforded for distinction to a knight of the shire or a burgess, in parliament? They, therefore, received pay from their constituents for taking upon themselves the trouble of watching over the interests of others while they neglected their own affairs.[1] But when better days dawned, and the

---

[1] The wages of a knight were four shillings a day, those of burgesses half that sum. They were fixed at this amount by writs *de levandis expensis* under 16 Ed. II. These were issued until the close of Henry VIII.'s reign; but instances of such payment occurred later, and Andrew Marvel is said to have been the last who received it.—See *Hallam's Midd. Ages*, vol. iii. 171, 6th edit. In 1681, however, when Lord Nottingham was Chancellor, a Mr. King, formerly M. P. for Harwich, presented a petition,

Commons of England began to feel and assert their power, such salaries were discontinued, and it became an object of ambition to be a member of parliament as the shortest and surest means of acquiring influence and station.

At the downfall of the Roman Republic a great change took place. The former motives which had led advocates to exert themselves for their clients gratuitously, had ceased to exist. The commons no longer had a voice in the distribution of public rewards. The Cæsar on the throne was the real fountain of honor, and the offices of state, which still retained their ancient names, as if in mockery of departed freedom, were comparatively valueless. Who cared to be one of the senators of Rome, after Domitian had convoked them in solemn conclave to determine how a turbot should be dressed? Who could be ambitious of the consulship, when he might, under a Caligula, have a horse for his colleague?

Hence the profession of an advocate, like other callings to which men devote themselves, began to be followed for the sake of its emoluments, and the Cincian law, though still unrepealed, became a dead letter soon after the change in the constitution of the Roman government. But Augustus revived and enforced it by a decree of the senate, prohibiting counsel from taking fees, under the penalty of forfeiting four times the amount they might receive from their clients. The temptation, however, was too strong to be resisted. Common sense was here on the side of self-interest, and

stating that he had served as burgess for that borough several years, but it had not paid him his wages, "though often requested so to do." Notice having been given to the Corporation of Harwich, and the facts having been proved, the Lord Chancellor ordered a writ *De expensis burgensium levandis* to issue.—See Lord Campbell's *Lives of the Lord Chancellors*, iii. 420. The learned author states that he knows no reason in point of law why any member of Parliament may not *now* insist on payment of his wages. The deputies in the French National Assembly are paid so much a day.

men naturally asked themselves why they might not turn their legal knowledge and powers of speaking to account, in the same way that other mental gifts were made available for the purposes of pecuniary profit. So long as public honors and influence in the state were to be gained by forensic oratory, they might well be content to forego payment of their services; but when these were no longer within their reach, what possible inducement could they have to exert themselves in the cause of others, if they were not permitted to reap any benefit from their labors? Hence the law of Augustus was practically disregarded, until the conduct of a vile and rapacious advocate, named Suilius, in the reign of the Emperor Claudius, directed the attention of the public to the subject. This man seems to have united in himself the offices of common informer and prosecuting counsel, and, in that capacity, caused the ruin of several members of the noblest families in Rome.

The senate at last took the matter up, and an interesting debate arose upon the question, whether the Cincian law ought not to be rigorously put in force.

Silius, who was then consul-elect, vehemently attacked the fees of counsel. He appealed to the example of the orators of old, who deemed fame with posterity a sufficient reward; and pointed out the temptations to dishonesty, where men occupied themselves in making haste to be rich. If there were no fees there would be fewer lawsuits; for private quarrels were fomented, and litigation was fostered, for the sake of gain. This abuse of the courts brought fees to the practitioner, just as the prevalence of disease benefited the physician. Let them call to mind the examples of Asinius and Messala, or, to speak of more recent times, of Aruntius and Æsernius, who had gained the highest honors, without the reproach of being mercenary in their profession.

But the other side had also warm supporters. "You talk," they said, "of fame as a sufficient reward; but who is vain enough to hope that his renown, as a speaker, will be carried down to distant times? The office of an advocate is necessary to protect the weak against the powerful: his eloquence and skill are not natural gifts, which require no cultivation, and entail no expense. Omitting the care of his own private affairs, he devotes himself to the interests of others. The soldier receives his pay, the agriculturist looks to the profits of his farm. No one follows a profession from which he does not expect to reap pecuniary benefit. It is easy to quote the examples of Asinius and Messala, who were enriched in the civil wars by other means than the profession of the bar. The Aruntii and Æsernini might well afford to be generous, and refuse fees, being, as they were, members of wealthy families. It is well known what kind of rewards Codius and Curio gained by their speeches in the Forum. As to ourselves, we are unambitious senators, only desirous in these 'piping times' of peace to gain a livelihood by our professional exertions. Consider the interest which the middle classes have in this question. The bar opens to them the road to honor. How can you expect that a learned profession will flourish when you take away all inducements to pursue it?"

The emperor was touched by this appeal, albeit it was in the judgment of the severe historian somewhat undignified, and he contented himself with a decree which limited the amount of fees to 10,000 sesterces, equivalent in English money to about seventy-five guineas,[1] and rendered advocates liable to an indictment for extortion if they received more than that sum.

At the beginning of the reign of Nero, which seemed to promise so well for the happiness of his subjects, a decree or resolution of the senate was passed, in effect reviving the Cincian law, and forbidding counsel to take

[1] The value of a sestertium or 1000 sesterces, after the reign of Augustus, was £7: 16: 3.

fees at all (*Tacit. Ann.* xiii. 4). Suetonius, however, informs us that afterwards, in the same reign, the Claudian law, which merely limited the *amount* of fees, was adopted.[1]

But abuses prevailed at Rome under the empire, which prove to how low an ebb the morality of some of the advocates had sunk. Grievous complaints were made that after receiving fees at the commencement of the trial of a cause, they abandoned it, or betrayed it for a bribe, either by going over to the other side, or purposely losing it. Thus Tacitus tells us, to the everlasting shame of the Roman bar in the time of Claudius, that "there was nothing so easily bought as the perfidy of advocates," and he mentions the case of Samius, a distinguished Roman knight, who, after he had paid the enormous fee of more than 3,000 guineas[2] to the infamous Suilius to conduct a cause for him, discovered that his counsel had perfidiously violated his confidence: and, being hopeless of success, he stabbed himself to the heart. Pliny has recorded a similar instance of dishonorable conduct on the part of an advocate named Nominatus, who had been retained by a deputation from the Vicentini to conduct a trial in which they were engaged against Solers, who claimed the right of holding a market in some of their lands. Nominatus received beforehand the full amount of the fees allowed by law, and afterwards declined to go on with the case, or, as we should say, threw up his brief without returning the fee.

---

[1] *Sueton. Nero*, c. 17. Brummer, in his *Commentarius ad Legem Cinciam*, thinks that Suetonius is mistaken in supposing that Nero limited the amount of fees, and that he confounded Claudius Nero with Tiberius Claudius. But I see no reason why the statements of both Tacitus and Suetonius should not be correct. Very probably Nero found it necessary to relax the severity of his first decree.

[2] *Ann.* xi. 5. Quadringentis nummorum millibus. 400 × 1000 sesterces would give about the sum mentioned in the text. The exact amount would be £3325.

In consequence of these scandalous occurrences Trajan caused a decree of the senate to be passed, by which parties to an action were obliged to take an oath, before it came on for trial, that they had neither given nor guaranteed any sum of money to the advocates whom they employed. When the cause, however, was at an end they were allowed to pay their counsel fees, not exceeding the amount fixed by the Claudian law. At the same time Licinius Nepos, the prætor, issued an edict, in which he gave public notice that he would vigorously enforce this decree.

Although we do not read of any express repeal of this law of Trajan, it certainly became obsolete, for we find in many passages of the Digest and Code of Justinian regulations enjoining advocates to return the fees which they had taken, if they did not afterwards conduct the case; and by an edict of the Emperor Severus it was provided that if a counsel died before the cause in which he was engaged was tried, the fees paid to him should not be recovered by the client from his representatives, since it was not his fault that he did not conduct the case,—which proves that it was a common practice to receive the money beforehand.

The mode in which Quintilian discusses the question, as it stood in his day, is curious, and though the argument he employs is obviously in favor of the theory of gratuitous services, his good sense points out some reasonable distinctions. From him we learn that counsel at Rome could not at that time claim fees as a debt, even though they were within the limit prescribed by law, but received them as a voluntary offering from their clients, in acknowledgment of benefits bestowed. He contends that it is a matter deserving of consideration whether advocates ought to undertake causes gratuitously, and this question ought by no means to be decided off hand. For all must admit, he says, that it is the most honorable course, and one most worthy of a man of liberal mind, not to sell his services, and thereby weaken the force of the obligation he confers, but this, he thought, was too clear for argument, nor could it be denied that any one who possessed a sufficient competency ought not, without meanness, to make a trade of his profession as an advocate. But if the state of his affairs required that he should earn a livelihood, then, according to all precedent and authority, he need not refuse to take pecuniary rewards for his exertions. Thus Socrates earned a subsistence, and Zeno, Cleanthus, and Chrysippus, received money from their pupils.

Quintilian then proceeds more boldly, and says, " Nor do I see what fairer or more proper mode of getting money can be suggested, than by means of a most honorable profession, and from those to whom we have rendered the most important services, and who, if they give nothing in return, must have been unworthy of our exertions. And this is not only right but necessary, since these very exertions, and the time devoted to the affairs of others, prevent counsel from increasing their fortunes by any other means. But moderation must be observed in this, and it is of the utmost consequence to observe from whom fees are received, and to what amount. For as to bargaining for fees, and taking advantage of the necessities of clients to extort money from them, this is a practice which none but the vilest will attempt : especially since an advocate who has good causes and respectable clients need not fear ingratitude. But if he meets with it, it is better that sin should lie at the door of his client than himself.

" A virtuous advocate, therefore, will not seek to get more than is sufficient for him, and even one whose poverty obliges him to receive fees will not take them as a debt due to him, but receive them as an acknowledgment, being well aware that the obligation is still on his side. For in truth the services of counsel ought not to be sold, nor, on the other hand, go unrewarded."

That this "debt of gratitude" was sometimes forgotten at Rome we know from an Epigram of Martial:

> Litigat et podagrâ Diodorus, Flacce, laborat,
> Sed nil patrono porrigit; hæc chiragra est.
>
> To law when Diodorus goes
> And limps, the gout is in his toes;
> But when he pays no counsel's fees,
> 'Tis plain his hands have the disease.

It is interesting to compare the above passage from Quintilian with the theory that has always prevailed at the English bar, as we find it stated by Sir John Davy's preface to his Reports:

" For the fees or rewards which they receive are not of the nature of wages, or pay, or that which wee call salary or hire, which are indeed duties certein, and grow due by contract for labour or service, but that which is giuen to a learned counsellor, is called honorarium and not merces, being indeed a gift which giueth honor as well to the taker as to the giuer: neither is it certein or contracted for, for no price or rate can be set vppon counsel, which is unvaluable and inestimable, so as it is more or less according to circumstances, namely the ability of the client, the worthiness of the counsellor, the weightyness of the cause, and the custom of the country. Briefly, it is a gift of such a nature, and giuen and taken upon such terms, as albeit the able client may not neglect to giue it, without note of ingratitude (for it is but a gratuity or token of thankfulness), yet the worthie counsellor may not demand it without doing wrong to his reputation: according unto that moral rule, *Multa honeste accipi possunt, quæ tamen honeste peti non possunt.*"

In England the rule has always been that which is here laid down by Sir John Davys. A barrister has no legal right to a fee.[1] He cannot sue for it in a court of law,

---

[1] The church, however, has taken more care of those who practice as advocates in the ecclesiastical courts, for she expressly requires that they shall not lose their reward. The 131st canon provides, that if any proctor " shall by any color whatsoever defraud the advocate of his duty or fee, or

and, as a consequence from this, he is not liable to an action, if through negligence or ignorance he injures the interest of his client. It has been decided that where a fee has been paid to a barrister, and he neglects to attend the case at the trial, no action will lie to recover the money back.[1] But such a state of things ought surely to render the members of the profession doubly cautious not to give just cause of complaint to those who have retained their services; and it will be difficult to persuade the public that no breach of duty is committed, where incompatible engagements are knowingly contracted, and the unfortunate suitor finds himself deserted by his counsel in the very crisis of the trial.

Whether it was that the heat of the sun made men more irritable and litigious in Africa than elsewhere, and that the inhabitants of the numerous towns on the southern shores of the Mediterranean, which have now utterly disappeared, had a system of local courts to bring home justice to every man's door, or for some other reason, which we cannot now accurately ascertain, it is certain that that province afforded such a field for the members of the legal profession as to be called by Juvenal *nutricula causidicorum*. Their zeal for the emoluments of their profession here too required to be checked. They appear to have not only received, but exacted large presents from their clients, in addition to the usual fees, and were entertained at their expense; while at the same time, as the imperial edict directed against them gravely complains, their horses were furnished with provender gratis, in the stables of their host, as they went from place to place.[2] One might almost fancy that

shall be negligent in repairing to the advocate, and requiring his advice, what course is to be taken in the cause, he shall be suspended from all practice for the space of six months, without hope of being thereunto restored before the said term be fully complete."

[1] Turner *v.* Philipps, *Peake's R.* 122. We have noticed, however, that in old times a different doctrine was upheld.

[2] Dum ipsis et animalibus eorundem alimoniæ sine pretio ministrantur.

these African barristers rode the circuit, as in the good old times in England.

A limitation upon the amount of fees that might be taken, continued as long as the Roman empire existed (*Dig.* 50, xiii. 1). And within the prescribed maximum the judge was to determine what was fairly and reasonably due from a client to his counsel, regard being had to the nature of the cause, the eloquence of the advocate, and the custom of the particular court where it was tried.

Among the capitularies of Charlemagne there are regulations concerning the conduct of advocates or " clamorers " (*clamatores*), as they are there called ; as, for instance, that if they were discovered to be influenced by undue eagerness for money in the causes they undertook, they were to be banished from the society of honorable persons, and to be, in fact, disbarred (*Cap.* vii, tit. 114); but we do not find any rules laid down as to the amount of fees they were permitted to receive.

In France, by a royal ordinance of Philip the Bold, in 1274, the honorarium was to be regulated by a regard to the importance of the cause and the ability of the advocate; but in no case was it to exceed thirty livres. Beaumanoir has a curious passage on the subject. "And they ought to be paid," he says, "according to their quality, and according as the quarrel (cause) is great or small, for it is not reasonable that an advocate, who goes *with one horse, should have as much as one who goes with who goes with two, or three, or more.*"[1] This seems to favor the idea of the knightly character of advocates in those days, to which we have before alluded. If the advocate and his client could not agree upon the amount, the judge who tried the cause was to determine it with due regard to equity. In this state matters seem to have remained for many years, until an ordinance was issued by Henry III., in 1579, known by the name of

[1] Coutumes de Beauvoisins, cited by Fournel, *Hist. des Avocats*, i. 89.

ordonnance de Blois, which enjoined advocates to put their names to all the papers which they drew up in a cause, and to subscribe the amount of fees they had received, in order that they might be taxed, if deemed exorbitant. An amusing anecdote is related of Pasquier, the famous French advocate, in connection with the subject of the present chapter. In 1583, while he was attending the assizes (*les grands jours*) at Troyes, he sat for his portrait, and after the painter had finished the likeness, which Pasquier had not yet examined, he asked him to represent him with a book in his hand. The painter said that it was too late, as the picture was completed without hands. Upon this the witty lawyer immediately wrote the following lines, as a motto for the portrait :—

> " Nulla hic Pascasio manus est : Lex Cincia quippe
> Causidicos nullas sanxit habere manus.

> " No hands has Pasquier ; for the Cincian law
> Forbids a lawyer to possess a paw."

The attempt at a later period to give effect to the De Blois ordinance was resolutely resisted by the Parisian bar, and they declared that they would rather throw up practice than condescend to sign receipts for their fees, which would give the profession the character of a servile calling. An order was then made, that all who refused to comply should give public notice of their intention, and should for the future be disbarred. At this crisis, Du Hamel, Chouart, and Loisel, advocates venerable in age, and of high character, in vain tried to induce the obstinate barristers to give way, and 307 of them met in the consultation room, *consultationum quam vocant camerâ*, and agreed that they would not exercise their profession so long as the obnoxious law was enforced. This caused an entire stay of all judicial proceedings, and there was such confusion, and such a ferment in the city, that De Thou says Paris was as if it were in a state of siege. The king and chancellor happened to be at

Poictiers, and an express was despatched there by some of the high functionaries of state, who pointed out the public scandal which this state of things occasioned, and urged that the law pressed too severely upon the modesty of the respectable members of the bar, and that if all modesty were removed, the *honorarium* would become the basest and most mercenary gain.[1] The king immediately sent a message post-haste back, confirming the order of the parliament, and enjoining the advocates on their allegiance to obey it. Those who had stripped off their gowns were, at the same time, commanded to resume their profession. The refractory barristers did not dare to disobey the royal mandate, but returned to their duties, and thus the tumult was appeased. The law, however, as De Thou informs us, fell into desuetude. Fournel, in his narrative of this *contretemps*, tries to make out that the advocates were successful in their resistance, and that the king gave way. This, however, is a mistake. With a pardonable zeal for the credit of his order, he represents the royal commands to the barristers to resume their gowns as a privilege accorded to them of practicing, notwithstanding that they had, by their own act, disbarred themselves. And he thus infers, that as no evil consequence resulted from their contumacy, the king never intended the ordinance to be obeyed.

[1] Such is the account given by De Thou; but it is not easy to see how the *modesty* of the bar was affected by this law, unless indeed the amount of fees was so large that the fortunate recipients were too bashful to acknowledge the high price at which their services were valued. Meyer, however, says, " Le refus des avocats au parlement de Paris de se soumettre à une taxe, était non seulement noble, mais beaucoup plus dans l'intéret des parties, que les ordonnances mesquines qui, sous prétexte de veiller à des exactions, décréditent la pratique judiciarie, et laissent le public en proie à l'avidité des patriciens subalternes."—*Inst. Jud.* vi. 554.

CHAPTER X.

FORENSIC CASUISTRY.

A WORK which professes to treat of the office of an advocate would be incomplete if it did not embrace what we may call the ethics of the question, and examine how far it is consistent with morality and good conscience, to be ready to espouse either side of an argument,—to lend the aid of great abilities to shelter guilt from punishment,—and become the consenting instrument whereby malice and iniquity are too often enabled to accomplish their designs.

For doubtless it does seem a startling fact, that there should exist in the community a body of men, pre-eminent in intellect, and held in honor and esteem, whose occupation it is to employ all the resources which wit and learning can supply, in advocating whatever cause they are paid to undertake, and in specious and plausible attempts to make the worse appear the better side; who throw the shield of their eloquence over the innocent and the guilty alike; and whose most signal triumphs frequently consist in arresting the arm of justice, when public expectation demands that it should strike the offending criminal.

If a traveler from Atlantis or Utopia were told that the man to whom he has lately been introduced—and who conversed with him so wisely and so well upon some of the deep questions in ethics and religion—who seemed to be an earnest inquirer after truth—whose character stands high for integrity, and who friendship is valued by all who know him—did, after quitting his society, immediately proceed to invest himself in a particular costume—and then, in the solemn temple of justice, successfully attempt to convince a jury that a culprit arraigned on the charge of murder, of whose guilt he had not himself the shadow of a doubt, was innocent—and afterwards, within a brief interval, exert all his ingenuity to prove that a will, by which a family would be disinherited and reduced to beggary, was valid, though in his own mind he was satisfied that the testator was at the time of the execution of it, insane—we may imagine the surprise and incredulity of the stranger, and how far from easy it would be to explain to him the apparent inconsistency.

The case is here stated strongly, for it is better not to conceal or disguise the difficulty. The venality of lawyers has been a favorite theme for declamation in every age, and in Pagan Rome and Christian England alike, has afforded ample materials for satire and reproach. In the following lines Ben Jonson has drawn a picture which few, I fear, will have charity enough to pronounce a caricature:—

> I oft have heard him say how he admir'd
> Men of your large profession, who could speak
> To every cause, and things mere contraries,
> Till they were hoarse again, yet all be law;
> That with most quick agility could turn
> And return, make knots and undo them,
> Give forked counsel, take provoking gold
> On either hand, and put it up. These men
> He knew would thrive with their humility—
> And for his part he thought he should be bless'd
> To have his son of such a suffering spirit;
> So wise, so grave, of so perplexed a tongue,
> And loud withal, that could not wag, nor scarce
> Lie still, without a fee.[1]

---

[1] Volpone, or the Fox.

And Bishop Hall thus disports himself in verse at their expense :—

> Woe to the weale where many lawyers bee;
> For there is no such store of maladie!
> 'Twas truly said, and truly 'twas foreseene
> The fat kine are devoured of the lean.[1]

So fair a mark for sarcasm was not likely to escape the caustic pen of Swift, who accordingly, in the voyage to the Houyhnhnms, makes Gulliver tell his master, the Grey Horse, that " there was a society of men among us, bred up from their youth in the art of proving, by words multiplied for the purpose, that white is black, and black is white, according as they are paid. To this society all the rest of the people are slaves. . . . . . . It is likewise to be observed, that this society has a peculiar cant and jargon of their own, that no other mortal can understand, and wherein all their laws are written, which they take especial care to multiply; whereby they have wholly confounded the very essence of truth and falsehood, of right and wrong, so that it will take thirty years to decide whether the field left me by my ancestors for six generations belongs to me or to a stranger three hundred miles off. . . . . . . Here my master interposing, said it was a pity that creatures endowed with such prodigious abilities of mind as these lawyers, by the description I gave of them, must certainly be, were not rather encouraged to be instructors of others in wisdom and knowledge. In answer to which, I assured his honor, that, in all points out of their own trade, they were usually the most stupid and ignorant generation among us,[2] the most despicable in common conversation, avowed enemies to all knowledge and learning, and equally disposed to pervert the general reason of mankind in every other subject of discourse, as in that of their own profession."

[1] Virgidemiæ or Satires.
[2] " Vous en ferez, je crois, d'excellents, avocats :
Ils sont fort ignorants."—*Les Plaideurs*, Act ii. Sc. 14.

Nor is the charge against them of moral obliquity confined to England. M. Cormenin, better known perhaps under his assumed name of Timon, in one of those brilliant sketches, entitled, *Etudes sur les Orateurs Parlementaires*, thus scoffs at the idea of any fixed principle or moral sense in an advocate :—" We are told that M. Sauzet has no principles ; but pray inform me where is the advocate to be found who has principles ? When one has been employed for twenty years of his life about the true and the false—and been occupied only in stitching up, as he best may, the holes in the coats of clients, through which their fraud and malice find vent, it is difficult,—nay, impossible, to have any fixity of principle."

Such passages might be easily multiplied ; but it would be an ungracious task, and it is impossible to read the current literature of the day, without seeing how prevalent is the opinion, that the profession of an advocate is inconsistent with a stern and strict sense of moral obligation. And it can not, I think, be denied, that, independently of what seems to be an erroneous view of the question of his duties, the practice and principles of some of its members sometimes give color to, if they do not justify, the accusation ; for they seem to view their profession as a kind of threatre, where they may personate any character as the actors of the hour, and not hold themselves responsible for what they do or utter, while keeping up the part they have assumed. But this is not so. The analogy fails in this essential respect, that in the one case all is notoriously fictitious, in the other all is real.[1] And whenever men imagine that

---

[1] *Nihil habeat forum ex scenâ* is one of Bacon's maxims ; but he there refers to fictitious cases, brought into the courts in order to determine points of law. See *De Augm. Scient.* lib. iii. cap. 3, aph. 91. Sergeant Maynard, who died in the reign of William III., is said to have had " the ruling passion strong in death" to such a degree, that he left a will purposely worded so as to cause litigation, in order that sundry questions which had been " moot points" in his lifetime, might be settled for the benefit of posterity.

the quality of an act, as regards right or wrong, can be altered by the capacity in which they perform it, the most dangerous consequences will be the result. If the legislator thinks that his conduct as a public man need not be governed by the same nice rules of religion and morality which he professes to take as the guide of his private life, he commits a grievous error, and throws open the door to every species of corruption in the state. Indeed it may be safely asserted, that no really honest—certainly no religious mind—can deceive itself by the sophistry of supposing that in such conduct there is no criminality. Can any man for a moment imagine that he is not equally accountable to God for his public as for his private actions?

It would be a melancholy fact, if true, that a class of men should exist, who thought themselves bound to palliate and defend every species of iniquity in a court of justice, provided their services were retained and paid for by the criminal. It would be an outrage upon common sense to argue that any conventional usage or supposed necessity could justify such a course. The advocate would indeed be a "chartered libertine," and a pest to society, if he might, without any imputation upon his honesty, support the principles of the wicked, which in his soul he abhorred. And, on the other hand, his condition would be that of a miserable slave, if he alone of all men were obliged to be at the command of every miscreant who might choose to employ him, and must surrender his free-agency as a Christian and a citizen to do the bidding of vice.

Far, however, is this from being the case. It is *not* the true theory of an advocate's profession, that he is bound to undertake any and every cause which is offered to him, in utter disregard of its nature or merits. If this proposition should be denied, its truth might be established by a chain of authorities extending from the most remote antiquity; but this would be to run into what

Milton calls a "paroxysm of citations." A few may be quoted to prove that the assertion is not made without warrant, and because it is most useful to be reminded of the view which men who were not moralists and divines, but lawyers and advocates themselves, have taken of a question on which it is to be feared that much error and misconception prevail.

The language of Cicero, with reference to this question, is remarkable for its caution, but clearly implies the right and duty of exercising a discretion in the defense of guilt. Having strongly reprobated the use of eloquence in oppressing the innocent, he says (*De Offic.* ii. 14), *Nec tamen ut hoc fugiendum est, ita habendum est religioni nocentem aliquando*, modo ne nefarium impiumque *defendere. Vult hoc multitudo; patitur consuetudo; fert etiam humanitas.* In conformity with this principle he refused to defend Autronius, who was implicated in the conspiracy of Catiline, which he himself had been so successful in defeating (*Pro Sulla*, 6): and in his speech against Verres he said that neither Antony nor Crassus would have undertaken the defense of such a man.

Quintilian employs a beautiful metaphor to express the rule which in his opinion ought to be observed. He says, " The advocate will not undertake the defense of every one; nor will he throw open the harbor of his eloquence as a port of refuge to pirates." And again, " Nor let any false shame prevent him from abandoning a cause in which he has engaged under an impression that it was just, when he discovers in the course of the trial that it is dishonest; but he ought previously to give notice to his client of his intention."

And by one of the edicts of Justinian it was ordered that, at the commencement of a trial, the advocates engaged in it should take a solemn oath upon the holy Gospels, that they would exert themselves for their clients to the utmost in all they believed to be right and just; but they were not to uphold a cause that was villanous, or supported by falsehood; and if, in the progress of the trial, they discovered that a case of that kind had been entrusted to their care, they were at once to abandon it. And in such an event the client was not allowed to avail himself of the services of any other counsel, *ne melioribus contemptis improba advocatio subrogetur* (*Cod.* III. i. 14).

In France it was one of the solemn obligations imposed upon every advocate by oath, that he would not maintain causes that were unjust; and Pasquier thus writes to his son:—" Do not undertake any cause which you do not believe to be good; for in vain will you attempt to persuade your judges if you are not first persuaded of the justice of your cause. Combat for truth and not for victory."[1] We have seen also that, at the present day, it is part of the duty of the president of the court to warn the counsel for a prisoner not to speak against his conscience, or the respect due to the laws.

The illustrious D'Aguesseau thus addresses the bar: " Never pride yourselves on the miserable honor of having thrown obscurity over truth; and, more sensitive to the interests of justice than the desire of a vain reputation, seek rather to make the goodness of your cause than the greatness of your genius appear. Let the zeal which you bring to the defense of your clients be incapable of making you the ministers of their passions, and the organs of their secret malignity."

Nor have our own lawyers, in earlier times, held a different theory from this. We may remember the noble saying of Queen Elizabeth, that she wished her advocates to remember that they were counsel, not so much *pro dominâ Regina* as *pro dominâ veritate*. And anciently every sergeant-at-law was obliged to take an oath that he would not maintain or defend a cause that

---

[1] A son fils sur le point de devenir advocat.—*Lettre* vi.

was unjust to his knowledge. *Chescun serjeaunt countor est chargeable per serement que il ne maintenera, ne defendera tort ne faixime son scient* (*Mirroir des Justices*, c. 2, § 5). Sir Edward Coke says, " Fraud and falsehood is against the common-law ; and, therefore, if the client would have the attorney to plead a false plea, he ought not to do it, for he may plead *quod non sum veraciter informatus, et ideo nullum responsum*, and that shall be entered into the roll to save him from damages in a writ of deceit : and if an attorney ought not wittingly to plead a false plea, *à fortiori*, a sergeant or an apprentice ought not to do the same " (*Second Inst.* 215).

Sir John Davys, in that preface to his Reports which has been quoted more than once in the present work, says, " But good lawyers have not with us that liberty which good physicians have. For a good physician may lawfully undertake the cure of a foul and desperate disease, but a good lawyer can not honestly undertake the defense of a foul and desperate cause. But if he fortune to be engaged in a cause, which seeming honest in the beginning, doth in the proceeding appear to be unjust, he followeth the good counsel of the schoolman Thomas Aquinas." The upshot of this " good counsel " is, that he must give up the cause, but take care not to betray its secrets to the adversary—having first endeavored to persuade his client to yield, or consent to a compromise.

And Cook, who was solicitor-general to the Regicides at the trial of Charles I., thus strongly and emphatically expresses his opinion : " For, truly, to speak well in a bad cause is but to go to hell with a little better grace without repentance : it is but a kind of juggling by an over-curious flourish to make a shadow seem a substance." [1]

Sir Matthew Hale, in his *Great Audit*, says, " I never thought my profession should either necessitate a man

[1] Vindication of the Professors and Profession of the Law, published in 1646.

to use his eloquence by extenuations or aggravations, to make anything worse or better than it deserves, or could justify a man in it: to prostitute my elocution or rhetoric in such a way I ever held to be most basely mercenary, and that it was below the worth of a man, much more of a Christian, to do so." And the following tribute, paid by a high living authority to the integrity and independence of the bar, is not merely gratifying as an eulogium upon its character, but valuable as a memento of its duties. They are the words of Lord Langdale, the present Master of the Rolls (*Hutchinson* v. *Stephens*, 1 *Keen*, 668): "With respect to the task, which I may be considered to have imposed upon counsel, I wish to observe that it arises from the confidence which long experience induces me to repose in them, and from a sense which I entertain of the truly honorable and important services which they constantly perform as ministers of justice, acting in aid of the judge before whom they practice. No counsel supposes himself to be the mere advocate or agent of his client, to gain a victory, if he can, on a particular occasion. The zeal and the arguments of every counsel, knowing what is due to himself and his honorable profession, are qualified not only by considerations affecting his own character as a man of honor, experience, and learning, but also by considerations affecting the general interests of justice."

By the ancient law of Scotland it was required that "advocates on the time of their admission, and yearly, should be sworn to execute their office of advocation diligently and truly; and that as soon as they understand their clients' cause to be unjust or wrongful, they should incontinent leave the same, and desist from all further pursuit and defense" (Statute of the Lords, 13th June, 1537). And the law of Spain imposes upon them an oath, that "they will conduct themselves faithfully, and will not defend unjust causes."[1]

[1] Institutes of the Civil Law of Spain, cited in *O'Brien's Lawyer*.

It would be needless to bring forward the opinions of Divines, for it will be readily supposed that they do not inculcate any less rigorous rule, but it may not be unseasonable to bear in mind the words of Bishop Sanderson, in an assize sermon preached by him at Lincoln, and addressed to the counsel upon circuit: "If thou comest hither as to thine harvest, to reap some fruit of thy long and expenseful study in the laws, and to assist thy client and his cause with thy counsel, learning, and eloquence, think not that because thou speakest for thy fee, that therefore thy tongue is not thine own, but thou must speak what thy client will have thee speak, be it true or false; neither think, because thou hast the liberty of the court, and perhaps the favor of the judge, that therefore thy tongue is thine own, and thou mayest speak thy pleasure to the prejudice of the adversary's person or cause. Seek not preposterously to win the name of a good lawyer by wresting and perverting good laws, or the opinion of the best counsellor by giving the worst and the shrewdest counsel. Count it not as Protagoras did the glory of thy profession, by subtilty of wit and volubility of tongue to make the worse cause the better, but, like a good man as well as good orator, use the power of thy tongue and wit to shame impudence and protect innocency, to crush oppressors and succor the afflicted, to advance justice and equity, and to help them to right that suffer wrong. Let it be as a ruled case with thee in all thy pleadings, 'not to speak in any cause to wrest judgment.'"

And those who are exposed to the temptation of making the worse appear the better cause, should ponder well the following stern denunciation by the same uncompromising moralist: "But what shall I say then of those, be they many or few, that abuse the gracefulness of their elocution (good speakers, but to ill purposes) to enchant the ears of an easy magistrate with the charms of a fluent tongue; or to cast a mist before the eyes of a weak jury, as jugglers may sport with country people, to make white seem black, or black seem white ; so setting a fair varnish upon a rotten post, and a smooth gloss upon a coarse cloth, as Protagoras sometimes boasted, that he could make a bad cause good when he listed, by which means judgment is perverted, the hands of violence and robbery strengthened, the edge of the sword of justice abated, great offenders acquitted, gracious and virtuous men molested and injured ? I know not what fitter reward to wish them for their pernicious eloquence, as their best deserved fee, than to remit them over to what David has assigned them in Psalm cxx.: 'What reward shall be given, or done unto thee, O thou false tongue? Even mighty and sharp arrows with hot burning coals.'"

But in opposition to this " cloud of witnesses," it can not be denied that a different theory has been maintained. And the opinions of Lord Erskine and Lord Brougham, each a mighty master in his art, may be cited to prove the contrary. The former, when he defended Thomas Paine, in 1792, against the charge of writing and publishing a seditious libel, gave utterance to the following remarkable words :—

" I will forever, at all hazards, assert the dignity, independence, and integrity of the English bar ; without which, impartial justice, the most valuable part of the English constitution, can have no existence. From the moment that any advocate can be permitted to say, that he *will* or will *not* stand between the crown and the subject arraigned in the court where he daily sits to practice, from that moment the liberties of England are at an end. If the advocate refuses to defend, from what *he may think* of the charge, or of the defense, he assumes the character of the judge ; nay, he assumes it before the hour of judgment ; and, in proportion to his rank and reputation, puts the heavy influence of, perhaps, a mistaken opinion into the scale against the accused, in whose favor the benevolent principle of English law makes all presumptions, and which commands the very judge to be his counsel."

It may also be mentioned that on Gerald's trial for sedition in the High Court of Justiciary in Edinburgh, in 1794, when the prisoner, or panel as he is called in Scotland, applied to the court to appoint him counsel, on the ground that he had besought the services of several advocates who had unanimously refused, the Lord Justice-Clerk said, " Even without the interference of the court, I think no gentleman ought to refuse to defend a panel, whatever the nature of his crime might be" (*State Trials*, xxiii. 806, 807). It was with reference to this occasion that Henry Erskine, the dean of the Faculty of Advocates, who would have enjoyed a wider reputation if he had not been thrown into the shade by the fame of his celebrated brother, in answer to an inquiry which was addressed to him by Mr. Howell, the editor of the *State Trials*, wrote the following reply : " I was not one of the counsel to whom Gerald applied, and who, he says, unanimously refused to undertake his defense. Had he wished my assistance, I should have certainly appeared for him, however inconvenient it might have been to me from the multiplicity of business in which I was in those days involved, for I ever felt (as the Lord Justice-Clerk well expresses it) that no gentleman ought to refuse to defend a panel, *whatever be the nature of his crime.* I should, at the same time, have qualified my compliance with this condition, that the conduct of the defense should be left entirely to me, knowing, as I did, that if he spoke for himself he would avow principles and views which would supply the counsel for the crown with the only thing they wanted to make out their case—the CRIMINAL INTENTION."

Now this is a striking passage, for it will be observed that the counsel was willing to undertake the defense of the accused, with a perfect conviction of his guilt. For the stipulation that the conduct of the defense should be left wholly to him, proceeded entirely upon the ground that the intentions of his client had been criminal, and that through incaution or impudence this fact would be betrayed by him if he spoke in his own behalf.

But the most highly colored picture of the devotion which an advocate is supposed to owe to his client is that drawn by Lord Brougham in the well-know and striking passage that occurs in his defense of Queen Caroline before the House of Lords: "I once before took occasion to remind your lordships, which was unnecessary, but there are many whom it may be needful to remind, that an advocate, by the sacred duty which he owes his client, knows in the discharge of that office but one person in the world, that client and none other. To save that client by all expedient means, to protect that client at all hazards and costs, to all others, and among others to himself, is the highest and most unquestioned of his duties; and he must not regard the alarm, the suffering, the torment, the destruction which he may bring upon any other. Nay, separating even the duties of a patriot from those of an advocate, and casting them, if need be, to the wind, he must go on reckless of the consequences, if his fate it should unhappily be to involve his country in confusion for his client's protection." [1]

---

[1] It will be interesting to quote, with reference to this passage, an extract from a letter I received from Lord Brougham in 1859. He says—

"I wish to mention to you, in reference to what you discuss in chapter 10 on the duties and rights of an advocate, and where you refer to what has been so often the subject of dispute, my statement in the Queen's case. The real truth is, that the statement was anything rather than a deliberate and well-considered opinion. It was a menace, and it was addressed chiefly to George IV., but also to wiser men, such as Castlereagh and Wellington. I was prepared, *in case of necessity*, that is, in case the Bill passed the Lords, to do two things—first, to resist it in the Commons *with the country at my back ;* but next, if need be, to dispute the King's title, to show he had forfeited the crown by marrying a Catholic, in the words of the Act 'as if he were naturally dead.' What I said was fully understood by Geo. IV.; perhaps by the Duke and Castlereagh, and I am

This is very different from the proposition of Lord Chancellor Nottingham, that an advocate should speak not so much to abet his client's guilt as to defend his innocence. But is it to be taken as the deliberate expression of the speaker's opinion or not? If the theory contained in the foregoing passage be true, he may, while he uttered it, have entirely disbelieved it. And this disbelief would be quite consistent with his argument, paradoxical as such an assertion may appear. For observe, it is the speech of an advocate for his client, and the assumption is, that in that character he may say and do anything, provided only it tends to exculpate his client. But if this be so, the very doctrine he promulgates with so much eloquence may have been adopted merely for the purpose of the moment, and no value can be attached to a statement that is made under circumstances, which, according to the hypothesis, absolve the author from the ordinary obligation to speak the truth. Cicero, indeed, without adopting any such overstrained view of an advocate's duty, does, in one passage of his orations, contend that a falsehood told to save an unfortunate fellow-citizen from ruin ought not to be too severely blamed.[1]

confident it would have prevented them from pressing the Bill beyond a certain point."

[1] Si honesto et misericordi mendacio saluti civis calamitosi consultum esse vellemus: tamen hominis non esset, in tanto discrimine et periculo civis repellere et coarguere *nostrum mendacium*.—*Cic. pro Ligario*, 5.

The question of how far, and in what circumstances, falsehood is justifiable, has much perplexed casuists. St. Augustin calls it *magna questio latebrosa tractatio ; disputatio inter doctos alternans*.—*De Mendacio*, cap. 1. He himself was inclined to maintain that it is sinful in any given state of things to tell an untruth. And yet even he asserted this, to use the words of Jer. Taylor, "as his manner is, with some variety. Physicians can never apply their remedies, unless they pretend warrants or compliances, and use little arts of wit and cozenage. This and the like were so usual, so permitted to physicians, that it grew to a proverb, *mentiris u. medicus*, which yet was always understood in the way of charity, and with honor to the profession."—Jer. Taylor, *Ductor Dubitantium*, Bk. iii. c. 2. The different opinions on the subject are collected by Grotius, *De jure Belli*

But although it is impossible to adopt the principles here laid down, a certain latitude must be allowed to an advocate, the limits of which it is not easy to define, and which must be left in a great degree to his own good sense and discretion. It would be rendering his office almost useless, if every impassioned speech which he delivers on behalf of another were to be tested by the same canons according to which we criticise the opinions expressed in an essay or a sermon. It is as true now as it was in the time of Cicero, that it would be a great mistake to look for the deliberate convictions of the man in the address of the counsel.

To a certain extent there may be the *suppressio veri*—for no one surely will contend that it is the duty of an advocate to bring forward facts of the existence of which he may be conscious, but which would be ruinous to his client—although there ought never to be the *suggestio falsi*. No doubt it is difficult to steer the right course between this Scylla and Charybdis, so as to avoid the infraction of a moral duty; and the temptation is sometimes great to overleap the boundaries that separate falsehood from truth. And herein consists one of the chief trials of the profession, and constant vigilance is required lest the speaker should be hurried away by his zeal for his client to misrepresent facts, or pledge himself to the belief of opinions which he does not entertain.

But it is worth while to consider whether the accusa-

et Pacis, lib. iii. c. 1, and Puffendorf, *De jure Naturæ et Gentium*, lib. iv. c. 1, both of whom admit that there are several occasions on which it is lawful to deceive. In the Old Testament there are many remarkable instances of this. The one most frequently cited is the falsehood of the Hebrew midwives, of whom we are told that "Therefore God dealt well with the midwives."—*Exod.* i. 20. On this passage even St. Augustin says, *O pium pro salute mendacium!* and compare 2 *Kings* viii. 10: "And Elisha said unto him, 'Go, say unto him, Thou mayest certainly recover;' howbeit the Lord hath showed me that he shall surely die." I do not find that any of these authors allude to the untruth told by the prophet Jeremiah, at the suggestion of King Zedekiah.—*Jer.* xxxviii. 24-27.

tion which is so commonly brought against lawyers, and especially in their character of advocates, that they violate a moral duty by being ready to espouse either side of a question in a court of justice, is, or is not, well founded. If it be true, as Junius has said, that "the indiscriminate defense of right and wrong contracts the understanding while it corrupts the heart," can such a blighting result flow from the profession of the law as it is practiced in this country? from

It would indeed be a humiliating reflection to think that the splendid triumphs of the bar have been achieved by a venal prostitution of the intellect, that the stream of its eloquence is polluted at the source, and that the wonderful ingenuity and skill which mark the higher efforts of forensic oratory are little better than elaborate perversions of fact. "To make the worse appear the better side," may be an intellectual, but can never be a moral victory. Success in such a conflict has no ennobling feature, and, happily, mankind are so constituted as to value the heart more than the head, and withhold approbation from those whose powers of argument are better than their principles. It is a remarkable, and perhaps a distinguishing feature of the present time, that public reputation and influence must rest on a substratum of moral worth. Private character is of more importance now than at any former period, and where motives are suspected, the degree of influence exercised by an individual is small indeed. If, then, there exists in the minds of many an opinion, and it can not be disguised that it does exist, that the profession of an advocate is inconsistent with the nice precepts of morality, it will have to undergo a more than ordinary share of odium. And, from this odium, it may not be unseasonable or impertinent briefly to attempt to vindicate the office.

It seems probable that such an unfavorable opinion has arisen from confounding two things totally distinct—the duty of the advocate and the office of the judge. It must never be forgotten that, in the case of pleading at the bar, these duties never coalesce. The individuals are different, and each has a separate province, within which he has to act. Other situations and other circumstances are not analogous. In almost every place except a court of justice, the speaker takes upon himself to decide upon matters of opinion and fact. If he be a member of a body in which the will of the majority is law, he is a party to the judgment which he has by his arguments supported. Without those arguments the particular decision would perhaps not have been arrived at. He does not appeal to that majority as a body distinct from himself. Whether they agree with him or not, his speech is the open expression of that opinion, which has determined him individually to vote in some particular way. If he sincerely believes that his views are correct and ought to be adopted, he is right in endeavoring to influence his hearers. If not, he is a hypocrite.

But the situation of the advocate is very different. His business is to supply materials out of which a decision is to be formed by others; but not *all* the materials —only those which relate to one side and view of the question; for he does not stand before the tribunal to array conflicting probabilities, and weigh minute differences, as though to him were committed the task of adjudicating between opposing claims. He is to urge as forcibly as he can all the arguments which may be suggested in favor of one particular side, and present them to the understanding of those whose duty and vocation it is to weigh everything that may be advanced on both sides, and carefully ascertain the validity of the reasoning by which they are respectively supported. All that an advocate undertakes to perform, in the point of view in which we are now considering him, is this: He says, " I will bring before the notice of the judge all that can be maintained in favor of one side of the question. The same will be done by my opponent, and the court will decide between us." He stands wholly separate and distinct from the tribunal, which pronounces its judgment upon the value it attaches to his arguments; and which recognizes their cogency by adopting them, or shows its sense of their insufficiency by rejecting them. The only case in which we can conceive such a situation as this being fairly open to objection on the ground of morality, would be where the attainments and intellectual power of the advocate were so vastly superior to those of the tribunal he was addressing, that he could as it were force it to surrender its own judgment to his, and extort from it any sentence which suited that side of the cause on which he happens to be retained.

But this is obviously a chimerical alarm. Such a phenomenon has never yet appeared in the courts of Westminster, and so long as the roll of judges continues to add to the list the brightest names among the members of the bar, we may safely predict never will. The motto of the Chevalier Bayard might well serve as the inscription over the gates of our courts of law—and " *sans peur et sans reproche,*" proclaim to the world that impartial justice will be there dealt out to all—alike indifferent to the frowns of power, the temptations of corruption, and the subtle artifices of practiced ingenuity. It is remarkable, however, that Puffendorf, in his *Law of Nature and Nations*, makes use of the argument derived from the difference between the functions of the advocate and the judge, to justify conduct revolting to common honesty, and contends for a degree of license in favor of the former, which the most unscrupulous would hardly venture to claim. He says (*Lib.* iv. 1. § 21), "For since the judge is supposed fully to understand the law, the advocate, *by producing false laws or false authorities*, is not likely to prevail to any purpose; and he is never credited upon his bare assertion, but obliged to produce sufficient proof. And therefore if a guilty person do *by this means* sometimes escape unpunished, *the fault is not to be charged on the advocate*, or on the prisoner, but on the judge who had not the wisdom to distinguish between right and wrong." In other words, a cunning counsel may falsify quotations, and impose upon the ignorance of a judge—and think that he shifts from himself the responsibility of a deliberate untruth on the plea that the court *ought* to be able to detect the fraud! A pickpocket might, with equal justice and logic, argue that he does not deserve punishment, because the person whom he has robbed ought to have been more vigilant in protecting his property.

But let us take a broader view of the question. One of the simplest principles of equity is, that an accused person should be permitted to defend himself, and that, for this purpose, he should be allowed every reasonable advantage. In a primitive state of society, where transactions are not intricate, nor interests complex, any and every kind of defense might be admitted, which suited the circumstances of each particular case. All kinds of evidence might be gone into, and the inquiry might be conducted in a mode similar to that which would, at the present day, be pursued by a jury of gentlemen, who consented to undertake the investigation of a disputed point. It might go further, and confessions might be made available, although drawn from the accused under false inducements. Where the character of a witness was good, hearsay evidence might be admitted equally with ocular observation. But in process of time it would become necessary to limit and curtail this privilege, and by the light of gradual experience to establish certain canons, within which both the accuser and the accused ought equally to confine themselves. It was soon seen that the uncertainty and confusion which arose from the want of settled principles of attack and defense produced great injustice, and these principles soon became laws applicable to all cases. In some few their operation might be injurious, and defeat their own object, namely, the elucidation of truth, but in the great majority of instances they would effectuate their end much better than any varying and capricious rules could possibly do. Hence, in every civilized community certain prescribed forms, the offspring of custom or statute, have been recognized as regulating the practice of the judicial tribunals; and in English jurisprudence there arose a system of pleadings and of evidence, for part of which, perhaps, it is not easy, at the present day, to assign a reason wholly satisfactory, and which partook of excessive sublety and refinement, but which were the established law of the courts. But in proportion to the complexity of these rules, and the nicety of the distinctions which were admitted to exist, the difficulty of rightly understanding them increased; and few or none of those whose attention had not been previously directed to the subject, could hope to disentangle themselves from the labyrinth in which legal proceedings were and are to a great extent involved. "The necessity of a distinct profession," says Mr. Chancellor Kent, "to render the application of the law easy and certain to every individual case, has always been felt in every country under the government of written law. As property becomes secure, and the arts are cultivated, and commerce flourishes, and when wealth and luxury are introduced, and create the infinite distinctions and refinements of civilized life, the law will gradually and necessarily assume the character of a complicated science, requiring the skill and learning of a particular profession" (*Kent* i. 306).

Hence has arisen the existence in every civilized community of a class of men

Qui juris nodos et legum ænigmata solvat—

who, by habits of previous application, have rendered themselves competent to carry litigated questions through the courts, and who, being acquainted with all the intricacies of the law, can lend a lantern to the feet of the unwary traveler. The services of such a body will be important, in proportion to the difficulty which an unprofessional person would feel in undertaking the management of his own cause, and this difficulty will depend, in a great measure, upon the simplicity or complexity of the rules according to which the law is administered, and the degree of latitude permitted in the conduct of a case in courts of justice. In all countries where jurisprudence has been cultivated as a system, it soon became impossible for any one who had not studied the law as a profession to plead his own cause with any hope of success; and what had at first been merely a matter of convenience, namely, the employment of some counsel learned in the law, became indispensable. The only practicable method of making complaints heard at the footstool of justice, or defending property and life from unprincipled attack, was through the medium of lawyers. They became the organs whereby the complicated wants of mankind reached the ear of Themis, and through them only could legal redress for wrongs be obtained. Let us consider, then, what would be the consequence if advocates might lightly refuse to undertake causes entrusted to their care. Let us suppose that a man who conceives himself aggrieved, and is anxious for redress, applies to a counsel to bring his cause before a legal tribunal, and support its merits to the best of his ability, would it be right that the person so applied to should refuse, because he is not satisfied in his own mind that his client has strict justice on his side? and ought he to anticipate the sentence of a court, and determine the question before it has been fairly heard? If one advocate is so justified in rejecting the application, the same privilege or obligation rests with all; and the unhappy suitor, who had fancied himself entitled to the benefit of that noble promise in Magna Charta, *nulli negabimus justitiam*, finds himself precluded from any attempt to obtain reparation for the wrong which he believes himself to have sustained. But even if *all* should not decline to undertake the cause, a grievous injury may be inflicted by the refusal of one eminent in character and station; and that result may happen which Cicero so strongly deprecates, when he exclaims, "If any one perchance shall say that Cato would not have undertaken the prosecution, if he had not first satisfied himself of its justice, this will be to introduce an unfair rule, and increase the misery of those who are in jeopardy, by affirming that the opinion formed by the accuser ought to prejudge the question of the guilt of the accused."[1]

It will be said, however, that this is not fairly meeting the question, and that by putting the hypothesis of a doubtful case, upon which there may be, previously to a judicial decision, considerable difference of opinion, we are avoiding the difficulty. Suppose the facts are such as to leave no doubt on the mind of the advocate that the cause of his client is morally unjust. Take for instance an informality in a will. The intention and wishes of the testator are clearly and unequivocally expressed, but there is a technical objection to the validity of the instrument, and the heir-at-law, or nearest of kin, seeks to take advantage of the mistake. What is the duty of the advocate then?

The answer, I think, is, that he may with a safe conscience undertake the cause of the party who seeks to set aside the instrument.[2] If the objection is presented

---

[1] *Pro Murena*, 28. We must therefore receive with caution the proposition of Camus, the French lawyer, in his *Profession d'Avocat*. "Son cabinet est un tribunal privé; il y juge les causes avant de se charger de les défendre." This is a different kind of "cabinet" from that noticed by old Fuller: "Some keep an assurance office in their chamber, and will warrant any cause brought to them."—*Holy State*, Bk. iii. ch. 1.

[2] Molena, however, in his treatise *De Justitiâ*, decides this question in the negative. He says that the advocate *non posse illis præstare patrocinium, utpote ad rem injustam*.

to the court, the judges are bound by their oaths to give effect to it, supposing it to be valid. And how can it be a wrong in an advocate to ask on behalf of another what the law says he has a right to receive?

"The law allows it, and the court awards it."

In such cases he does no more than point out the requirements of the law—just as he would, if consulted by a client on the question, give an opinion in conformity with that law, without reference to the practical consequences that might flow from it. It seems absurd to contend that he ought to decline to give a legal opinion at all in such a case; and if he is justified in doing that which first gives the client confidence in his claim, why may he not go one step further and support his own opinion by argument in a court of justice? But it does not follow from this that in all cases where the law is in favor of a party, an advocate is *bound* to render his services to that party if he applies for them. He may well refuse to become the instrument to work out the ends of mean and unprincipled malignity. He is not, of all men, to be left without discretion in the employment of the talents with which God has entrusted him. *Dabitur licentia sumpta* PUDENTER.

The information given him may be so clear, and thereby the turpitude of his client so manifest, that he may be compelled to refuse the aid of his ingenuity. All must have read with pleasure of instances where advocates have indignantly thrown up their briefs when facts of an atrocious nature have been unexpectedly elicited, and they have found that they have been unwittingly engaged in the support or defense of villany.[1]

Still less may he, under any pretence, or under any circumstances, connive at fraud. Let us put the case of a party who has been paid a debt due to him from

---

[1] Certainement l'avocat a le droit et meme l'obligation d'abandonner une cause sur la nature de laquelle il reconnaît s'etre abusé.—*Meyer*, vi. 544.

another; but who has omitted to give a receipt, and knows that his former debtor has no means of proving the payment. Suppose he were to bring an action against the latter, and these facts were communicated to a counsel with his brief, and he knew that his client was seeking to recover his debt twice over,—his duty is clear and imperative. He must decline to appear in such a cause, and leave the dishonest creditor to enforce his claim as he best may.[1]

Jeremy Taylor, in his *Ductor Dubitantium, or Rule of Conscience*, puts a case arising out of the absence of a receipt; but it is of a different kind, and certainly seems to savor of excessive refinement.—"Agricola borrows of Sempronius five hundred pounds, and pays him at the day, but without witness: Sempronius sues him for the money: Agricola owes him none, but can not prove the payment; but, yet may not, when he particularly interrogated, to save himself from injury, deny that he ever received any. He must confess the truth, though he pay the money again. Covaruvius affirms that he may in this case lawfully deny that ever he received any, because he is not indebted: he received none that remains in his hand; and to other purposes the judge can not question him; and if he does, he is unjust, and, therefore, Agricola is not tied to answer rightly. But this is not well said nor well considered. For the judge, being competent, may require him to answer; and the intention of the question is not to know whether Agricola

[1] It is to be hoped that such a case could not occur, for the counsel receives his instructions solely through the medium of an attorney; and it would be equally the duty of the latter to refuse to be employed in the service of iniquity. So that the fraudulent attempt would be stopped *in limine*. Suppose, however, that a receipt has actually been given, of which the counsel has heard nothing, but when produced in court it turns out either that there is no stamp upon it, or an improper one. Ought he to take the objection, and thus enable his client to win the verdict, thereby in effect pocketing the money twice over? This is, I think, a question of some nicety, especially if the objection has occurred only to the advocate himself, and is not perceived by either the court or the client.

has paid the money, yea or no ; but whether he borrowed it, for, if he did, the judge is afterward to enquire concerning the payment ; and as Sempronius was tied to prove *that*, so is Agricola tied to prove *this ;* and a lie is not to be confuted by a lie, nor the error of Agricola in not taking witnesses or an acquaintance, to be supplied by a direct denial of a truth." This is a wire-drawn illustration,—for Agricola must be a simpleton, indeed, not to plead in confession and avoidance, to use a legal expression, and answer at once, *uno flatu*, when asked whether he had received the money—" Yes : but I paid it back again to the lender."

But cases of patent fraud do not often occur, and they create no difficulty when they do. In the vast majority of instances where the services of an advocate are required, he may without scruple render them ; and this will, I think, appear from considerations derived from the nature of civil and criminal jurisprudence.

Society necessarily requires some abridgment of perfect liberty, and contracts within the limits of beneficial operation the acts of its members. For this purpose it frames a code of laws, and establishes rules, which are the measure of the legal right of the citizens of the community. The eye of the law makes no distinction between *mala prohibita* and *mala in se*. An artificial system is established, having its foundations in the eternal principles of right ; but owing to the imperfection of general rules, when applied to the infinitely varying nature of different transactions, frequently defeating the ends of justice. Maxims which suited the simplicity of a former age are retained and acted upon ; but in order to meet a change of circumstances, nice and subtle distinctions are eagerly laid hold of, and admitted by the legal tribunals. The doctrine of legal rights becomes gradually more complicated, and they are made to depend upon technical considerations, which a plain understanding would reject as frivolous ; but which in courts of law are regarded with the most reverential respect. Any one at all conversant with the Reports, in which are enshrined the mysteries of English Law, will at once admit the truth of these remarks. At the same time that rights are circumscribed and defined, remedies are given which are liable to become anxiliary to the cause of wrong. The law gives an adversary salient points of attack which he would not otherwise possess; but at the same time affords bulwarks and buttresses behind which a defendant may shelter himself successfully. Cases constantly occur,—indeed the majority of litigated questions are of this nature,—in which beforehand it is impossible to say on which side the legal right lies. And even where the justice of the case is apparent, the law itself, and not the lawyer, often enables a man to defeat it. *Aliter leges, aliter philosophi tollunt astutias* (*Cic. de Off*, iii. 17). A sense of honor may sometimes induce a man to renounce the advantages afforded him by law; as, for instance, in the case of a bankrupt who pays his creditors in full, although their claims are barred by his certificate. But this is an obligation which rests wholly upon the conscience of the individual; and it would be quixotic to say that an advocate is conniving at fraud, because in such a case he interposes on behalf of his client the defenses behind which the law permits him to retire. All that he is concerned to ascertain is, what is the condition of his client relatively to the law? If the facts come within its beneficial operation, how can he take upon himself to decide that the protection which it is ready to bestow ought to be denied? The equity of the case rests not with him, but with the jury or the judge, if it is one in which the exercise of any discretion can be admitted.

But besides this, the exertions of an advocate often actually effect a change in the application of the law. As the whole fabric of civil jurisprudence is an artificial structure based upon the foundation of natural equity, and every year in this country adds to its complicated architecture, the difficulty of anticipating what will be the decision of the court in a particular case becomes very great. There is perhaps a conflict of authorities, or hints have been thrown out that some doctrine hitherto recognized and admitted ought to receive qualification, and final judgment may depend upon a most careful examination and comparison of analogous cases, and an appeal to general principles. Each side of the question may fairly admit of copious argument. The necessity of upholding general rules may be urged on the one side, the hardship of the particular case on the other, and each counsel may cite numerous decisions which appear to favor the side he is interested in maintaining. These opposite views are presented to the court, whose duty it is narrowly to watch the tremulous and dancing balance of authorities, and decide according to the best of its judgment. In cases like these it cannot be asserted that an advocate is venal, who is prepared to advance the claims of either of the contending parties. He stands merely in the situation of a man possessed of a certain quantity of information and knowledge of precedents applicable to both views of the question; and he is called upon to lay before the consideration of those whose province it is to weigh and decide all that can be said in favor of one of these views. Here then there can be no ground for applying to the profession the hard names which ignorance so liberally bestows; and yet any one who attends to the cases that are discussed in the courts of law in this country, will find that instances such as the above form a very large proportion of the cases in which professional skill and ingenuity are employed. As Sir Thomas Browne, the good knight of Norwich, says, "There are yet, after all the decrees of councils and the niceties of the schools, many things untouched, unimagined, wherein the liberty of an honest reason may play and expatiate with security, and far without the circle of a heresy." So also there is a very wide circle indeed, within which a counsel may exercise his ingenuity without being guilty of moral dereliction.

But it is urged that of two sides of an argument one only is right, and that to be equally prepared to maintain either evinces a reckless indifference to truth. This is a plausible objection, but will be found to have little real relevancy to the subject. In all arguments where the abstract merits of a question are under discussion, and our own opinion is to be exercised on those merits, we at once assume the functions of a judge, and, after examining the whole bearings of the case, decide according to our convictions. Here we are, the last *court of appeal*, and we assume that we are competent, to the best of our judgment, to determine the contested point. But how does this apply to the professional advocate? It would be, as we have endeavored to show, mere tyranny and injustice, if the decisions of courts were to be anticipated by private opinions, and lawyers were to assume that they could divine the verdict or judgment, and consequently refuse, on such grounds, the aid of their professional skill. And the fact is that they cannot, in the great majority of litigated cases, know what will be the issue of the trial; and that issue may very much depend on their own individual exertions, presenting the subject in a point of view which may not previously have struck the court, but which general principles or a close analysis of previous authorities may warrant them in exhibiting. At all events, if that view be an erroneous one, such error is either corrected by the judges, or is acquiesced in and adopted as a principle, which will be a guide for subsequent decisions; for it is a maxim of the common law that "*communis error facit jus*"—a maxim which, however paradoxical it may seem, and open to a sneer, amounts merely to this, that a received doctrine in law shall not be overturned or abandoned, even although its soundness in principle may be questioned;

and on the ground stated on one occasion by Lord Eldon, namely, that it is more material that the law should be settled than how it is settled.

In the English courts, where no codification of laws exists, and where (except in the case of statutes) the body of legal jurisprudence gradually evolves itself by the application of general principles to varying conditions of facts, it is by the elaborate arguments and subtle distinctions of advocates at the bar, that admitted principles can be brought to bear upon the constantly changing and infinitely diversified relations of social and commercial life. The struggle generally is to bring the facts of the particular case within the scope of the principle; and in a very large proportion of the questions which are litigated, it is by no means easy to predict beforehand what will be the ultimate decision. If this be so, it follows, I think, irresistibly that as a general rule an advocate may in most cases, with a safe conscience, take either side on which he happens first to be retained.

The mode in which Sir John Davys seeks to resolve the difficulty is perhaps not very satisfactory. He says, "But there is yet another exception against the professors of our law, namely, that wittingly and willingly they take upon them the defense of many bad causes, knowing the same to be unjust when they are first consulted with and retained. And this is objected by such as presume to censure our profession, in this manner. In every cause between party and party (say they) there is a right, and there is a wrong; yet neither the one party nor the other did ever want a counsellor to maintain his cause. This may be true, for the most part, and yet in truth the learned counsel, whose fortune it is to light on the wrong side, may be free from imputation of any blame. For when doth the right or wrong in every cause appear? When is that distinguished and made manifest? Can it be discovered upon the first commencement of the suit, and before it be known what can be alleged and proved by either party? Assuredly it can not: and therefore the counsel, when he is first retained, cannot possibly judge of the cause, whether it be just or unjust, because he hears only part of the matter, and that also he receives by information from his client, who doth ever put the case with the best advantage to himself." It is obvious that this is what logicians call an *ignoratio elenchi*; for the hypothesis upon which the argument of the objector proceeds is that the counsellor *kuows* that the cause of which he undertakes the defense is unjust; but the answer assumes that owing to the representations of his client he either remains in doubt, or believes the contrary. If so, *cadit quæstio*, and the sternest moralist will concede that he may without scruple support the claim.

But it is not in civil causes, where the rights of parties depend so much upon technical and conventional rules, but in criminal cases, that the chief odium is incurred by the profession. And if the license which we sometimes see boldly challenged on its behalf, to sacrifice every consideration to the one object of enabling a client to escape conviction, were necessary for its exercise, it is not easy to see how that odium could be repelled. Such a license all right-thinking men must repudiate, and it tends only to the dishonor of a noble calling to represent it as requiring and justifying the use of trickery and falsehood. The principle is as clear as noon-day, that no man ought to do for another what that other can not, without moral turpitude, do for himself. The advocate stands before the tribunal to plead the cause and represent the person of his client, *utimur enim fictione personarum, et velut ore alieno loquimur* (*Quintil. Inst. Orat.* xi. 1), but he cannot possibly by virtue of his agency acquire rights greater than are possessed by his principal. He may not assert that which he knows to be a lie. He may not connive at, much less attempt to substantiate a fraud. He may not avail himself of the wretched sophistry of Paley, and say, " that there are falsehoods which are not lies, that is which are not criminal; as where no one is deceived, which is the case in . . . . a prisoner's pleading not guilty—an advocate asserting the justice, or his belief of the justice, of his client's cause. In such instances no confidence is destroyed, because none was reposed; no promise to speak the truth is violated, because none was given or understood to be given." Every man is under an obligation to speak the truth if he speaks at all, and virtually promises to do so every time that he opens his lips. "For there is in mankind," says Jeremy Taylor, " an universal contract implied in all their intercourses; and words being instituted to declare the mind, and for no other end, he that hears me speak hath a right in justice to be done him, that as far as I can what I speak be true, for else he by words does not know your mind, and then as good and better not speak at all." If an advocate does not expect to be believed when he asserts his conviction of the innocence of his client, why does he volunteer the assertion at all? His only object must be to persuade the jury, by throwing into the balance the weight of his own asseveration, in order to make it incline in favor of a verdict of acquittal.

Where, however, a moralist will ask, is the difference between appearing to countenance an untruth, and actually doing so, between the practical and verbal falsehood? and how can a counsel, under any circumstances, without a dereliction of moral duty, appear on behalf of a prisoner whom he *knows* to be guilty of the crime of which he is accused?

The reasoning of Quintilian on this part of the question is weak, and somewhat deficient in candor. For he pretends that as the guilt of a falsehood depends upon the *motive* with which it is uttered, many laudable reasons may induce an advocate to undertake the defense of a criminal. For instance, he may wish to preserve the life of such a man, in order that he may be reclaimed from his evil ways, and become a useful citizen. Or, although his client is clearly guilty, he may think that the state has need of his services, and that a public benefit will be conferred by rescuing him from the arm of the law; on the same principle that led Fabricius to vote in favor of Rufinus as consul, because, although the latter was a man without principle, and his own enemy, he believed him to be an able general, and war was then impending over Rome. The reply to such an argument is, that causes are not undertaken on this principle, and perhaps no such instance has occurred since courts of justice have existed.

The real answer to the objection is not difficult. "Let the circumstances against a prisoner be ever so atrocious, it is still the duty of the advocate to see that his client is convicted according to those rules and forms, which the wisdom of the legislature has established, as the best protection of the liberty and security of the subject."[1]

Every man charged with an offense in a court of law stands or falls according to the evidence there produced. If that which is brought forward against him is weak and insufficient, or the charge itself is so inartificially framed, that the law, if appealed to, must relax its hold upon its prisoner, it can be no violation of moral duty to point out these deficiencies to the court, although the effect must be that the criminal will escape. Nor does this apply to the advocate alone. If a juryman who is sworn to "make a true deliverance *according to the evidence*," had heard a prisoner confess that he was guilty, but the witnesses called for the prosecution entirely failed to bring the charge home to him—he would be bound, notwithstanding his own knowledge to the con-

---

[1] Note by Professor Christian in his edition of *Blackstone*, iv. 356.

trary, to bring in a verdict pronouncing the prisoner innocent.[1]

The question may be further illustrated by supposing some radical defect in the authority of the court which tries the offender; as, for instance, to take a familiar example, the prosecution of a man for perjury at the quarter sessions. Here there is a want of proper jurisdiction, and if the charge were capital, execution following conviction in such a case would, in the eye of the law, be murder. To object, therefore, to the competency of a court to try a criminal, may be a clear and positive duty. But not only must the court have jurisdiction, but the indictment must be drawn in a legal form, otherwise the prisoner is entitled to an acquittal. Can it be wrong then to show that it does not contain a sufficient statement of the charge, or is in other respects imperfect? or that the particular statute upon which it has been framed is inapplicable to the peculiar nature of the offense? And if the evidence is really weak and unsatisfactory, although the counsel may know that his client is guilty, it is hardly going a step further to insist before the jury that they ought not to convict upon the testimony, with which alone they have to deal.

But it can not be denied that the utmost circumspection is necessary to prevent the zeal of the advocate from hurrying him too far. He must keep within certain prescribed limits, and stand strictly, in such cases as we are now considering, upon the defensive. He may honorably say to the accuser: "Prove my client guilty if you can: You use the law as a sword,—I will take it as a shield;" and so long as he keeps within the lines which the law has traced for the protection of the accused, he may—nay, he must—afford his client the

---

[1] The proper course in such a case would be for the juryman to tender himself as a witness for the crown. But if he had only *heard* from another that the prisoner had confessed, although he might have no doubt of the fact, he could not make use of it.

benefit of its shelter. If the law allows a loophole of escape, he is a traitor to his trust if he does not bring this before the attention of the judge. He would incur a fearful responsibility indeed, if, knowing an objection, which, if taken, would be fatal to an indictment, he were to suppress it, because he was satisfied of the fact of his client's guilt.

It is no doubt difficult to observe the proper medium, and herein, in a moral point of view, consists one of the chief trials of the profession. All who have attended courts of justice must have been struck with the ingenious perversions of evidence which are there adopted and urged by advocates, in civil as well as in criminal cases. Expressions are misinterpreted, wrong motives are attributed, and glaring misconstructions are put upon actions of the most ordinary and unsuspicious character. The hypothesis by which an attempt is made to explain away the force of unfavorable facts, is often such as to draw largely upon the credulity of the jury, and certainly experience has proved that it is difficult to assign limits to the extent of that credulity.

If, owing to the imperfection of human memory, an adverse witness has been betrayed into some slight discrepancies of statement, an attack is made upon his veracity, and the jury are called upon to believe that he has committed perjury. Some counsel adopt it as an axiom, that a police officer can not speak the truth, and accordingly they think themselves at liberty to deal with his evidence as in every case utterly unworthy of credit, if it happens to be unfavorable to their view of the case. But this is dangerous ground. The feelings of the jury revolt at such an assumption, and in their sympathy with the witness whose character is thus causelessly assailed, they are apt to conceive prejudice against the party whose case seems to require the aid of untruth to support it. *Quocirca astutiæ tollendæ sunt, eaque malitia, quæ vult illa quidem videri se esse prudentiam; sed abest ab eâ distatque plurimum* (*Cic. de Off.* iii. 17).

Quintilian lays down the rule which in such cases ought to be observed, and it is founded on discretion and good sense. "Sometimes the duty imposed upon an advocate compels him to make strictures upon a whole class of men, as, for instance, of freedmen, or soldiers, or farmers of the revenue, or such like. In all which cases the general rule is to appear reluctant to say anything offensive, and to make no indiscriminate attacks, but confine one's self to the proper object, and where censure is bestowed, to compensate this by some words of panegyric" (*Inst. Orat.* xi. 1).

But, independently of this, advocacy exists for nobler uses than to construct fictions or scatter calumnies, and these can not be described better than in the words of one of our old divines. · "That winning and persuasive faculty," says Bishop Sanderson (*Ad Magistratum*), "which dwelleth in the tongues of some men, whereby they are able not only to work strongly upon the affections of men, but to arrest their judgments also, and to incline them whither way they please, is an excellent endowment of nature, or rather, to speak more properly, an excellent gift of God;—which whosoever hath received is by so much the more bound to be truly thankful to him that gave it, and to do him the best service he can with it by how much he is enabled thereby to give more glory to God, and to do more good to human society than most of his brethren are. And the good blessing of God be upon the heads of all those, be they few or many, that use their eloquence aright, and employ their talent in that kind for the advancement of justice, the quelling of oppression, the repressing and discountenancing of insolence, and the encouraging and protecting of innocence."

This is an impressive admonition to lay to heart, and well worthy of the consideration of a profession which ought to be above suspicion or reproach. Each member of it ought not only to be impressed " with a profound sense of the ample instruction and glorious rewards which await his future enterprise and patient devotion in the study of the first of human sciences,—the law " (*Story's Eq. Juris.* ii. 687), but dwell upon the thought that he belongs to an Order in which have been enrolled the names of some of not only the most eloquent, but the wisest and most virtuous of men. And he may, when he calls to mind their high destinies and great achievements, exclaim with Berryer—" Noble profession que celle de l'avocat!"—To justify, however, such a title, it behoves him to cherish that " chastity of honor which feels a stain like a wound," and never for a moment imagine himself released from the obligations of Christian morality. Others may outstrip him in the arduous race, and reach triumphantly the goal towards which he pants in vain. But it is no disgrace nor dishonor to fail in a conflict in which

> non tam
> Turpe fuit vinci, quam contendisse decorum.

The same path has been trod by Demosthenes and Cicero,—by L'Hopital and D'Aguesseau,—by Hale, Mansfield, and Erskine,

> equall'd with us in fate,
> So were we equall'd with them in renown!

each of whom, in various measure and degree, had to surmount difficulties, trials, and discouragements.

And if it were not presumptuous to speak of our own times, it would be no more than the truth to say that we have seem among us some, whose names as advocates might challenge a comparison with the greatest of those which have been mentioned in these pages. Of one who has not long since died, and with whom I had the happiness of being on terms of intimate friendship, I mean the late Lord Brougham, it was said by a Right

Reverend Prelate, himself not unworthy to encounter him in debate, that he was "the most eloquent of living men;" nor was he more conspicuous for the power of his oratory than the grasp of his intellect and the extent of his acquirements. From the ranks of advocates also have been taken those who adorn the Bench, which is occupied by Judges distinguished for their learning, their independence, and their integrity.

www.ingramcontent.com/pod-product-compliance
Lightning Source LLC
Chambersburg PA
CBHW030238170426
43202CB00007B/42